D0385131

AIRCRAFT OF THE WORLD

Mud Puddle Books, Inc.
54 West 21st Street
Suite 601
New York, New York 10010
info@mudpuddlebooks.com

Cover picture: Dassault Rafale F2
Three-sided profile: Aeromedia Anton E. Wettstein

ISBN: 1-59412-017-X

Printed in China

AIRCRAFT OF THE WORLD

CLAUDIO MÜLLER

MUD PUDDLE BOOKS, INC.
New York, New York

➤ **Aircraft of the World** has become the standard aviation yearbook in German speaking countries. For the 44 years it has appeared, it has introduced every significant aircraft model currently in production as well as the substantial upgrades on older models. Space is also reserved for some exotic models. The most interesting of these are always those models that are soon expected to take their first flights. They are always an important indicator of what direction the aviation industry is moving in. Under the category "Aircraft projects of tomorrow", I would, however, like to expand the horizon even more and highlight future projects whose first flights are still a long way off - or may even stay on paper. These projects are important because they demonstrate what has already been thought of in aviation and where the developments could lead. The Boeing Sonic Cruiser is a very suitable example of this. Even if the project is halted, or perhaps temporarily abandoned, it still represents a truly innovative step and is thus worth presenting.

In 2003, we celebrated the 100th birthday of flying. What began as the adventure of a few daredevils in 1903 has developed into one of the world's most important industries. Flying has become something that is natural. The technical evolution that began with a few flying carpentry products held together by wood, fabric and wires to today's standard aircraft is overwhelming. This evolution occurred in stages. Usually wars, primarily the Second World War, were responsible for many of the leaps in development. Still, the past few years have been characterized by great evolutionary developments. Where does air travel stand today? And where is it headed?

The industry as a whole is currently in the midst of a difficult phase and parts of the industry are again going through a crisis. The industry as an economic sector is hardly producing satisfactory results. Further, the effects of the present political and economic conditions have probably not yet been fully felt. Thanks to a high inventory of orders for transportation aircraft, the large manufacturers Boeing and Airbus have been able to hold back the tide to some extent and are still producing satisfactory production figures. However, manufacturers must go to extremes in order to obtain any new orders. They do this by announcing "catalog prices" and then offering deep discounts on those prices. The practice becomes cloudy when orders are announced and the only price quoted is the "catalog price", not the discounted price actually paid. Enormous price reductions are ensured. This may well be why low-cost carriers such as EasyJet and Ryanair are able to place so many large orders for new aircraft. In addition, it's not uncommon for rates to drop further when it comes time to renew leasing contracts. We all know where these kinds of developments may lead. Companies become financial shaky.

For some time it looked as if the boom in business aircraft would hardly be affected. Enormous orders of the so-called network providers were supposed to provide healthy production figures for manufacturers for years to come. But this segment, too, has been caught up in the current economic realities. Most manufacturers have had to lower their production rates.

Development of new models is becoming increasingly difficult. Few new types of aircraft have emerged and the time between the first flight and readiness for use - particularly with military aircraft - is getting longer and longer. Ten years or more between the first flight and putting an aircraft into service has become the norm - consider, for example, the F/A-22. Technical difficulties, substantial model adaptations and the explosion of development costs accompany almost every demanding military project. What is happening? We've already had a phase like this in the 1970's. What is interesting now is the so-called "follow the sun development method". In the future, in order to drastically shorten development time projects may be worked on at the same time worldwide. A day has 24 hours and therefore, e.g., a project is begun daily in Australia and then "follows the sun" to Europe, and finally to the USA. Modern communication technology allows this to happen on a daily basis - what an amazing idea!

Currently, there are fewer new projects than in past years. Truly new elements can only be observed in the area of UAV (**u**nmanned **a**ir **v**ehicles) and in the great number of small, particularly economical business aircraft. Belonging to the first group are the Boeing X-45A, the Bell Eagle Eye and the Northrop Grumman Fire Scout; in the second group, the Eclipse 500 and the Safire S-26 are worth mentioning. Generally, the shelf-life of aircraft is increasing, seemingly without limit. In addition to the mentioned development times, production times for smaller annual units are also getting longer and longer (see Eurofighter, Rafale, Hawkeye, etc.). A consequence of this is that the lifespan of older models is being substantially extended. However, even if these models appear to be "the same" on the outside, their inner life is routinely adapted to developments. Thus, the same aircraft are actually very different in the end. It is therefore interesting to describe these mutations over the course of the lifespan of a model.

Technological momentum can be observed, however, in several areas of aviation. I would like to mention only one innovation as an example of this. Under the term "Connexion by Boeing", the Internet has made its way into the passenger cabin. In cooperation with the satellite operator Intelsat, the use of mobile broadband service - for the time being restricted to North Atlantic flights - is being introduced to civilian air travel. Several companies, including Lufthansa as one of the first customers, are equipping all their long-haul fleets with Connexion.

Currently, the airline industry is associated with many negative headlines. However, negativism often provides a spark for positive development. Can the air travel industry remain exempt from the current international climate? Let's stay optimistic! No matter what, the industry will remain exciting, fascinating and technically interesting. I would like to share this excitement with you in the first English language edition of **Aircraft of the World**.

Claudio Müller
2004

➤ Boeing Sonic Cruiser

Fasten your seat belt.

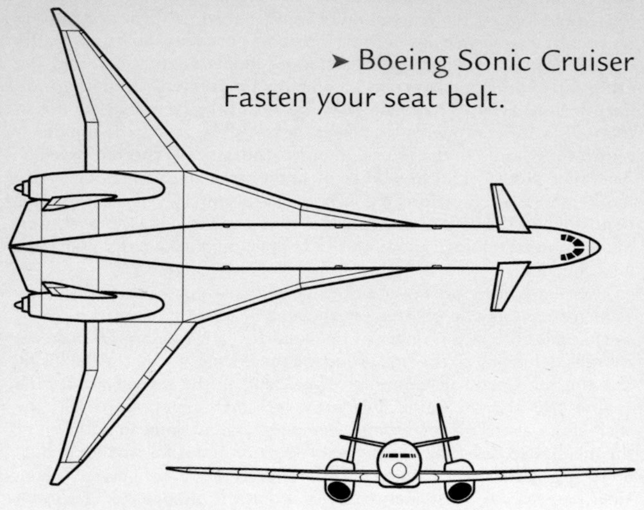

Country of origin: USA.
Type: Long-range airliner.
Power Plant: Two turbofan engines with a medium-sized secondary current ratio each at least 89,924 lbs (41,000 kp/400 kN) static thrust.
Performance: Maximum cruising speed of 0.95 to 0.98 Mach at an altitude of 39,369 to 49,212 ft (12,500 to 15,000 m), cruising range between 7,456 to 10,253 miles (12,000 and 16,500 km).
Weight: No data available yet.
Payload: Two-person cockpit and 200 to 250 passengers in two classes.
State of development: At this time, the project has been suspended. It was originally intended, provided that were a sufficient number of customers, to launch a prototype in 2006 followed by the introduction of scheduled air service in 2008.
Manufacturer: The Boeing Company, Commercial Airplane Group, Seattle, Everett plant, Washington, USA.

Dimensions:
Wingspan approximately 183 ft (56 m)
Length approximately 229 ft (70 m)

BOEING SONIC CRUISER

At the end of 2001, Boeing proposed an interesting alternative to supersonic aircraft with its Sonic Cruiser. Because this project initially appears prohibitive for both economic and, particularly, ecological reasons, the velocity range is being kept below the sound barrier (transonic range) for now. In order to develop an economically competitive model, substantial innovations are necessary in the following four fields: engines, aerodynamics of the wings, configuration of the aircraft cells and materials. Variables derived from current engine models are currently being examined to enable higher compressions in case of a smaller engine diameter. The fuselage has a diameter similar to that of the B767; however, it would be longer and considerably tapered at the rear. A completely new path was taken in the design of wing. It features a triple-delta shape and would only be half as thick as today's models. Almost the entire structure would consist of composite materials such as carbon fiber. The designs presented so far are still evolving and many more changes may occur.

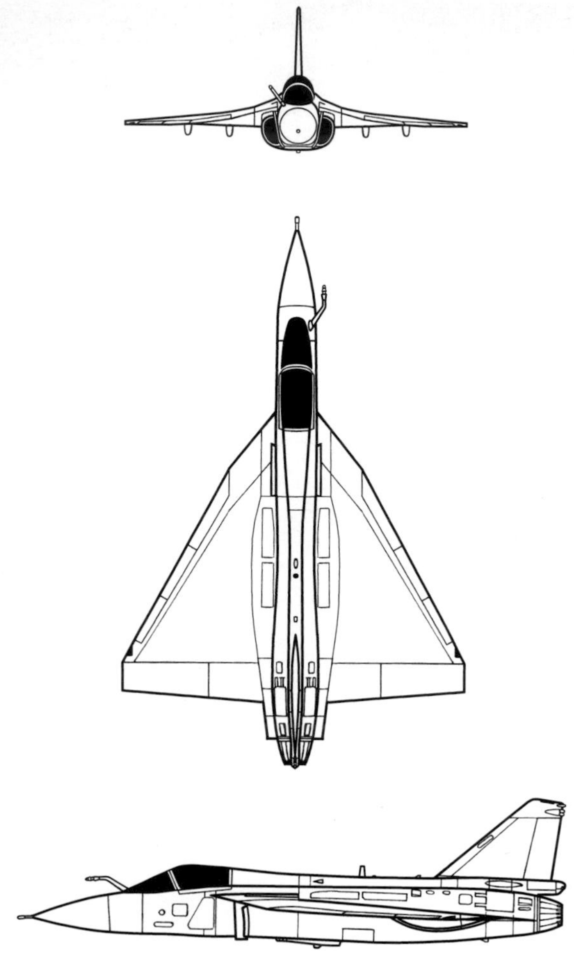

Dimensions:
Wingspan 26.24 ft (8.20 m)
Length 43.30 ft (13.20 m)
Height 14.43 ft (4.40 m)
Wing area approximately 413.33 sq. ft (38.40 m^2)

ADA (HAL) LCA

Country of origin: India.
Type: One and two-seat lightweight multiple purpose fighter.
Power Plant (trial version TD-1/2 + prototypes): One General Electric F404-F2J3 turbofan engine with 18,097 lb (8,210 kp/80.50 kN) static thrust with afterburner, (serial machine) one Kaveri GTX-35VS turbofan engine with 11,789 lbs (5,270 kp/52.44 kN) without afterburner and 18,138 lb (8,170 kp/(80.68 kN) with afterburner.
Performance (estimated): Maximum speed at high altitudes Mach 1.8+, service ceiling above 49,212 ft (15,000 m).
Weight: Empty weight approximately 12,125 lbs (5,500 kg), take-off weight without external load 18,739 lbs (8,500 kg), with external load up to 28,659 lbs (13,000 kg).
Armament: One double loop 23-mm GSh-23 cannon with 200 shots as well as weapons weighing up to 8,818 lbs (4,000 kg) at seven suspension points.
State of development: On January 6, 2001, five years after the rollout, the first of two trial versions, TD-1, was taken on a flight test. A second flight test using the second trial version, TD-2, followed on June 6, 2002. Later, five prototypes are to be built: three one-seat, one two-seat and one naval model (first flight 2004). The Indian armed forces have ordered eight units and plan to order about 200 units in total as replacements for the MiG-21. Delivery is not expected until approximately 2007.
Remarks: The LCA is a small, agile and cost-efficient multiple purpose combat aircraft. The use of the most modern composite materials and aluminum/lithium compounds make this prototype very light. Initially, the electronics were developed in cooperation with Western companies. However, these companies withdrew for political reasons and India was forced to replace the electronic systems with its own systems. Thus, the multifunctional Doppler radar is of Indian origin. The project is still suffering from long delays due to the insufficient performance of the Indian Kaveri engine and problems with the digital fly-by-wire system. Because of this, the commissioning date keeps moving further and further into the future. The model for the Indian Navy will be deployed from aircraft carriers.
Manufacturer: ADA Aeronautical Development Agency of the Hindustani Aeronautics Ltd., Bangalore, India.

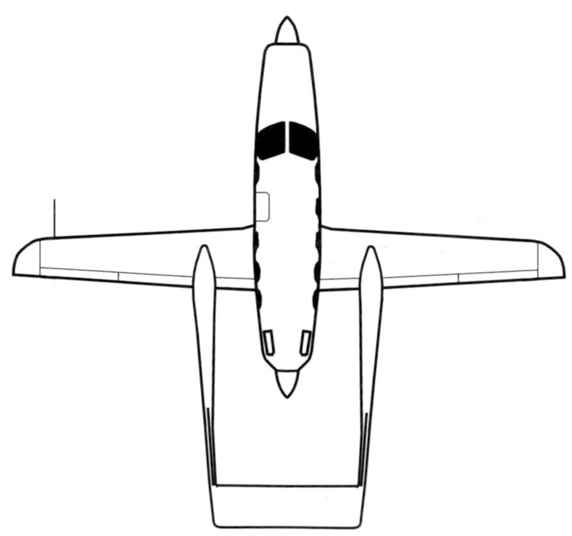

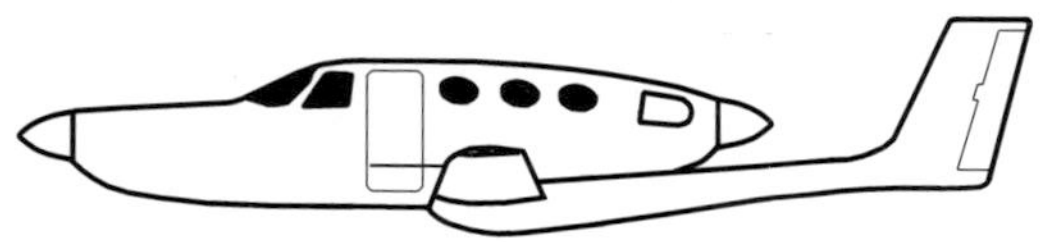

Dimensions:
Wingspan 43.96 ft (13.40 m)
Length 36.58 ft (11.15 m)
Height 9.38 ft (2.86 m)

ADAM A500

Country of origin: USA.
Type: Lightweight corporate aircraft.
Power Plant: Two air-cooled six-cylinder horizontally opposed Teledyne Continental TSIO-550E engines each with 350 SHP (260 kW) performance.
Performance (according to data provided by the manufacturer): Maximum cruising speed at 75% performance 288 mph (463 km), economic cruising speed at 60% performance 255 mph (410 km/h), initial take-off speed 30 ft (9 m)/sec, service ceiling 24,999 ft (7,620 m), maximum cruising range with IFR-reserves 1,324 miles (2,130 km).
Weight: Take-off weight 6,300 lbs (2,858 kg).
Payload: One pilot and five passengers in the standard model, maximum payload 2,094 lbs (950 kg).
State of development: A trial version designated as M-309 flew for the first time on March 21, 2000. The first of three reengineered prototypes was flight tested on July 11, 2002. There have been few sales for the first 50 units. Delivery dates are expected to be in the near future.
Remarks: Few changes have been made from the M-309 trial version to the A500. The fuselage has become a little longer in order to create space for a ventral stair. Also the wingspan has increased slightly in size. Thanks to the engine arrangement at the front and rear end of the fuselage, this two-engine aircraft shows the flight qualities of a single-engine aircraft. The design of the wing, which is made of carbon, is remarkable. Designed as a low-wing airplane, the aircraft's main wing is connected with the horizontal and vertical tail by means of double hulls. The cockpit has contemporary flat screens. Compared to other airplanes of this class, the cabin is truly spacious with an internal length of 14 ft (4.11 m), a width of 4 ft (1.33 m), and a height of 4 ft (1.29 m). The A500 has an attractive purchase price of US$935,000. The jet-operated A700 had its maiden flight on Sunday, July 27, 2003.
Manufacturer: Adam Aircraft Industries, Denver, Centennial Airport plant, Englewood, Colorado, USA.

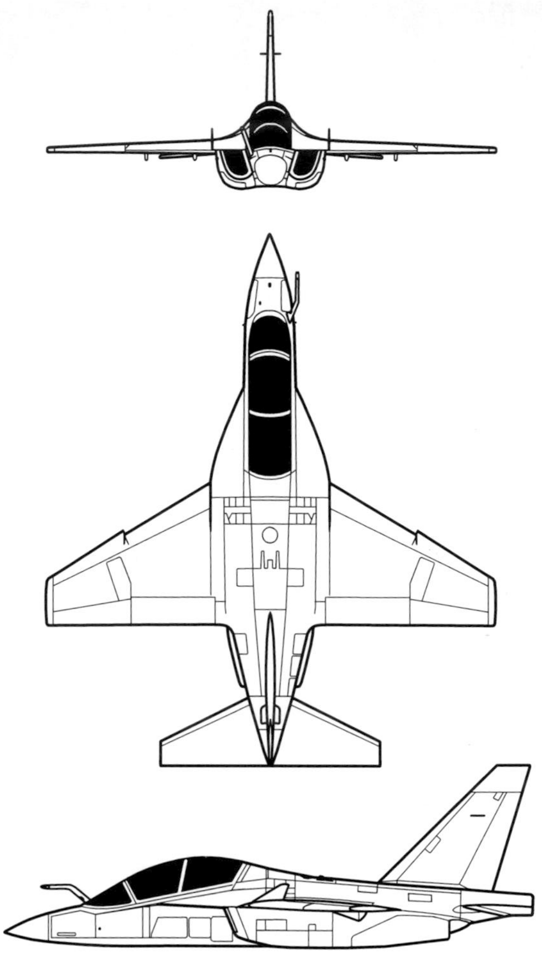

Dimensions:
Wingspan 31.88 ft (9.72 m)
Length 37.69 ft (11.49 m)
Height 15.32 ft (4.76 m)
Wing area 253.16 sq. ft (23.52 m^2)

AERMACCHI M-346

Country of origin: Italy.
Type: Advanced trainer.
Power Plant: Two Honeywell F124-GA-200 turbofan engines each with 6,249 lbs (2,830 kp/27.80 kN) performance.
Performance (according to the manufacturer): Maximum speed 673 mph (1,083 km/h) at 4,986 ft (1,520 m), initial rate of climb 335 ft (102 m)/sec, service ceiling 44,946 ft (13,700 m), cruising range with maximum internal fuel 1,174 miles (1,890 km), with two external additional tanks and 10% reserve 1,578 miles (2,540 km).
Weight: Empty weight 10,196 lbs (4,625 kg), take-off weight for training deployment 14,770 lbs (6,700 kg), with full armament 20,943 lbs (9,500 kg).
Armament (according to the manufacturer): A weapons load of up to 6,613 lbs (3,000 kg) can be carried.
State of development: Should the upcoming test flight of the first of three prototypes generate sales, the first model could be delivered in 2007.
Remarks: The M-346 is a derivative of the Russian-Italian co-project Yak/AEM-130. Although it looks similar to the test model from the outside, the new construction has slightly smaller dimensions. The structure primarily consists of light aluminum. Parts of the wings as well as the horizontal and vertical tail are made of composite materials. A substantial innovation is the fly-by-wire delivered by Teleavio/Marconi that can be programmed in varying ways according to deployment. It can be implemented manually or up to the fly-by-wire configuration. As a result, an optimal training effect can be achieved The twofold redundant Avionics structure is based on a MIL-STD-1553B databus and comprises TACAN, IFF, IN/GPS, etc. Thanks to these assets, the M-346 is one of the most advanced training systems of its time for prospective combat pilots of the world. Yakowlew continues the further development of the output prototype YAK/AEM-130.
Manufacturer: Aermacchi SpA, Varese-Venegono, Italy.

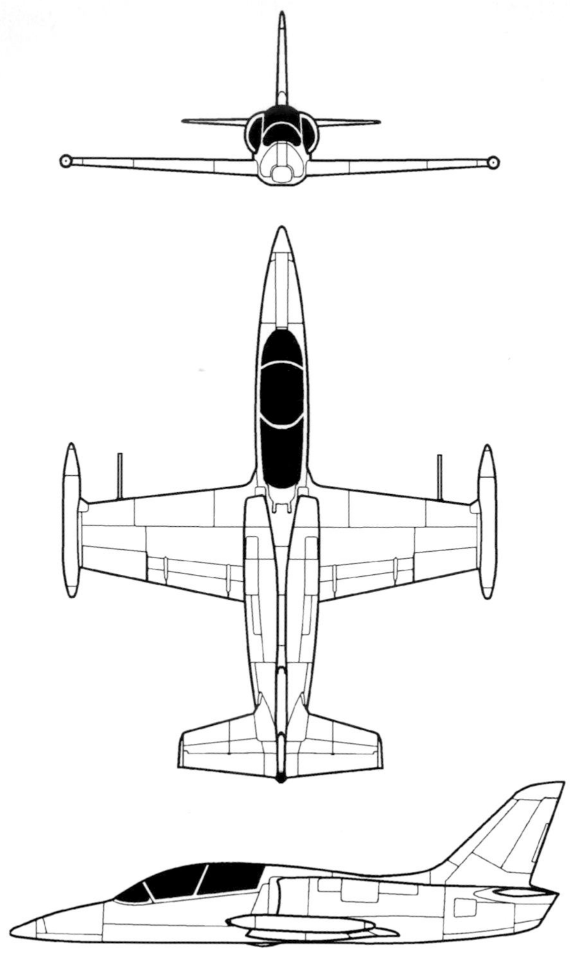

Dimensions:
Wingspan including wing end tanks 31.29 ft (9.54 m)
Length 41.76 ft (12.73 m)
Height 15.68 ft (4.78 m)
Wing area 202.36 sq. ft (18.80 m^2)

AERO L159 ALBATROS

Country of origin: Czech Republic.
Type: Light one-seat (L 159A) and two-seat (L 159B) combat aircraft and mission-trainer.
Power Plant: One AlliedSignal/ITEC F124-GA-100 turbofan engine with 6,295 lbs (2,850 kp/28 kN) static thrust.
Performance: Maximum speed 582 mph (936 km/h [Mach 0.82]) at sea-level, 567 mph (912 km/h) at 1,640 ft (500 m), initial take-off speed 155 ft (47 m)/sec, service ceiling 43,306 ft (13,200 m), cruising range with maximum internal fuel and 10% reserve 976 miles (1,570 km), with additional tanks 1,572 miles (2,530 km).
Weight: Empty weight 9,171 lbs (4,160 kg), maximum take-off weight 17,636 lbs (8,000 kg).
Armament: Combination of weapons at one station underneath the fuselage and six under the wings for air-to-air guided missiles, air-to-ground guided missiles, bombs and electronics box with a total weight of 5,158 lbs (2,340 kg).
State of development: The first two-seat prototype completed a flight test on August 2, 1997 followed by a one-seat prototype on August 18, 1998. The mission-trainer model L-159B has been flying since July 23, 2002. Contrary to earlier information, all 72 units ordered by the Czech Air Force were model L-159A (approximately 50 have been delivered). Subsequently, two L-159B trainers have been ordered.
Remarks: Although this aircraft is derived from the well-known L39/L59, the L159 is a new development in many aspects. The stretched out fuselage was completely reengineered in the front area in order to make room for the modern Rockwell-Collins avionics system, consisting of the multi-role FIAR Grifo-L Doppler radar, MIL-STD-1553B-databus, H-764G-navigation system with GPS, Head-Up Display, etc. Thanks to the Western engine with a thrust increased by 30%, all airplane performances could be remarkably enhanced. The cockpit with liquid crystal displays is widely armored. Two models are manufactured: the two-seat L159B as well as the one-seat L159A with an additionally built-in tank instead of the second seat.
Manufacturer: Aero Vodochody a.s., Odolena Voda, Prague, CFR.

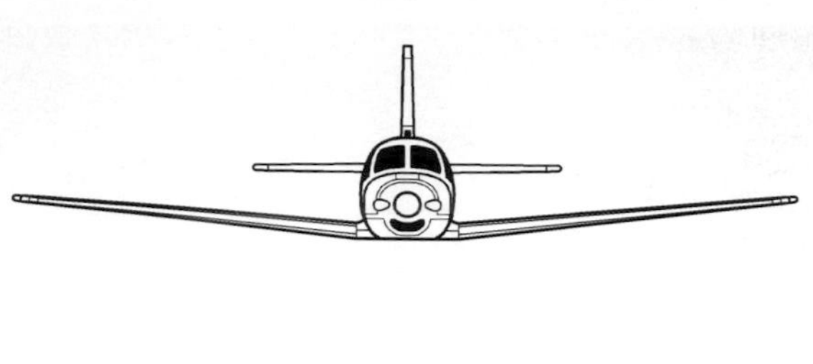

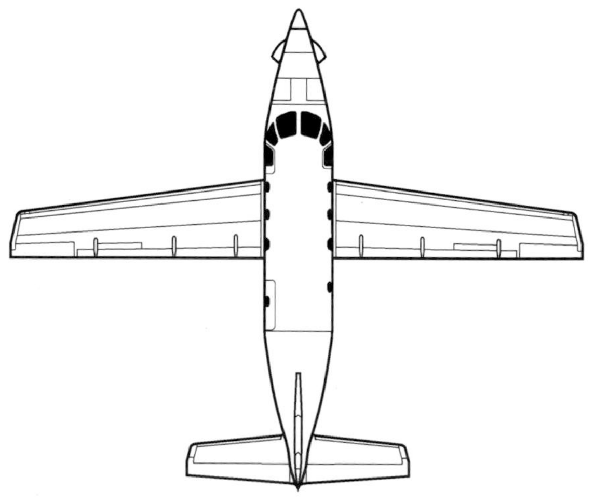

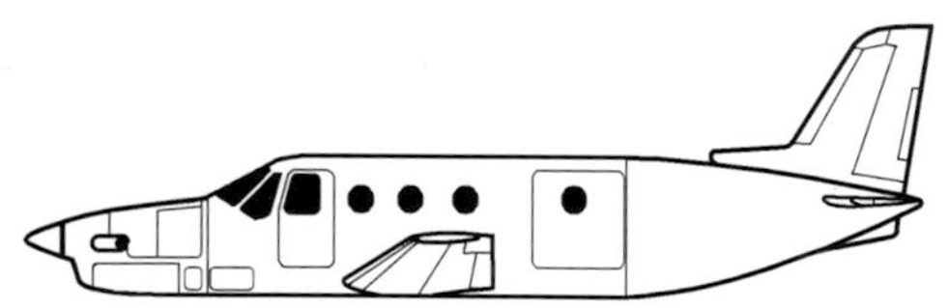

Dimensions:
Wing span 45.34 ft (13.82 m)
Length 40.12 ft (12.23 m)
Height 15.68 ft (4.78 m)
Wing area 226.04 sq. ft (21 m^2)

AERO AE 270

Country of origin: Czech Republic.
Type: Light multi-purpose airplane.
Power Plant: (Ae270P) One Pratt & Whitney Canada PT6A-42A propeller turbine with 850 SHP (634 kW) performance or (Ae270W) Walter M 601F with 777 SHP (580 kW) performance.
Performance (Ae270P). Maximum cruising speed of 13,123 ft (4,000 m) 253 mph (407 km/h), normal cruising speed 242 mph (390 km/h), initial rate of climb 27 ft (8.2 m)/sec, service ceiling 24,999 ft (7,620 m), cruising range with maximum payload 292 miles (470 km), maximum cruising range 1,473 miles (2,370 km).
Weight (Ae270P): Empty weight 5,026 lbs (2,280 kg), maximum take-off weight 8,157 lbs (3,700 kg).
Payload: One to two people in the cockpit and up to eight passengers or up to 2,645 lbs (1,200 kg) freight.
State of development: After many years of inactivity, the first prototype Ae270P had its initial flight test on July 25, 2000. Three flying prototypes were built. Deliveries of the 70 units on order will start in the near future.
Remarks: The Ae270P is a 50/50 joint venture between Aero and the AIDS in Taiwan. The Aero270W features the Czech Walter-engine, domestic electronics and fixed alighting gear as well as the substantially more efficient Ae270P Ibis with a power plant from Pratt & Whitney Canada, avionics of AlliedSignal Bendix/King, retractable landing gear and pressure cabin. AIDS manufactures the wings and alighting gear while Aero takes care of the rest of the structure and is responsible for the final assembly. As a multi-role airplane, the Ae270 is designed for both passenger and freight transport as well as for transport of business executives. Two models are currently being developed: the Ae270HP will have a more powerful Pratt & Whitney power plant and a second model has been designed with buoyancy chambers. The basic model Ae270P is priced at about US$1.9 million.
Manufacturer: Aero Vodochody a.s., Odolena Voda, Prague, CFR.

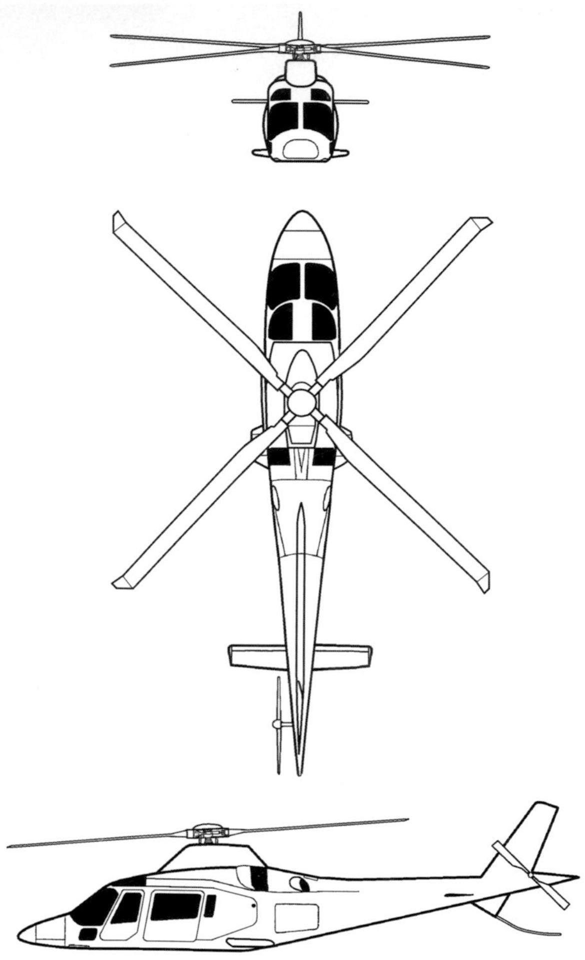

Dimensions:
Rotor diameter 36.08 ft (11.00 m)
Fuselage length 37.53 ft (11.44 m)
Height 11.48 ft (3.50 m)

AGUSTA WESTLAND A109 POWER

Country of origin: Italy.
Type: Light multi-purpose helicopter.
Power Plant: Two Pratt & Whitney Canada PW206C turboshaft engines each with 640 SHP (477 kW) performance.
Performance: Maximum speed 193 mph (311 km/h), maximum cruising speed 186 mph (300 km/h) at 4,986 ft (1,520 m), maximum diagonal take-off speed 34 ft (10.5 m)/sec, hovering altitude with ground effect 18,995 ft (5,790 m), without ground effect 13,300 ft (4,054 m), cruising range 516 miles (830 km), maximum flight duration 4 hours and 20 minutes.
Weight: Empty 3,428 lbs (1,555 kg), maximum take-off weight 6,283 lbs (2,850 kg) with internal payload and 6,613 lbs (3,000 kg) with external payload.
Payload: One pilot and seven passengers. As an ambulance helicopter, two recumbent patients and two medics. Maximum payload 2,491 lbs (1,130 kg).
Armament (A109KM): Up to eight wire guided TOW-guided missiles, one 7.62-mm machine gun mounted underneath the fuselage or a 12.7-mm cannon attached to the doors.
State of development: This version has been flying since February 8, 1995. Upon obtaining certification, deliveries started mid-1996. Since then Agusta has obtained more than 200 definite orders (130 have been delivered), among the orders are 30 A109 LUH (+ 10 options) for the South African Air Force (under license by Denel), 20 HPK15 for the Swedish Air Force, 3 for the navy of Nigeria and 8 MH-68A for the US Coast Guard.
Remarks: The latest design, Power, has a new all-embracing main rotor head consisting of few parts with a titanium hub and elastomer beds, which is easy to maintain. The high-capacity engines are equipped with FADEC, an electronic engine management system. The retractable alighting gear has been reengineered. Finally, the cabin has been made roomier. Thanks to a 1553 MIL-STD databus, a multitude of additional systems can be made compatible. The power is also obtainable by means of French Turbomeca Arrius 2K1 engines each 670 SHP (500 kW). In short, an A109 "stretched" by about 8 inches (20 cm), flies with stronger PW207-engines with a slightly increased take-off weight and a tail rotor made of composite material.
Manufacturer: AgustaWestland Ltd., Vergiate plant, Italy.

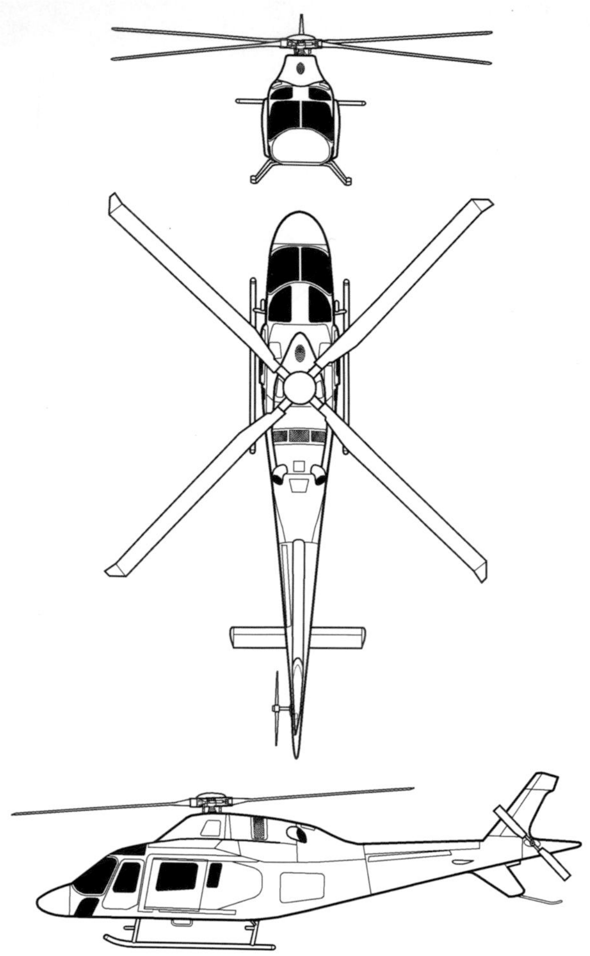

Dimensions:
Rotor diameter 36.08 ft (11.00 m)
Fuselage length 36.31 ft (11.07 m)
Height 10.82 ft (3.30 m)

AGUSTA WESTLAND A119 KOALA

Country of origin: Italy.
Type: Light multi-purpose helicopter.
Power Plant: One Turbomeca Arriel 1K1 turboshaft engine (prototype) with 800 SHP (596 kW) continuous power and (series) Pratt & Whitney Canada PT6B-37A engine with 1,000 SHP (747 kW) continuous power.
Performance (with PT6B-37 engine): Maximum speed 173 mph (278 k/hm), maximum cruising speed 162 mph (260 km/h), hovering altitude with ground effect 10,892 ft (3,320 m), without ground effect 8,037 ft (2,450 m), service ceiling 17,913 ft (5,460 m), maximum flight duration 3 hours and 40 minutes and maximum cruising range 385 miles (620 km).
Weight: Empty weight 3,417 lbs (1,550 kg), maximum take-off weight 5,996 lbs (2,720 kg), later up to 6,613 lbs (3,000 kg).
Payload: Pilot and up to seven passengers with a maximum payload 2,546 lbs (1,155 kg).
State of development: The first two prototypes have been flying since April 1995. Following certification delays through mid-1999, the first deliveries were made to customers at the end of that year. To date 30 units have been ordered, options exist for about 30 more. The Italian Carabinieri may obtain up to 50 units. A purchasing decision is still outstanding. A second assembly line has been established at Denel, South Africa.
Remarks: The A119 Koala is the most cost-efficient model of the A109. It can be obtained at a price of US$1.78 million. The cells and the rotor have been modeled on the A109. As far as the cabin volume is concerned, the A119 is, at this time, the largest single-motor helicopter. Eight persons can be seated and, when used as an ambulance helicopter, the A119 can additionally accommodate up to two stretchers for recumbent patients. Also, this helicopter has a voluminous luggage compartment of 34 cubic feet (0.95 m^3). Economic efficiency and robustness in the entire design add value.
Manufacturer: AgustaWestland Ltd., Vergiate plant, Italy.

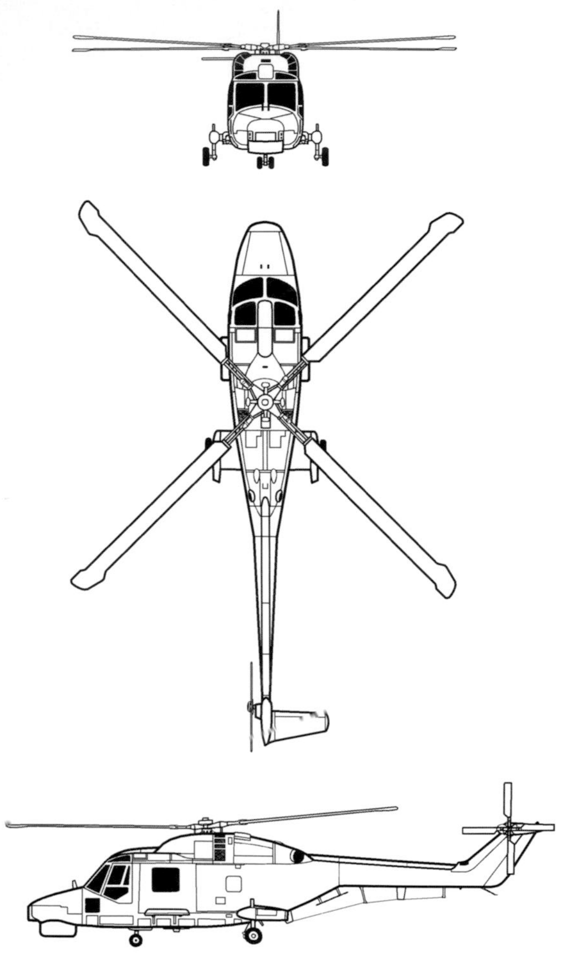

Dimensions:
Rotor diameter 41.99 ft (12.80 m)
Fuselage length with folded rotor blades 43.43 ft (13.24 m)
Height including rotor head 12.04 ft (3.67 m)

AGUSTA WESTLAND SUPER LYNX 300

Country of origin: United Kingdom.
Type: Military multi-purpose helicopter for Army (Battlefield Lynx) and Navy missions (Super Lynx).
Power Plant: Two Honeywell LHTEC CTS800-4N turboshaft engines each with 1,620 SHP (1,207 kW) or Rolls-Royce Gem 42-1 each with 1,120 SHP (835 kW) performance.
Performance (Gem 42-1): Maximum cruising speed 159 mph (256 km/h) at sea-level, normal cruising speed 143 mph (230 km/h), diagonal take-off speed 33 ft (10 m)/sec, cruising range during tactical missions with 20 minute reserve 426 miles (685 km). The duration of an antitank mission conducted 29 miles (46 km) from base: 2 hours.
Weight (Super Lynx 300): Empty weight 8,692 lbs (3,943 kg), maximum take-off weight 11,750 lbs (5,330 kg).
Payload: One to two pilots and, depending on the purpose of the mission, up to 12 people in the cabin. Three to eight including patients and medics when used as a rescue helicopter. Rescue winch with lifting capacity of 600 lbs (272 kg).
Armament: As an antitank helicopter up to eight suspension points TOW-, HOT- or hellfire guided missiles, as an anti-ship helicopter up to four guided missiles Sea Skua, AS12TT or two Penguins.
State of development: The latest version of the Lynx has been flying since 2001. As a serial helicopter for the navy of Malaysia, it has been flying since May 2002. More than 430 units of all models have been delivered to three armies and 14 navies.
Remarks: At this time the British Army is testing Battlefield Lynx helicopter versions AH7/9 equipped with Honeywell-T800 engines. First and foremost, all helicopters will receive improved navigation and communication systems such as a laser-target display device. A new model described as AH10 will be better suited to fulfill the support function for the WAH-64D (see pages 100/101). The navy version Super Lynx is currently offered in three models: Srs.100 with Rolls-Royce Gem 42-1 engines and a main rotor made of composite material, 360°-Seaspray-Radar in the bow of the fuselage and in the conventional cockpit; Srs.200 in similar configuration, though with LHTEC-CTS800 engines and FADEC-system; Srs.300 the top model with additional Night-Vision-Goggles (NVG), glass cockpit, digital avionics and double redundant databus MIL-STD-1553D.
Manufacturer: AgustaWestland Ltd., Yeovil plant, Somerset, United Kingdom.

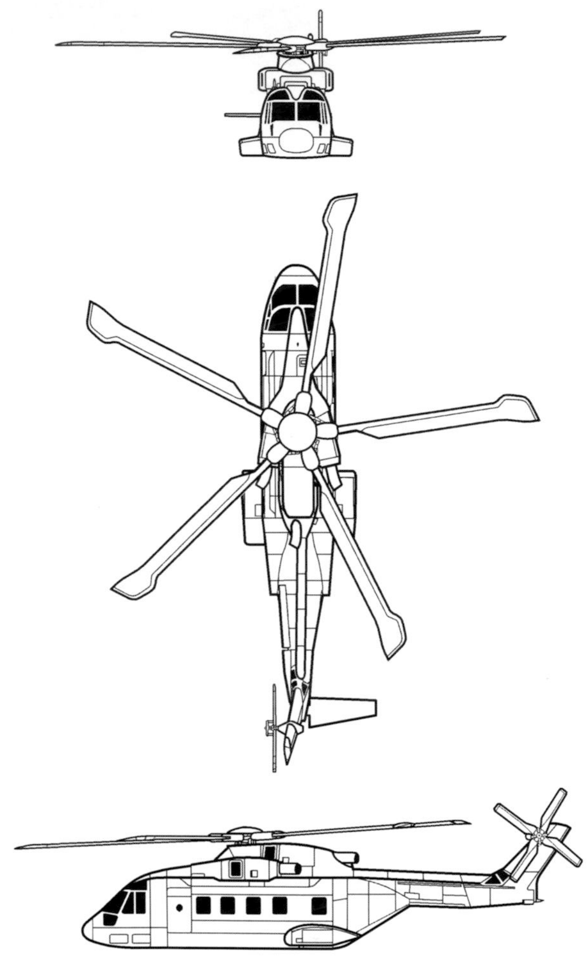

Dimensions:
Rotor diameter 60.99 ft (18.59 m)
Fuselage length 64.00 ft (19.51 m)
Height, including rotor head 17.09 ft (5.21 m)

AGUSTA WESTLAND EH101

Country of origin: United Kingdom and Italy.
Type: Submarine fighter and transport helicopter.
Power Plant: (RN) Three Rolls Royce Turbomeca RTM 322 turboshaft engines each with 2,241 SHP (1,671 kW) or (Italian Navy) General Electric CT7-6A1 each with 2,040 SHP (1,521 kW) performance.
Performance (CT7-6): Maximum cruising speed 191 mph (308 km/h), economic touring speed 166 mph (267 km/h), hovering altitude with ground effect 9,005 ft (2,745 m), without ground effect 5,495 ft (1,675 m), maximum flying altitude 15,091 ft (4,600 m), cruising range with 30 passengers 575 miles (926 km), deployment cruising range with additional tanks 1,093 miles (1,760 km).
Weight: Empty weight ASW-model 20,447 lbs (9,275 kg), multi-purpose version 19,841 lbs (9,000 kg), civilian model 19,825 lbs (8,993 kg), maximum take-off weight ASW-model 29,828 lbs (13,530 kg), others 31,499 lbs (14,288 kg).
Payload: Two pilots and 30 passengers, maximum payload 14,770 lbs (6,700 kg).
Armament (HM Mk.1): Four lightweight Stingray torpedoes or anti-ship guided missiles of the Exocet-Harpoon class.
State of development: The first of nine aircraft in development flew for the first time on October 9, 1987. Until now a total of 130 orders have been placed: Denmark 14 multi-role-/SAR-version, United Kingdom 66 (44 ASW-version for RN, 22 multi-role version for RAF), Italy 20 for the navy (8 ASW, 4 AEW and 8 multi-role version), Canada 15 SAR-version AW520 Cormorant, Portugal 14 SAR (+ 2 options), Tokyo Police 1 of the civilian model.
Remarks: Westland will test the development of an optimized version for amphibious missions that could launch from helicopter carriers. This design would have a greater take-off weight of about 35,273 lbs (16,000 kg) thanks to powerful RTM322-04 engines. It would also have new slightly larger rotors. In conjunction with Lockheed Martin, an additional US-version with the designation US101 is offered.
Manufacturer: AgustaWestland (EH Industries Ltd.), London, UK.

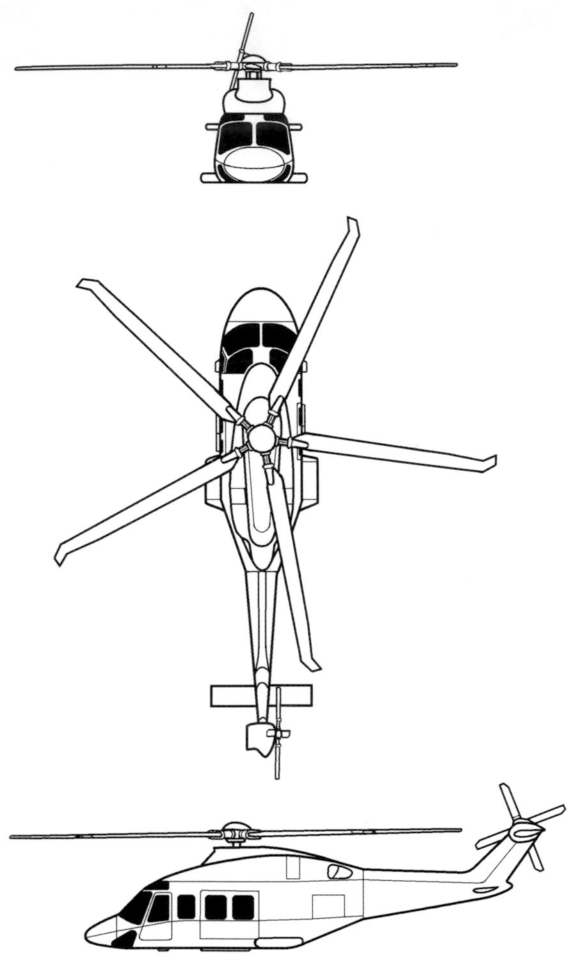

Dimensions:
Rotor diameter 45.27 ft (13.80 m)
Fuselage length 54.62 ft (16.65 m)
Height above empennage 16.23 ft (4.95 m)

AGUSTA WESTLAND BELL AB139

Country of origin: Italy and USA.
Type: Mid-weight multi-purpose helicopter.
Power Plant: Two Pratt & Whitney Canada PT6C-67C turboshaft engines each with 1,679 SHP (1,250 kW) performance.
Performance: Maximum speed 193 mph (310 km/h), maximum cruising speed 180 mph (290 km/h), diagonal take-off speed 33 ft (10 m)/sec, hovering altitude with ground effect 11,810 ft (3,600 m), without ground effect 9,579 ft (2,920 m), service ceiling 19,402 ft (5,914 m). Flight duration 4 hours, cruising range with 10 passengers 404 miles (650 km), maximum 466 miles (750 km).
Weight: Maximum take-off weight 13,227 lbs (6,000 kg).
Payload: Two pilots and between 12 and 15 passengers or, for rescue operations, six recumbent patients and four medics, maximum payload internal 5,511 lbs (2,500 kg), external 5,952 lbs (2,700 kg).
State of development: The prototype had its flight test on February 3, 2001 followed by a serial model on June 24, 2002. Thus far, 50 units have been ordered. Delivery began in 2003. The US Coast Guard will purchase 34 AB139 as a search and rescue helicopter.
Remarks: The AB139 is a community project of Agusta (75%) and Bell (25%) whereby the first named company holds the lead in this enterprise. Also GKN Westland (tail), PZL Swidnik (fuselage components) and Honeywell (Primus Epic Avionics) are participating in this project. The new model will be manufactured simultaneously on both sides of the Atlantic as the successor to the successful Bell-205-412 family. The following fields of application are planned for the AB139: transport of business people and VIPs, surveillance duties, EMS-transport and supply for offshore oil-drilling platforms. Also armed models for military missions are planned. The AB139 stands out with a very roomy cabin for its class. The electronic equipment corresponds with today's standards.
Manufacturer: AgustaWestland Ltd., Vergiate plant, Italy and Bell Helicopter, Textron, USA.

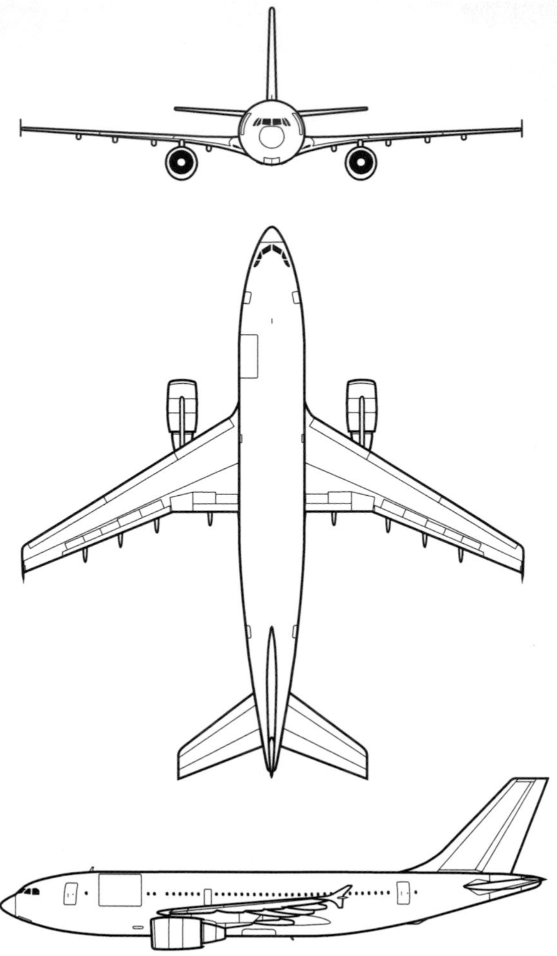

Dimensions:
Wingspan 144.02 ft (43.90 m)
Length 153.08 ft (46.66 m)
Height 51.83 ft (15.80 m)
Wing area 2,357 sq. ft (219.00 m^2)

AIRBUS A310 MRTT ◄

Country of origin: European Consortium.
Type: Military multi-purpose transporter and tanker.
Power Plant: Two General Electric CF6-80C2 turbofan engines each with 58,988 lbs (26,760 kp/262.39 kN) static thrust.
Performance: Maximum cruising speed 553 mph (890 km/h) at 24,999 ft (7,620 m), normal cruising speed 544 mph (875 km/h [Mach 0.80]) at 31,003 ft (9,450 m), service ceiling 40,025 ft (12,200 m), cruising range with maximum number of passengers 4,598 miles (7,400 km), deployment cruising range 8,055 miles (12,964 km), action radius as tanker with 126,764 lbs (57,500 kg) fuel 1,149 miles (1,850 km).
Weight: Empty weight 158,378 lbs (71,840 kg), maximum take-off weight 361,554 lbs (164,000 kg).
Payload: Two-person cockpit and up to 214 passengers or combination of passengers and freight. Maximum payload 86,199 lbs (39,100 kg).
State of development: First flight of the standard model on December 5, 1985. The air forces of the following countries are using various versions of the A310: France (2, VIP), Germany (7) and Canada (5) as transporter, freighter and partially as tanker. The A310-300 of Belgium (2) and Thailand (1) are configured for VIP and passenger flights. Additional reconstruction orders are taken into account. The civilian version is built in small quantities. 255 of the 260 orders have already been delivered.
Remarks: Increasingly, the A310 is being used for military missions. Germany and Canada have some of their units reconstructed to so-called Mutli-Role-Transport-Tankers (MRTT). Two hoses can be reeled out for refueling from each of the MK32B-907 pods supplied by Flight Refueling (part of the UK Cobham Group) and positioned under the wings. Airbus also offers a AEW&C-version furnished with the Israeli early warning radar Elta-EL/M-2075 Phalcon above the fuselage as well as additional defense electronics. So far no orders have been placed for this variation.
Manufacturer: Airbus Industrie, Blagnac, France, part of the EADS (European Aeronautic Defence and Space Company).

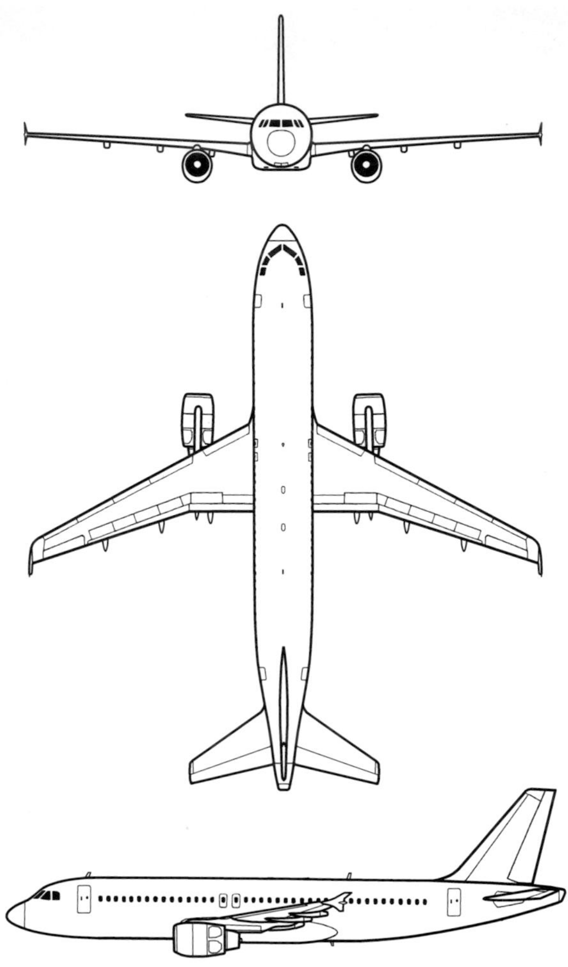

Dimensions:
Wingspan 111.84 ft (34.09 m)
Length (A320) 123.25 ft (37.57 m), (A321) 145.99 ft (44.50 m)
Height 38.71 ft (11.80 m)
Wing area 1,317 sq. ft (122.40 m^2)

AIRBUS A320-200

Country of origin: European Consortium.
Type: Short and long-range commercial airplane.
Power Plant: Two CFM International CFM56-5B4 turbofan engines each with 26,505 lbs (12,020 kp/117.9 kN) static thrust or IAE V2500-A1 each with 26,505 lbs (12,020 kp/117.9 kN) static thrust.
Performance: Maximum cruising speed Mach 0.82, economic cruising speed 525 mph (845 km/h), service ceiling 39,008 ft (11,890 m), cruising range with maximum number of passengers including reserves 3,125 miles (5,030 km).
Weight: Empty weight 92,152 lbs (41,800 kg), maximum take-off weight 169,798 lbs (77,020 kg).
Payload: Two-person cockpit and multiple-class seating for 150 passengers, single class interior design for maximum 179 passengers, maximum payload 47,619 lbs (21,600 kg).
State of development: The prototype of the A320 had its first flight test on February 22, 1987 and initial deliveries took place in March 1988. Orders through December 2002 totaled 2,958 units of the models A318/319/320/321, which included 1,597 A320, 421 A321 and 856 A319. About 1,880 of those (A320: 1,128) have been delivered.
Remarks: The A320 is the basic model of the "small fuselage family" of Airbus. Even without the ongoing production figures, this model has already proven to be one of aviation's greatest commercial successes. See pages 32/33 for specifications for the A318. EADS/Alenia offers a maritime surveillance model based on the A320 that is designated as "**M**aritime **M**ultirole **A**ircraft (MMA)". The navies of Italy (14 units) and Germany (10) have similar needs. The mission system is supposedly equipped with L-3 communications with maritime surveillance radar and sensors. The fuselage would be completed with a weapons bay underneath it. For this purpose, two-suspension apparati would be provided under the wings to carry guided missiles. The decision for this kind of development should come shortly.
Manufacturer: Airbus Industrie, Blagnac, France, (A320) Toulouse-Blagnac plant, (A321) Hamburg-Finkenwerder, Federal Republic of Germany, part of the EADS (European Aeronautic Defence and Space Company).

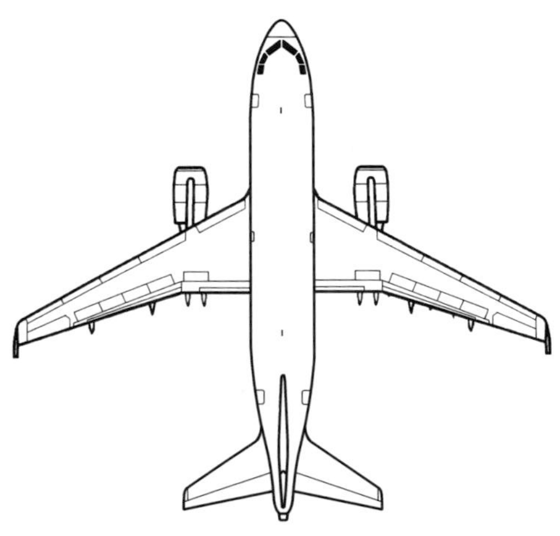

Dimensions:
Wingspan 111.87 ft (34.10 m)
Length 103.14 ft (31.44 m)
Height 41.20 ft (12.56 m)
Wing area 1,317 sq. ft (122.40 m^2)

AIRBUS A318

Country of origin: European Consortium.
Type: Short to medium-range airliner.
Power Plant: Two CFM 56-5 International or Pratt & Whitney PW6000 turbofan engines, each featuring between 20,008 to 22, 998 lbs (9,070 and 10,430 kp/89.0 to 102.3 kN) static thrust.
Performance (according to manufacturer's information): Maximum cruising speed Mach 0.82, flight range with maximum payload 1,739 miles (2,800 km), option for maximum cruising range of 3,293 miles (5,300 km).
Weight: Empty weight 84,656 lbs (38,400 kg), take-off weight 130,071 lbs (59,000 kg), option for maximum take-off weight of 145,503 lbs (66,000 kg).
Payload: Two-person cockpit team, and, depending on the version of interior equipment, up to 107 passengers in two classes or 117 passengers in a single class.
State of development: The construction of the A318 with PW6000 engines was completed on January 15, 2002 and the first prototype equipped with CFM-5 engines followed on August 29, 2002. Delivery has been considerably delayed due to continuing difficulties regarding the PW6000 engines. In addition, several contracts have been canceled, so the present volume of orders has been reduced to only 84 units.
Remarks: The A318 type was mainly developed as competition for the Boeing 717 (see pages 82/83). It is the newest and smallest version of the A320-family and serves to fill the needs of short-range traffic. Compared to the A319, it features a shortened fuselage by 8 ft (2.40 m), engines with reduced power and with the PW6000 it constitutes an alternative model with lower weight. It fits smoothly into the modular construction principle of the A319, A320, and the A321. A larger vertical tail has been designed due to ensure direction stability. Finally, the manufacturer offers two versions featuring different take-off weights and flight ranges.
Manufacturer: Airbus Industries, Blagnac, France, Airbus Hamburg-Finkenwerder, Federal Republic of Germany, subsidiaries of EADS (European Aeronautic and Space Company).

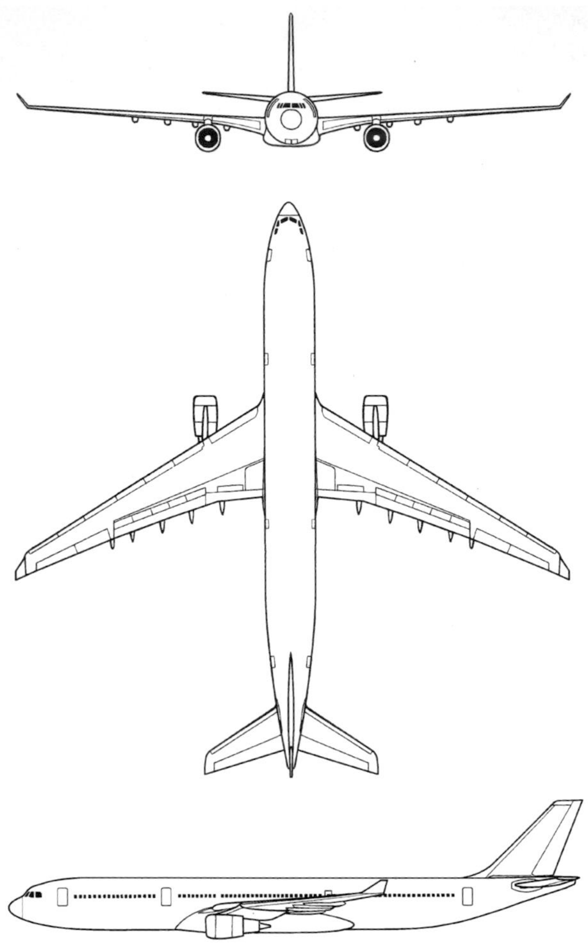

Dimensions:
Wingspan, including winglets 197.83 ft (60.30 m)
Length 193.50 ft (58.98 m)
Height 58.69 ft (17.89 m)
Wing area 3,908 sq. ft (363.10 m^2)

AIRBUS A330-200

Country of origin: European Consortium.
Type: Long-range airliner.
Power Plant: Two Rolls-Royce Trent 772, General Electric CF6-oE1, or Pratt & Whitney PW4168 turbofan engines featuring between 67,893 and 71,034 lbs (29,600 and 31,000 kp/302 and 316 kN) static thrust.
Performance: Maximum cruising speed 559 mph (900 km/h), economic cruising speed 547 mph (880 km/h), service ceiling 39,369 ft (12,000 m), flight range with 293 passengers 7,457 miles (12,000 km), with 380 passengers 6,151 miles (9,900 km).
Weight: Empty weight 264,552 lbs (120,000 kg), maximum take-off weight 507,058 lbs (230,000 kg).
Payload: Two-person cockpit team and, employing three-class seating, 16, 36 and 205 passengers in the first, second and tourist classes respectively in six- or eight-seat arrangements with two aisles. A maximum of 380 passengers in a nine-seat arrangement with a maximum payload of 80,248 lbs (36,400 kg).
State of development: The first flight of the 330-200 prototype took place on August 13, 1997. Deliveries started in April 1998. By the end of 2002, 21 airlines or leasing companies have ordered about 210 units (+ options). Currently, about 200 planes constitute the number of orders of the initial type. So far about 250 planes of both versions have been delivered.
Remarks: The A330-200 is the long-range version of the A330 family. This is why the fuselage has been shortened by 18 ft (5.33 m) and the fuel capacity increased to 36,720 gallons (139,000 l). Additionally, there have been minor revisions to the vertical tail. In all other aspects this version is largely identical with the A330-300 featuring the same wings, vertical tail, cockpit design and all other systems as the A340-300. Currently in development is an A330-200F cargo version as well as a military variant MRTT for mid-air fueling, designed for carrying 36,984 gallons (140,000 l). See photo of experimental carrier.
Manufacturer: Airbus Industries, Blagnac, France, subsidiary of EADS (European Aeronautic Defense and Space Company).

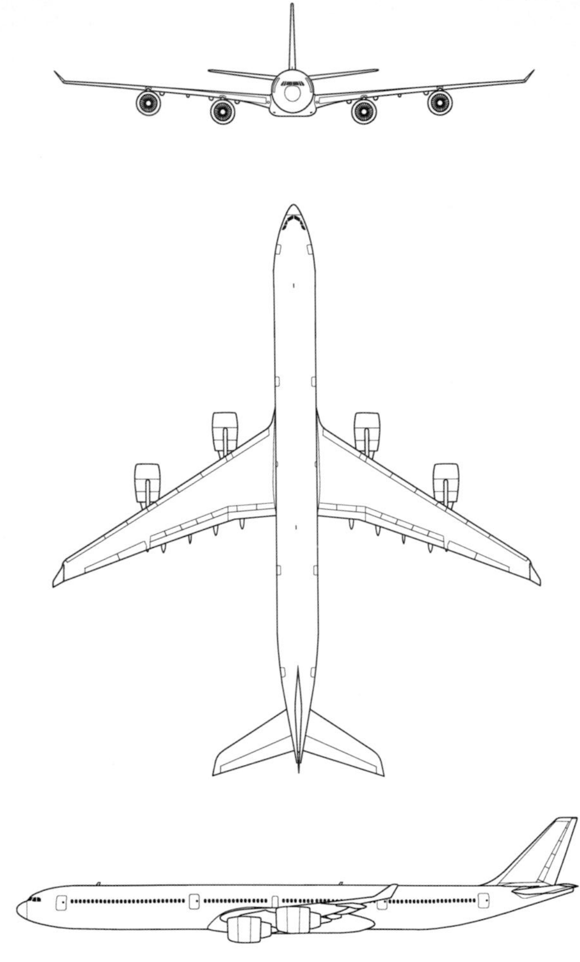

Dimensions:
Wingspan including winglets 208.16 ft (63.45 m)
Length (-600) 247.04 ft (75.30 m), (-500) 222.76 ft (67.90 m)
Height 56.71 ft (17.29 m)
Wing area 4,729 sq. ft (439.40 m^2)

AIRBUS A340-600/-500

Country of origin: European Consortium.
Type: Long-range airliner.
Power Plant: (-600) Four Rolls-Royce or Trent 556 turbofan engines each featuring static thrust of 55,978 lbs (25,380 kp/249 kN) or (-500) Trent 553 each featuring static thrust of 53,055 lbs (24,050 kp/236 kN).
Performance (according to manufacturer's information): Maximum cruising speed 578 mph (930 km/h [Mach 0.86]), economic cruising speed 553 mph (890 km/h [Mach 0.83]), service ceiling 41,010 ft (12,500 m), flight range (-600 / -500) with normal amount of passengers 8,637 miles (13,900 km)/9,973 miles (16,050 km).
Weight (-600 /-500): Empty weight 390,214 lbs (177,700 kg)/374,782 lbs (170,000 kg), maximum take-off weight 804,679 lbs (365,000 kg), option for 811,292 lbs (368,000 kg).
Payload (-600 / -500): Two-person cockpit team and, employing three-class seating, 12, 54/47 and 314/259 passengers in first, second and tourist classes respectively in six-, eight-or nine- seat arrangements totaling 380/318 passengers respectively, employing single-class seating in a nine-seat arrangement 485 /440. Maximum payload (-600) 137,346 lbs (62,300 kg), (-500) 112,875 lbs (51,200 kg).
State of development: The latest version of the A340-600 had its test flight on April 23, 2001 followed on February 11, 2002 by the first A340-500. The -600 was initially delivered in mid-2002, the -500 followed at the beginning of 2003. Orders received through 2002 for all versions of the A340 numbered 320, of which 230 units have already been delivered.
Remarks: The versions of A340-600 (see three-sided diagrams) and -500 (see photo) constitute a considerable advancement for the A340 family. The -600 variant features a fuselage lengthened by 37 ft (11 m) and is, at present, the longest airliner in the world. The -500, with only a minor lengthening of its fuselage, is meant for longer flight ranges. Both types are equipped with a new wing and engines that provide a considerably higher performance than earlier models. The entire horizontal tail is made of carbon fibers. The remaining parts and systems are largely identical to those of the A330. A -600 version featuring an increased take-off weight of 81,571 lbs (37,000 kg) is currently in the planning stage.
Manufacturer: Airbus Industries, Blagnac, France, subsidiary of EADS (European Aeronautic Defense and Space Company).

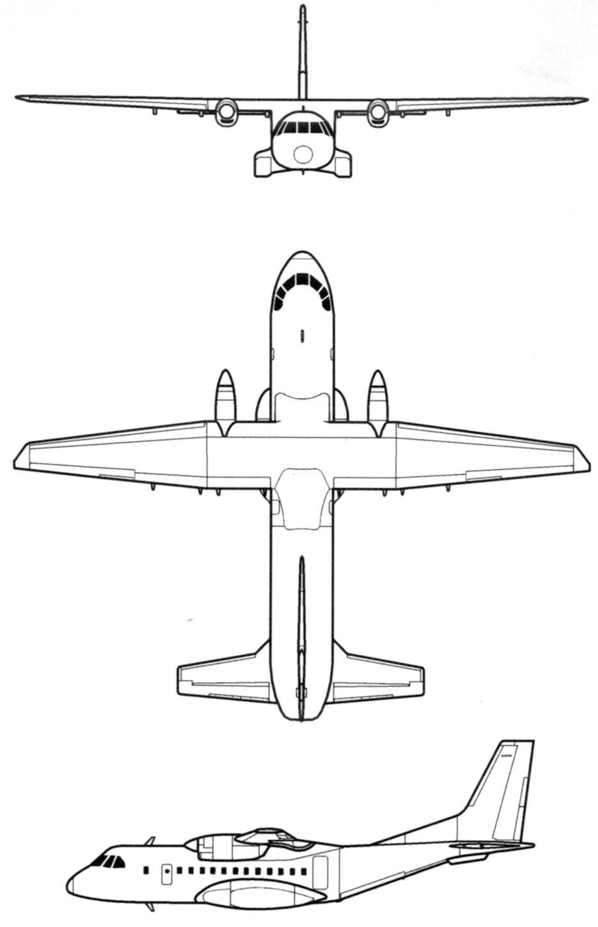

Dimensions:
Wingspan 84.67 ft (25.81 m)
Length 70.04 ft (21.35 m)
Height 26.83 ft (8.18 m)
Wing area 636.15 sq. ft (59.10 m^2)

AIRTECH (CASA/IPTN) CN-235-200

Country of origin: Spain and Indonesia.
Type: Regional airliner and multi-purpose transport plane, as well as military cargo plane (CN-235M) and naval patrol craft (CN-235MPA).
Power Plant: Two General Electric CT7-9C turboprop engines each featuring 1,750 SHP (1,305 kW) performance.
Performance: Maximum cruising speed 286 mph (460 km/h) at an altitude of 15,009 ft (4,575 m), initial rate of climb 25 ft (7.75 m)/sec, service ceiling 24,999 ft (7,620 m), flight range with maximum payload and 45-minute reserve 1,101 miles (1,773 km), with 5,291 lbs (2,400 kg) and maximum fuel load 2,273 miles (3,658 km).
Weight: Empty weight 21,605 lbs (9,800 kg) (CN-235M) 18,960 lbs (8,600 kg), maximum take-off weight 34,832 lbs (15,800 kg) (CN-235M) 36,376 lbs (16,500 kg).
Payload: Two pilots and standard interior equipment for 40 to 44 passengers in a standard four-row seat configuration, in the CN-235QC multi-role version payload up to 9,479 lbs (4,300 kg), in the CN-235QC multi-role version 18 passengers and two LD-3 containers, in the military transport plane (CN-235M) 53 soldiers or a payload up to 13,227 lbs (6,000 kg).
State of development: The maiden flight of the first prototype took place on November 11, 1983. Initial delivery to clients began on December 15, 1986. About 275 combined units of the civilian and military versions have been ordered through December 2002, about 250 of which have been delivered. Turkey is the largest single customer with an order for 61 CN-235M's. Latest repeat order comes from France for 3 CN-235-200's bringing their total to 20 units. 35 CN-235ER's are expected to be purchased by the U.S. Coast Guard.
Remarks: Construction of the CN-235 is a joint venture of Spanish CASA and Indonesian IPTN. An ASW/naval patrolling version CN-235MPA with a 360° search radar, flying since 1991, has been ordered by Brunei, Indonesia, Ireland, Spain and Turkey. It is capable of carrying two AM-39 Exocet guided anti-ship missiles or two Mk-46 torpedoes. The most recent version, the CN235-300, features more powerful CT7-9C3 engines with a 1,900 SHP (1,400 kW) performance, Honeywell avionics and ARL-2002 EW self-defense system.
Manufacturer: Airtech, Aircraft Technology Industries, Madrid, Spain, plants in Sevilla, Spain and Bandung, Indonesia.

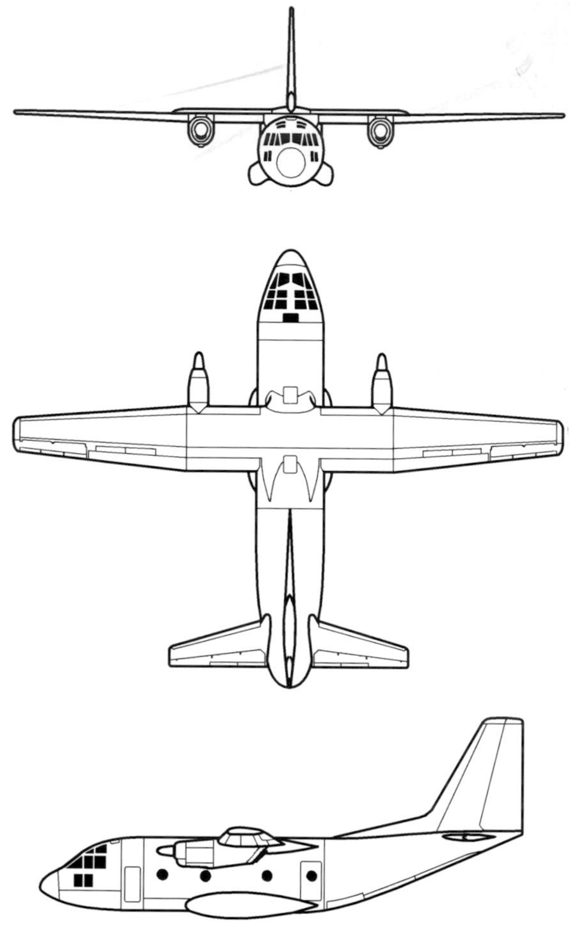

Dimensions:
Wingspan 94.15 ft (28.70 m)
Length 74.47 ft (22.70 m)
Height 31.82 ft (9.70 m)
Wing area 882.64 sq. ft (82.00 m^2)

ALENIA C-27J SPARTAN

Country of origin: Italy and USA.
Type: Military multi-role and STOL transport plane.
Power Plant: Two Allison AE2100-D2 turboprop engines each featuring 4,640 SHP (3,460 kW).
Performance: Maximum cruising speed 374 mph (602 km/h), long-range cruising speed 311 mph (500 km/h) at an altitude of 19,684 ft (6,000 m), initial rate of climb 33 ft (10+ m)/sec, service ceiling 30,019 ft (9,150 m), flight range with 22,040 lbs (10,000 kg) payload 1,099 miles (1,770 km), with 13,227 lbs (6,000 kg) 2,392 lbs (3,850 km), flight range under best flying conditions 3,200 miles (5,150 km).
Weight: Empty weight 36,376 lbs (16,500 kg), maximum take-off weight 70,107 lbs (31,800 kg).
Payload: Two-person cockpit team and, in the troop transport version, either 53 fully equipped soldiers or 46 paratroopers or 36 wounded men up to 25,353 lbs (11,500 kg).
State of development: The initial prototype of C-27J began flying September 25, 1999, the first series-produced unit followed on May 12, 2000. So far, the Italian Air force has ordered 5 units (with an option for 7 more). Greece also has recently purchased 12 planes. 111 units of the original version of C-27A/G.222 have been delivered to ten air forces.
Remarks: The C-27J is a considerably more advanced version of the original G.222. It was developed as a 50/50 joint venture with Lockheed Martin and features many characteristics of the mid-heavy transport plane C-130J Hercules II (see pages 224/225). The engines, six-blade propellers and avionics are largely identical. The manufacturers are confident that sales of both types would assure the profitability of the enterprise. Based upon civilian considerations, the C-27J was certified in June 2001. The first deliveries took place in 2002. Additionally, an AEW version featuring APS-145 radar is being developed.
Manufacturer: Alenia, Rome, Italy and Lockheed Martin Marietta Corp., Marietta, Georgia, USA.

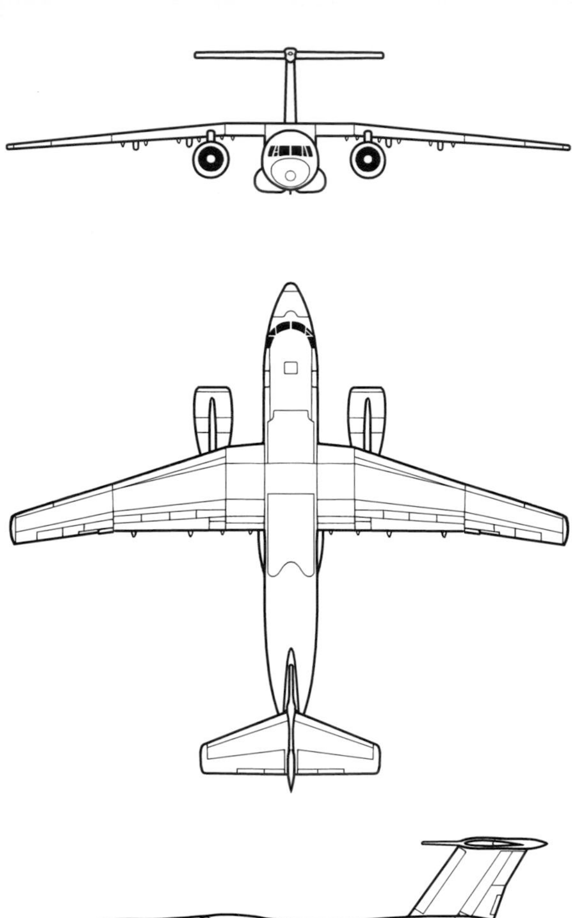

Dimensions:
Wingspan 104.62 ft (31.89 m)
Length 92.09 ft (28.07 m)
Height 28.37 ft (8.65 m)
Wing area 1,061 sq. ft (98.62 m^2)

ANTONOW AN-74TK-300

Country of origin: Ukraine.
Type: Civilian and military STOL transport plane for short- and medium-range flights.
Power Plant: Two ZMKB Progress/Ivchenko D-36A-4A turbofan engines each with 14,320 lbs (6,500 kp/63.7 kN) static thrust.
Performance: Maximum cruising speed 451 mph (725 km/h), service ceiling 33,136 ft (10,100 m), flight range with 52 passengers and normal reserves 2,299 miles (3,700 km), maximum flight range 3,262 miles (5,250 km).
Weight: Maximum take-off weight 82,672 lbs (37,500 kg).
Payload: Two-person cockpit team and, depending on designation and interior equipment, up to 68 persons on folding seats along the cabin walls or 57 paratroopers. The ambulance version holds 24 stretchers, 12 wounded persons in sitting position and a medic. Maximum payload 22,046 lbs (10,000 kg).
State of development: The first prototype of the An-74TK-300 flew on April 20, 2001. It was certified on September 9, 2002. Two planes have been ordered so far. The Aeroflot Company signed a letter of intent for an additional 25. More than 170 units of the original version of the An-72/74, still being offered for sale, have been manufactured.
Remarks: Further advances in development of the An-74TK-300 highlight two new engines conventionally placed under the wings. This should make it considerably more cost efficient. According to the manufacturer's general information, the fuel consumption has been reduced by 29%. Although it does not feature the extraordinary short take-off characteristics of the An-72/74 version, the -300 can still take-off and land on short runways. Additionally, the option of offering a lengthened version, the An-74-400, is being examined. Its fuselage would be 26 ft (8 m) longer and equipped with more powerful Progress D-436 T1 engines.
Manufacturer: Antonov Aeronautical Scientific Complex, Kiev and other plants in Arsenyev and Omsk, Ukraine.

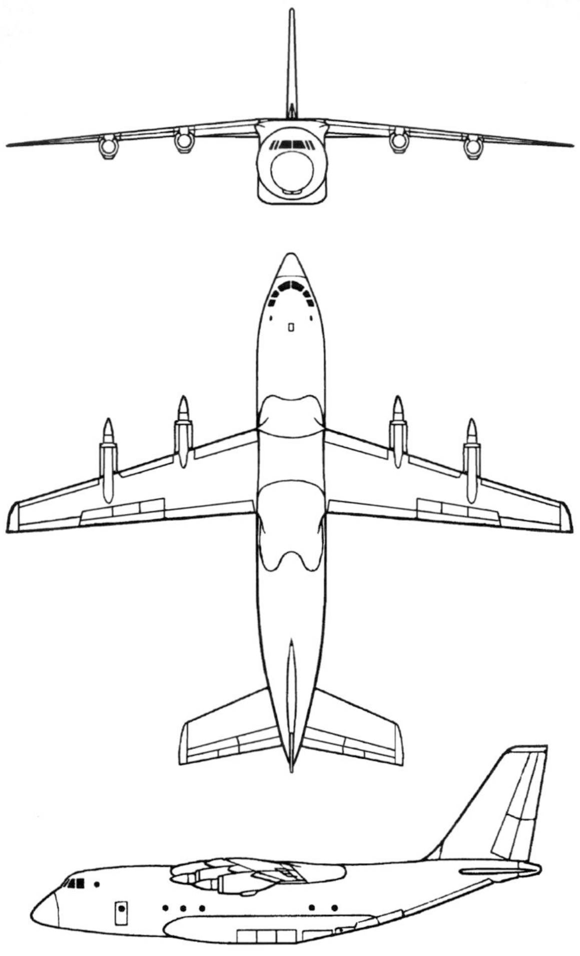

Dimensions:
Wingspan 144.25 ft (44.06 m)
Length 133.62 ft (40.73 m)
Height 53.73 ft (16.38 m)

ANTONOW AN-70

Country of origin: Ukraine.
Type: Military and civil medium- and long-range cargo plane.
Power Plant: Four counter-rotating Progress/Motor Sich D-27 turboprop engines each with 14,000 SHP (10,440 kW) performance.
Performance: Normal cruising speed 466 mph (750 km/h) at an altitude of 31,495 ft (9,600 m), cruise ceiling 39,369 ft (12,000 m), flight range with 77,161 lbs (35,000 kg) payload 2,174 miles (3,500 km), with maximum payload 839 miles (1,350 km), maximum flight range 4,846 miles (7,800 km).
Weight: Empty weight 160,935 lbs (73,000 kg), normal take-off weight 246,915 lbs (112,000 kg), maximum take-off weight 297,621 lbs (135,000 kg).
Payload: Three-person cockpit team and 170 soldiers or a 103,616 lb (47,000 kg) cargo in a ventilated freight hold with a length of 63 ft (19.10 m) not including the platform, a width of 13 ft (4 m) and height of 13.45 ft (4.1 m).
State of development: The first prototype, flight-tested on December 16, 1994, crashed on February 10, 1995. The second prototype flew for the first time on April 24, 1997. Five units will be manufactured for the Ukrainian Air Force that wishes, as of 2003, to purchase an additional 65 planes. Depending on the availability of funds, Russia is scheduled to receive 164 An-70's, of which 10 have been ordered. The Czech Republic is set to receive two or three planes from the Russian production.
Remarks: The An-70 is offered either as a military or civilian cargo plane. In the construction of the plane, the Antonov Company has emphasized cost efficiency and safety considerations. A high durability is expected because of the application of composite materials. In terms of the construction, the most interesting device has turned out to be the engines, applied here for the first time in a series-produced plane. The counter-rotating propellers have eight anterior and six posterior blades. Carrying its maximum flight weight the An-70 reportedly is able to take off after 4,921 ft (1,500 m). Several additional developments are currently being explored: An-70-100 equipped with state-of-the-art avionics which will reduce the size of the cockpit team; An-70PS, a search and rescue (SAR) version; An-70T, a civilian cargo plane; and AN-70TK, a dual-purpose version carrying both civilian passengers and cargo.
Manufacturer: Antonov Aeronautical Scientific Complex, Kiev, Ukraine, Aviacor plant in Samara, Russia.

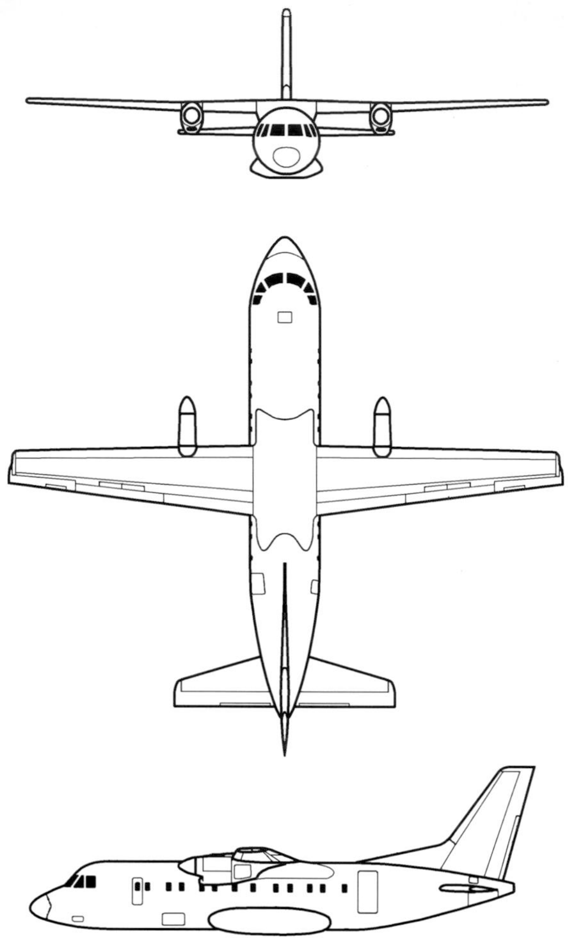

Dimensions:
Wingspan 79.55 ft (24.25 m)
Length 73.68 ft (22.46 m)
Height 26.34 ft (8.03 m)

ANTONOW AN-140

Country of origin: Ukraine (Iran).
Type: Civil and military short-range passenger and cargo plane.
Power Plant: Two Kaemov NPPTV3-117VMA turboprop engines each with 2,600 SHP (1,838 kW) performance or, alternatively, two Pratt & Whitney PW127A engines each with 2,415 SHP (1,800 kW) performance.
Performance (according to manufacturer's data): Maximum cruising speed 357 mph (575 km/h), service ceiling 23,622 ft (7,200 m), flight range with 52 passengers and 45- minute reserve 1,305 to 1,647 miles (2,100 to 2,650 km), maximum flight range 2,361 miles (3,800 km).
Weight: Maximum take-off weight 42,219 lbs (19,150 kg).
Payload: Two pilots and, depending on interior equipment, (An-140) up to 52 passengers in a four-seat arrangement with a central aisle, or (An-140TK) 20 passengers and 8,047 lbs (3,650 kg) of cargo. The military cargo plane (An-140T) has a maximum payload of 13,228 lbs (6,000 kg).
State of development: The first prototype was flight-tested on September 17, 1997, the second followed at the end of 1997, and the first series-produced plane at the beginning of 2000. The initial unit was delivered to Odessa Airlines (see photo) in the summer of 2002. Delivery was followed by an additional four units by the end of 2002. The Iranian Government ordered 80 An-140's (under a construction license) of which the first unit flew on February 7, 2001.
Remarks: The An-140 is a sturdy passenger and cargo airliner featuring good STOL characteristics and considerable passenger comfort. It's capable of taking off and landing on unprepared runways. Extra effort has produced an aircraft that requires simple maintenance and provides cost-efficient operation. Production took place first in Iran, subsequently in Ukraine and finally expanded to the Aviacor plant in Samara, Russia. Several versions are currently in development including the An-140-100 featuring a 13 ft (3.8 m) longer fuselage and room for 68 passengers. A second aircraft in the planning stage, the military An-140T, has a loading platform at the rear end. The Iranian Navy is examining an AEW version with a 360° panoramic radar placed on the fuselage.
Manufacturer: Antonov ACTC, Kiev, Ukraine, Isfahan plant, Iran, and Kharkov State Aircraft Production Company, Ukraine.

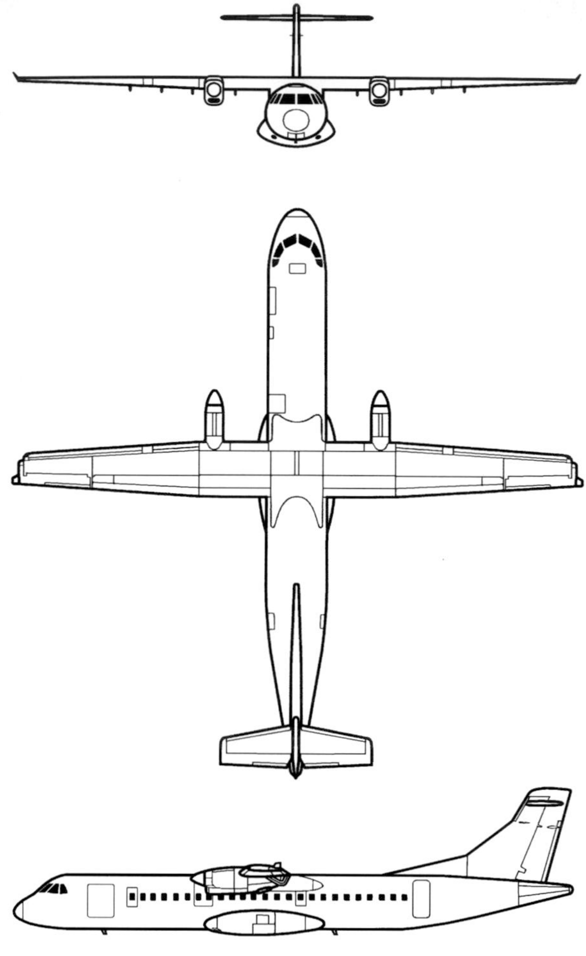

Dimensions (ATR 42-500/ATR 72-500):
Wingspan 80.60/88.74 ft (24.57/27.05 m)
Length 74.37/89.13 ft (22.67/27.17 m)
Height 24.90/25.09 ft (7.59/7.65 m)
Wing area 586.63/656.60 sq. ft (54.50/61.00 m^2)

ATR 42-500/ATR 72-500

Country of origin: France and Italy.
Type: Regional airliner.
Power Plant (ATR 42-500/ATR 72-500): Two Pratt & Whitney Canada PW127E turboprop engines each with 2,400 SHP (1,790 kW) performance or two PW127F engines each with 2,750 SHP (2,050 kW) performance.
Performance (ATR 42-500/ATR 72-500): Maximum cruising speed 345/318 mph (555/511 km/h) at an altitude of 25,000 ft (7,620 m), economic cruising speed 280 mph (450 km/h) at an altitude of 25,000 ft (7,620 m), flight range with 48/68 passengers and maximum baggage 963/1,025 miles (1,550/1,650 km), with no payload more than 2,485 miles (4,000 km).
Weight (ATR 42-500/ATR 72-500): Equipped weight 24,802/28,550 lbs (11,250/12,950 kg), maximum take-off weight 41,006/49,604 lbs (18,600/22,500 kg).
Payload: Two-person cockpit team and, depending on the interior configuration, (ATR 42-500 see photo) a maximum of 48 passengers, (ATR 72-500, see silhouette) 64 to 74 passengers in a four-seat arrangement with central aisle. Payload (ATR 42-500) 12,016 lbs (5,450 kg), in the cargo-plane version 12,787 lbs (5,800 kg), (ATR 72-500) 16,170 lbs (7,350 kg).
State of development: The first flight of the latest version of ATR 42-500 took place on September 16, 1994 with the second flight following a short while later. Through September 2002, 672 units of the various versions (ATR-42 369, ATR-72 303) have been ordered, about 642 have already been delivered.
Remarks: The ATR 42/72-500 has enriched the already large ATR family. It features the same dimensions as the previous ATR-42 versions but its six-blade propeller makes it a more powerful aircraft. The cabin interior has been revised and equipped with an Active Noise-Control System to reduce the noise level. With the exception of length and wingspan, the ATR 72-500 is exactly identical to the ATR 42-500. The ATR 42-400MP is a sea-monitoring version of the ATR-42 equipped with Rayteon SV2022 radar beneath the fuselage, FLIR and ESM equipment. The Italian Guarda di Finanza received two units and the Coast Guard received one. Recently the ATR42/72 has been offered as a cargo plane with a lateral gate and strengthened cabin floor. The first reconstructed ATR-72-201F was delivered to FanAir in July 2002.
Manufacturer: Avions de transport regional (ATR), Aerospacial Matra, Toulouse-Blagnac (France) and Alenia, Naples (Italy).

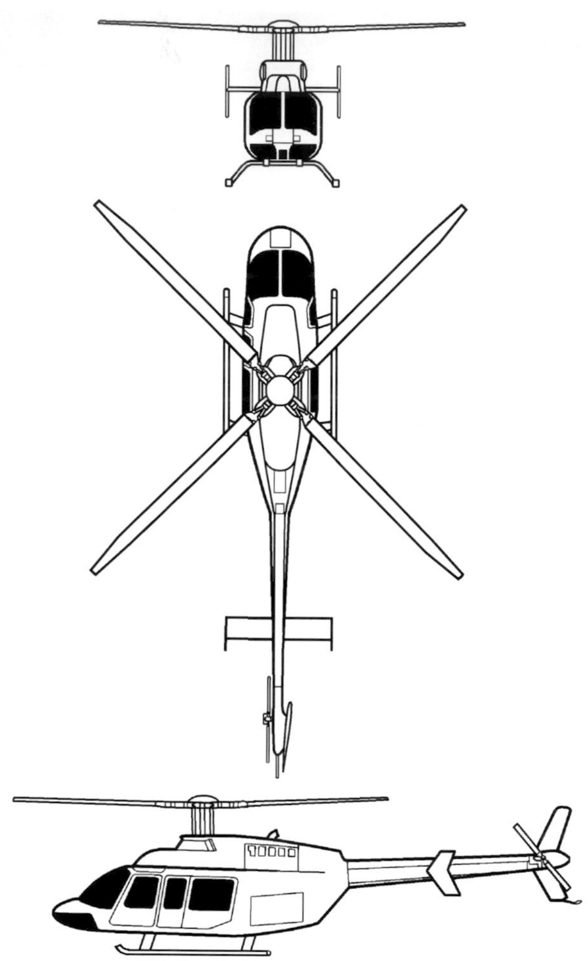

Dimensions:
Rotor diameter 34.97 ft (10.66 m)
Fuselage length 34.18 ft (10.42 m)
Height, including rotor head 10.17 ft (3.10 m)

BELL 407

Country of origin: USA (Canada).
Type: Light, multi-purpose helicopter.
Power Plant: One Allison 250 C47 turboshaft engine with 674 SHP (5.03 kW) performance.
Performance: Maximum speed 162 mph (260 km/h), with maximum payload 149 mph (240 km/h), maximum diagonal climbing speed 21 ft (6.4 m)/sec, service ceiling 13,500 ft (4,115 m), hovering altitude in ground effect 12,795 ft (3,900 m), out of ground effect 10,500 ft (3,200 m), flight range without reserves 360 miles (580 km).
Weight: Standard empty weight 2,597 lbs (1,178 kg), maximum take-off weight 5,249 lbs (2,381 kg), with external payload 6,000 lbs (2,722 kg).
Payload: Pilot and six passengers, maximum external payload 2,646 lbs (1,200 kg).
State of development: An experimental 407 unit has been flying since April 21, 1994. The first of two real prototypes was flight-tested in June 1995. Delivery began later that year. To date, about 600 units have been ordered by about 80 operators. The 500th unit was delivered at the end of 2001. 10 aircraft are produced each month.
Remarks: The 407 with its single engine replaced the successful 206 JetRanger and TwinRanger models. In addition to considerably more powerful engines, the 407 features a four-blade rotor stemming from the OH58D model and manufactured from synthetic materials. The dynamic system has also been adopted from this model. Also, FADEC, a fully digital engine management system, has been installed. Because of these measures the 407 flies with much less vibration and is more cost-efficient. The 206 model has a cabin is that is 7 inches (18 cm) wider than its predecessor. It also features larger windows and doors. The models currently being delivered are characterized by some improvements concerning reliability and comfort, such as, among other things, a new rear hoist arm, redesigned cooling system, starter generator, folding rotor blades, new seats, etc.
Manufacturer: Bell Helicopter Textron Inc., Canadian Division, Mirabel, Montreal, Canada.

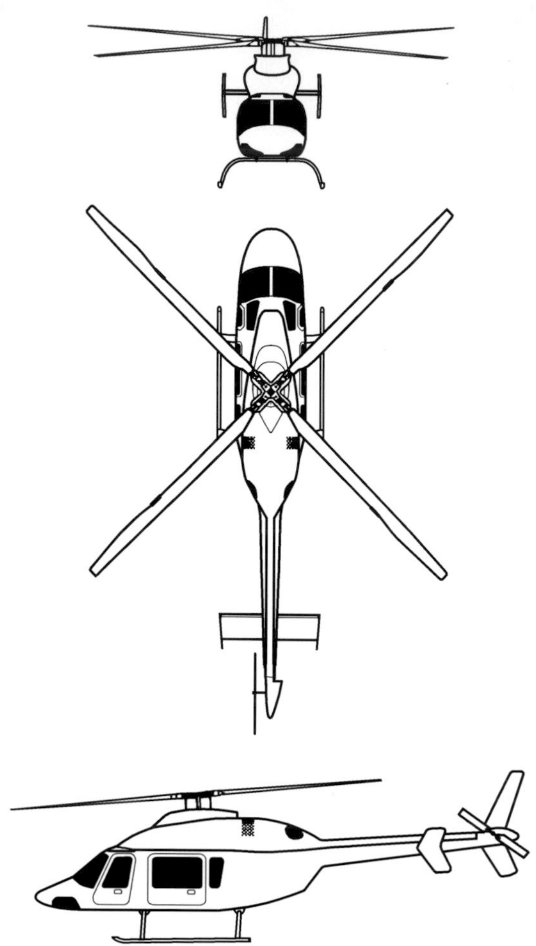

Dimensions:
Rotor diameter 37 ft (11.28 m)
Fuselage length 35.26 ft (10.75 m)
Height 11.44 ft (3.49 m)

BELL 427VFR

Country of origin: USA (Canada, South Korea).
Type: Light, multi-purpose helicopter.
Power Plant: Two Pratt & Whitney PW207D turboshaft engines each with 625 SHP (466 kW) performance.
Performance: Maximum speed 159 mph (256 km/h), normal cruising speed 154 mph (248 km/h), service ceiling 18,898 ft (5,760 m), hovering altitude out of ground effect 13,879 ft (4,230 m), within ground effect 16,175 ft (4,930 m), flight range 449 miles (722 km), maximum flight duration 4 hours.
Weight: Empty weight 3,682 lbs (1,670 kg), maximum take-off weight with internal load 6,349 lbs (2,880 kg), with external load 6,499 lbs (2,948 kg).
Payload: One pilot and up to seven passengers or a payload of 2,249 lbs (1,020 kg). The ambulance version is capable of carrying two recumbent patients.
State of development: The first of two prototypes flew in December 1997. Bell started delivery at the end of 1999. The current number of orders is about 70.
Remarks: The Bell 427VFR is based on the 407 model (see pages 50/51), and was developed in cooperation with Samsung Aerospace Industries Ltd, Korea. The dynamic system (rotor head, transmission and rotors) stems from the 407 model; however, the rotor blades are 16 inches (40 cm) longer and 1 inch (25 mm) broader. The fuselage, manufactured from composite materials, was redesigned and is about 13 inches (33 cm) longer than that of the 407. The cabin can actually be altered and adjusted for various purposes. The large doors (sliding doors are an option) facilitate loading and unloading of freight. All seats are crash resistant, all cockpit instruments are digital. The selling price is about US$2.7 million. Samsung manufactures the cabin and rear of all the 427's, the rotor system is produced by Bell, Fort Worth. The final assembly takes place in the Mirabel plants, Canada, and by Samsung, Sachon for the units designated for the Korean and Chinese markets. An optimized version for rescue actions (EMS operations) is in development.
Manufacturer: Bell Helicopter Textron Inc., Canadian Division, Mirabel, Montreal, Canada.

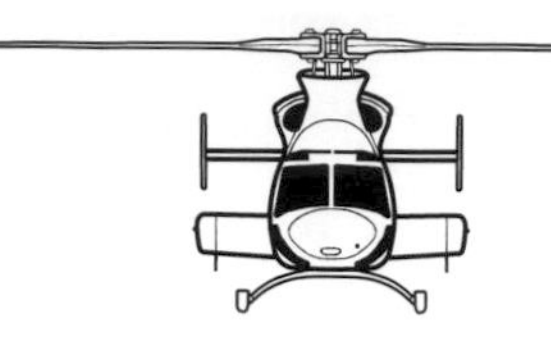

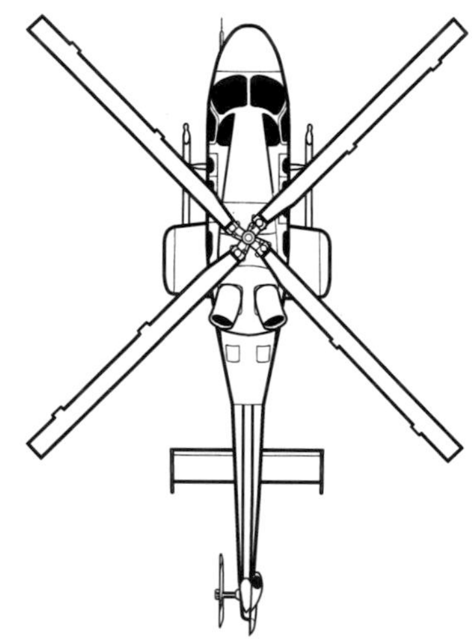

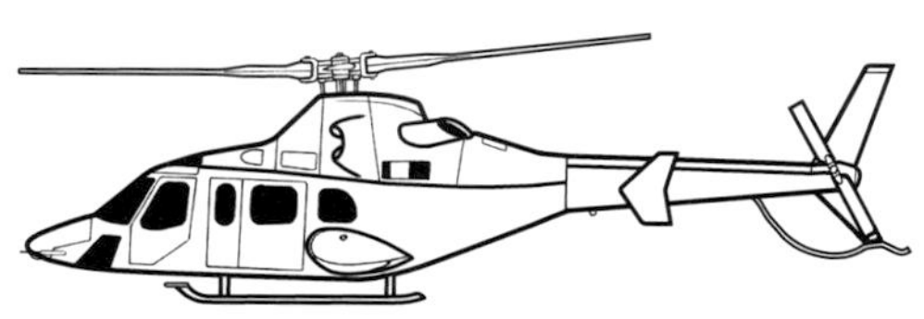

Dimensions:
Rotor diameter 41.99 ft (12.80 m)
Fuselage length 42.55 ft (12.97 m)
Height, including rotor head (with vats) 13.22 ft (4.03 m)
(with landing gear) 12.20 ft (3.72 m)

BELL 430

Country of origin: USA (Canada).
Type: Multi-purpose and transport helicopter.
Power Plant: Two Allison 250-C40B turboshaft engines each with 808 SHP (603 kW) performance.
Performance: Maximum speed 169 mph (272 km/h), cruising speed 153 mph (246 km/h), hovering altitude within ground effect 17,192 ft (5,240 m), out of ground effect 14,567 ft (4,440 m), service ceiling 20,000 ft (6,096 m), flight range 329 miles (530 km).
Weight (with runners): Empty weight 5,327 lbs (2,430 kg), maximum take-off weight 92,99 lbs (4,218 kg).
Payload: One or two pilots and six to eight passengers, in EMS rescue operations one or two recumbent patients and two to three medics, maximum external payload 3,497 lbs (1,586 kg).
State of development: The newest 430 version was flight-tested on October 25, 1994. The first customer delivery took place in mid-1996. So far about 70 units have been ordered, most of which have been delivered. The Bell 430 is still being manufactured.
Remarks: The Bell 430 model is a better performing version of the Bell 230. It differs from its predecessor by featuring a four-blade rotor with highly reduced vibrations, a fuselage lengthened by nearly 2 ft (0.45 m) with 23% larger cabin space, more powerful Allison engine with Fadec system, and, finally, Rogerson liquid crystal displays in the cockpit. As in the 230 model, the customer has the option to choose between runners and a wheel system. Although constructed as a multi-purpose helicopter, most of the Bell 430's have been purchased for medical transportation and search-and-rescue operations. The purchase price for a basic version is about US$4.9 million.
Manufacturer: Bell Helicopter Textron Inc., Canadian Division, Mirabel, Montreal, Canada.

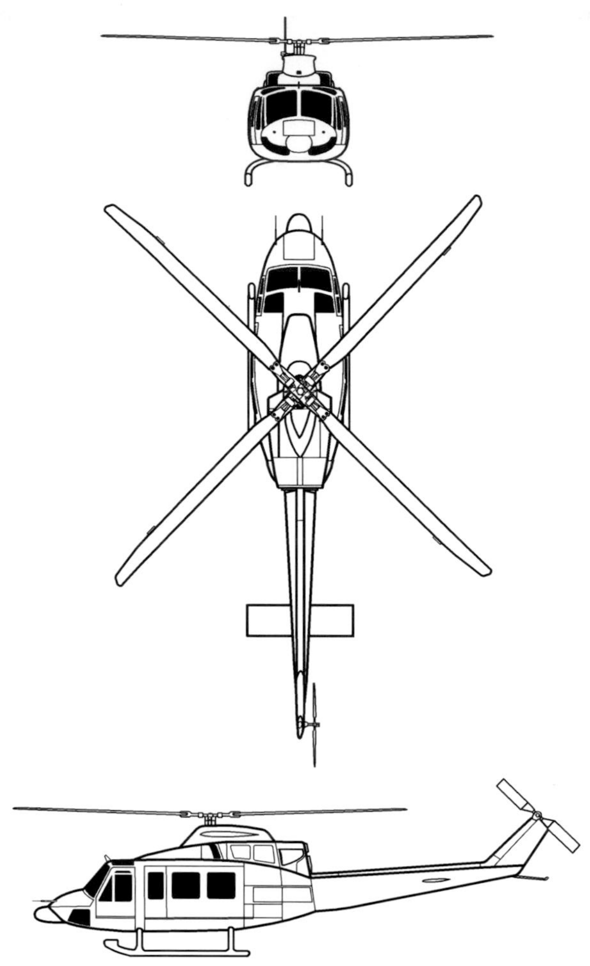

Dimensions:
Rotor diameter 45.99 ft (14.02 m)
Fuselage length 42.38 ft (12.92 m)
Height, including rotor head 11.41 ft (3.48 m)

BELL 412EP/UH-1Y

Country of origin: USA (Canada).
Type: Multi-purpose and transport helicopter.
Power Plant: One Pratt & Whitney Canada PT6T-3D-Turbo Twin Pac turboshaft engine with 1,800 SHP (1,347 kW) performance.
Performance: Maximum speed 161 mph (259 km/h) at sea level, cruising speed 143 mph (230 km/h), maximum diagonal climbing speed 23 ft (6.86 m)/sec, service ceiling 16,503 ft (5,030 m), hovering height within ground effect 10,203 ft (3,110 m) with 10,498 lbs (4,762 kg), out of ground effect 5,200 ft (1,585 m), maximum flight range 463 miles (745 km) without additional tanks at 5,003 ft (1,525 m).
Weight: Empty weight 6,788 lbs (3,079 kg), maximum take-off weight 11,898 lbs (5,397 kg).
Payload: One or two pilots and 13 or 14 passengers, maximum payload 4,500 lbs (2,041 kg).
State of development: The latest version -EP was approved in February 1991. 24 countries have received military versions of the -412 from either Bell or Augusta; the most recent orders include the RAF (repeat order) and the Venezuelan Navy, 3. Additionally, some 470 civilian 412's have also been ordered. About 24 units are produced annually. The first reconstructed UH-1Y (see photo) was flight-tested on December 20, 2,001.
Remarks: The Bell 412EP is the latest version of the 412 model to be placed in production. It features more powerful engines with corresponding transmissions and increased take-off weight. In addition to the Bell plant in Mirabel, it is also being constructed at AugustaWestland in Italy. Recently, an ASW version 412EP Sentinel has been offered. It features Telephonic RDR1500 360° Radar and an infrared container at the anterior tip of the fuselage. It can be armed, among other things, with torpedoes and anti-ship guided missiles. The performance of 100 USMC UH-1N units, marked as UH-1Y (first flight: December 21, 2001) will be considerably upgraded during the coming years with two GE T 700-GE-401 engines, a new Hexbeam rotor fastened without bearings, four-blade rotors made of synthetic material, a fuselage lengthened by about 20 inches (50 cm) and a longer rear extension arm with a four-blade rear rotor etc.
Manufacturer: Bell Helicopter Textron Inc., Canadian Division, Mirabel, Montreal, Canada.

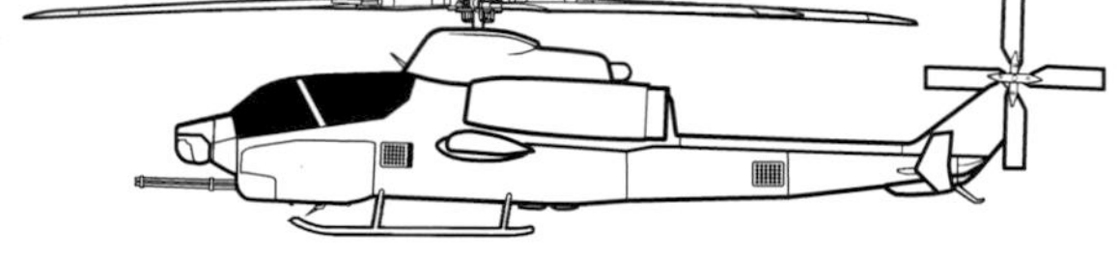

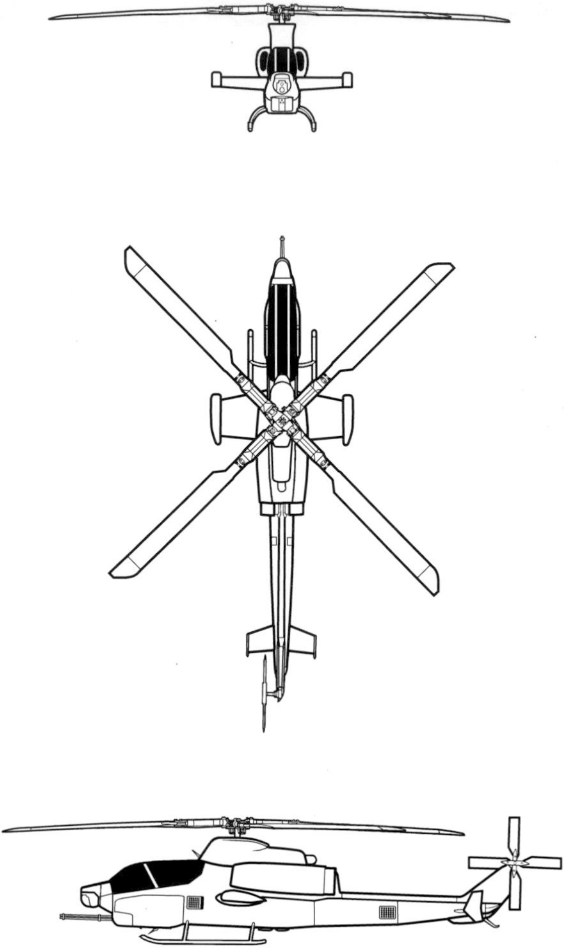

Dimensions:
Rotor diameter 58.16 ft (17.73 m)
Fuselage length 45.50 ft (13.87 m)
Height above tail rotor 12.41 ft (3.78 m)

BELL AH-1Z

Country of origin: USA.
Type: Two-seat combat helicopter.
Power Plant: Two General Electric T700-401 turboshaft engines each with 1,773 SHP (1,285 kP) performance.
Performance: Maximum operation radius speed 185 mph (298 km/h), typical combat speed 165 mph (265 km/h), operation radius with 2,500 lbs (1,134 kg) of armament 145 mph (234 km/h), flight range with maximum internal fuel load and armament 438 miles (705 km), maximum flight duration 3.7 hours.
Weight: Empty weight 12,302 lbs (5,580 kg), maximum take-off weight 18,500 lbs (8,391 kg).
Armament: General Electric M197 triple 20-mm cannon and weapon systems fastened to the wings which may contain four containers for non-guided missiles, eight to sixteen guided anti-tank AGM-114 hellfire missiles or two guided air-to-air AIM-9L Sidewinder missiles.
State of development: First flight of the prototype (the reconstructed AH-W) took place on December 7, 2000. Three units are currently test flying. The USMC is expected to receive 180 units in annual deliveries of 12 to 36 units. Since considerable technical problems have been encountered, operability is not likely to occur before 2007.
Remarks: The new AH-1Z, a much more powerful model than the AH-1W, is equipped with a rigid rotorhead with a four-blade rotor made of composite materials. In addition to a glass cockpit, this version features a new, fully integrated navigation system from Northrop Gruman/Litton. It is placed along with a Hawkeye multifunctional target acquisition system in the anterior tip of the fuselage. The latter features target search functions such as FLIR, TV and laser. The AH-1Z is able to carry significant number of additional weapons.
Manufacturer: Bell Helicopter Textron Inc., Canadian Division, Mirabel, Montreal, Canada.

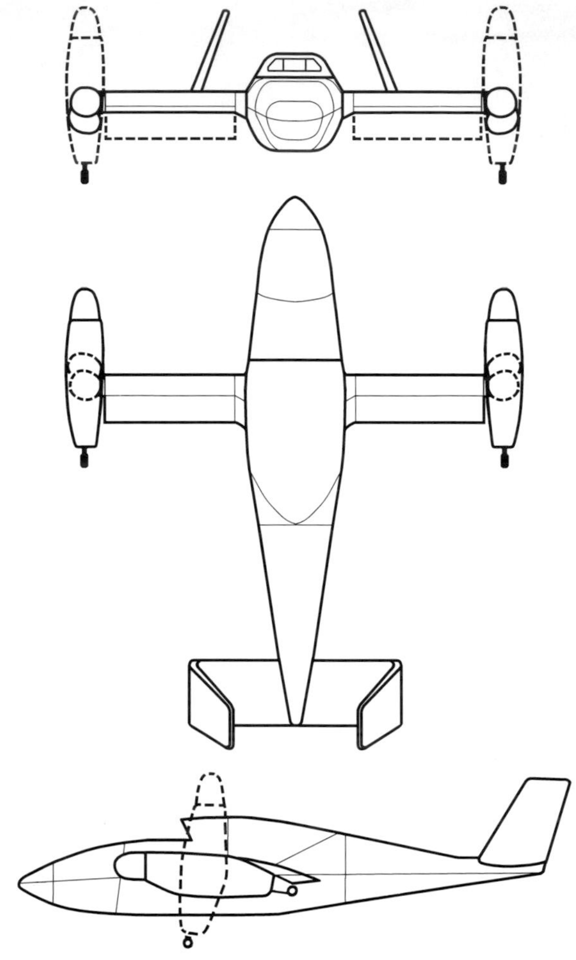

Dimensions:
Wing span 15.19 ft (4.63 m)
Length 17.91 ft (5.46 m)
Height 5.67 ft (1.73 m)
Diameter of each individual rotor 9.51 ft (2.90 m)

BELL HV-911 EAGLE EYE

Country of origin: USA.
Type: Unmanned test air vehicle with tilt rotors.
Power Plant: Two propeller turbines each with 425 SHP (315 kW) performance.
Performance: Maximum speed in horizontal flight 233 mph (375 km/h), service ceiling 20,012 ft (6,100 m), maximum flight time 8 hours, action radius 124 miles (200 km), cruising range 320 miles (515 km).
Weight: Empty weight 1,300 lbs (590 kg), maximum take-off weight 2,248 lbs (1,020 kg).
Payload: Payload of 198 lbs (90 kg) consisting mainly of reconnaissance systems.
State of development: A test carrier has been flying since 1992. After years of delay, the project is now moving forward. The U.S. Coast Guard is planning to acquire a series of 69 economy planes for use as ship supported reconnaissance drones starting in 2007.
Remarks: The only tilt rotor equipped unmanned aircraft up to this time (UMAV-\TDL unmanned air vehicle) is primarily intended to launch from ships. Therefore it is outfitted with a new kind of automatic recovery system for landing on warships. It can use the STOL (**s**hort **t**ake-**o**ff and **l**anding) or the TOL (**t**ake-**o**ff and **l**anding) method. This model is a cost-effective, simple and sturdy machine designed for reconnaissance, surveillance and the identification of ocean targets. For this reason, it is equipped with a data link system, which can transfer information online to the mother ship. For the Coast Guard, the Eagle Eyes would be intended for deployment from offshore patrol cutters. The series design would have a revised fuselage and presumably other engines.
Manufacturer: Bell Helicopter, Textron, Fort Worth, Texas, USA.

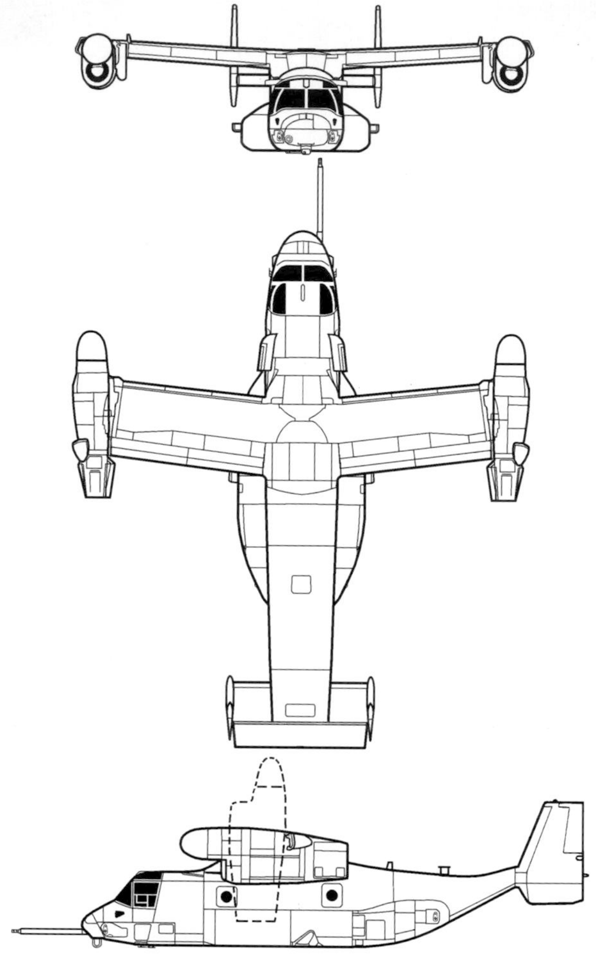

Dimensions:
Wingspan, including rotors 84.54 ft (25.77 m), without rotors 50.91 ft (15.52 m)
Length with folded rotors 62.99 ft (19.20 m), without 57.31 ft (17.47 m)
Height above everything 22.07 ft (6.73 m)

BELL-BOEING CV-22B OSPREY

Country of origin: USA.
Type: Tilt rotor aircraft for special military purposes.
Power Plant: Two Rolls-Royce AE 1107C propeller turbine engines each with 6,180 SHP (4,590 kW) performance.
Performance: Maximum cruising speed as surface aircraft 342 mph (550 km/h) at optimal height in helicopter configuration 115 mph (185 km/h) at sea level, maximum speed with external cargo of 15,000 lbs (6,804 kg) 230 mph (370 km/h); maximum take-off speed 18 ft (5.53 m)/sec, service ceiling 26,000 ft (7,925 m), range on vertical take-off with a payload of 11,999 lbs (5,443 kg) 1,381 miles (2,224 km), on a short take-off with a payload of 20,000 lbs (9,072 kg) 2,072 miles (3,336 km), surface range 2,418 miles (3,892 km).
Weight: Empty weight 33,139 lbs (15,032 kg), normal take-off weight in VTO conditions 52,590 lbs (23,855 kg), maximum weight under STO conditions 60,498 lbs (27,442 kg).
Payload: Three person crew and up to 24 equipped soldiers or 12 stretchers for the wounded plus medical attendants. Maximum payload 20,000 lbs (9,072 kg).
State of development: The test flight of the first of six prototypes was on March 28, 1989. Flight tests for four more prototypes modeled on the first Osprey followed in 1996. About 20 aircraft have been manufactured to date. The U.S. military intend to acquire about 458 22-Vs. Of that number the United States Marine Corps will receive 360 22M's, the United States Navy 48 HV-22B's and the United States Air Force 50 CV-22B's for special missions. Because of emerging problems, considerable modifications have been made and the delivery of the aircraft has been delayed until sometime in 2004.
Remarks: The CV 22B, intended for special applications, was presented as the latest design. It differs from the CV-22 in its additional avionics and communications systems. Raytheon's APQ-135, a terrain following radar system, and the ITT ALQ-221, an electronic defense system, were incorporated in the design. In order to increase the mission radius to 575 miles (925 km) there are eight additional fuel tanks in the wings and two fuel tanks on the side of the fuselage. At the present time, experiments are being conducted on a CV-22 version equipped with an MV 127- mm cannon at the front of the fuselage.
Manufacturer: Bell Helicopter, Textron, Fort Worth, Texas, USA and Boeing Helicopter Company, Philadelphia, USA, Amarillo plant, Texas, USA.

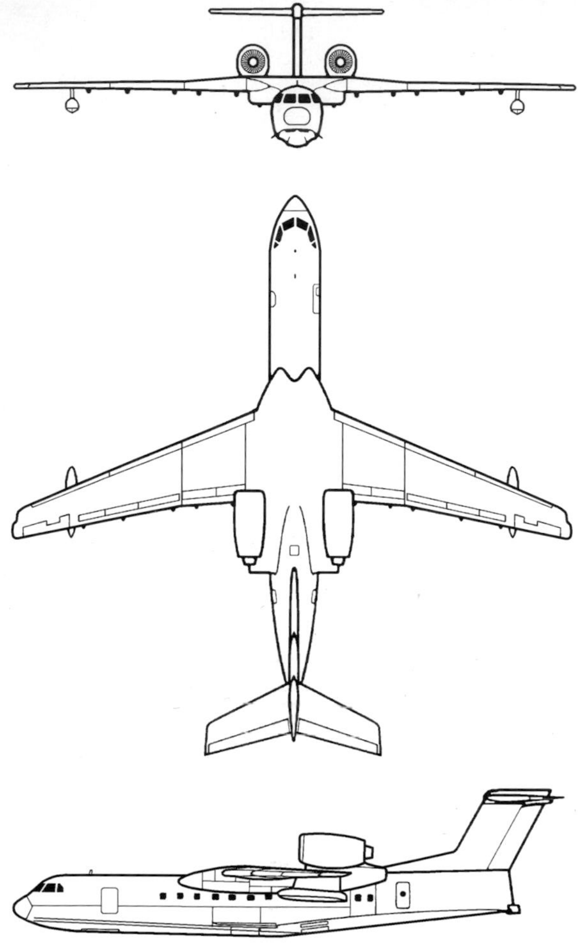

Dimensions:
Wingspan 107.54 ft (32.78 m)
Length 105.14 ft (32.05 m)
Height 29.19 ft (8.90 m)
Wing area 1,264 sq. ft (117.44 m^2)

BERIEW BE-200

Country of origin: Russia.
Type: Amphibious aircraft.
Power Plant: Two ZMKB Progress 4367 turbofan engines each with 16,546 lbs (7,500 kp/73.60 kN) static thrust.
Performance (estimated): Maximum speed at 22,965 ft (7,000 m) 466 mph (750 km/h), maximum cruising speed at 26,246 ft (8,000 m) 441 mph (710 km/h), initial take-off speed 46 ft (14 m)/sec, service ceiling 36,088 ft (11,000 m), range with a payload of 6,613 lbs (3,000 kg) 1,553 miles (2,500 km), maximum 2,237 miles (3,600 km).
Weight: Empty weight 55,379 lbs (25,120 kg), maximum take-off weight 79,365 lbs (36,000 kg) or 94,797 lbs (43,000 kg) for discharge operations.
Payload: Two pilots and up to 72 passengers in tourist class or up to 17,637 lbs (8,000 kg) payload as a freighter.
State of development: The first prototype undertook its test flight on September 24, 1998 and the second followed on August 27, 2002. In mid-2002, the BE-200 was certified in Russia. The first series of aircraft are now in production. The Russian Civil Defense Ministry has placed an official order for seven of these aircraft (+options) for rescue and fighting forest fires. Delivery of the aircraft is imminent. In addition, the fire-fighting version of this model is generating increasing interest in the European Union countries.
Remarks: The BE-200 is a considerably revised and clearly smaller design of the initial model Beriew Be-42/A-40 Mermaid. The BE-200 incorporates all the essential elements of its predecessor. Several designs are available including a fire fighting version with a water tank load of 26,455 lbs (12,000 kg), a pure passenger transport, a freighter as well as a version for search and rescue and excursion purposes. For a possible export version, BMW Rolls-Royce BR715 or Allison GMA-2100 engines will be offered.
Manufacturer: OKB Georgi Beriew, Taganrog, APK plant, Suchoj, Irkutsk, Russia.

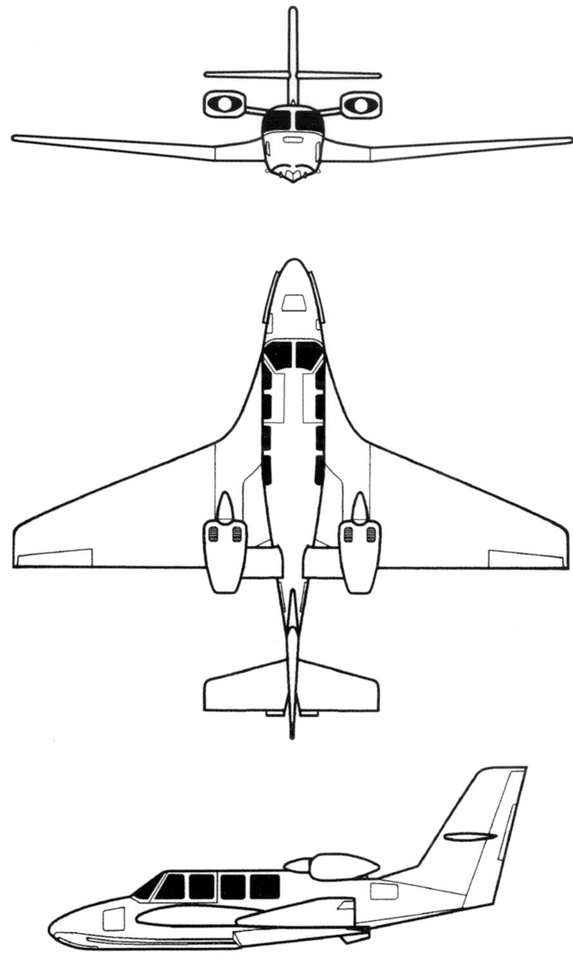

Dimensions:
Wingspan 34.30 ft (12.72 m)
Length 33.60 ft (10.65 m)
Height 12.50 ft (3.76 m)
Wing area 124.60 sq. ft (25.10 m^2)

BERIEW BE-103

Country of origin: Russia.
Type: Amphibious aircraft for civil and military applications.
Power Plant: Two Teledyne-Continental TCM 10-360ES4 six-cylinder air-cooled horizontally opposed engines each with 210 SHP (156 kW) performance or Kolesow M-17F-engines of similar output.
Performance: Maximum speed 177 mph (285 km/h), maximum cruising speed 162 mph (260 km/h), economic cruising speed 137 mph (220 km/h), service ceiling 9,842 ft (3,000 m+), cruising range with maximum payload 311 miles (500 km), with full fuel tanks 777 miles (1,250 km).
Weight: Empty weight 3,395 lbs (1,540 kg), maximum take-off weight 5,004 lbs (2,270 kg).
Payload: Six people including pilot or, when used as a freighter, 849 lbs (385 kg).
State of development: The first flight took place on July 15, 1997. Before the year was out a second model had its flight test. To date five more aircraft have been built. The Be-103 was certified at the end of 2001. The Russian border patrol, which reportedly intends to order 200 of these aircraft, has placed a provisional order for 30. Private individuals are acquiring seven more.
Remarks: The development of this aircraft was based on the easiest, most cost effective and most robust principles possible. Therefore, the Be-103 can be offered for sale at a price of only US$700,000. The fuselage and wings are constructed of several watertight sections that are subdivided to reduce the risk of the aircraft going down in the event of damage. Thanks to its retractable landing gear the Be-103 can take off from and land on water as well as land. The technology originates with Bendix/King. A prototype of a more economical design SA-20P with a Vedeneyev M-14P radial engine with an output of 360 PS (268 kW) mounted on the fuselage was presented in September 2002.
Manufacturer: OKB Georgie Beriew, Taganrog, Komsomolsk-Amur plant, Russia.

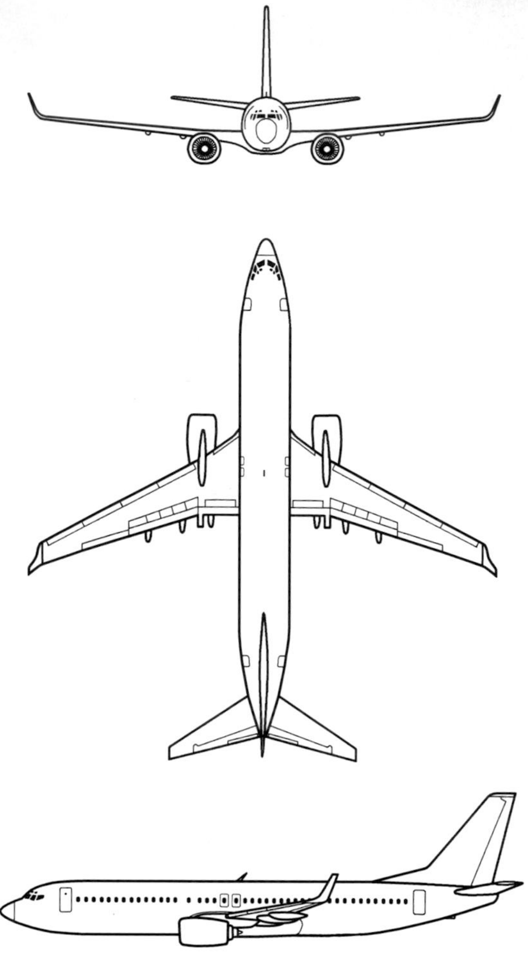

Dimensions:
Wingspan 41.73 ft (12.72 m)
Length 34.94 ft (10.65 m)
Height 12.33 ft (3.76 m)
Wing area 270.2 sq. ft (25.10 m^2)

BOEING 737BBJ/BBJ2

Country of origin: USA.
Type: Long haul commercial aircraft.
Power Plant: Two CFM International CFM 56-7B24 turbofan engines each with 23,999 lbs (10,886 kp/106.75 kN) static thrust.
Performance (estimated): Maximum cruising speed 567 mph (912 km/h [Mach 0.8]), normal cruising speed 519 mph (835 km/h), service ceiling 41 ft (12,500 m), maximum range 7,084 miles (11,400 km).
Weight: Empty weight 89,596 lbs (40,540 kg), take-off weight 170,991 lbs (77,560 kg).
Payload: Two-man cockpit crew and 20 to 100 passengers depending on the internal configuration of the aircraft.
State of development: The first model had its flight test on September 4, 1998 and the initial sales occurred in 1999. To date, around 85 BBJ1's and 10 BBJ2's have been ordered including one for Boeing itself. Almost 70 aircraft are now in use.
Remarks: Boeing incorporated the BBJ1 into the design of the 737, which was intended exclusively for commercial travel. It combines the fuselage length of the 700 version with the wings and the framework of the 800. In order to achieve a greater range, they are all equipped with 9 inch (2.6 m) high winglets. The BBJ2 incorporates the fuselage of the 737-800, which has been lengthened by 19 inches (5.80 m) to offer more passenger room and almost double the freight capacity. Boeing delivers the aircraft in a "raw state" for a price of US$32 million. A customized interior configuration is available (for example, for Jet Aviation, Basel and Lufthansa Technik, Hamburg). The interior is custom designed based on the needs of the customers. Boeing has developed a sea reconnaissance and ASW version MMA based on the BBJ (**M**ultimission **M**aritime **A**ircraft). In addition, Boeing, along with the Airbus A321 model, has entered the competition to create a successor to the Lockheed P-3 Orion.
Manufacturer: The Boeing Company, Commercial Airplane Group, Seattle, Renton plant, Washington, USA.

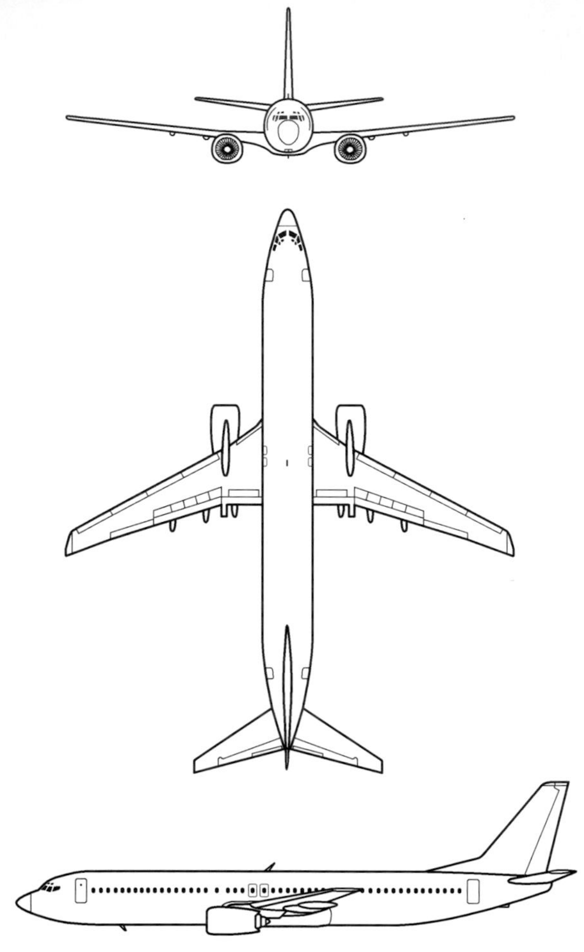

Dimensions:
Wingspan 112.5 ft (34.30 m)
Length 138.1 ft (42.10 m)
Height 41 ft (12.50 m)
Wing area 1,341.2 sq. ft (124.60 m^2)

BOEING 737-900

Country of origin: USA.
Type: Short and medium haul commercial aircraft.
Power Plant: Two CFM International CFM 56-7B turbofan engines each with 24,010-27,292 lbs (10,800-12,370 kp/106.8-121.4 kN) static thrust.
Performance: Maximum cruising speed 567 mph (912 km/h [Mach 0.82]), normal speed 519 mph (835 km/h) at 38,976 ft (11,880 m), service ceiling 41,010 ft (12,500 m), range 3,157 miles (5,080 km).
Weight: Empty weight 91,290 lbs (41,410 kg), maximum take-off weight 172,490 lbs (78,240 kg).
Payload: Two-man cockpit crew and 177 passengers using various cabin configurations, maximum number of passengers 189.
State of development: Considered the final design of the 737's current generation, the -900 version undertook its test flight on August 3, 2000. Alaska Airlines, Continental, KLM and Korean Airlines have ordered 46 aircraft. These were put into service in the early part of 2001. By October 2002, about 2,040 aircraft (+ options) of the -600/-700/-800 and -900 versions have been ordered and 1,200 have been delivered. To date, Boeing has received commissions for over 5,170 B737 aircraft of all designs.
Remarks: The -900 version is Boeing's longest aircraft in the 737 series. It is 5 ft (1.47 m) longer than the -800 version in front of the wings and nearly 4 ft (1.07 m) behind them. This version essentially records the same performance data as the -800 while providing the passengers with greater comfort. The cargo space is 18% greater. Presently, Boeing is conducting tests on the -900X, a new version that can carry up to 220 passengers and has a longer range and a greater take-off weight of 184,526 lbs (83,700 kg).
Manufacturer: The Boeing Company, Commercial Airplane Group, Renton plant, Washington, USA.

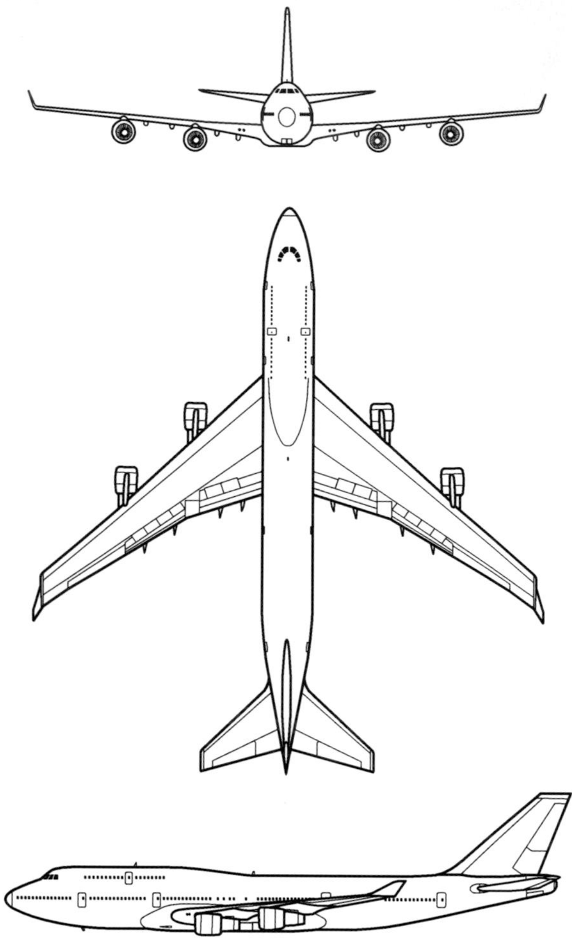

Dimensions:
Wingspan 211.4 ft (64.44 m)
Length 231.8 ft (70.67 m)
Height 63.7 ft (19.41 m)
Wing area 5,825 sq. ft (541.16 m^2)

BOEING 747-400ER

Country of origin: USA.
Type: Long haul commercial aircraft.
Power Plant: Four General Electric CFM International CF60-80C2B5F turbofan engines each with 62,108 lbs (28,165 kp/276.27 kN) static thrust.
Performance: Long haul cruising speed 567 mph (912 km/h) at 35,000 ft (10,668 m), cargo plane range with maximum payload 5,039 miles (8,110 km), range with maximum fuel load 8,831 miles (14,212 km).
Weight: Maximum take-off weight 910,000 lbs (412,800 kg).
Payload: Two-man cockpit and 450 passengers in three classes. As a 400F cargo plane 249,100 lbs (113,000 kg) payload.
State of development: The first flight of the 747-400ER version took place on July 31, 2002. Eight units (6 for Qantas and 2 for Air France) went into service in October and November 2002. Counting all versions of the 747's, about 1,370 aircraft were ordered by 35 companies (about 1,320 have been delivered), of which 540 were the -400 version and 105 were -400F cargo conversions. Presently, production is proceeding at a rate of two aircraft per month.
Remarks: To date, the latest long haul design for the 747-400ER designation features considerable improvements while retaining the same external measurements. It is a passenger aircraft as well as a cargo plane and provides reinforcement of the outer wings in the upper and lateral parts of the craft. In the main wings, the tank capacity has been increased to 63,700 gallons (241,140 l). Because of this as well as a sturdier chassis, the maximum take-off weight is considerably higher than other aircraft in the -400 series. These measures have led to an ability to transport larger payloads over longer distances. Additionally, the cockpit and the comfort of the passenger cabin are comparable to those of the 777 designation. The manufacturer is presently developing a quiet, long range variant of the -400ER called the -400XQLR (**Q**uiet **L**ong **R**ange). This is being tested with aerodynamic refinements to the wings and the fuel tanks.
Manufacturer: The Boeing Company, Commercial Airplane Group, Seattle, Everett plant, Washington USA.

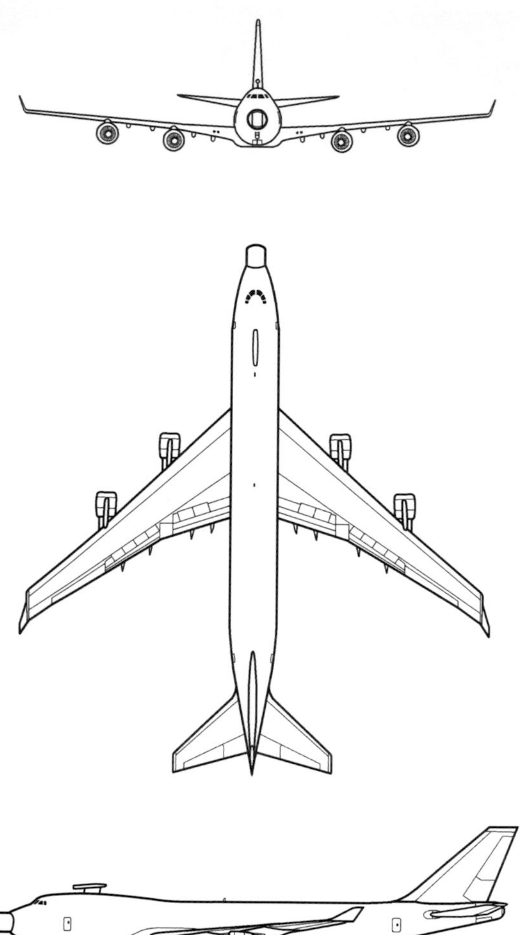

Dimensions:
Wingspan 211.4 ft (64.44 m)
Length 231.95 ft (70.70 m)
Height 63.7 ft (19.41 m)
Wing area 5,825 sq. ft (541.16 m^2)

BOEING YAL-1A AIRBORNE LASER

Country of origin: USA.
Type: Strategic anti-missile defense system.
Power Plant: Four General Electric CFM International CFM 60-80C2 turbofan engines each with 63,165 lbs (28,644 kp/280.97 kN) of static thrust.
Performance (provisional data): Normal patrol speed 584 mph (939 km/h), range 9,675 miles (15,570 km).
Weight: Empty weight 289,100 lbs (181,120 kg), maximum take-off weight 871,500 lbs (395,300 kg).
Payload: Six-person occupancy includes two pilots and four operators with ammunition for 20 laser rounds. The entire laser system, including the accompanying chemicals, weighs around 178,574 lbs (81,000 kg).
Armament: There is a specific chemically based oxygen iodine laser in the rear of the fuselage that can be activated by means of a moveable optical device in the nose of the fuselage.
State of development: The first partially equipped YAL-1A prototype began its test flight on July 18, 2002. The remaining systems were built in by the middle of 2003. The testing of the laser weapons will begin before the end of 2004. The United States Air Force plans to acquire seven of these aircraft by 2008.
Remarks: The YAL-1A is planned as one element of the anti-missile defense system of the United States. An essentially modified 747-400F serves as a basis for this. The design centerpiece is a chemical oxygen iodine laser in the megawatt class incorporated in the fuselage. Using the aircraft's optics, enemy medium- and long-range missiles can be attacked from up to 373 miles (600 km) away. Up to 30 targets can be handled simultaneously. The YAL-1A features numerous changes from the initial model 747-400F. For example, the radar, which is normally positioned in the fuselage, is in a container in the undercarriage. Because of the great weight of the entire system and the release of hot gasses, parts of the structure are reinforced with titanium. One such structure is the interior of the laser control center that is also separated by a pressure frame. Behind the cockpit, on the upper part of the fuselage, a laser range finder is installed for the detection of targets.
Manufacturer: The Boeing Company, Defense & Space Group, Seattle, Washington, USA.

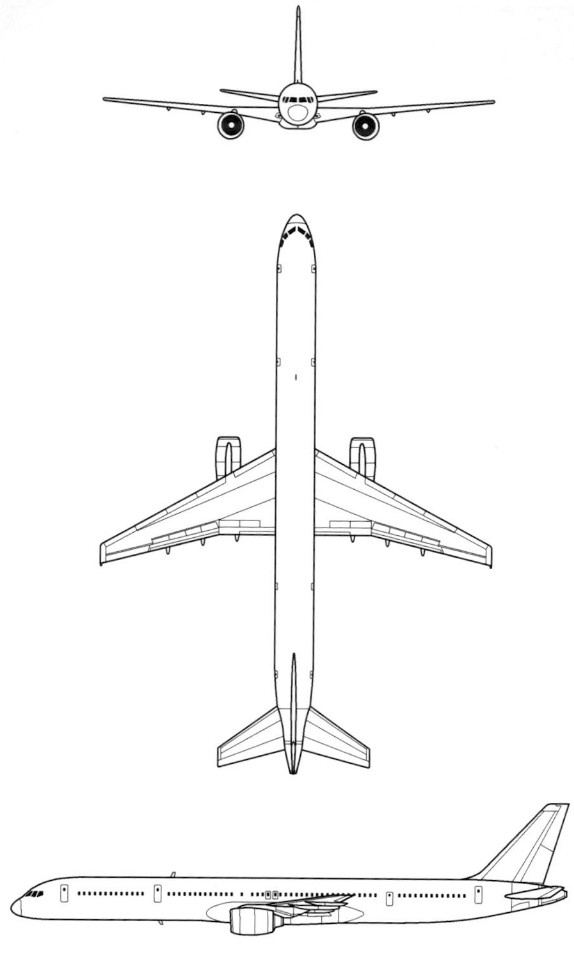

Dimensions:
Wingspan 124.84 ft (38.05 m)
Length 178.48 ft (54.40 m)
Height 44.49 ft (13.56 m)
Wing area 1,994 sq. ft (185.25 m^2)

BOEING 757-300

Country of origin: USA.
Type: Middle-range airliner.
Power Plant: Either two Rolls-Royce RB.211-535E4B turbofan engines each with 42,939 lbs (19,470 kp/191 kN) or two Pratt & Whitney PW2040 engines each with 41,590 lbs (18,860 kp/185 kN) static thrust.
Performance: Maximum cruising speed 581 mph (935 km/h [Mach 0.86]) at 30,020 ft (9,150 m), economic cruising speed 528 mph (850 km/h) at 39,042 ft (11,900 m), service ceiling 42,030 ft (12,810 m), maximum cruising range 3,977 miles (6,400 km).
Weight: Empty weight 141,300 lbs (64,105 kg), maximum take-off weight 270,000 lbs (122,470 kg).
Payload: Two pilots and (-757-300) 240 to a maximum of 289 passengers using a typical interior design, as a cargo plane (-757-200) 67,020 lbs (30,400 kg).
State of development: The first flight of the Boeing 757-300 took place on August 2, 1998 and, by the end of 2002, orders were placed by more than 60 operators for approximately 1,050 units of all versions. More than 1,020 have been delivered. 63 units of the -300 have been ordered. Lacking further new orders, Boeing has reduced the monthly production. Many older 757's were reconstructed into cargo planes including 84 for DHL.
Remarks: The model -757-300 distinguishes itself by an enlarged 23 ft (7.11 m) fuselage of which 13 ft (4.06 m) is in the front and 10 ft (3.05 m) is behind the wing. Due to the increased weight, the pitch elevators, parts of the area structures and the alighting gear have been strengthened accordingly. In addition to the higher number of passengers, the freight capacity has become 40% larger. Boeing has launched a long-range model 757-200ERX with a higher fuel capacity that is evident by the fuselage of the -200 and the reinforced wing and other components of the -300. This model can fly for 5,748 miles (9,250 km) with a maximum take-off weight of 272,271 lbs (123,500 kg) and two additional tanks in the cargo compartment. Although it's available for immediate delivery, no orders have yet been placed. A business version 757BBJ3 will be derived from this model.
Manufacturer: The Boeing Company, Commercial Airplane Group, Seattle, Renton plant, Washington, USA.

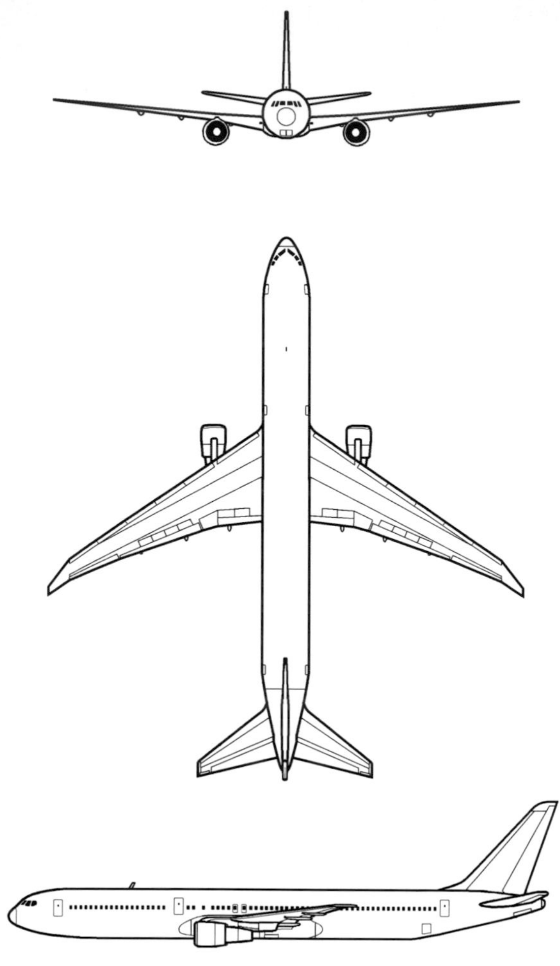

Dimensions:
Wingspan 170.34 ft (51.92 m)
Length 201.34 ft (61.37 m)
Height 55.35 ft (16.87 m)
Wing area 3,129 sq. ft (290.70 m^2)

BOEING 767-400ER

Country of origin: USA.
Type: Medium- to long-range commercial aircraft.
Power Plant: Two Pratt & Whitney PW 40E2 turbofan engines each with 68,117 lbs (32,890 kp/303 kN) or two General Electric CF6-80C2 engines each with 61,373 lbs (27,830 kp/273 kN) static thrust.
Performance: Cruising speed 528 mph (850 km/h [Mach 0.80]), service ceiling 43,127 ft (13,145 m), maximum cruising range 6,493 miles (1,0450 km).
Weight: Empty weight 227,300 lbs (103,100 kg), maximum take-off weight 450,000 lbs (204,120 kg).
Payload: Two pilots and, with a typical multi-class interior configuration, 245 to a maximum of 375 passengers in eight-seat rows.
State of development: The first flight of the basic Boeing 767 airframe took place on September 26, 1981. The test flight of the latest -400ER version occurred on October 9, 1999. Delivery started in August 2000. Through 2000 the number of orders stood at around 930 aircraft of all versions for almost 80 customers of which 900 have been delivered. There are firm orders from Delta, Continental and Korean Airways for 50 of the -400ER aircraft. Presently, four 767's are manufactured each month.
Remarks: The 767-400ER designation is the largest design offered for sale so far. It has both a 15 to 20% increase in seating capacity and the lowest operating costs. It is 22 ft (6.7 m) longer with a slightly larger wingspan and a reinforced undercarriage with the B777 wheels. A military design of the 767-200ER, the E-767T-T, flew in 2003 for the first time. The Italian Air Force has been first to order this combined military transport plane and tanker which is equipped with a flying boom and two fuelling pods under the wings (4 ordered + 2 options). The United States Air Force has been leasing 757 designated aircraft for 10 years. Japan plans to acquire 4 of these.
Manufacturer: The Boeing Company, Commercial Airplane Group, Seattle, Everett plant, Washington USA.

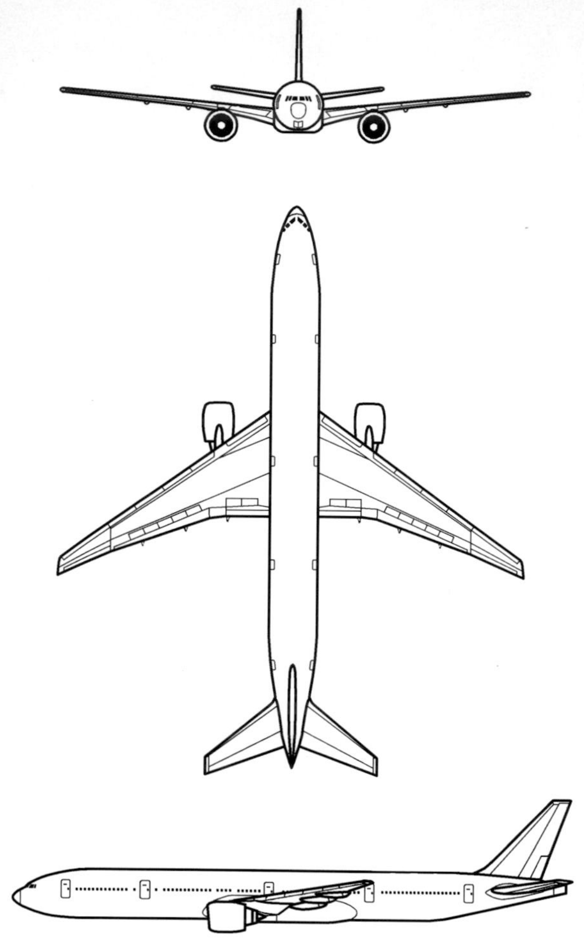

Dimensions:
Wingspan (-300) 200 ft (60.93 m), (-200LR/300ER) 212.6 ft (64.80 m)
Length (-300/-300ER) 242.1 ft (73.80 m), (-200 LR) 209 ft (63.70 m)
Height 60.5 ft (18.44 m)
Wing area (-300) 4,604.8 sq. ft (427.80 m^2)

BOEING 777-300

Country of origin: USA.
Type: Medium- to long- range commercial aircraft.
Power Plant: Two Rolls-Royce Trent 892 or Pratt & Whitney PW4090/4098 turbofan engines each with 91,947 to 98,017 lbs (41,700 to 44,460 kp/409 to 436 kN) static thrust.
Performance: Maximum cruising speed 590 mph (950 km/h [Mach 0.87]), long range cruising speed 556 mph (895 km/h [Mach 0.35]), service ceiling 43 ft (13,100 m), range with 368 passengers up to 6,462 miles (10,400 km).
Weight: Empty weight 343,304 lbs (155,720 kg), maximum take-off weight 660,000 lbs (299,370 kg).
Payload: Two pilots and, in a typical three class configuration, 368 to 394 passengers with a maximum of 550 passengers, maximum payload 120,400 lbs (54,603 kg).
State of development: The first test flight of the 777-300 was on October 16, 1997. The 777-300ER, which by then had been ordered by six airlines (46 aircraft), followed in February 2003. Including all the variants, 30 customers have ordered around 620 aircraft by the end of 2002. Of these, 107 were the -300 version. At this time five 777's were produced a month and around 420 aircraft had been delivered.
Remarks: The 777-300 is 33 ft (10 m) longer than the original model. A long distance design, 777-300ER, will be delivered in 2004 to Air France, its first customer. The span values are greater by 1,004 ft (306 m) and the take-off weight increased to 749,637 lbs (340,030 kg). Ranges up to 8,326 miles (13,400 km) should be achieved. The newest technological advances are factored into the construction of the aircraft including a newly developed wing profile, fly-by-wire system, aluminum alloy with the best pressure and fatigue characteristics, vertical tail which consists primarily of composite materials and the most modern avionics and materials. The 777-200LR ultra long haul aircraft, planned by Boeing, will soon be a reality. Only five have been ordered so far and its launch is planned for 2004. Carrying 250 passengers, it aims to reach a range up to 10,150 miles (16,330 km). As an option, there is a dormitory for up to 40 people in the cargo area and one for the crew above the passenger area. A cargo model is also under consideration.
Manufacturer: The Boeing Company, Commercial Airplane Group, Seattle, Everett plant, Washington, USA.

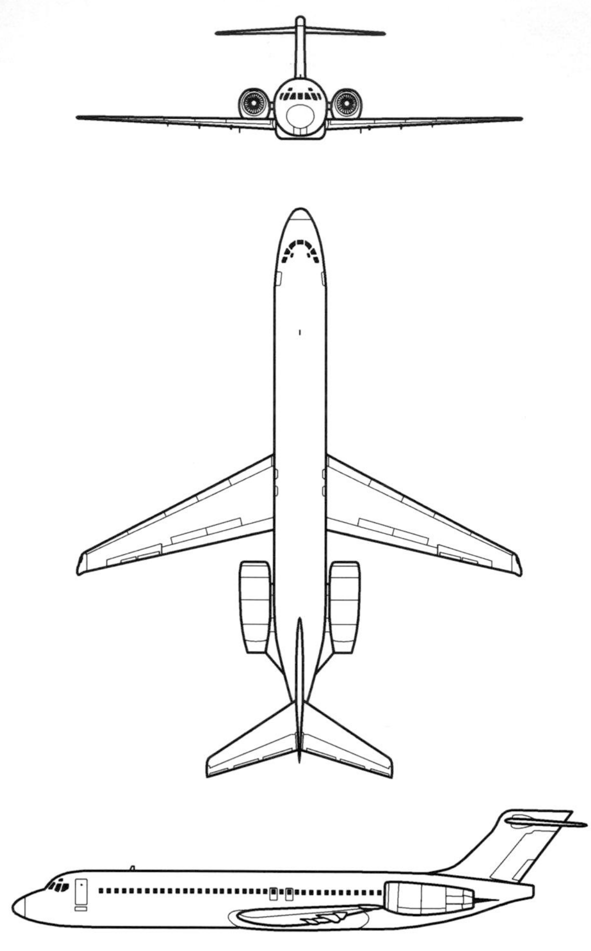

Dimensions:
Wingspan 93.34 ft (28.45 m)
Length 124.05 ft (37.81 m)
Height 29.26 ft (8.92 m)
Wing area 1,000.8 sq. ft (92.97 m^2)

BOEING (MDD) 717-200

Country of origin: USA.
Type: Short to medium-range commercial aircraft.
Power Plant: Two BMW/Rolls Royce BR 715 turbofan engines each with either 18,502 lbs (8,390 kp/82.3 kN) or 20,008 lbs (9,073 kp/89.0 kN) with an option for 20,997 lbs (9,525 kp/93.4 kN) static thrust.
Performance: Cruising speed 505 mph (812 km/h [Mach 0.76]) at 35,010 ft (10,670 m), service ceiling 4,052 ft (1,235 m), range with full passenger load (-200) 1,805 miles (2,905 km), (-200HGW) 2,299 miles (3,700 km).
Weight: Empty weight (-200) 69,831 lbs (31,675 kg), (-200HGW) 70,790 lbs (32,110 kg), maximum take-off weight (-200) 114,000 lbs (51,710 kg) (-200 HGW) 121,000 lbs (54,885 kg).
Payload: Two-person cockpit and 106 passengers in a two class configuration or 129 passengers in five-seat rows with a middle aisle, maximum payload 26,965 lbs (12,231 kg).
State of development: The first flight of the prototype took place on September 2, 1993. Deliveries to the initial customers (Valujet and AirTran) began on September 23, 1999. By the end of 2002, orders increased to 153 aircraft (of which 110 have been delivered). The principal customers were AirTran, which increased their order to 23 B717s, Capital, Hawaiian and Midwest.
Remarks: The 717 was launched on the market as the latest version of an already long list of DC-9 derivatives. Equipped with a particularly low-emission and quiet version of the BMW/Rolls-Royce BR 715 engine, it provides a shorter fuselage than that of the MD30 family. The cockpit has six state-of-the-art liquid crystal display screens. At the moment, it's not clear if the proposed shorter or longer version of the 717 design will be pursued.
Manufacturer: The Boeing Company, Commercial Airplane Group, Seattle, Washington, Long Beach plant, California, USA.

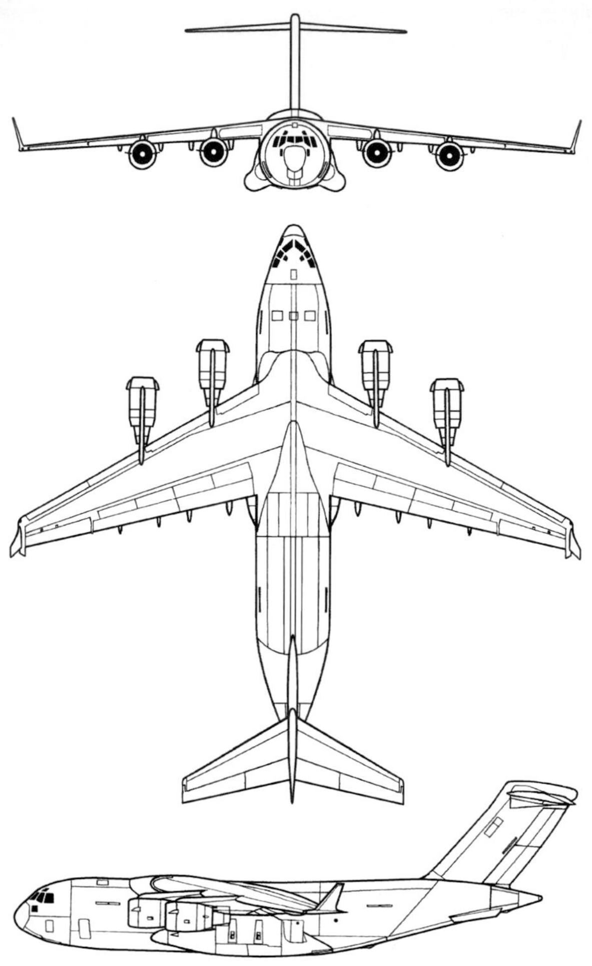

Dimensions:
Wingspan 165 ft (50.29 m)
Length 174 ft (53.04 m)
Height 55.08 ft (16.79 m)
Wing area 3,800.8 sq. ft (353 m^2)

BOEING (MDD) C-17A GLOBEMASTER III

Country of origin: USA.
Type: Heavy military cargo plane.
Power Plant: Four Pratt & Whitney F 117 -PW 100 turbofan engines each with 41,702 lbs (18,914 kp/ 165.5 kN) static thrust.
Performance: Cruising speed 508 mph (818 km/h [Mach 0.77]) at 36,000 ft (10,975 m), 404 mph (650 km/h) at a lower altitude, service ceiling 44,950 ft (13,700 m), range with a payload of 129,200 lbs (58,605 kg) 3,225 miles (5,190 km), with a payload of 158,500 lbs (71,895 kg) 3,108 miles (5,000 km) and with a payload of 167,000 lbs (75,750 kg) 2,762 miles (4,445 km).
Weight: Empty weight 48,540 lbs (22,016 kg), maximum take-off weight 58,610 lbs (26,583 kg).
Payload: Two pilots and 2 cargo personnel. The 88 ft (26.83 m) long 18 ft (5.49 m) wide and 13 ft (4.11 m) high cargo space can carry a payload of 167,000 lbs (75,750 kg). A typical load might include three AH-64 attack helicopters or a fully equipped M-1 Abrams battle tank and up to 102 paratroopers. Single loads of 60,000 lbs (27,215 kg) or large pallets with a maximum 110,000 lbs (49,895 kg) can be dropped in flight.
State of development: The prototype first flew on September 15, 1991 and the first delivery was made to the United States Air Force in July 1993. Shortly thereafter, the Air Force increased its order to 180 aircraft to be delivered in 2007. An additional order of 42 is presently under negotiation. The RAF took delivery of four leased C-17's in 2001.
Remarks: What distinguishes the C-17A is its special ability to transport heavy cargo over strategic distances and to place it directly into the combat zone. Sturdily built with this task in mind it is adaptable for runways only 3,000 ft (915 m) long. The absolutely crucial wing assembly with a sweep of 25° is equipped with winglets and a blown flap system. The stable chassis allows the craft to maneuver under its own power on the ground. Since 2001, all C-17's are equipped with an additional tank with a capacity of 10,303 gallons (39,000 l). This feature allows the aircraft to achieve meaningfully greater ranges. The development of BC-17X, a civilian version, which, because of its internal outfitting, could accommodate a payload of 173,283 lbs (78,600 kg) is presently being dropped due to lack of demand.
Manufacturer: The Boeing Company, Defense & Space Group, Seattle, Washington, Long Beach plant, California, USA.

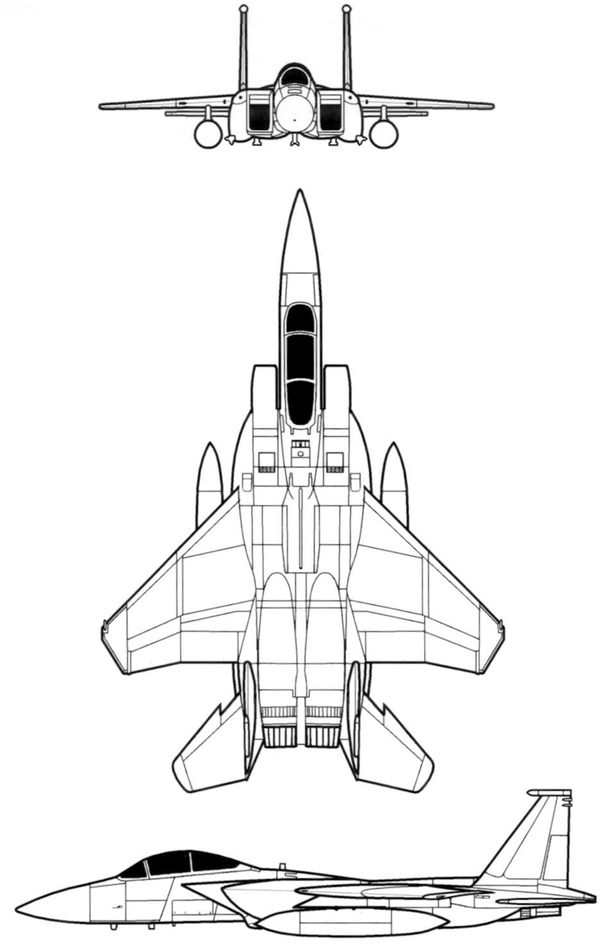

Dimensions:
Wingspan 42.81 ft (13.05 m)
Length 63.75 ft (19.43 m)
Height 18.47 ft (5.63 m)
Wing area 608.2 sq. ft (56.50 m^2)

BOEING (MDD) F-15E EAGLE

Country of origin: USA.
Type: Two-seat air superiority fighter and ground combat support aircraft.
Power Plant: Two Pratt & Whitney F100-PW-229 turbofan engines each with 17,805 lb (8,073 kp/79.20 kN) static thrust without afterburners and 29,090 lb (13,200 kp/129.40 kN) with afterburners.
Performance: Peak speed reachable for a short burst 1,676 mph (2,698 km/h [Mach 2.54]) at 39,990 ft (12,190 m), maximum sustained speed 1,518 mph (2,443 km/h [Mach 2.4]) at 39,993 ft (12,190 m), service ceiling 60,039 ft (18,300 m), maximum tactical operation radius 789 miles (1,270 km), deployment range with supplementary tank 2,762 miles (4,445 km).
Weight: Empty weight 31,700 lbs (14,379 kg), maximum take-off weight 80,960 lbs (36,721 kg).
Payload: (ground combat) A six barrel M61A1 20-mm revolving cannon with external weapons load of 24,500 lbs (11,113 kg), (air superiority missions) either four each of AIM-7F Sparrow air-to-air guided missiles and AIM-9LM Sidewinder or up to 8 AIM-120.
State of development: The first F-15E's began testing on December 11, 1986. Delivery of 245 aircraft to the United States Air Force began in 1989. Manufacturing continues in small quantities. Israel and Saudi Arabia have ordered similar versions of the F-15E (Israel 25 F-15I and Saudi Arabia 99 F-15S). South Korea has recently acquired 40 F-15K's.
Remarks: The F-15E is a version of F-15C optimized for ground combat support with a reinforced structure, higher acceleration limits, threefold electrical control system and expanded avionics for all weather low altitude flight (Hughes APG-70 radar, the infrared FLIR system, LANTIRN low altitude navigation and night flight system). The F-15K design for South Korea is different because, among other things, it uses General Electric F-110 GE 129 engines, has a new cockpit and improved sensors and avionics. However, the new APG-63V1 or -V2 radar permits tracking of moving targets on land or sea. Deliveries will begin in 2005.
Manufacturer: The Boeing Company, Defense and Space Group, Seattle, Washington, St. Louis plant, Missouri, USA.

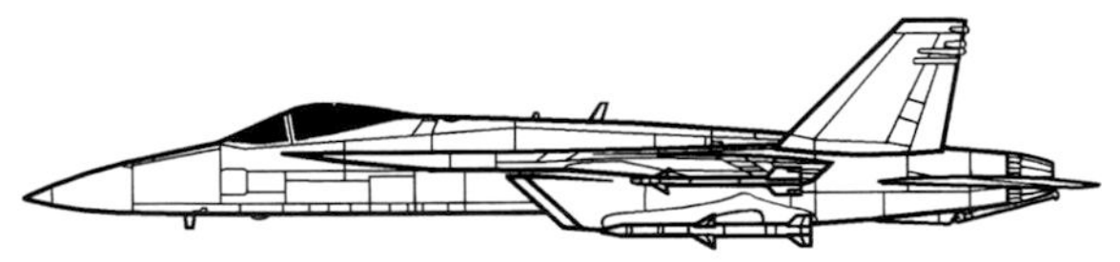

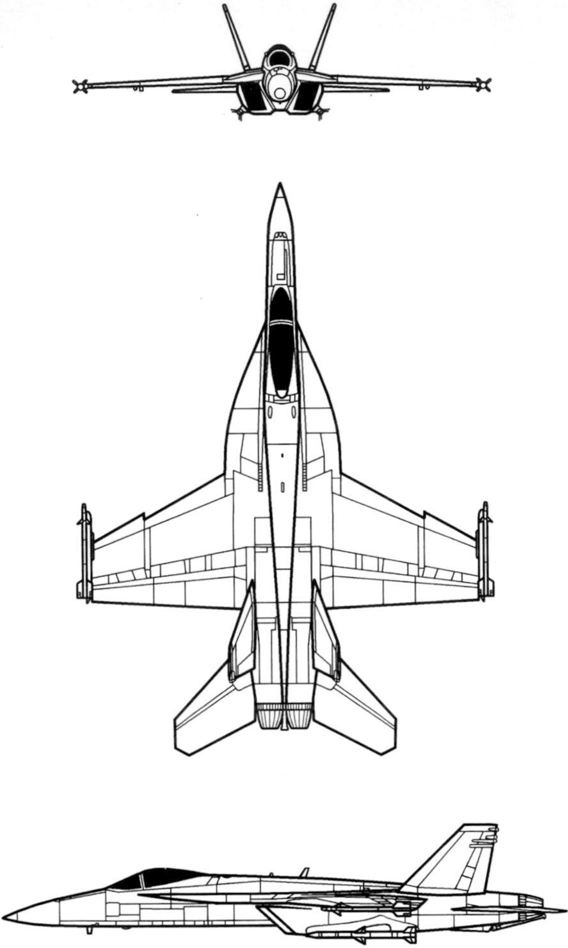

Dimensions:
Wingspan 44.95 ft (13.70 m)
Length 60.37 ft (18.40 m)
Height 16.01 ft (4.88 m)
Wing area 500 sq. ft (46.45 m^2)

BOEING (MDD) F/A-18E/F SUPER HORNET

Country of origin: USA.
Type: Multi-purpose one and two-seat ship and land based electronic fighter aircraft.
Power Plant: Two General Electric F414-GE-400 turbofan engines each with 22,000 lbs (9,978 kp/97.86 kN) static thrust with afterburners.
Performance: Maximum speed at optimal height Mach 1.8+, service ceiling 50,000 ft (15,240 m), mission radius with two each Sidewinder air-to-air missiles and AMRAAM 472 mph (760 km/h), during low-level attack missions with four 1,000 lb (450 kg) bombs, two Sidewinders and two 480-gallon (1,818 l) external tanks (high-low-low-high) 449 mph (722 km).
Weight: Empty weight 23,670 lbs (10,735 kg), normal take-off weight 51,900 lbs (23,541 kg), maximum weight 65,180 lbs (29,564 kg).
Armament: One M61A1 20-mm revolving cannon and various weapons totaling 17,750 lbs (8,050 kg).
State of development: The first of seven prototypes flew on November 29, 1996. The United States Navy and the United States Marine Corps together have expressed an interest in about 548 F/A-18E/F's of different designs. 284 of them are on order. The 100th completed aircraft was handed over to the United States Navy on June 14, 2002.
Remarks: The F/A-18E/F Super Hornet is an advanced version of the F/A-18C/D Hornet. Its main wings are larger and the fuselage has been lengthened by adding a 34-inch (86 cm) section. About one third of the airframe consists of composite materials, mainly carbon fiber. The engine intakes are rectangular in shape. The Super Hornet is 25% larger than the original model. The contour reflections are kept to a minimum so that the radar signature can be smaller. Because the engines are 35% stronger, the fuel capacity is one-third higher in all areas resulting in a considerably better flight performance and higher range. To replace the EA-6B Prowler, Boeing is developing a design for an EA-18 Growler for electronic battle control. A corresponding test vehicle has been flying since November 15, 2001.
Manufacturer: The Boeing Company, Defense & Space Group, Seattle, Washington, St. Louis plant, Missouri, USA.

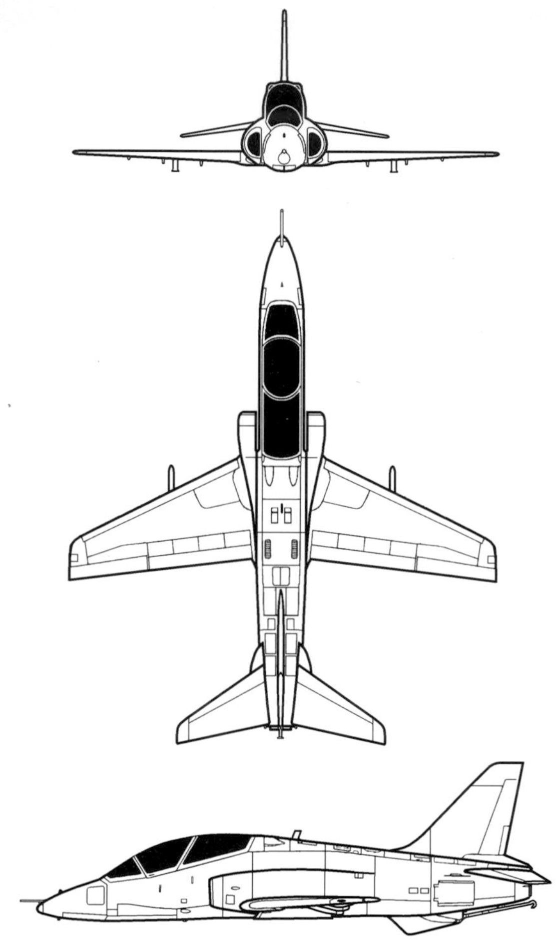

Dimensions:
Wingspan 30.8 ft (9.39 m)
Length 39.27 ft (11.97 m)
Height 13.42 ft (4.09 m)
Wing area 179.65 sq. ft (16.69 m^2)

BOEING (MDD / BAe) T-45C GOSHAWK

Country of origin: USA and Great Britain.
Type: Two-seat ship and land based advanced trainer aircraft.
Power Plant: One Rolls-Royce Turboméca F405-RR-401 (Adour Mk. 871) turbofan engine with 5,481 lbs (2,648 kp/25.98 kN) static thrust.
Performance: Maximum speed 625 mph (1,006 km/h) at 8,202 ft (2,500 m), 573 mph (922 km/h) at 30,020 ft (9,150 m), take-off speed 166 ft (35.47 m)/sec, service ceiling 42,500 ft (12,955 m), climb time to 30,020 ft (9,150 m) 7.20 minutes, transportation range with internal fuel tank 1,150 miles (1,850 km).
Weight: Empty weight 9,398 lbs (4,263 kg), maximum take-off weight 14,080 lbs (6,337 kg).
Armament (as a weapons trainer): One station under each wing and one under the fuselage for missile pod, practice bomb container, etc.
State of development: The first of two prototypes of the T-45A flew for the first time on April 16, 1988. The deployment tests began in the fall of 1993. The United States Navy acquired 169 T-45's in yearly consignments of 6 to 12 aircraft. The 150th aircraft was handed over to the United States Navy on August 8, 2002 (see photo).
Remarks: The T-45A Goshawk is part of an integral training system (T-45 Training System), which incorporates, in addition to the aircraft, simulators, infrastructure and logistical support. Differences between this aircraft and the British Hawk (see pages 120/121) include additional arresting hook, newly installed and positioned air brakes, compartmentalization under the fuselage, a reinforced chassis for carrier take-off and landing and a stronger engine as well as some changes in the wing flap system. The first T-45 C (73rd aircraft in the series) with a digitally equipped cockpit carried out a test flight in March 1994 and the first delivery was in October 1997. All earlier units will be converted to this standard.
Manufacturer: The Boeing Company, Defense and Space Group, Seattle, Washington, St. Louis plant, Missouri, USA and British Aerospace PLC, Military Aircraft Division, Warton, Lancashire, Great Britain.

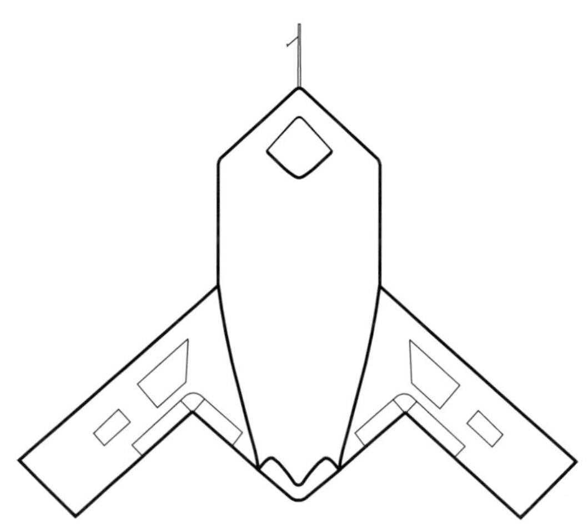

Dimensions:
Wingspan 33.46 ft (10.20 m)
Length 26.25 ft (8.00 m)
Height approximately 3.77 ft (1.15 m) without landing gear

BOEING X-45A SPIRAL 0

Country of origin: USA.
Type: Unmanned test carrier for combat applications.
Power Plant: An Allied Signal F 124 turbofan engine with vector control.
Performance (very provisional information): Maximum speed just under Mach 1.0, tactical operation radius of about 746 miles (1,200 km).
Weight: Empty weight 8,000 lbs (3,628 kg), maximum take-off weight 15,000 lbs (6,804 kg).
Payload: Test equipment and experimental weapons up to a weight of 1,984 lbs (900 kg) can be carried in two internal compartments.
State of development: The X-45A technology demonstrator flew for the first time on May 22, 2002. A second model undertook its test flight on November 21, 2002.
Remarks: This UCAV (**U**nmanned **C**ombat **A**ir **V**ehicle) opens a new dimension in this category. The X-45A is the first model designed for actual combat tasks. Former models were mainly used for reconnaissance and interception. Testing is concentrated on the feasibility of combat missions under near war conditions. In 2004, Boeing is going to produce two units of a somewhat larger design, X-45B Spiral 1. They will be fitted with General Electric F-404-102D engines. For the actual weapons testing, they are equipped with a fully integrated avionics and weapons system, aperture radar and electronic defenses. The contours of the fuselage, wings, openings and antennas are displayed in accordance with the stealth principle. A provisional serial model, designated as X-45 Spiral 2, is slated to be introduced in 2008.
Manufacturer: The Boeing Company, Military Aircraft and Missile Systems, Phantom Works, St. Louis, Missouri, USA.

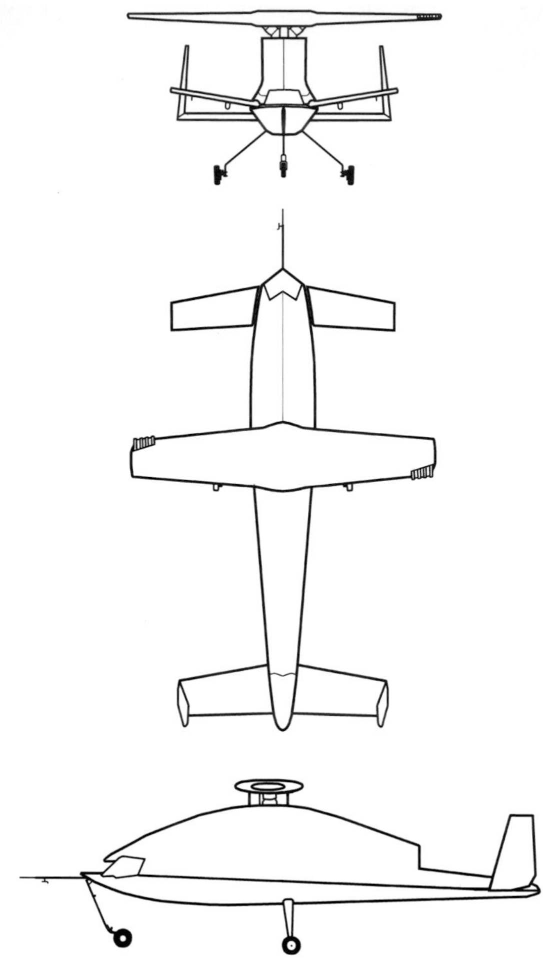

Dimensions:
Wingspan duck-wings 8.89 ft (2.71 m)
Main wings/rotor 11.97 ft (3.65 m)
Length 17.26 ft (5.26 m)
Height 6.63 ft (2.02 m)

BOEING X-50A DRAGONFLY

Country of origin: USA.
Type: Unmanned experimental aircraft with rotor-wings.
Power Plant: One Williams F-112 turbofan engine with nozzles at the wing tips for the conversion of the wings into a rotor configuration.
Performance (very provisional information): Maximum speed about 174 mph (280 km/h). In the rotor configuration, speeds about 68 mph (110 km/h) should be reached. Changing the rotorcraft to the surface configuration takes place at 149 mph (240 km/h).
Weight: No information available.
State of development: The first of two prototypes was presented in July 2002 and the first experimental flight took place on December 3, 2003.
Remarks: With the X-50A, Boeing is breaking completely new ground. An attempt is being made to combine the attributes of a rotorcraft with those of a fixed wing airplane. However, in contrast to models with tilt rotors (cf. Bell/Boeing V-22, pages 62/63), the X-50A wings take over the function of the rotors. On take-off and landing, the rotors turn like those of a helicopter. In flight, these are locked into a fixed position and allow, together with the wings towards the front of the fuselage, the vehicle to function as a fixed wing aircraft. Boeing has coined the term CRW (**C**anard **R**otor/**W**ing) to describe this principle. If the testing were successful, a whole new generation of fast aircraft would be produced to replace today's VTOL-models. The United States Navy intends to commission a larger CRW-design based on the X-50A that would be stationed on ships.
Manufacturer: The Boeing Company, Military Aircraft and Missile Systems, Phantom Works, Mesa, Arizona, USA.

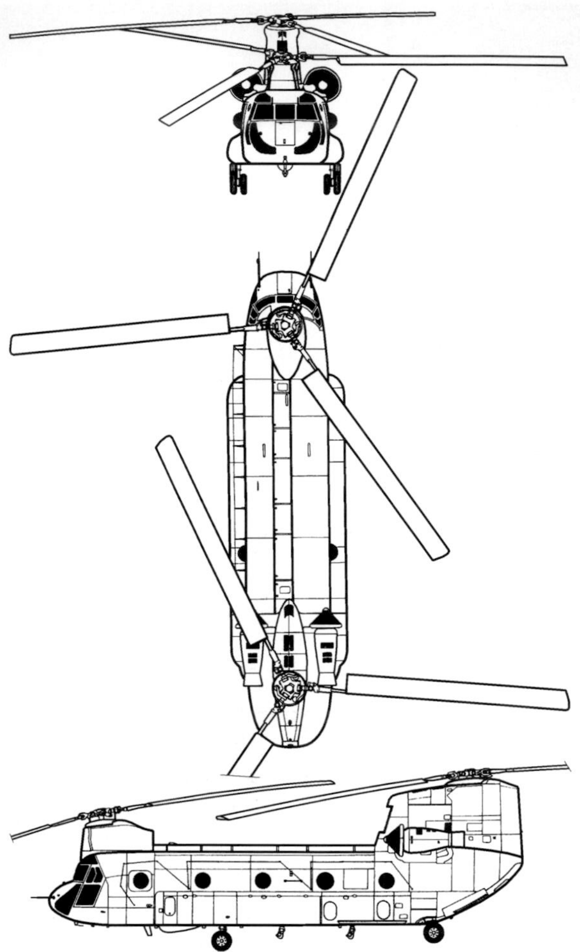

Dimensions:
Diameter of each of the two rotors 60 ft (18.29 m)
Fuselage length without refueling pipe 52 ft (15.84 m)
Fuselage height without rotor 17.06 ft (5.20 m)

BOEING CH-47SD/F CHINOOK

Country of origin: USA.
Type: Heavy transport helicopter.
Power Plant: Two Allied Signal T55- 714A gas turboshaft engines each with 4,733 SHP (3,529 kW) performance.
Performance: Maximum speed 185 mph (298 km/h) at sea level, average speed 152 mph (245 km/h), maximum diagonal climb rate 31 ft (9.38 m)/sec, cruising altitude with ground effect 6,027 ft (1,837 m), without ground effect 5,495 ft (1,675 m), maximum altitude 11,099 ft (3,383 m), maximum mission radius 373 miles (600 km).
Weight: Empty weight 25,463 lbs (11,550 kg), maximum take-off weight 54,000 lbs (24,495 kg).
Payload: Two pilots and 45 personnel or, as an ambulance helicopter, 22 patients plus two medical attendants. Maximum external load 28,000 lbs (12,700 kg).
State of development: The first flight of the CH47 SD's latest design took place on August 25, 1999. Singapore placed 6 orders for this version and Taiwan 9. The United States Army would like to acquire 25 more of the CH-47F compatible MH-47G version for United States Special Operations. The first CH-47D converted into a CH-47F Chinook was handed over to the United States Army in May 2002.
Remarks: The CH-47SD (**S**uper **D**) is a considerably upgraded design. The United States Army equivalent is called the CH-47F and flew for the first time on June 25, 2001. The most important new features are the substantially improved avionics systems with a MIL-STD-1553 databus and a fully integrated glass cockpit that is very suitable for NVG applications. The engines produce roughly a 22% higher performance. In addition, larger fuel tanks have been incorporated. For increased longevity and to lower the level of vibration, the skin has been reinforced and stiffened. Finally, new retractable hoists can be used to reach the rotor heads. Reliability increases with this feature in place and it facilitates maintenance on demand. The United States Army wants to convert about 300 CH-47Ds into the CH-47F version by the year 2013. Then, with the exception of the fuselage, practically all components will be new. Orders have been received for seven helicopters by the end of 2003.
Manufacturer: The Boeing Company, Helicopter Division, Philadelphia, Pennsylvania, USA.

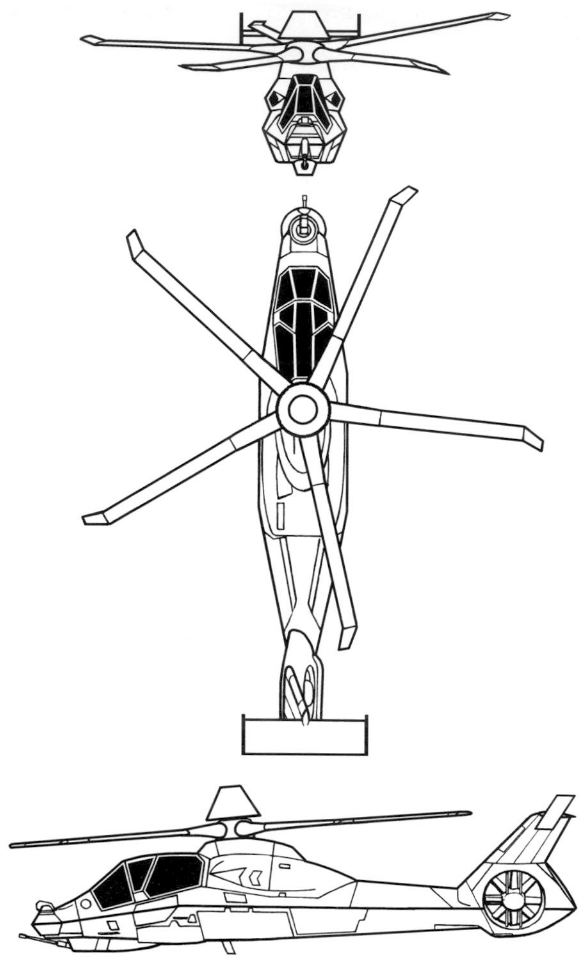

Dimensions:
Rotor diameter 39.04 ft (11.90 m)
Length without canon 43.37 ft (13.22 m)
Height above tail unit 11.12 ft (3.39 m)

BOEING / SIKORSKY RAH-66 COMANCHE

Country of origin: USA.
Type: Two-seat stealth combat helicopter.
Power Plant: Two LHTEC T800-LHT-800 gas turboshaft engines (prototypes) each with 1,344 SHP (1,202 kW) or two T800-LHT-801 turboshaft engines (series) each with 1,563 SHP (1,165 kW) performance.
Performance (estimated): Maximum speed 204 mph (328 km/h), vertical climb rate 20 ft (6 m)/sec, transportation range 1,451 miles (2,335 km), normal flight duration with internal fuel 2 hours 30 minutes.
Weight: Empty weight 7,749 lbs (3,515 kg), normal take-off weight 10,013 lbs (4,587 kg), maximum take-off weight for transportation 17,170 lbs (7,790 kg).
Armament: A General Electric/Giat 3 barreled 20 mm-revolving cannon in a turret under the fuselage nose and up to six Hellfire anti-tank guided missiles and Stinger air-to-air missiles in two closed weapon bays. Further weapons can be carried on removable wing pylons.
State of development: The first of two YRAH-66A prototypes undertook its test flight on January 4, 1996. After that, five pre-series machines were manufactured. The United States Army had envisioned a fleet of 675 Comanches. However, the start of production was postponed once again to January 2005 pushing the introduction of the aircraft into service to 2009 at the earliest (13 years after its maiden flight!). Recently the Pentagon requested that the U.S. Congress cancel the order. The future of the Comanche is, to say the least, up in the air.
Remarks: The RAH-66 was intended to replace the AH-1 Cobra and the OH-58 Kiowa for the United States Army. For the main task of armed reconnaissance, the Comanche is constructed from composite materials and is therefore less observable by radar. In addition, the silhouette is designed as much as possible in accordance with the so-called stealth criteria. Thus, for example, the weaponry can be deployed from internal compartments that can be snapped open to the outside. The landing gear is completely retractable. Surveillance electronics include, among others, a second-generation forward-facing infrared night vision navigational device combined with a TV camera in the fuselage nose, a millimeter wave radar and diverse sensors. Longbow fire control radar and infrared jammers will reportedly be incorporated in later production series.
Manufacturer: Boeing Helicopters and Sikorsky Aircraft, LH Program Office, Philadelphia, Pennsylvania, USA.

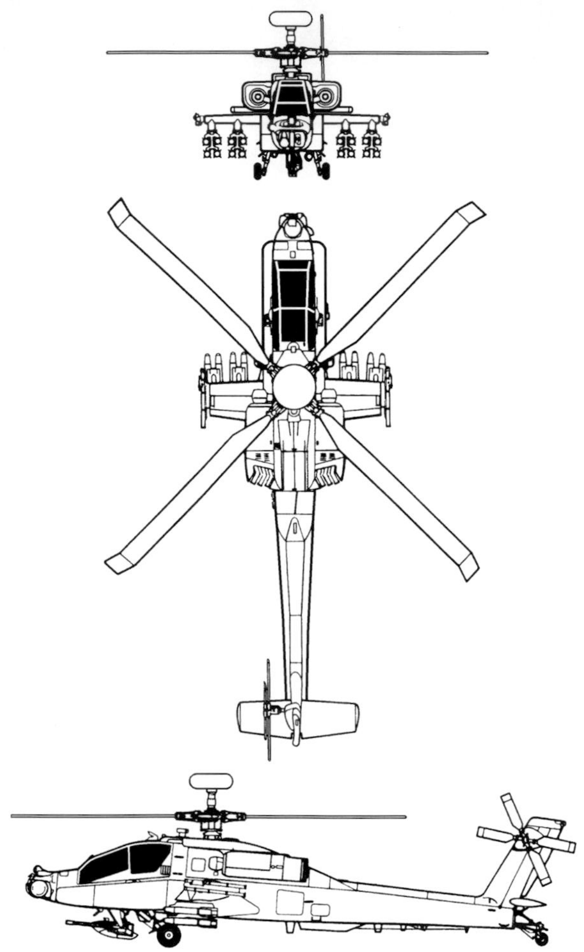

Dimensions:
Rotor diameter 47.99 ft (14.63 m)
Fuselage length 48.22 ft (14.70 m)
Height including mast mounted-radar 16.07 ft (4.90 m)

BOEING (MDD) AH-64D LONGBOW APACHE

Country of origin: USA.
Type: Two-seat combat helicopter.
Power Plant: Two General Electric T700-GE-701C turboshaft engines each with 1,890 SHP (1,409 kW) performance.
Performance (at 14,445 lbs/6,552 kg): Maximum speed 184 mph (296 km/h), typical flight speed at 15,780 lbs (7,158 kg) 169 mph (272 km/h), maximum rate of climb 42 ft (12.7 m)/sec, hover ceiling with in-ground effect 17,211 ft (5,246 m), hover ceiling without ground effect 13,530 ft (4,124 m), radius of action at maximum internal fuel intake 253 miles (407 km), transportation range 1,057 miles (1,701 km).
Weight: Empty weight 11,799 lbs (5,352 kg), maximum take-off weight 20,999 lbs (9,525 kg).
Armament: A 30-mm "fire and forget" cannon underneath the front fuselage and up to 16 laser-guided hellfire antitank defense rockets or 76 unguided 70-mm rockets. Air to air missiles such as the Stinger, Sidewinder or Mistral can be carried along as defense weapons.
State of development: The AH-64D Longbow Apache had its first flight on April 15, 1992. The first units have been in use since mid-1998. Including all the AH-64 variants, there are currently approximately 1,085 (+ options) orders placed by 12 air forces (642 of the AH-64D model). The latest orders are for 16 from Kuwait. The US Army is upgrading its 501 AH-64A to meet the new standards set by the AH-64D.
Remarks: Unlike earlier designs, the AH-64D has mast-mounted radar (Longbow millimeter wave radar) for all around battlefield observation. The Longbow can detect more than a dozen targets at the same time. A stronger MIL-Std-1553B data bus is built-in for processing relevant data. The AH 64D is also equipped with a more efficient engine and can carry the latest radio-guided Hellfire missiles. The British WAH-64D (first flight September 25, 1998) has been licensed for manufacturing at Westland with 67 ordered. It is equipped with a Rolls Royce/Turboméca RTM322 engine.
Manufacturer: The Boeing Company, Helicopter Division, Philadelphia, Pennsylvania, Mesa plant, Mesa, Arizona, USA.

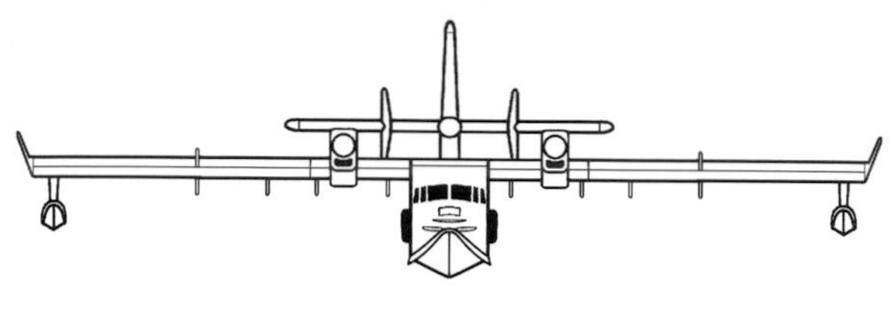

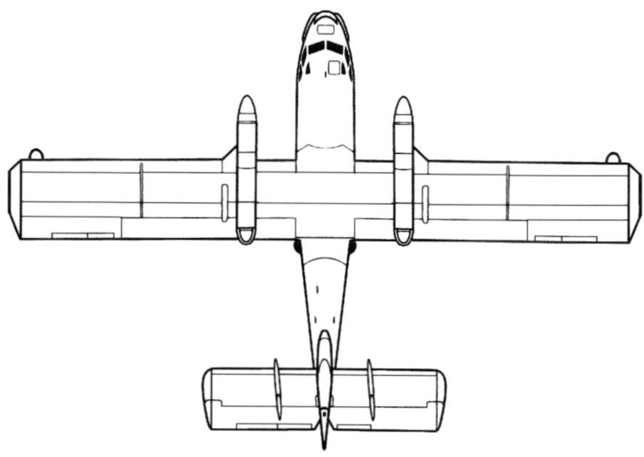

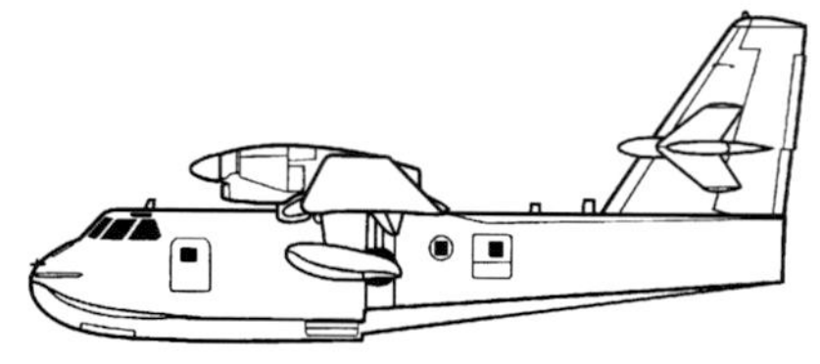

Dimensions:
Wingspan 93.83 ft (28.60 m)
Length 65.02 ft (19.82 m)
Height (on the ground) 29.46 ft (8.98 m)
Wing area 1,079.95 sq. ft (100.33 m^2)

BOMBARDIER (CANADAIR) 415 MR

Country of origin: Canada.
Type: Multi-purpose amphibious aircraft.
Power Plant: Two Pratt & Whitney Canada PW123AF propeller turbine engines each with 2,380 SHP (1,775 kW) performance.
Performance: Maximum cruising speed at 32,498 lbs (14,741 kg) 233 mph (375 km/h) at 5,003 ft (1,525 m), normal cruising speed 178 mph (287 km/h), normal patrolling speed at 35,000 lbs (15,876 kg) 127 mph (204 km/h) at sea level, vertical rate of climb at 45,999 lbs (20,865 kg) 23 ft (7 m)/sec, transportation range 1,508 miles (2,427 km).
Weight: Empty weight for multi-purpose tasks 25,990 lbs (11,789 kg), as water bomber 26,550 lbs (12,043 kg), maximum take-off weight on land 43,651 lbs (19,800 kg), in the water 37,699 lbs (17,100 kg), maximum flying weight after picking up water 46,297 lbs (21,000 kg).
Payload: Two-man crew and, as a transporter, 32 to 35 passengers. Maximum payload of 10,560 lbs (4,790 kg) in multi-role configuration, 13,499 lbs (6,123 kg) as a water bomber. For marine patrolling there are two other stations, one for a flight engineer/navigator and one for two observers.
State of development: The first flight of the 415 MR was in March 2002 with deployment the following year. To date, Greece has ordered two aircraft in this design. There have been 55 orders for the 415 fire-fighting version and all have been delivered: France Sécurité Civile 12, Greece 10 415 GRs, Province of Québec 8, Ontario 9, Sorern Italy 13, Croatia 3. The most recent order comes from the Mexican Coast Guard.
Remarks: In addition to the fire-fighting abilities of the earlier version, the latest variant of the 415 MR (**M**ulti-**R**ole) can be used for general maritime monitoring tasks, search and rescue missions and coastal protection. The 415 MR is differentiated by, among other things, the Primus 660 radar mounted in the nose. In addition, radar antennas from Ericsson have been horizontally installed on both sides of the fuselage. Finally, the tail cone has a SeaFLIR infrared system.
Manufacturer: Bombardier (Canadair), Station Centreville, Montréal, Québec, Canada.

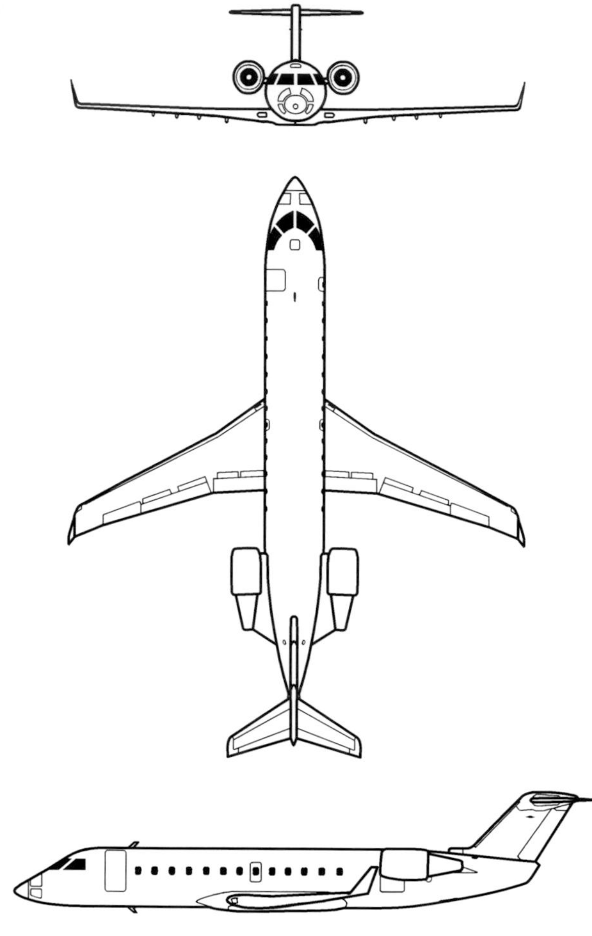

Dimensions:
Wingspan 69.61 ft (21.22 m)
Length 87.82 ft (26.77 m)
Height 20.40 ft (6.22 m)
Wing area 520 sq. ft (48.31 m^2)

BOMBARDIER (CANADAIR) REGIONAL JET CRJ200/440

Country of origin: Canada.
Type: Regional airliner.
Power Plant: Two General Electric CF34-3B1 turbofan engines each with 8,729 lbs (3,959 kp/ 38.83 kN) performance or 9,217 lbs (4,182 kp/41.0 kN) including automatic reserve thrust.
Performance: Maximum cruising speed 529 mph (851 km/h [Mach 0.8]) at 36,007 ft (10,975 m), long-haul cruising speed 488 mph (786 km/h [Mach 0.74]) at 36,007 ft (10,975 m), vertical climb rate 58 ft (17.8 m)/sec, climbing time to 35,006 ft (10,670 m) 23 minutes, service ceiling 41,000 ft (12,497 m), range at maximum payload 973 miles (1,566 km), maximum range 1,633 miles (2,628 km), RJ 200 ER version 1,892 miles (3,045 km).
Weight: Empty weight 30,104 lbs (13,655 kg), maximum take-off weight (RJ 100) 47,697 lbs (21,635 kg), (RJ 200 ER) 51,001 lbs (23,134 kg).
Payload: Two pilots and 50 passengers in the standard design of four-seat rows. Maximum payload 13,501 lbs (6,124 kg).
State of development: The first pre-production machines were flight-tested on May 10, 1991. Delivery began in the fourth quarter of 1992. By the end of 2002, about 940 (+ options) CRJ100/200/440s were ordered by 25 airlines and about 540 have been built. Monthly production is about twelve units.
Remarks: The regional jet, or RJ for short, is a modification of the company's Challenger aircraft. In addition to the extension of the fuselage, various other modifications were necessary in order to convert a business aircraft into a regional airliner. The basic design is designated as the 100 series while longer-range aircraft are part of the 200 ER series. A business aircraft version of the 200 ER is also available as well as a LR (**l**ong **r**ange) model with an increased take-off weight of 52,899 lbs (23,995 kg) and a maximum range of 2,175 miles (3,500 km). A more recent development is a lighter design of the CRJ440. This is set up for only 44 passengers while the dimensions remain the same. Northwest Airlines has ordered 75 units with delivery starting in the third quarter of 2002.
Manufacturer: Bombardier (Canadair), Station Centreville, Montréal, Québec, Dorval plant, Québec, Canada.

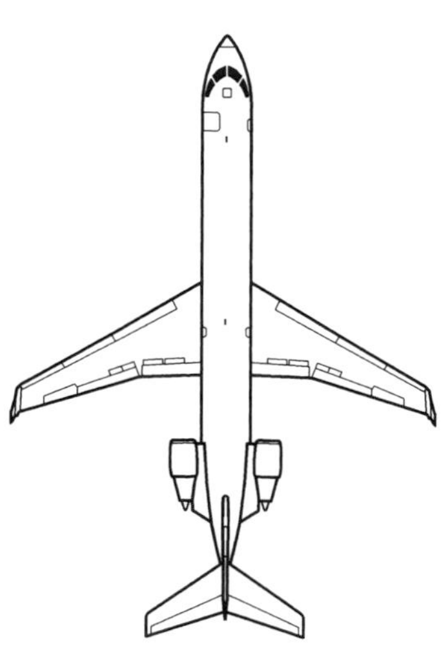

Dimensions:
Wingspan 76.24 ft (23.24 m)
Length 106.65 ft (32.51 m)
Height 24.63 ft (7.51 m)
Wing area 738.73 sq. ft (68.63 m^2)

BOMBARDIER (CANADAIR) REGIONAL JET CRJ700

Country of origin: Canada.
Type: Regional airliner.
Power Plant: Two General Electric CF34-8C1 turbofan engines each with 13,781 lbs (6,250 kp/ 31.30 kN) static thrust.
Performance: Maximum cruising speed 534 mph (860 km/h [Mach 0.81]), normal cruising speed 508 mph (818 km/h [Mach 0.77]), service ceiling 41,010 ft (12,500 m), range (700) 1,957 miles (3,150 km), (700ER) 2,237 miles (3,600 km).
Weight: Empty weight 43,499 lbs (19,731 kg), maximum take-off weight (700) 72,498 lbs (32,885 kg), (700ER) 74,998 lbs (34,019 kg).
Payload: Two pilots and up to 70 passengers in four-seat rows, maximum payload 18,799 lbs (8,527 kg).
State of development: Flight-testing of five prototypes began on May 27, 1999. To date, orders have been received for over 200 CRJ700s (+ options) from six airlines. The first deliveries were made in the first quarter of 2001. About 50 units had been delivered by the end of 2002. Taking into account the entire CRJ family from the 100's to the 900's, there are orders or options for about 2,500 units. About 730 of these have been delivered.
Remarks: The CRJ700 is a further development of the CRJ200 (see pages 104/105). For the CRJ700, the fuselage has been extended by 16 ft (4.72 m), the wingspan has been made larger by 6 ft (1.82 m) and the wing surface is about 40% larger than the CRJ200. The CRJ700 has also been given some aerodynamic optimizations. Slats have been mounted on the entire wing front in order to improve uplift. Additionally, the CRJ700 has the high performance CF34-8C1 engine. Due to the greater weight, new landing gear from Menasco has been built in. Two designs are offered: the normal design of the CRJ700 and the heavier CRJ700 ER with greater range performance. Two modifications are currently being tested: an updated avionics program and the installation of the wings of the larger CRJ900 to allow for a greater take-off weight.
Manufacturer: Bombardier (Canadair), Station Centreville, Montréal, Québec, Montréal-Mirabel plant, Québec, Canada.

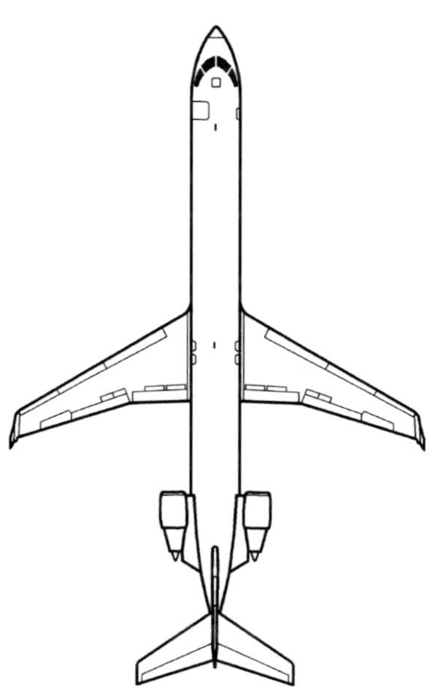

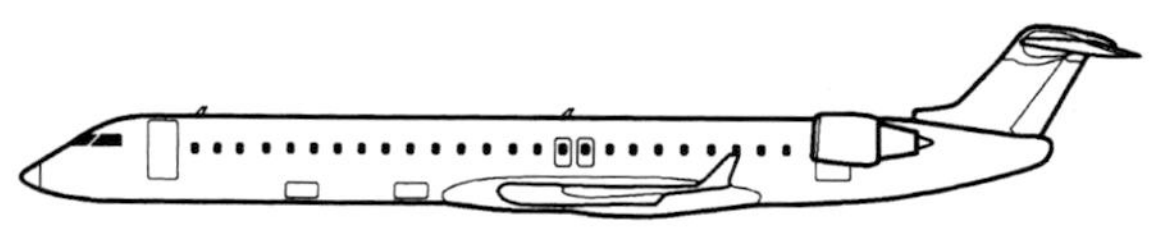

Dimensions:
Wingspan 46.24 ft (23.24 m)
Length 119.42 ft (36.40 m)
Height 24.63 ft (7.51 m)
Wing area 738.73 sq. ft (68.63 m^2)

BOMBARDIER (CANADAIR) REGIONAL JET CRJ900

Country of origin: Canada.
Type: Regional airliner.
Power Plant: Two General Electric CF34-8C5 turbofan engines each with 14,500 lbs (6,575 kp/ 64.5 kN) static thrust.
Performance: Maximum cruising speed 534 mph (860 km/h [Mach 0.81]), normal cruising speed 515 mph (829 km/h [Mach 0.78]), service ceiling 40,997 ft (12,496 m), range with 86 passengers 1,724 miles (2,774 km), ER 1,993 miles (3,208 km).
Weight: Empty weight 47,500 lbs (21,546 kg), maximum take-off weight (900) 80,500 lbs (36,514 kg), (CR900 ER) 82,498 lbs (37,421 kg).
Payload: Two pilots and up to 86 passengers in four-seat rows, maximum payload of 22,500 lbs (10,206 kg).
State of development: The first test models, a redesign of the CRJ700, flew on February 21, 2001. This led to the creation of a new prototype in the middle of 2002. The first series model was deployed in the first quarter of 2003. By the end of 2002, there were solid orders for 30 units (+ options) including 12 Tyrolean orders.
Remarks: While the development of the CRJ900 remained as close as possible to the CRJ700 model, some important differences evolved. The fuselage has been extended in front of and behind the wings by a total of 13 ft (3.86 m). The wings have been structurally strengthened while maintaining the same wingspan. The landing gear has been more robustly designed in order to handle greater weight. Finally, another baggage door has been added at the front and an emergency exit added above the wings. The cockpit is equipped with the avionics Collins Pro Line4 with six EFIS screens. As with the initial model, two versions are planned: one standard and one long-haul version (the CRI900 ER). The maximum take-off weight has been increased to 84,436 lbs (38,300 kg) and, as a result, the range will increase to 2,231 miles (3,590 km).
Manufacturer: Bombardier (Canadair), Station Centreville, Montréal, Québec, Montréal-Mirabel plant, Québec, Canada.

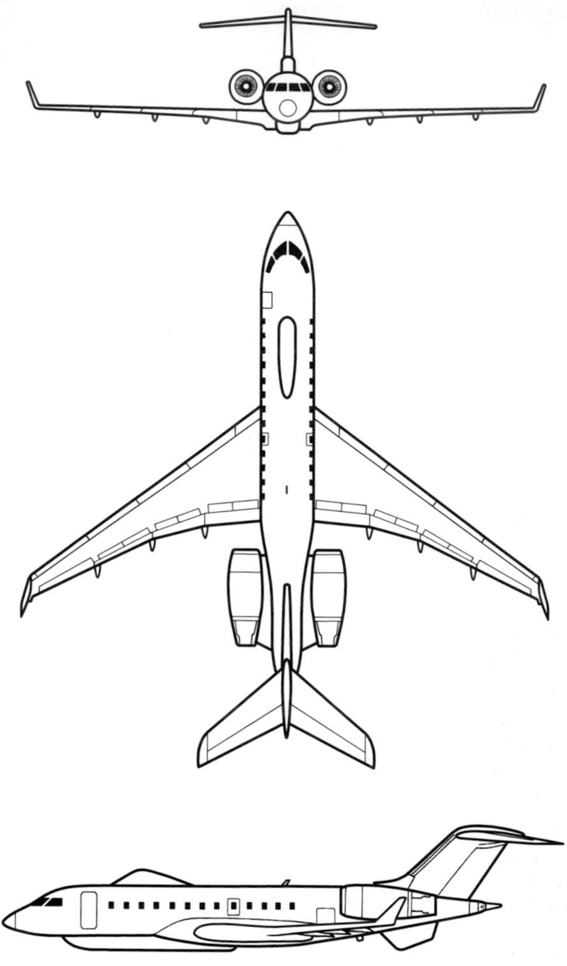

Dimensions:
Wingspan including winglets 93.99 ft (28.65 m)
Length 99.40 ft (30.30 m)
Height 24.83 ft (7.57 m)
Wing area 1,021.93 sq. ft (94.94 m^2)

BOMBARDIER (CANADAIR) GLOBAL EXPRESS ASTOR ◄

Country of origin: Canada.
Type: Flying radar station.
Power Plant: Two BMW/Rolls-Royce BR710-48A2-20 turbofan engines each with 14,748 lbs (6,690 kp/65.6 kN) static thrust.
Performance (Global Express): Maximum cruising speed 581 mph (935 km/h [Mach 0.88]), long-haul cruising speed 547 mph (880 km/h), maximum vertical rate of climb 60 ft (18.3 m)/sec, service ceiling 51,000 ft (15,545 m), range with 8 passengers 7,270 miles (11,700 km), maximum range 7,710 miles (12,408 km).
Weight: Empty weight 48,501 lbs (22,000 kg), maximum take-off weight 93,497 lbs (42,410 kg).
Payload: Two pilots and four to six system operators.
State of development: Test flights took place on August 3, 2001, and the first fully equipped model followed in October 2003. The only orders to date have been for five units from the RAF with delivery to begin at the end of 2004. About 110 units (almost 90 delivered) of the initial model of the Global Express business jet have been ordered by, among others, VW and Deutsche Telekom.
Remarks: Bombardier developed the military design of the ASTOR (**A**irborne **St**and-**o**ff **R**adar) based on the Global Express and equipped it with the surveillance and imaging system SAR/MIT from Raytheon systems. This enables monitoring of fixed and movable objects on the ground from the air using real-time methods. When flying at a height of 49,212 ft (15,000 m), the aircraft can survey an area with a diameter of 186 miles (300 km). Visible parts of this system include a 15-ft (4.6 m) long SAR radar (**S**ynthetic **A**perture **R**adar/Moving Target Indicator) underneath the fuselage and a satellite broadcast antenna above the fuselage. Recently, Bombardier began offering a version with the ground observation GSARS radar (**G**round **S**urveillance **A**irborne **R**adar **S**ystem).
Manufacturer: Bombardier (Canadair), Station Centreville, Montréal, Québec, and/or (system) Raytheon Corp., Greenville, Texas, USA.

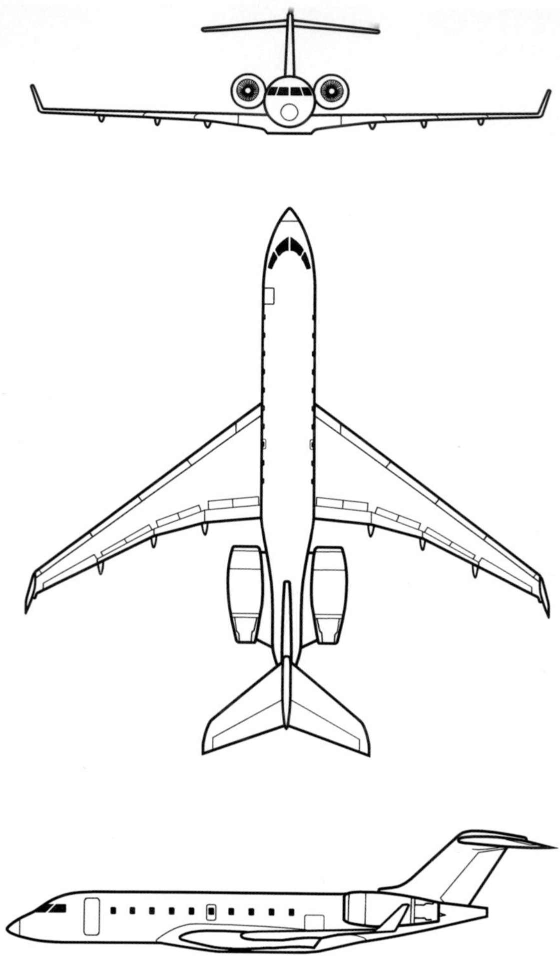

Dimensions:
Wingspan including winglets 94 ft (28.65 m)
Length 80.34 ft (29.49 m)
Height 24.83 ft (7.57 m)
Wing area 1,021.93 sq. ft (94.94 m^2)

BOMBARDIER GLOBAL 5000

Country of origin: Canada.
Type: Business aircraft.
Power Plant: Two BMW/Rolls-Royce BR710-48A2-20 turbofan engines each with 14,746 lbs (6,690 kp/65.6 kN) static thrust.
Performance (provisional data): Maximum cruising speed 590 mph (950 km/h [Mach 0.89]), normal cruising speed 562 mph (904 km/h [Mach 0.85]), service ceiling 50,852 ft (15,500 m), maximum range 5,524 miles (8,890 km).
Weight: Empty weight 50,265 lbs (22,800 kg), maximum take-off weight 87,699 lbs (39,780 kg).
Payload: Two-man cockpit crew and generally eight passengers depending on internal configuration, with tighter seating up to 19 passengers, maximum payload of 5,650 lbs (2,563 kg), with full tanks 1,601 lbs (726 kg).
State of development: The first prototype of the Global 5000 had its initial test flight on March 7, 2003 followed by the second prototype in January 2004. To date, 15 parties have expressed interest in purchasing the aircraft. Customer delivery will start at the end of 2004.
Remarks: The Global 5000 is based on the Global Express and uses the same wings. The fuselage, however, is 32 inches (81 cm) shorter. By leaving off the fuel tanks on the vertical stabilizer and by limiting the tank capacity in the wings, it is designed for shorter ranges than the Global Express. The remainder of the aircraft is basically the same. Synergy effects are promised, particularly to those customers that already have the initial model in use and now need a smaller version for continental use. The Global 5000 is viewed as competition to the family of "wide fuselage business jets", i.e., Gulfstream IV-SP. The starting purchase price for an average equipped unit is US$33 million.
Manufacturer: Bombardier (Canadair), Toronto plant, Toronto, Ontario, Canada.

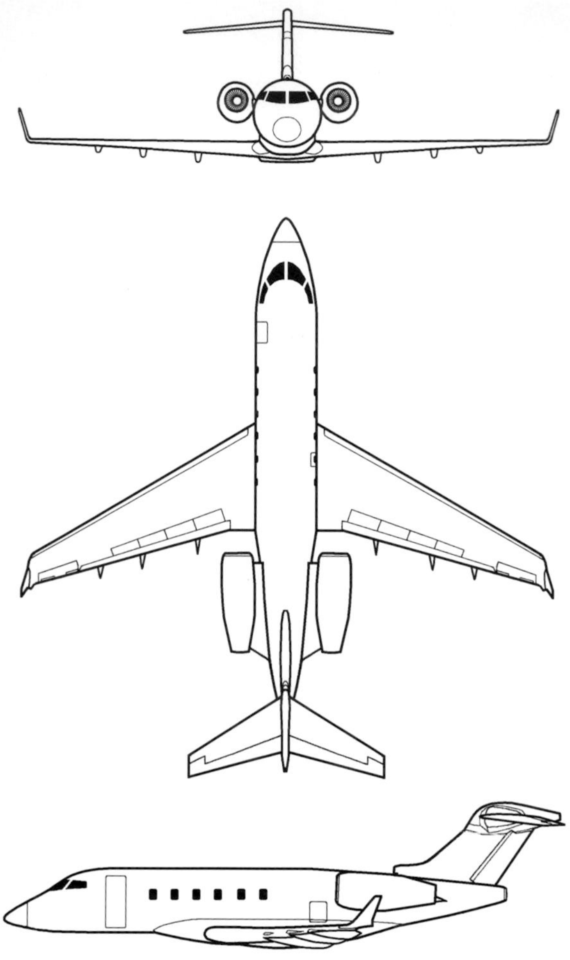

Dimensions:
Wingspan including winglets 63.84 ft (19.46 m)
Length 68.79 ft (20.97 m)
Height 20.40 ft (6.22 m)
Wing area 522.05 sq. ft (48.50 m^2)

BOMBARDIER CHALLENGER 300

Country of origin: Canada.
Type: Business aircraft.
Power Plant: Two Honeywell AS907 turbofan engines each with 6,500 lbs (2,950 kp/28.91 kN) static thrust.
Performance: Maximum cruising speed 541 mph (870 km/h [Mach 0.82]), normal cruising speed 528 mph (850 km/h [Mach 0.80]), service ceiling 45,000 ft (13,716 m), range with eight passengers and IFR reserves 3,573 miles (5,750 km).
Weight: Empty weight 22,350 lbs (10,138 kg), maximum take-off weight 37,500 lbs (17,010 kg).
Payload: Two pilots and 8 to 16 passengers depending on internal configuration, maximum payload of 2,998 lbs (1,360 kg).
State of development: The first prototype, which was called the BD-100 Continental, had its test flight on August 14, 2001, followed by a second test flight on October 8, 2001. A total of five prototypes are scheduled. Certification came in the fall of 2002. The first deliveries to customers were made in the first quarter of 2004. To date, orders have been placed for about 125 units including 25 for Bombardier's own Flexjet program. About 60 units should be manufactured annually.
Remarks: Bombardier's latest medium haul business aircraft has been renamed the Challenger 300 and is intended to close the gap between the Learjet 60 and the Challenger 604. Technically, the Challenger 300 has the latest state-of-the-art technology. For its class, it has a very large fuselage cross-section (internal dimensions 7 ft/2.18 m wide, 6 ft/1.85 m high) so that continuous standing height is possible. Normally, the internal furnishings include eight individual seats, a small kitchen in the front and a toilet in the back as well as direct access to the baggage space. The avionics Pro Line 21 comes from Rockwell Collins. Priced at US$14.25 million, it should prove to be particularly economical for its class.
Manufacturer: Bombardier, Wichita plant, Kansas, USA, Station Centreville, Montréal, Québec, Canada.

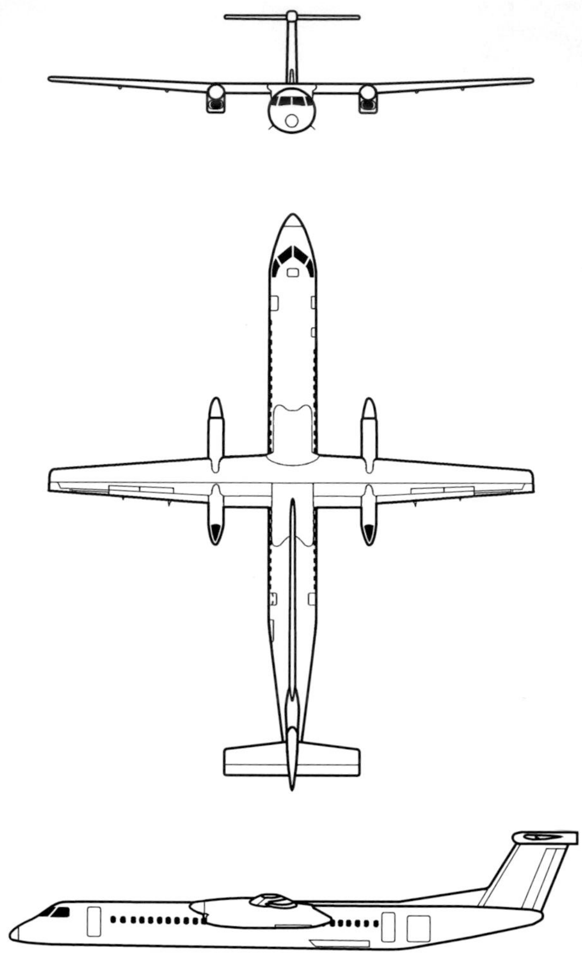

Dimensions:
Wingspan 93.24 ft (28.42 m)
Length 107.74 ft (32.84 m)
Height 27.42 ft (8.36 m)
Wing area 678.99 sq. ft (63.08 m^2)

BOMBARDIER (DE HAVILLAND CANADA) DASH 8 Q400 ◄

Country of origin: Canada.
Type: Regional airliner.
Power Plant: Two Pratt & Whitney Canada PW150A propeller turbine engines each with 4,580 SHP (3,415 kW) performance.
Performance: Maximum cruising speed 415 mph (667 km/h), economic cruising speed 351 mph (565 km/h), service ceiling 25,000 ft (7,620 m), range with maximum payload 992 miles (1,596 km), with 70 passengers 1,567 miles (2,522 km).
Weight: Empty weight 37,716 lbs (17,108 kg), maximum take-off weight 64,500 lbs (29,257 kg).
Payload: Two pilots and 70 passengers in the standard internal configuration of four-seat rows, maximum payload 19,283 lbs (8,747 kg).
State of development: The first Dash 8-400 (recently renamed the Dash 8 Q400) made its initial flight at the end of 1997 with delivery in January 2000. By the end of 2002, about 670 Dash 8's were on order (+ options) and about 650 were shipped to over 70 customers. To date, 79 units (+ options) of the 400-model have been ordered, and about 60 of these have already been manufactured. The largest order so far has been SAS with 20 Q400's. Production of all Dash 8 designs may be in jeopardy unless the number of orders increase.
Remarks: The Dash 8 Q400 is a larger version of the basic Dash 8 model. The fuselage is 15 ft (4.60 m) longer than that of the Dash 8-300 and it has a more powerful engine and a strengthened wing centerpiece. Particularly quiet six-blade rotors from Dowdy have been placed about 8 ft (20 cm) further from the fuselage. To greatly reduce noise, an active cabin-noise control system has been built-in which substantially absorbs noise penetrating the cabin to 77 dBs – thus the name change to the model Q400 (Q = quiet).
Manufacturer: Bombardier (The de Havilland Aircraft Corporation of Canada Ltd.), Downsview, Ontario, Canada.

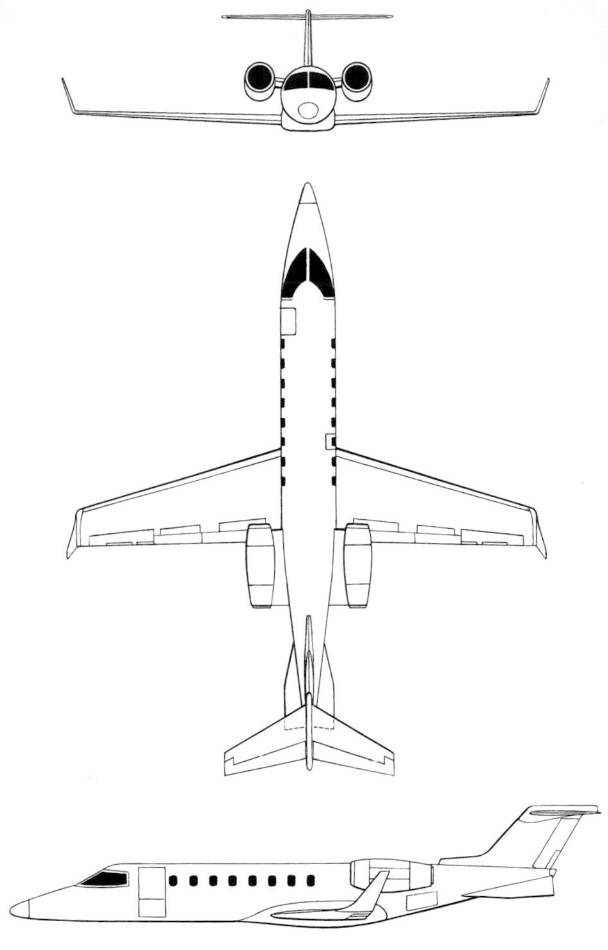

Dimensions:
Wingspan including winglets 47.80 ft (14.57 m)
Length (45XR) 57.61 ft (17.56 m), (40) 55.47 ft (16.91 m)
Height 14.10 ft (4.30 m)
Wing area 311.61 sq. ft (28.95 m^2)

BOMBARDIER LEARJET 45 XR/40

Country of origin: USA.
Type: Business aircraft.
Power Plant: Two Garrett (45 XR) TEF731-23BR, (40) TEF731-20AR turbofan engines each with 3,485 lbs (1,590 kp/15.5 kN) performance.
Performance: Maximum cruising speed 526 mph (847 km/h), normal cruising speed 479 mph (770 km/h), service ceiling 51,000 ft (15,545 m), maximum range with four passengers (45 XR) 2,414 miles (3,885 km), (40) 2,075 miles (3,339 km).
Weight (45 XR): Empty weight 11,700 lbs (5,307 kg), maximum take-off weight 20,194 lbs (9,160 kg).
Payload (45 XR): Two pilots and, normally, 8 to a maximum of 10 passengers in the cabin, maximum payload 3,306 lbs (1,500 kg).
State of development: The first flight of the Learjet 40 took place on August 31, 2002. There will not be any actual prototypes of the 45 XR. Both variants were ready for delivery in the first quarter of 2004. Future order status is unknown. By the end of 2002, over 200 units of the Learjet 45 have been delivered. Production is continuing.
Remarks: In 2002, Bombardier simultaneously launched two further developments of the initial Learjet 45 model, the 45 XR (see drawing) and the 40 (see photo). While the XR exceeds the 45 in terms of performance, the Learjet 40 provides a viable alternative for lower performance aircraft. Eventually the 40 should replace the Learjet 31A that is still in production. While the 45 XR has the same external measurements as the 45, the 45 XR has a better range/payload ratio. In terms of performance, the new engine corresponds to that of the 45, but still has better short-term take-off performance. The previous Learjet 45 can be converted into this variant. The main difference in the latest design of the Learjet 40 compared to the 45 XR is a fuselage that is 24 inches (60 cm) shorter. Thanks to lesser weight and a smaller payload, it can manage with a runway of only 3,691 ft (1,125 m). New internal furnishings have been built into both variants.
Manufacturer: Bombardier (Learjet Inc.), Wichita, Kansas, USA.

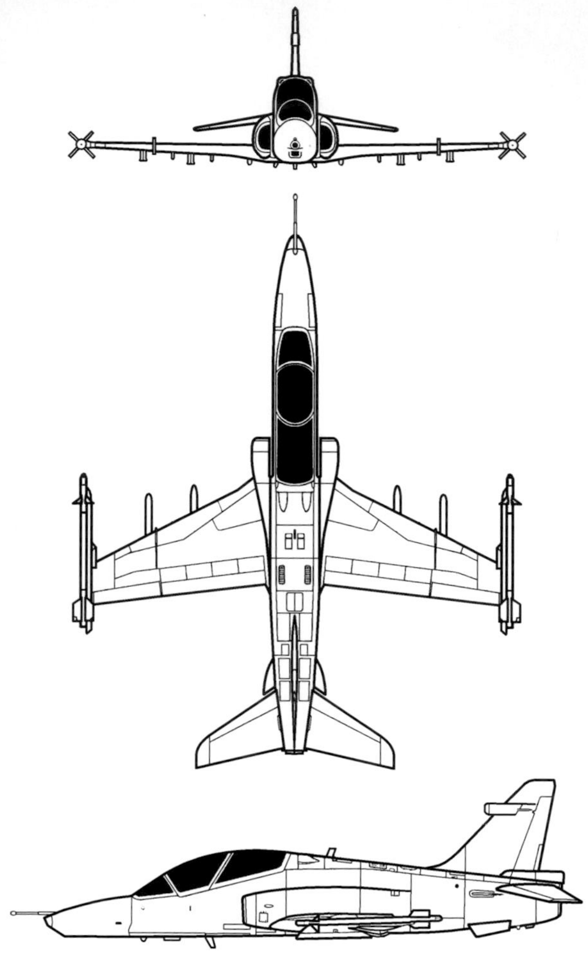

Dimensions:
Wingspan, including guided missiles, 32.61 ft (9.94 m)
Length 37.33 ft (11.38 m)
Height 13.64 ft (4.16 m)
Wing area 179.65 sq. ft (16.69 m^2)

BRITISH AEROSPACE HAWK LIFT 100/200

Country of origin: Great Britain.
Type: Two-seat advanced trainer and easy ground fighter.
Power Plant: One Rolls-Royce/Turboméca Adour 871 turbofan engine with 5,845 lbs (2,650 kp/26.0 kN) static thrust.
Performance: Maximum cruising speed 634 mph (1,021 km/h [Mach 0.83]), maximum speed at mean sea level 633 mph (1,019 km/h), economic cruising speed 495 mph (796 km/h) at 41,010 ft (12,500 m), initial rate of climb 192 ft (58.5 m)/sec, service ceiling 50,032 ft (15,250 m), combat radius 200 miles (322 km) with 500 lb (227 kg)-bombs, ferry range with two 227 gallon (860 l) and one 156 gallon (590 l) additional tanks 2,240 miles (3,606 km), without additional tanks 554 miles (892 km).
Weight: Empty weight 8,752 lbs (3,970 kg), maximum take-off weight 18,738 lbs (8,500 kg).
Payload: Two 25 mm-Aden or two 27 mm-Mauser cannons and a maximum 6,834 lbs (3,100 kg) of external weapons arranged on seven stations under the wings and the fuselage.
State of development: The first flight of the 200 prototype took place on May 19, 1986. It is technically equivalent to the two-seat 100-version that, designed to correspond to the series-standard, first flew in 1990. A test model of the latest model LIFT has been flying since 1998. Altogether, (without the T-45 of the USN; see pages 90/91) more than 600 aircraft of all versions have been ordered by 17 air forces. Almost all have been delivered. Latest customer: Bahrain 6.
Remarks: The LIFT (**L**ead-**I**n- **F**ighter **T**rainer) is the latest Hawk model. It shows some significant improvements in avionics such as MIL-Std-1553B database, revised cockpit with three flat screens and HUD, night-vision monitors, INS/GPS and further electronic aids. The cell has been reinforced for a longer lifespan and the nose landing gear can be actively steered. Moreover, an APU (**A**uxiliary **P**ower **U**nit) booster has been installed. A new model, the Mk.120, has been flying since the middle of August 2002. This version features a fully digitized cockpit and Adour 951 engines.
Manufacturer: British Aerospace PLC, Military Aircraft Division, Warton, Preston, Lancashire, Great Britain.

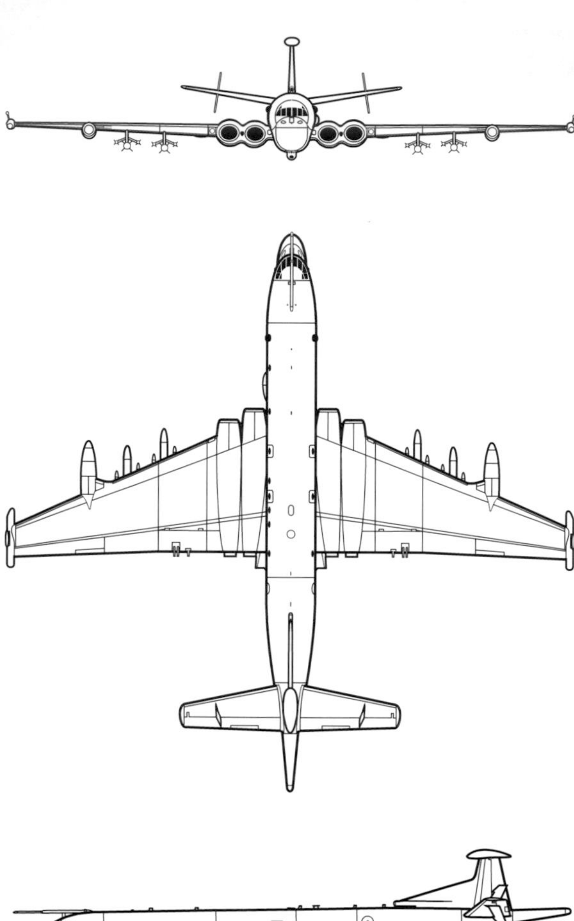

Dimensions:
Wingspan, including pods at the wing tips, 127.85 ft (38.71 m)
Length without fueling tube 126.77 ft (38.63 m)
Height 30.47 ft (9.29 m)
Wing area 2,538 sq. ft (235.80 m^2)

BRITISH AEROSPACE NIMROD MRA.4 (NIMROD 2000)

Country of origin: Great Britain.
Type: Sea reconnaissance and assault plane.
Power Plant: Four BMW Rolls-Royce BR710 turbofan engines each with 15,500 lbs (7,030 kp/ 68,95 kN) static thrust.
Performance: Maximum speed Mach 0.77, service ceiling 41,994 ft (12,800 m), range with maximum internal fuel 6,959 miles (11,200 km), maximum flight time up to 15 hours.
Weight: Empty weight 102,513 lbs (46,500 kg), maximum take-off weight 231,229 lbs (104,885 kg).
Payload: More than 12,125 lbs (5,500 kg) including air-air and air-ground guided missiles, torpedoes, mines and bombs arranged in four stations located below the wings in the internal weapon shaft.
State of development: The initial flight of the first of two completely rebuilt test designs took place in mid-2003. By the end of 2004, the RAF is expected to get 18 units, which originate from the remaining stock of 46 original MRA Mk.1/2 units.
Remarks: Only the fuselage has been kept from the original design. However, the fuselage has been structurally revised and reinforced in order to increase the lifespan 25 years. With 80 percent of the aircraft redesigned, the MRA.4 is essentially a new airplane including a completely new wing with larger span and new and very powerful mission avionics. The supervision radar is a Searchwater 2000MR made by Racal-Thorn. The new cockpit, suitable for two pilots, is equipped with flat screens. As the main supplier, Boeing is responsible for the most important parts of surveillance and weapon electronics. The new undercarriage is manufactured by Messier-Dowty.
Manufacturer: British Aerospace PLC, Military Aircraft Division, Warton, Preston, Lancashire, Great Britain.

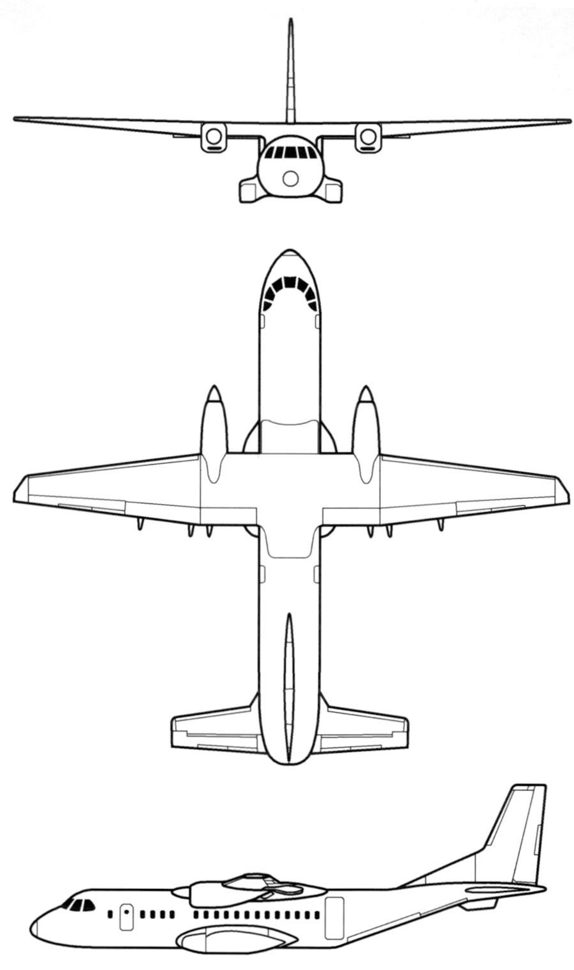

Dimensions:
Wingspan 84.67 ft (25.81 m)
Length 80.21 ft (24.45 m)
Height 28.21 ft (8.60 m)
Wing area 636.15 sq. ft (59.10 m^2)

CASA C-295

Country of origin: Spain.
Type: General purpose transporter.
Power Plant: Two Pratt & Whitney Canada PW127G propeller turbine engines each with 2,645 SHP (1,972 KW) performance.
Performance (according to the manufacturer): Maximum cruise speed 299 mph (481 km/h) at 24,999 ft (7,620 m), range with maximum payload 828 miles (1,333 km), maximum range 3,279 miles (5,278 km).
Weight: Empty weight 24,250 lbs (11,000 kg), maximum take-off weight 51,146 lbs (23,200 kg).
Payload: Two pilots and normally 69 or up to 78 fully equipped soldiers, for evacuation missions 27 recumbent people and four helpers, when operating as a freighter five standard containers or three lightweight vehicles, maximum payload 21,384 lbs (9,700 kg).
State of development: The first prototype corresponding to the series standard had its test flight on December 22, 1998. Deliveries began in October 2001. Current order status. twelve for the Brazilian Air Force, eight for the Polish Air Force, and nine units for the Spanish Air Force.
Remarks: The C-295 was developed solely by CASA based on the CN-235 (see pages 38/39). Judging from size and power, the C-295 is superior to the CN-235 and can be regarded as a direct competitor to the Alenia C-27J (see pages 40/41). Because fuselage segments have been inserted in front of and behind the wing, the external length has been extended by 10 ft (3.10 m) and the cabin length extended by 10 ft (3 m). More powerful engines have been combined with Hamilton's latest six-leaf propeller technology. The increased weight has required the reinforcing of the wings and undercarriage. Because of these measures, the cargo capacity has increased by approximately 50% compared to the initial design. Lastly, the C-295 has a new Avionik Topdeck from Sextant and is equipped with an aerial tanking feature. A sea surveillance and submarine combat version ("Persuader") is also offered. The United Arabic Republic has ordered four units.
Manufacturer: CASA, Seville plant, Madrid (Spain).

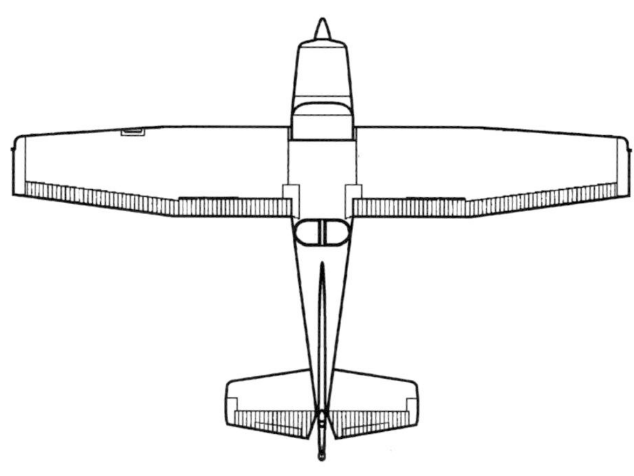

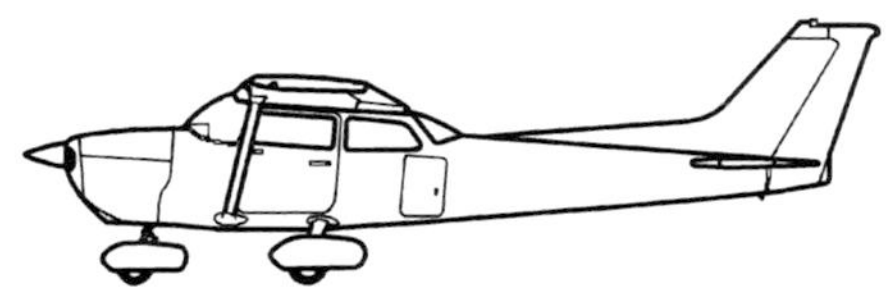

Dimensions:
Wingspan 35.99 ft (10.97 m)
Length 28.24 ft (8.61 m)
Height 9.28 ft (2.83 m)
Wing area 173.83 sq. ft (16.15 m^2)

CESSNA 172SP SKYHAWK

Country of origin: USA.
Type: Sport and travel airplane.
Power Plant: A Textron-Lycoming IO-360-L2A air-cooled four cylinder horizontally opposed engine with 180 SHP (134 kW) performance.
Performance: Maximum speed at sea level 145 mph (233 km/h), cruising speed at 75 percent performance at 8,497 ft (2,590 m) 142 mph (228 km/h), initial rate of climb 12 ft (3.55 m)/sec, service ceiling 13,999 ft (4,267 m), range with 75 percent of performance and normal reserves at 8,497 ft (2,590 m) 516 miles (830 km).
Weight: Empty weight 1,430 lbs (649 kg), maximum take-off weight 2,400 lbs (1,089 kg).
Payload: Pilot and three passengers, payload 915 lbs (415 kg).
State of development: The new Cessna 172SP has been flying since April 16, 1996. First deliveries to customers were made in January 1997. To date, over 3,000 airplanes have been produced.
Remarks: Based on the successful design of the 60's/70's, Model 172 remained unchanged in basic construction but featured revised avionics and other segments. A cost-effective production and operation were taken into account. There are two models of the Cessna. The 172R is the basic model (from US$145,000), and the 172SP is an upgraded version (basic configuration starting at US$152,300). Based on this version, a whole family of one-engine aircraft has been developed. The Cessna 182T Skylane is essentially the same as the Cessna 172 in its basic design. The differences can be found in the interior and in the motorization. The six-seat 206H Stationair (price US$322,000) and the T206H Turbo Stationair (price US$365,000) are the remaining models in the upper ranks of Cessna's lightweight aircraft. A larger volume in the fuselage provides more space in the passenger area. Depending on the intended purpose of the aircraft, fashionable interior equipment or, for carrying freight, a much simpler interior setting may be selected. As a new option, the 172SP will be available with a Thielert TAE 125 diesel engine.
Manufacturer: Cessna Aircraft Company, Wichita, Independence plant, Kansas, USA.

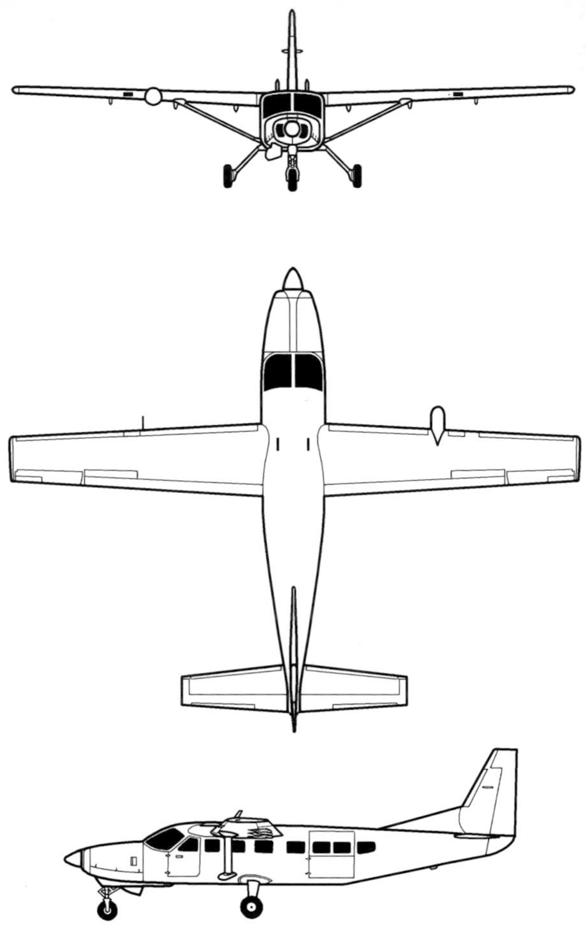

Dimensions:
Wingspan 52.06 ft (15.87 m)
Length 41.56 ft (12.67 m)
Height 14.82 ft (4.52 m)
Wing area 279.43 sq. ft (25.96 m^2)

CESSNA 208B GRAND CARAVAN

Country of origin: USA.
Type: Multiple-purpose airplane.
Power Plant: A Pratt & Whitney Canada PT6A-114A turboprop engine with 675 SHP (503 kw) performance.
Performance: Maximum cruising speed 211 mph (340 km/h) at 10,006 ft (3,050 m), 183 mph (295 km/h) at 19,996 ft (6,095 m), initial rate of climb 16 ft (4.9 m)/sec, service ceiling 24,999 ft (7,620 m), maximum range with 45 minutes of reserves 1,665 miles (2,680 km) at 10,006 ft (3,050 m).
Weight: Empty weight 4,103 lbs (1,861 kg), maximum take-off weight 8,750 lbs (3,969 kg).
Payload: One to two pilots and nine passengers in the standard configuration to a maximum of 14 passengers or 3,498 lbs (1,587 kg) of freight.
State of development: The prototype of the 208 flew for the first time on December 9, 1982 and the deliveries to customers began in February 1985. The military version U-27A was introduced in 1986. The improved 208B version recorded its first flight on March 3, 1986, followed by the Grand Commander in 1991. To date, over 1,200 Caravan of all versions, including approximately 500 of the 208B version, have been delivered. The principal buyer has been Federal Express with 309 units (299 of which are the 208B Super Cargomaster version).
Remarks: The latest version of the Cessna 208B, the Grand Commander, has been extended by 4 ft (1.22 m), and has a more powerful engine at its disposal. Accordingly, flight performance has improved. A model with floaters is also available. Specifically for this version, Aero Twin offers a conversion set with the more powerful Honeywell TPE331-12 engine with 850 SHP (633 kw) performance and a four-sheet propeller (see photo). As a result, the start performance has been especially improved. The Caravan has proven to be a real "workhorse" and has been utilized for the widest variety of different tasks from freight carrier to passenger airplane with VIP furnishings.
Manufacturer: Cessna Aircraft Company, Wichita, Kansas, USA.

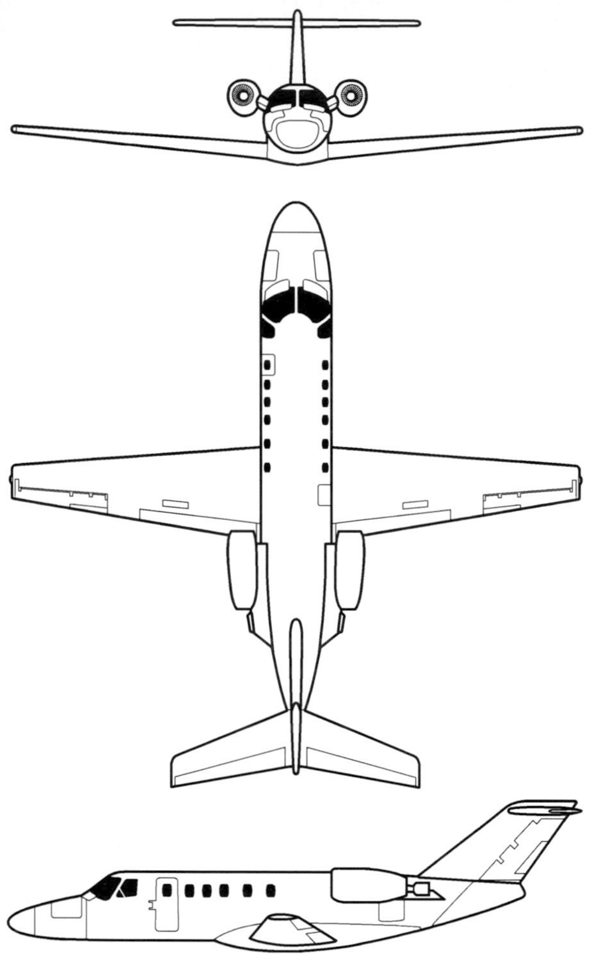

Dimensions:
Wingspan 49.50 ft (15.09 m)
Length 46.91 ft (14.30 m)
Height 13.91 ft (4.24 m)
Wing area 263.71 sq. ft (24.50 m^2)

CESSNA 525 CITATION CJ2

Country of origin: USA.
Type: Corporate airplane.
Power Plant: Two William Rolls-Royce FJ44-2C turbofan engines each with 2,299 lbs (1,050 kp/10 kN) performance.
Performance: Maximum cruising speed 472 mph (760 km/h), initial rate of climb 64 ft (19.55 m)/sec, service ceiling 44,999 ft (13,716 m), maximum range 1,988 miles (3,200 km).
Weight: Empty weight 7,358 lbs (3,338 kg), maximum take-off weight 12,425 lbs (5,636 kg).
Payload: Pilot and co-pilot/passenger in the cockpit and up to six passengers in the cabin, payload with full fuel tank 840 lbs (381 kg), maximum payload 1,600 lbs (726 kg).
State of development: The first of three CJ2 prototypes completed its initial flight on April 27, 1999. More than 100 units have been delivered since the start of the production.
Remarks: As the name already indicates, the CJ2 is a further enhancement of the CJ1 model. Thanks to a larger wingspan, a tail unit increased by 15%, a fuselage that has been extended by 4 ft (1.32 m) and stronger engines, the CJ2 is clearly a more efficient aircraft when compared to the original design. Although it is a small company airplane, the passenger cubicle is quite spacious with a length of 19 ft (5.76 m), a width of 5 ft (1.49 m) and a height of 5 ft (1.45 m). The remaining installation characteristics and the avionics are identical to the CJ1. In the basic design, the Citation CJ2 costs US$4.3 million. Cessna has recently announced the CJ3, a new design based on the CJ2. However, it is 2 ft (60 cm) longer and features more powerful FJ44-3A engines. Delivery of the CJ3 is expected in the first quarter of 2005. Already over 150 units have been ordered with a purchase price of US$5.795 million.
Manufacturer: Cessna Aircraft Company, Wichita, Kansas, USA.

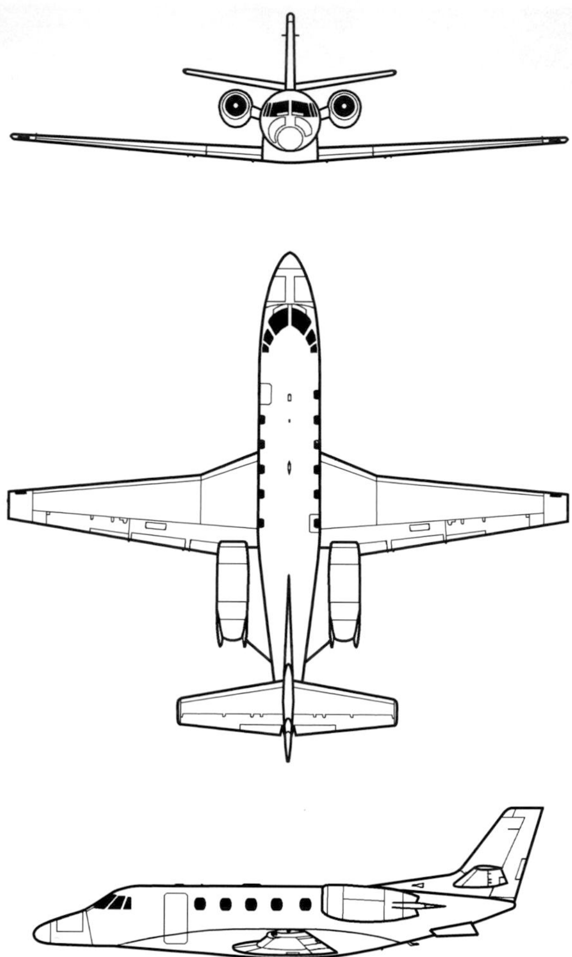

Dimensions:
Wingspan 55.70 ft (16.98 m)
Length 51.77 ft (15.78 m)
Height 17.19 ft (5.24 m)
Wing area 369.74 sq. ft (34.35 m^2)

CESSNA 560XL CITATION EXCEL

Country of origin: USA.
Type: Corporate airplane.
Power Plant: Two Pratt & Whitney Canada PW545A turbofan engines each with 3,804 lbs (1,725 kp/16.92 kN) static thrust.
Performance: Maximum cruising speed 498 mph (802 km/h [Mach 0.77]), normal speed at 35,000 ft (10,668 m) 495 mph (797 km/h), initial rate of climb 62 ft (18.8 m)/sec, service ceiling 45,000 ft (13,716 m), range with four passengers and 45 minutes of reserves 2,224 miles (3,580 km).
Weight: Standard empty weight 11,710 lbs (5,312 kg), maximum take-off weight 19,199 lbs (8,709 kg).
Payload: Two-man cockpit crew and normally six passengers in single-seats. Maximum payload up to eight passengers.
State of development: The Excel took its test flight on February 29, 1996, and became available in the second quarter of 1998. Over 240 units are in use. The largest individual customer is Executive Jet with 50 Excels. Recently, the Swiss Confederacy also obtained an Excel for the Federal Council.
Remarks: The simpler intermediate design of the Cessna 560XL Citation Excel combines the non-pointy wing of the Citation V Ultra with the shortened fuselage of the Citation X (see Pages 136/137). The Excel enables the passengers to stand up throughout the cabin without difficulty. This happens, also, because the wing spar runs continuously under the fuselage. The cockpit is equipped with the Honeywell Primus 1000 avionics package that includes three EFIS-screens among other things. Because sturdiness and cost-effectiveness have been considered in all construction characteristics, the purchase price is around US$7 million.
Manufacturer: Cessna Aircraft Company, Wichita, Kansas, USA.

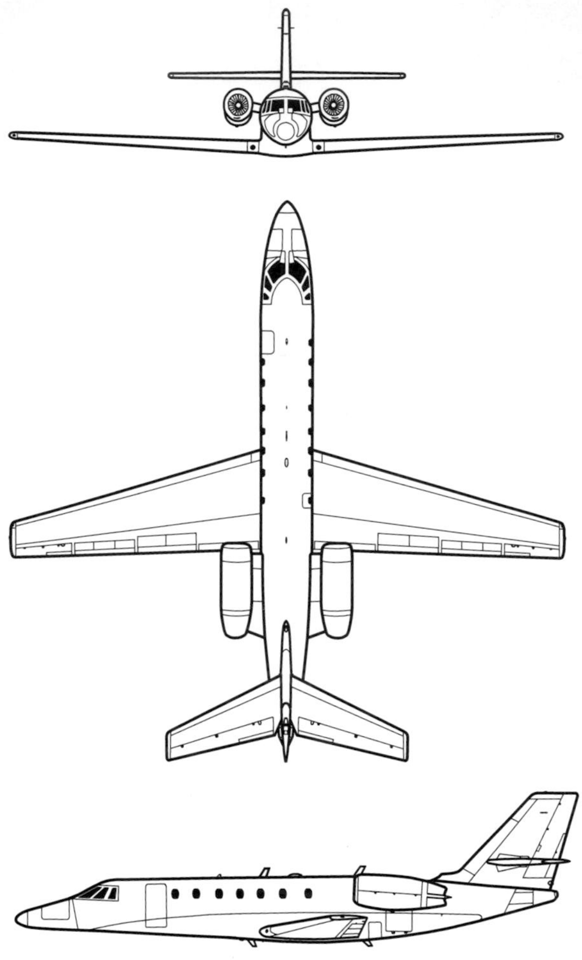

Dimensions:
Wingspan 63.12 ft (19.24 m)
Length 63.54 ft (19.37 m)
Height 19.88 ft (6.06 m)
Wing area 516.02 sq. ft (47.94 m^2)

CESSNA 680 CITATION SOVEREIGN

Country of origin: USA.
Type: Corporate airplane.
Power Plant: Two Pratt & Whitney Canada PW306C turbofan engines each with 5,778 lbs (2,617 kp/25.70 kN) static thrust.
Performance: Maximum cruising speed 513 mph (826 km/h) at 35,104 ft (10,700 m), time to reach 42,978 ft (13,100 m) 26 minutes, service ceiling 46,997 ft (14,325 m), range with eight passengers and with IFR reserves 2,858 miles (4,600 km), under VFR 3,243 miles (5,220 km)
Weight: Empty weight 17,398 lbs (7,892 kg), maximum take-off weight 29,998 lbs (13,607 kg).
Payload: Two pilots and up to ten passengers, payload with maximum fuel 1,598 lbs (725 kg), maximum payload 2,500 lbs (1,134 kg).
State of development: The prototype of the Sovereign recorded its test flight on February 27, 2002 followed by the first production model on June 27, 2002. Delivery began mid-2004. There are orders for more than 125 units, including 100 Sovereigns for the American company Executive Jet.
Remarks: Cessna launched the new Sovereign as a response to the new competitive models in the field of medium-sized business aircraft. In order to keep its purchase price as low as possible (fully equipped, approximately US$13.3 million), its construction is based on the Cessna Excel (see pages 132/133). However, its much larger size allows for a very roomy cabin. The fuselage has been made 6 ft (1.80 m) longer compared to the initial model. New features include the supercritical wing with a light sweep of 16.1° and a particularly small aerodynamic resistance. As a result, high cruising speeds can be obtained. For the same reason, the vertical tail and elevator are slightly swept. The Sovereign maintains the good take-off and landing characteristics of the Citation family (take-off approximately 4,101 ft/1,250 m, landing distance approximately 3,198 ft/ 975 m). The Epic CDS avionics is from Honeywell and the cockpit is equipped with four large multi-functional flat screen monitors.
Manufacturer: Cessna Aircraft Company, Wichita, Kansas, USA.

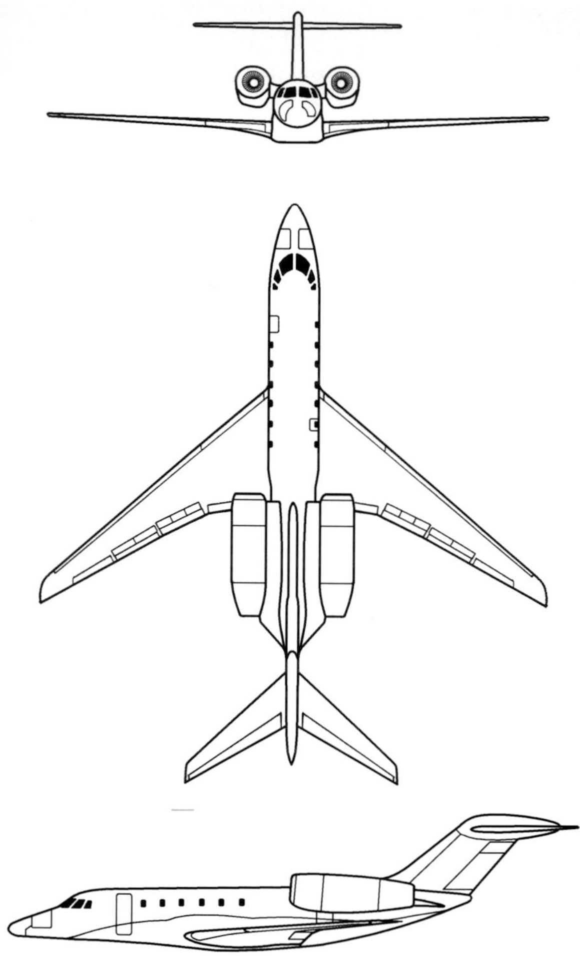

Dimensions:
Wing span 63.97 ft (19.50 m)
Length 72.17 ft (22.00 m)
Height 16.69 ft (5.09 m)
Wing area 527 sq. ft (48.96 m^2)

CESSNA 750 CITATION X

Country of origin: USA.
Type: Corporate plane.
Power Plant: Two Allison GMA 3007C-1 turbofan engines each with 6,765 lbs (3,068 kp/30.09 kN) static thrust.
Performance: Maximum speed Mach 0.92, maximum cruising speed at 36,991 ft (11,275 m) 580 mph (934 km/h [Mach 0.88]), long-range cruising speed 529 mph (851 km/h), initial rate of climb 74 ft (22.4 m)/sec, service ceiling 51,000 ft (15,545 m), VFR range at Mach 0.82 with six passengers and 45-minutes reserve 3,799 miles (6,115 km), IFR range 3,452 miles (5,556 km).
Weight: Empty weight 18,999 lbs (8,618 kg), maximum take-off weight 36,098 lbs (16,374 kg).
Payload: Two-person cockpit crew and eight to a maximum of 12 passengers in single seats and a 3-seat couch, maximum payload 2,599 lbs (1,179 kg).
State of development: A flight test for the first of three models took place on December 21, 1993. After registration, deliveries to customers commenced in June 1996. To date, about 200 orders have been placed for the Citation X, 31 of which are from Executive Jet. The monthly production is two units. Around 180 are currently in service.
Remarks: The Citation X reaches the highest cruising speed of all commercial planes with the exception of the Concorde. For that purpose, it is designed with a novel and highly developed wing displaying a 35° sweep. It is the first Cessna plane equipped with servo-assisted flight control. The cross section profile of the fuselage allows for end-to-end headroom. The cockpit is equipped with the EFIS Honeywell Primus 2000 digital system. Beginning in 2002 Citations X models have a power plant that is 397 lbs (180 kp) more powerful and have a higher maximum weight than previous models. The Honeywell avionics have been upgraded as well. The price for the basic version is approximately US$19 million.
Manufacturer: Cessna Aircraft Company, Wichita, Kansas, USA.

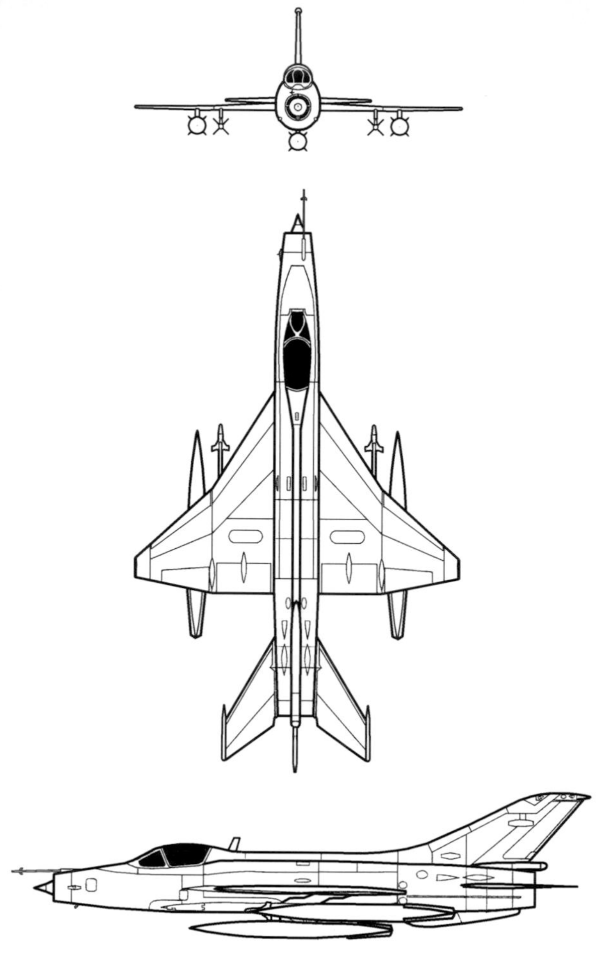

Dimensions:
Wingspan 27.29 ft (8.32 m)
Length 48.85 ft (14.89 m)
Height 13.45 ft (4.10 m)
Wing area 267.80 sq. ft (24.88 m^2)

CHENGDU F-7MG/PG

Country of origin: People's Republic of China.
Type: Lightweight 1-seat multi-purpose fighter (F-7MG) and 2-seat trainer (FT-7P).
Power Plant: One Wopen WP-13F turbojet engine with 7,608 lbs (3,450 kp/33.84 kN) static thrust with afterburner and 14,554 lbs (6,600 kp/64.74 kN) without afterburner.
Performance: Maximum speed at high altitudes Mach 2.0, at sea level 746 mph (1,200 km/h), initial rate of climb 641 ft (195 m)/sec, service ceiling 57,414 ft (17,500 m), action radius (high-high-high) with two AIM-9P missiles and three additional tanks with 110 gallons (500 l) each 528 miles (850 km), maximum range 1,367 miles (2,200 km).
Weight: Empty 11,666 lbs (5,292 kg), maximum take-off weight 20,061 lbs (9,100 kg).
Payload (F-7MG): Two 30-mm cannons in the nose and five weapon stations for a weapon load up to 3,968 lbs (1,800 kg) including four air-air missiles and air-ground missiles as well as bombs and a variety of rocket launchers. The 2-seat FT-7P has only four weapon stations.
State of development: The F-7MG was shown to the public for the first time in November 1996. Pakistan obtained 57 units of the version F-7PG, the latest version of the Chinese F-7, and put its first machines in service during 2002. Bangladesh reportedly received 20 units.
Remarks: There is little noticeable relationship between the F-7MG and the initial model MIG-21. It is based on the F-7M Airguard, a further development of the MIG-21 by the Chinese. With the exception of the silhouette, it is a completely new product. Thanks to the new delta double wings with fore flaps, the aerodynamic characteristics have been greatly enhanced. The avionics and cockpit design for the F-7MG are totally new featuring cost-effective FIAR GRIFO S7 multi-purpose radar with "look down capability", HUD, weapons computer, TACAN, GPS, EFIS, etc. Nearly all performance data exceed that of the earlier F-7M versions. The 2-seat FT-7P is roughly 24 inches (60 cm) longer.
Manufacturer: CAC/Chengdu Aircraft Industrial, Chengdu , Sichuan, PRC.

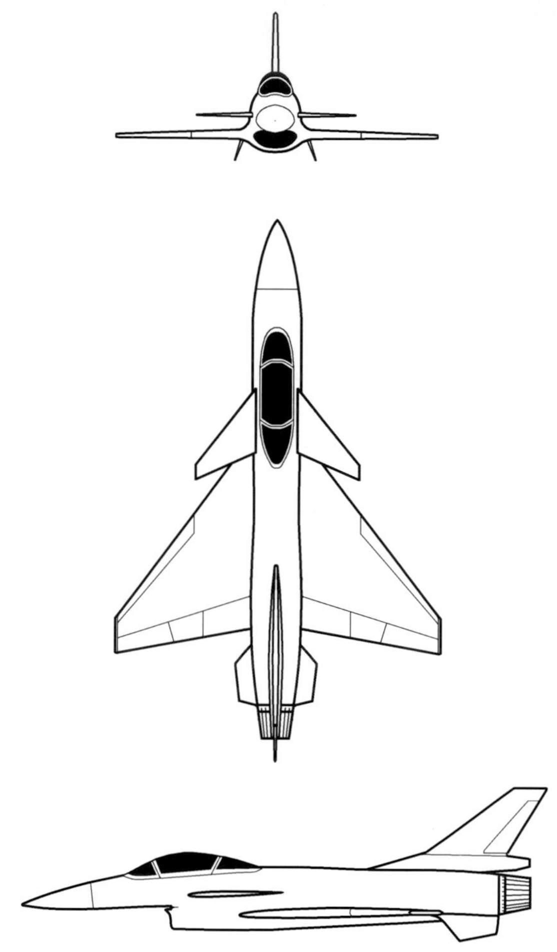

Dimensions:
Wingspan main wing 28.80 ft (8.78 m)
Length 47.80 ft (14.57 m)
Height 15.74 ft (4.80 m)
Area of main wing 355.21 sq. ft (33 m^2), front wing 58.66 sq. ft (5.45 m^2)

CHENGDU AIRCRAFT F-10

Country of origin: People's Republic of China.
Type: 1-seat multi-purpose fighter.
Power Plant: One Saturn/Lyulka AL-31FN turbofan engine with 19,334 lbs (8,800 kp/86 kN) static thrust with afterburner and 27,562 lbs (12,500 kp/122.60 kN) without afterburner, alternatively with a Chinese WPS-12 turbofan engine.
Performance: Maximum speed Mach 1.8, action radius 342 miles (550 km), range 1,149 miles (1,850 km).
Weight: Empty weight 15,299 lbs (6,940 kg), maximum take-off weight 40,564 lbs (18,400 kg).
Armament: A combination of short range air-air PL-8 missiles, medium range air-air PL-11 missiles and additional tanks, air to ground rockets, bombs and a minimum of seven to a maximum of eleven weapon stations. Maximum weapon load around 18,518 lbs (8,400 kg). Presumably 23- or 30-mm cannon are built-in.
State of development: The first of four prototypes flew on March 24, 1998. Production began in 2003 and the first deliveries are expected in 2005.
Remarks: The F-10 is the result of a joint development of Chengdu and the Israel IAI. The latter brought its experience manufacturing the Lavi interceptor fighters into the project. Because of that, both models look very much alike. Three manufacturers are in fierce competition to supply the airborne radar with the decision not yet made. The companies are Elta EL/M2035 of Israel, the Russian Phazotron-Zhemcoug sytem or a separately constructed Chinese Doppler-Pulse-radar JL-10A. The F-10 carries a fly-by-wire control. The development of the F-10 system was marked by long delays due to technical difficulties leading to, among other things, a reconstruction of the cell. The air intake very much resembles that of the Eurofighters (see pages 184/185). All the information is based on estimates.
Manufacturer: CAC, Chengdu Aircraft Industrial Corporation, Chengdu, Sichuan, PRC.

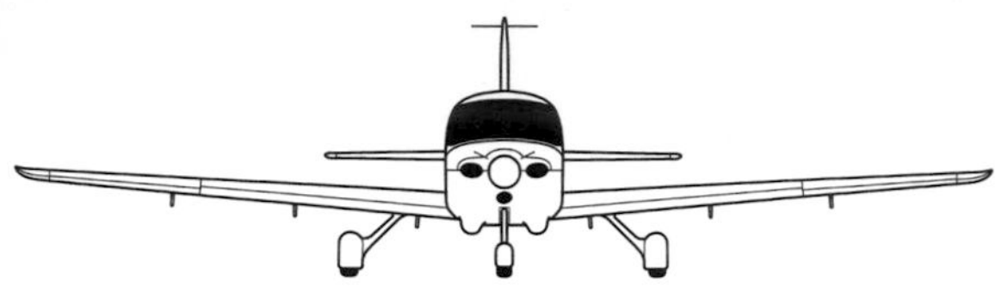

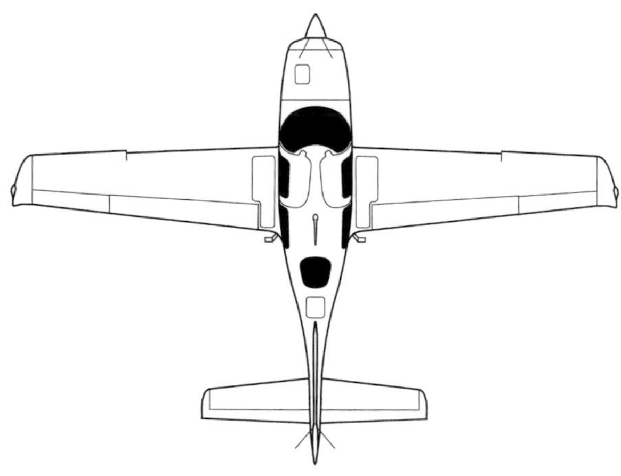

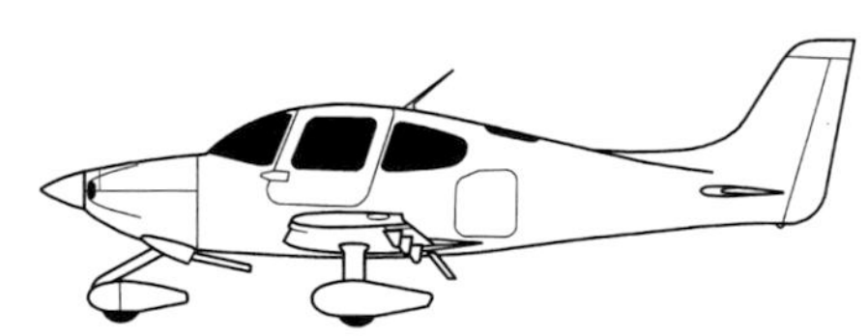

Dimensions:
Wingspan 38.48 ft (11.73 m)
Length 25.98 ft (7.92 m)
Height 9.18 ft (2.80 m)
Wing area 145 sq. ft (13.46 m^2)

CIRRUS SR22

Country of origin: USA.
Type: Travel and sports plane.
Power Plant: One Teledyne Continental IO-550-N air-cooled 4-cylinder horizontally opposed engine with 310 PS (230 kW) performance.
Performance: Maximum permissible speed 235 mph (378 km/h), maximum cruising speed 208 mph (335 km/h), initial rate of climb 23 ft (7 m)/sec, service ceiling 16,666 ft (5,080 m), maximum range with IFR reserve 994 miles (1,600 km).
Weights: Empty weight 2,250 lbs (1,021 kg), take-off weight 3,399 lbs (1,542 kg).
Payload: Pilot and three passengers, maximum payload around 1,102 lbs (500 kg).
State of development: The SR22 has been flying since the middle of 2000. To date, more than 500 SR22 have been ordered. The first units were delivered in February 2001. The 500th unit of the SR22 model was delivered in the middle of 2002. Three SR20 and/or SR22 leave the factory each business day.
Remarks: The Cirrus SR22 is a further development of the Cirrus SR20. It has the same attributes of the first model which include the usage of the latest technologies, cabin and wings with special chassis completely manufactured of a compound material (Epoxyd-fiberglass) in sandwiched construction, and extensive avionics consisting of a ICDS 2000-multifunction cockpit with autopilot and GPS for flight under IFS conditions. The otherwise conventional two command sticks are replaced by "Sidesticks". Also, the unique "Ballistic Recovery System" has been adopted. This will take the aircraft safely to the ground by means of parachute in case there's a danger of crashing. In addition, the SR22 is equipped with a more powerful power plant and a newly conceived wider wingspan. The fuel tank takes in 84 gallons (320 l), which enables a wider range. Finally, part of the airframe and the chassis are reinforced for coping with a larger take-off weight. The SR22 will also be offered with the SMA SR21tdi diesel power plant with 230 PS (170 kW) performance. Beginning in 2003 the SR22 became available with a multifunction cockpit from Avidyne and a de-icer system.
Manufacturer: Cirrus Design Corp., Duluth, Minnesota, USA.

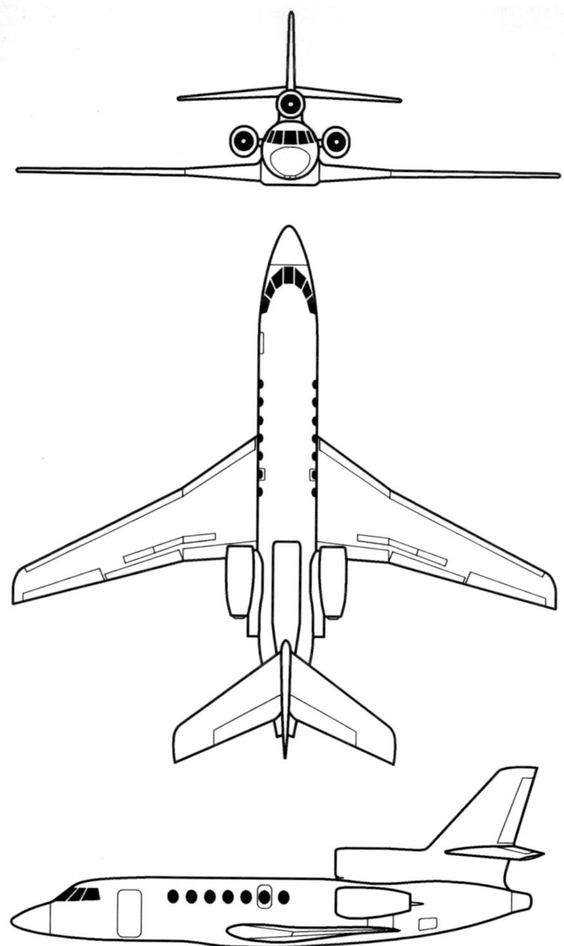

Dimensions:
Wingspan 61.87 ft (18.86 m)
Length 60.76 ft (18.52 m)
Height 22.89 ft (6.98 m)
Wing area 504 sq. ft (46.83 m^2)

DASSAULT FALCON 50EX

Country of origin: France.
Type: Corporate plane.
Power Plant: Three AlliedSignal/Garrett TFE731-40 turbofan engines each with 3,703 lbs (1,678 kp/1,6.47 kN) static thrust.
Performance: Maximum speed Mach 0.86, maximum cruising speed 547 mph (880 km/h), time for reaching 41,010 ft (12,500 m) 23 minutes, range with eight passengers and IFR reserves 3,756 miles (6,046 km).
Weight: Empty weight 21,175 lbs (9,605 kg), maximum take-off weight 39,704 lbs (18,010 kg).
Payload: Two men in the cockpit and, depending on the internal configuration, from nine passengers in club seating to a maximum of 19 people, maximum payload 3,769 lbs (1,710 kg).
State of development: The initial long-range version of the Falcon 50 first flew on April 10, 1996. Customer deliveries started in February 1997. Around 300 Falcon 50 and Falcon 50ER have been delivered since. The production continues. Aéronavale received five Falcon 50EX (coast guard version) in 1998.
Remarks: Compared to the Falcon 50, the Falcon 50EX possesses more economical and powerful power plants, which allow the range to expand by around 230 miles (370 km) at a reasonable cost. Other parameters are also enhanced such as the new Collins ProLine 4 avionics with EFIS screens. The planes for the Aéronavale are equipped with surveillance radar, along with containers under the fuselage for Search and Rescue devices, including an infrared camera.
Manufacturer: Dassault Aviation, Vaucresson, France.

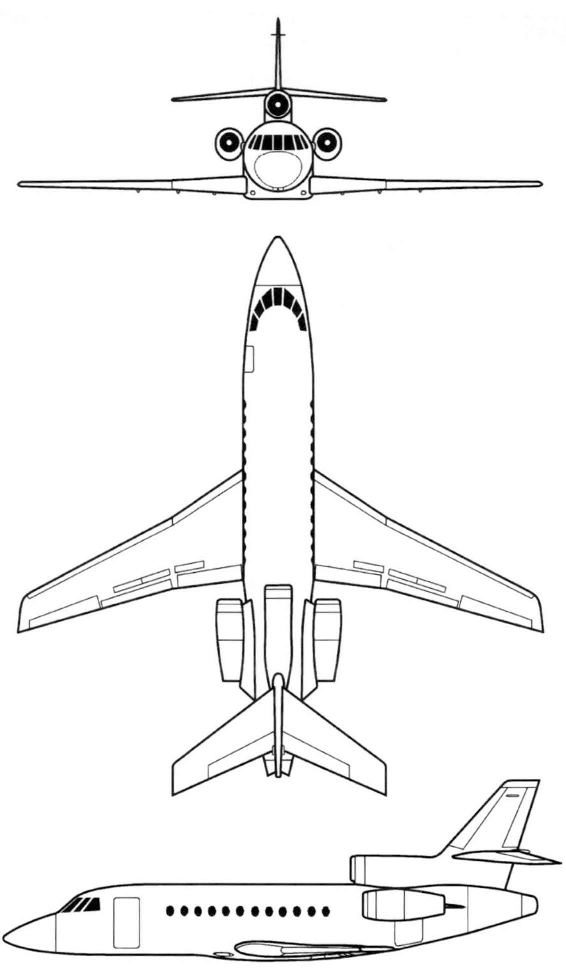

Dimensions:
Wingspan 63.41 ft (19.33 m)
Length 66.30 ft (20.21 m)
Height 24.77 ft (7.55 m)
Wing area 528 sq. ft (49.03 m^2)

DASSAULT FALCON 900C

Country of origin: France.
Type: Corporate plane.
Power Plant: Three AlliedSignal TFE731-5BR turbofan engines each with 4,775 lbs (2,165 kp/ 21.27 kN) static thrust.
Performance: Maximum speed with 27,000 lbs (12,250 kg) 574 mph (924 km/h [Mach 0.87]) at 36,000 ft (10,975 m), maximum cruising speed 555 mph (893 km/h [Mach 0.84]) at 39,000 (11,890 m), long range cruising speed 495 mph (797 km/h [Mach 0.75]) at 36,991 ft (11,275 m), service ceiling 51,016 ft (15,550 m), range with five passengers and maximum fuel load 4,607 miles (7,410 km), with 15 passengers 4,329 miles (6,968 km).
Weight: Empty weight 22,608 lbs (10,255 kg), maximum take-off weight 45,502 lbs (20,640 kg).
Payload: Two pilots and 8 to 15 passengers depending on the internal layout. Maximum passenger capacity 19 people in three-seat rows, maximum payload 4,783 lbs (2,170 kg).
State of development: The prototype of the Falcon 900 flew for the first time on September 21, 1984. Production followed, producing the first plane in March 1986. The version 900C flew for the first time on December 17, 1998. It was certified on August 26, 1999. Dassault started delivering this version in early 2000. Counting all variants, more than 300 Falcons have been delivered, of these 30 were ordered by the French government.
Remarks: As replacement for the Falcon 900/900B Dassault offers the new Falcon 900C. It takes the Honeywell Primus 2000 avionics and the EFIS cockpit from the -EX, but offers the same features of the 900/900B for the rest. Compared to the -EX, the 900C is a bit lighter and more economical to operate but it cannot achieve the same range. At present Dassault only manufactures the versions 900EX and 900C. All feature a very comfortable cabin 39 ft (11.9 m) long, 6 ft (1.87 m) high and nearly 8 ft (2.34 m) wide. Dassault has announced a substantial further development of the Falcon 900 under the preliminary name Falcon 7X. This new version will feature three more powerful power plants PW307A, a longer fuselage, maximum speed up to Mach 0.9 and fly-by-wire control. Scheduled availability is 2006.
Manufacturer: Dassault Falcon Jet Corporation, Vaucresson, France.

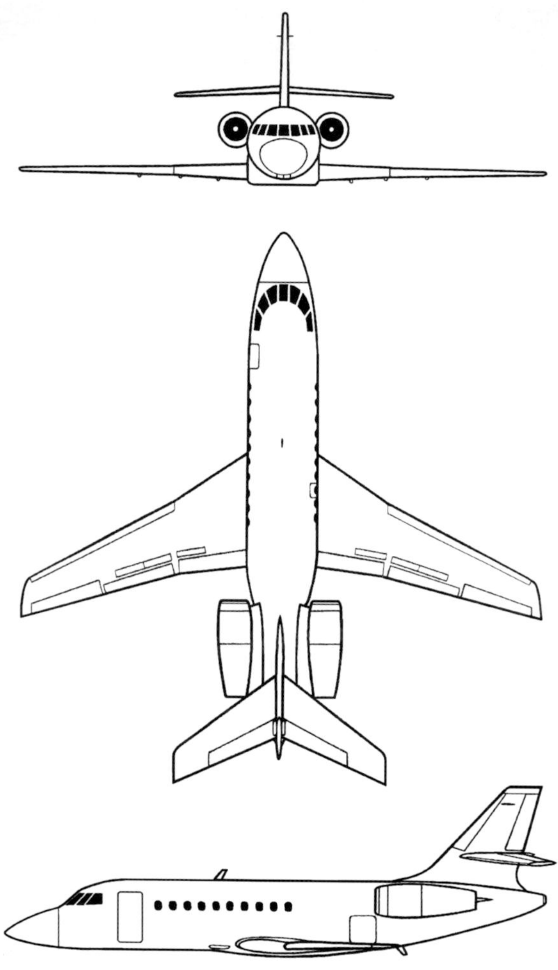

Dimensions:
Wingspan 63.41 ft (19.33 m)
Length 66.37 ft (20.23 m)
Height 23.16 ft (7.06 m)
Wing area 528 sq. ft (49.02 m^2)

DASSAULT FALCON 2000/2000EX

Country of origin: France.
Type: Corporate plane.
Power Plant (2000): Two General Electric/Garrett CFE 738-1-1B turbofan engines each with 5,724 lbs (2,596 kp/25.46 kN) static thrust.
Performance (2000): Maximum cruising speed at 39,008 ft (11,890 m) 561 mph (903 km/h [Mach 0.85]), rate of climb 57 ft (17.4 m)/sec, service height 46,915 ft (14,300 m), range with eight passengers and maximum fuel load and NBAA reserve 3,451 miles (5,555 km), with maximum payload 1,149 miles (1,850 km).
Weight (2000): Empty weight 20,734 lbs (9,405 kg), maximum take-off weight 35,802 lbs (16,240 kg).
Payload: Two pilots in the cockpit and eight to 12 passengers in the cabin depending on the internal configuration or, with narrow seating, 19 passengers.
State of development: The first flight of the Falcon 2000 test model took place on March 4, 1993. Registration and the start of customer deliveries were in February 1995. The latest Falcon 2000Ex flew for the first time in October 25, 2001. Through 2002, 400 of both versions had been ordered, 200 having been delivered. The monthly production of the models 900 and 2000 combined comes to around eight units.
Remarks: The Falcon 2000 is based on the same comfortable cross section of the body with uninterrupted standing height as the Falcon 900C/900EX (see pages 146/147). The length of the cabin is a bit shorter at 31 ft (9.46 m). By carrying only two power plants the Falcon 2000 can operate more economically than similar models. The cockpit is equipped with four CRT EFIS displays of the Collins Pro Line 4 type. A HUD is available as an option. All Falcon 2000 models since 1999 are equipped with thrust reversal. The improved 2000EX version began deliveries in May 2004. It has the more powerful Pratt & Whitney PW308C power plants each with 7,037 lbs (3,175 kp/31.3 kN) static thrust. With 31% higher fuel capacity, a range of up to 4,350 miles (7,000 km) is expected. Given the greater weight, selective reinforcements are necessary, i.e., at the chassis. Beginning in 2004, the interactive cockpit "EASy" will be offered as standard equipment.
Manufacturer: Dassault Falcon Jet Corporation, Vaucresson, France.

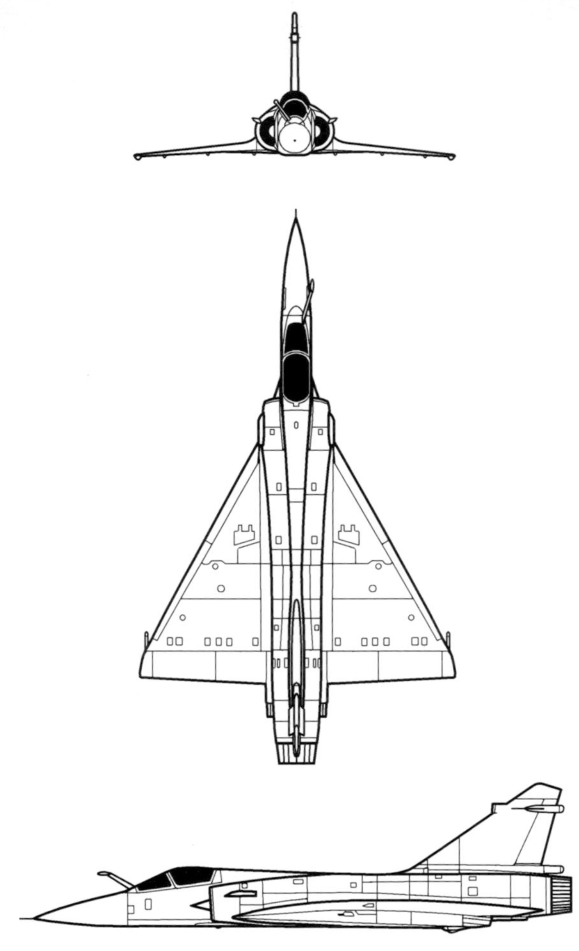

Dimensions:
Wingspan 29.95 ft (9.13 m)
Length 47.11 ft (14.36 m)
Height: 16.47 ft (5.02 m)
Wing area 441.3 sq. ft (10.76 m^2)

DASSAULT MIRAGE 2000-5MK.II/-9

Country of origin: France.
Type: 1- or 2-seat multi-purpose fighter.
Power Plant: One SNECMA M53-P2 turbofan engine with 14,455 lbs (6,558 kP/64.3 kN) static thrust without afterburner and 21,379 lbs (9,700 kP/95.1 kN) with afterburner.
Performance: Short term top speed 1,485 mph (2,390 km/h [Mach 2.25]) above 36,090 ft (11,000 m), maximum sustained speed 1,385 mph (2,230 km/h [Mach 2.1]) or 695 mph (1,118 km/h [Mach 0.91]) without afterburner, maximum rate of climb 1,296 ft (395 m)/sec, time to reach 49,212 ft (15,000 m) while accelerating to Mach 2.0 four minutes, range with maximum internal and external fuel load 2,085 miles (3,355 km), tactical operation radius with two additional 450 gallon (1,700 l) tanks and 2,205 lbs (1,000 kg) of weapons 932 miles (1,500 km).
Weight: Empty weight 16,535 lbs (7,500 kg), take-off weight without external load 20,944 lbs (9,500 kg), maximum take-off weight 38,580 ft (17,500 kg).
Armament: As a fighter, two DEFA 30-mm cannons, two short range air-air Magic missiles and four middle-range Mica air-air missiles equipped with active radar. Weapon load up to 14,330 lbs (6,500 kg), distributed at five stations at the fuselage and four at the wings.
State of development: The latest Mirage 2000-9 flew for the first time on December 14, 2001. The first order was for 30 units of this model from the United Arab Republic. To date, 612 units of all Mirage 2000 models have been ordered.
Remarks: The 2000-9 (sometimes referred to as -5Mk.II) is an improved version of the Mirage 2000-5. Given its updated electronics, it possesses improved night flight capability. In addition, it incorporates the powerful RDY-2 radar and a complete system for electronic combat control (IMEWS). Finally, the maximum take-off weight has been increased. Based on the two-seat model, the Mirage 2000AT will soon be offered as an advanced trainer. It will have the same cockpit as the Mirage 2000-9. However, all the combat electronics will be removed.
Manufacturer: Dassault Défense, Vaucresson, France.

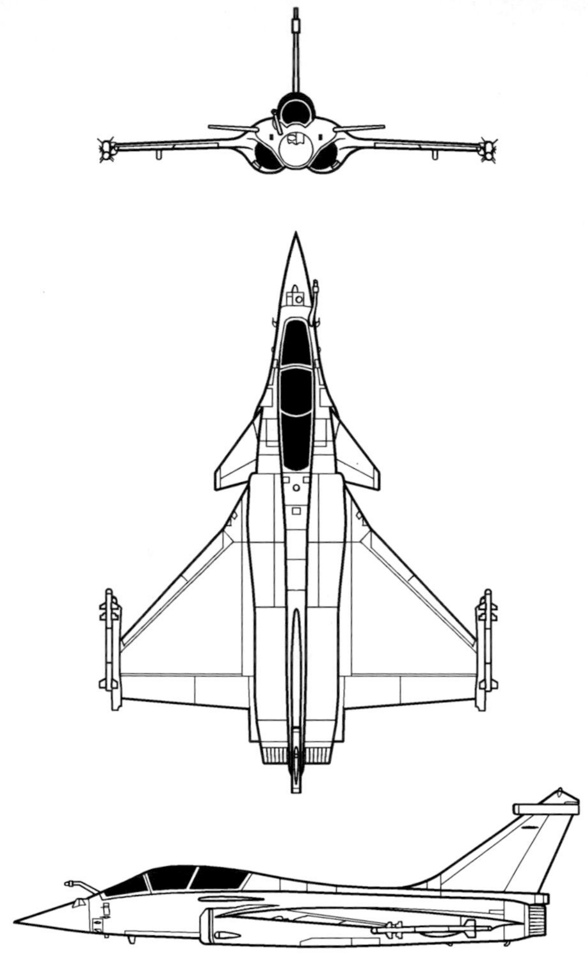

Dimensions:
Wingspan including missiles at wingtips 29.95 ft (10.90 m)
Length 50.20 ft (15.30 m)
Height: 17.52 ft (5.34 m)
Wing area 491.90 sq. ft (45.70 m^2)

DASSAULT RAFALE F1/F2

Country of origin: France.
Type: Two-seat multi-purpose F2 fighter, one-seat carrier-based interceptor and multi-purpose fighter.
Power Plant: Two SNECMA M88-2 turbofan engines each with 10,948 lbs (4,966 kP/48.7 kN) static thrust without afterburner and 16,387 lbs (7,438 kP/72.9 kN) with afterburner.
Performance: Maximum speed 1,320 mph (2,124 km/h [Mach 2.0]) above 36,000 ft (10,975 m), 864 mph (1,390 km/h [Mach 1.15]) in low flight, initial rate of climb 1,000 ft (305 m)/sec, service ceiling 55,036 ft (16,775 m), tactical combat radius during intercept mission with eight Mica air- air missiles and one additional tank of 449 gallons (1,700 l) under the fuselage and one 344 gallon (1,300 l) tank under each of the wings 1,151 miles (1,853 km), with a high-low-low-high mission profile and 12 551+ lb (250+ kg) bombs and four Mica Missiles and a total of 1,136 gallons (4,300 l) in external tanks 679 miles (1,093 km).
Weight: Empty weight (F2) 18,956 lbs (8,600 kg), (F1) 21,600 lbs (9,800 kg), maximum take-off weight 42,990 to 49,600 lbs (19,500 to 22,500 kg).
Armament: One 30-mm GIAT-DEFA cannon and a weapons load of maximum 20,944 lbs (9,500 kg), distributed at 13 pylons under the fuselage and wings as well as the wingtip rails.
State of development: The initial flight of the first of four prototypes (Rafale C) took place on May 19, 1991. The French Air Force plans to obtain 235 2-seat Rafale F2's (at present 87 have been ordered) and the French Navy plans to obtain 60 Rafale F1's (38 ordered thus far, 18 delivered). The first serial aircraft, an F1, was delivered to the Navy on July 7, 1999. The first squadron, the Flotilla 12F, has been operational since mid-2002.
Remarks: Both the Rafale F2 and the Navy Rafale F1 are equipped with the latest GIE RBE2 airborne radar with electronic scan antenna. Almost the entire airframe is manufactured of composite materials with a Kevlar nose and tail. Titan is used for parts especially subject to wear. Controls adhere to the fly-by-wire principle. At present, a test model is flying equipped in the upper part of the fuselage with integrated (so-called conforming) fuel tanks holding 304 gallons (1,150 l) each. With the delivery of its 21st unit, the French Navy will change over to the two-seat Rafale.
Manufacturer: Dassault Défense, Vaucresson, France.

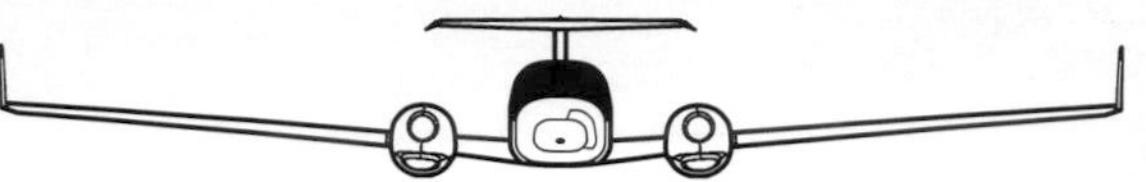

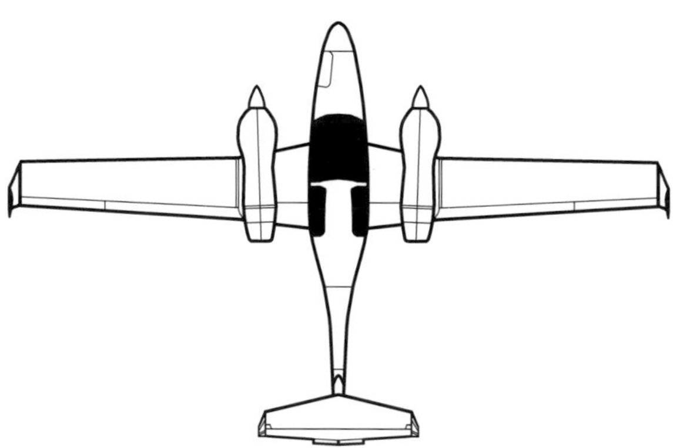

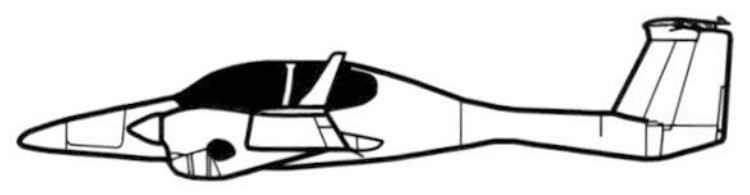

Dimensions:
Wingspan 44 ft (13.41 m)
Length 27.6 ft (8.43 m)
Height: 8.4 ft (2.56 m)
Wing area 115.8 sq. ft (10.76 m^2)

DIAMOND DA-42 TWIN STAR

Country of origin: Austria.
Type: Sport and travel plane.
Power Plant: Two Thielert TAE air-cooled turbo-diesel engines each with 135 PS (100 kW) performance.
Performance (estimated): Top speed 233 mph (375 km/h) at 12,500 ft (3,810 m), maximum cruising speed 193 mph (310 km/h), initial rate of climb rate 29 ft (8.7 m)/sec, service ceiling 20,012 ft (6,100 m), normal range 1,217 miles (1,960 km), range with optional reserve tank 1,708 miles (2,750 km).
Weight: Empty weight 2,270 lbs (1,030 kg).
Payload: Four people including pilot.
State of development: The prototype was presented in May 2002 at the Berlin ILA and made its test flight on December 9, 2002. No confirmed order information is available at present although there are thought to be about 324 backorders waiting for the aircraft's government certification, which was achieved in May 2004. The first deliveries are planned for late-2004. Reportedly Lufthansa intends to take 15 units for their flying schools.
Remarks: The diesel engines are certainly the most interesting aspect of the Twin Star. Developed by the Liechtenstein-based Thielert Aircraft Engines Company, the engines are distinguished by their low noise and exhaust values and their exceptionally economic consumption figures. Fuel consumption per hour is just 4.62 gallons (17.5 l) at the speed of 124 mph (200 km/h). Apart from diesel, they can also be fuelled with A-1 jet fuel or any mixture of both. Moreover, the DA-42 exhibits a very aerodynamic and individual form. Its avionics comply with today's standards. Optionally, the cockpit can be equipped with three multi-function displays. The price of the basic version is around US$360,000.
Manufacturer: Diamond Aircraft, Flugplatz Wiener-Neustadt, Austria.

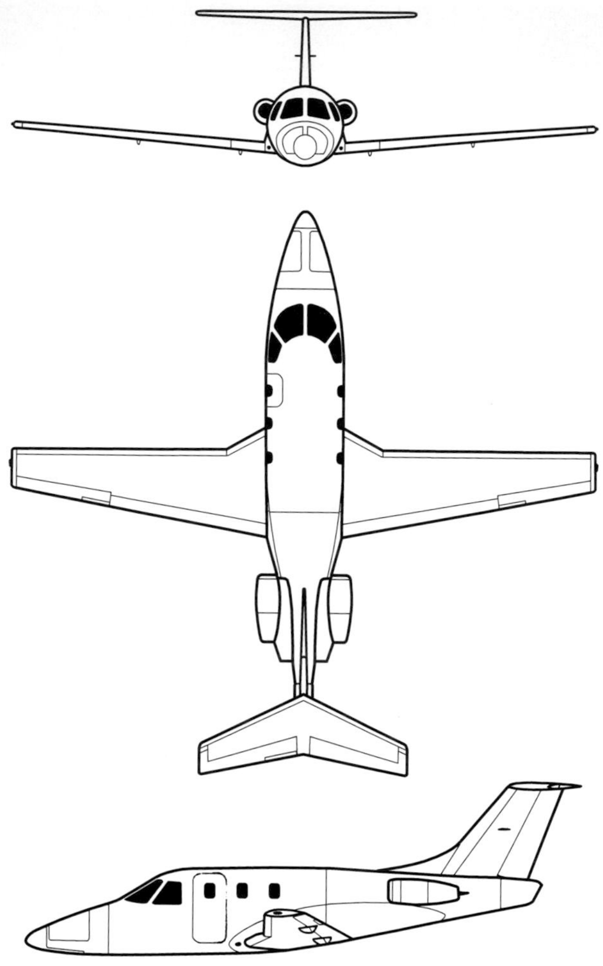

Dimensions:
Wingspan 36.09 ft (11.00 m)
Length 33.14 ft (10.10 m)
Height 10.83 ft (3.30 m)

ECLIPSE AVIATION ECLIPSE 500

Country of origin: USA.
Type: Air taxi and corporate plane.
Power Plant: Two Williams International EJ22 turbofan engines each with 771 lbs (336 kp/3.43 kN) performance.
Performance (according to manufacturer's data): Maximum cruising speed 409 mph (658 km/h), service ceiling 41,010 ft (12,500 m), maximum range 1,496 miles (2,409 km).
Weight: Empty weight 2,700 lbs (1,225 kg), maximum take-off weight 4,700 lbs (2,132 kg).
Payload: Pilot and three to five passengers.
State of development: The prototype's maiden flight was on August 26, 2002. A total of eight aircraft will be taking part in the test flights. According to the manufacturers, contracts for around 1,400 units are on the table (plus a further 715 purchase options), among them an order from the Swiss company Aviace for 112 Eclipse 500's for the expansion of a "private jet club". Delivery is scheduled to begin in March 2006. The original order from the Nimbus Group for 1,000 units for a region-wide air taxi service inside the US has recently been canceled.
Remarks: The concept for the Eclipse envisages a low cost and economical "people's jet". Initially the purchase price is about US$837,000. Customers will be recruited from among the owners of single engine sport and touring aircraft. Eclipse claims that their jet has lower operating costs than some single-piston-engine aircraft. The whole construction is aluminum. Although composite materials have been avoided for cost considerations, the Eclipse is surprisingly light in relation to its size, i.e., an EJ22 engine from Williams weighs only 100 lbs (45 kg). The avionics from Avio include, among other things, a GPS based flight management system and FADEC digital engine monitoring. It is expected that the standard version will be equipped with engines from a different manufacturer.
Manufacturer: Eclipse Aviation Corp., Albuquerque, New Mexico, USA.

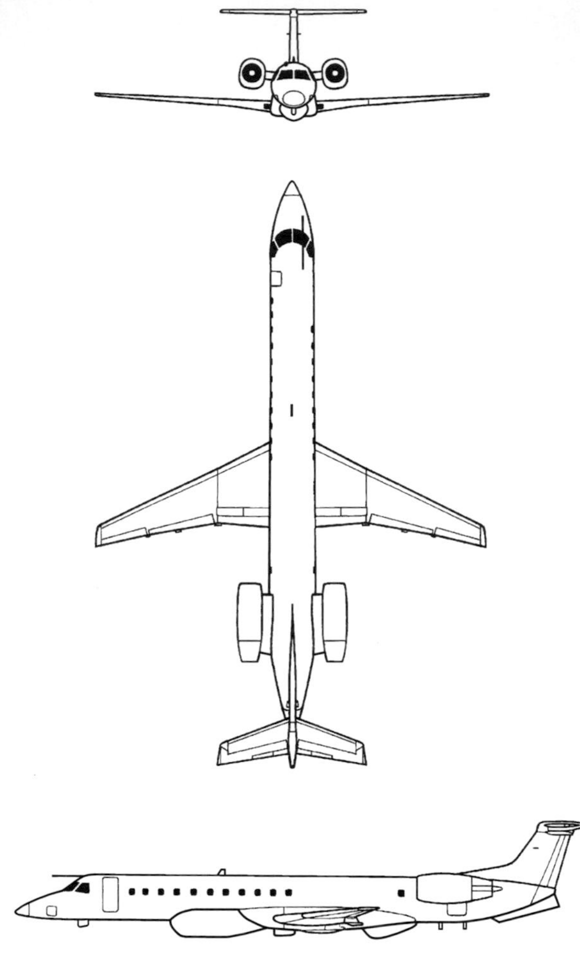

Dimensions:
Wingspan 65.75 ft (20.04 m)
Length 98 ft (29.87 m)
Height 22.14 ft (6.75 m)
Wing area 550.9 sq. ft (51.18 m^2)

EMBRAER ERJ-145SA/RS

Country of origin: Brazil.
Type: (ERJ-145SA/R-99A) radar and command aircraft (AEW&C) and (ERJ-145RS/R-99B) electronic surveillance aircraft.
Power Plant: Two Allison AE3007A1P turbofan engines each with 7,419 lbs (3,391 kp/3.00 kN) static thrust.
Performance: Maximum cruising speed 495 mph (796 km/h) at 35,000 ft (10,668 m), service ceiling 36,974 ft (11,270 m), maximum flying time 9 hours.
Weight: Empty weight approximately 30,864 lbs (14,000 kg), maximum take-off weight 51,587 lbs (23,400 kg).
Payload: Two pilots and (ERJ-145SA) four system operators.
State of development: The first flight of the ERJ-145SA (see photo) took place on May 22, 1999. To date, Brazil has ordered five, Greece four and Mexico three (one ERJ-145SA and two ERJ-145MPA) planes. In addition, the Brazilian Air Force is procuring three ERJ-143RS's. Following certification in mid-2002, Embraer started delivering the first units. By the end of 2002, 583 orders and 301 purchase options for the civilian model ERJ-145 had been received, 475 of which were delivered.
Remarks: The AEW&C version ERJ-145SA was developed by the Brazilian government for the "Amazon Surveillance System" project. This aircraft, together with the A-29/AT-29 (see pages 164/165), is intended to combat drug dealing, smuggling and environmental crime from the air in this vast area. To this end, Ericsson Erieye side-view radar is mounted over the fuselage. This system, weighing 2,865 lbs (1,300 kg), can detect low flying targets within a range of 217 miles (350 km). Additional electronic systems and sensors are used for further military tasks such as sea surveillance, SAR deployment and air-space management. Alternatively, the ERJ-145RS (see silhouette) constitutes an electronic ground surveillance, defence and disruption aircraft. The radar above the fuselage has been replace by synthetic aperture ground surveillance radar from Raytheon, an FLIR system Star Safir, infrared sensing and COMINT/ELINT equipment. Finally, there is also an armed marine patrol version RJ-145MPA that is equipped with a 360° scanning radar in addition to the AEW radar.
Manufacturer: EMBRAER (**Emp**rêsa **Br**asileira de **Aer**onautica SA), Sao José dos Campos, Brazil.

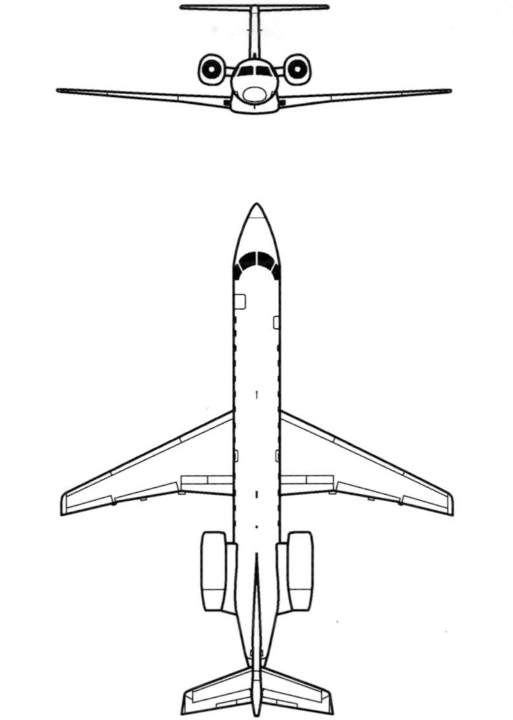

Dimensions:
Wingspan 65.75 ft (20.04 m)
Length 7.64 ft (2.33 m)
Height 22.01 ft (6.71 m)
Wing area 550.9 sq. ft (51.18 m^2)

EMBRAER LEGACY

Country of origin: Brazil.
Type: Corporate aircraft.
Power Plant: Two Rolls Royce Allison AE3007-A1P turbofan engines each with 7,954 lbs (3,600 kp/35.38 kN) static thrust.
Performance: Maximum speed Mach 0.80, maximum cruising speed 518 mph (833 km/h [Mach 0.78]), service ceiling 35,104 ft (10,700 m), range with ten passengers 3,561 miles (5,732 km).
Weight: Maximum take-off weight 49,603 lbs (22,500 kg).
Payload: Two pilots and up to 16 passengers depending on configuration, as a corporate shuttle up to 37 persons, maximum load capacity 6,635 lbs (3,010 kg).
State of development: The business jet model Legacy has been flying since March 31, 2001. Orders for 73 units plus 91 options were received by the end of 2002. EMBRAER began delivery in the autumn of 2002. To date, 122 orders (plus 6 options) have been received for the initial model ERJ-135, and 174 orders (plus 45 options) for the ERJ-140 model. So far, 90 of the former and 60 of the latter aircraft have been delivered.
Remarks: Three models are available: a 10 to 16-seat executive version, a 16 to 37-seat corporate shuttle and a government aircraft model. The Legacy, although derived from the ERJ-135, has new engines and a different interior configuration. Moreover the cargo hold has been reconstructed to accommodate an additional 1,051 gallon (3,978 l) fuel tank. For the most part, the remainder of the aircraft is uniform with the initial model. The price for a basic model is about US$19 million, which is inexpensive for this type of corporate aircraft.
Manufacturer: EMBRAER (**Em**prêsa **Br**asileira de **Aer**onautica SA), Sao José dos Campos, Brazil.

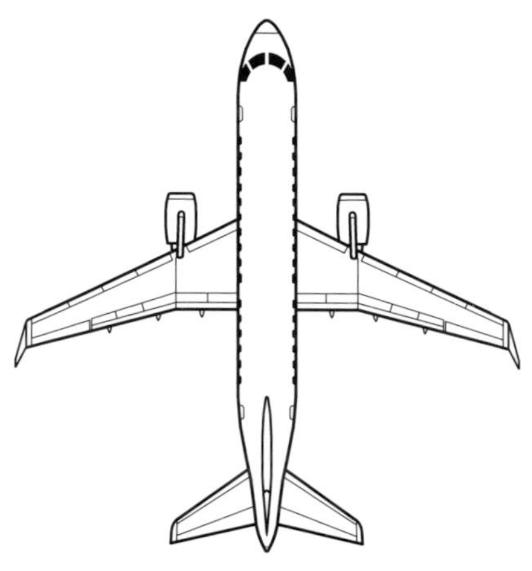

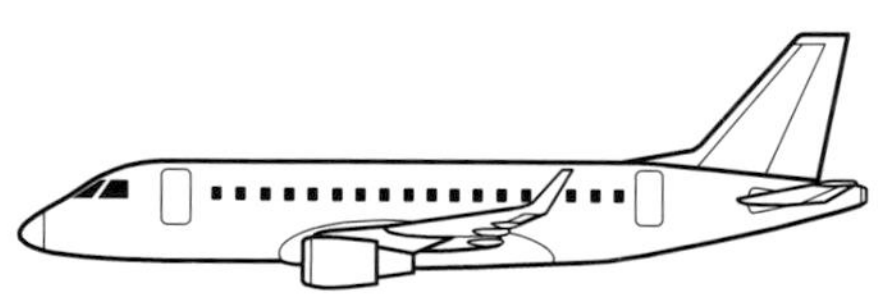

Dimensions:
Wingspan including winglets 85.30 ft (26 m)
Length (170) 98.09 ft (29.90 m), (175) 103.90 ft (31.67 m)
Height 31.72 ft (9.67 m)

EMBRAER 170

Country of origin: Brazil.
Type: Regional commercial aircraft.
Power Plant: Two General Electric CF34-8E turbofan engines each with 14,006 lbs (6,350 kp/ 62.3 kN) static thrust.
Performance: Maximum cruising speed 541 mph (870 km/h [Mach 0.80]), range with full passenger capacity (170STD) 2,071 miles (3,334 km), (170LR) 2,416 miles (3,889 km), (175STD) 1,491 miles (2,400 km), (175LR) 1,839 miles (2,960 km).
Weight: Empty weight (170) 44,422 lbs (20,150 kg), (175) 46,693 lbs (21,180 kg), maximum take-off weight (170STD) 78,153 lbs (35,450 kg), (170LR) 81,239 lbs (36,850 kg), (175STD) 79,409 lbs (36,020 kg), (175LR) 82,562 lbs (37,450 kg).
Payload: Two pilots and up to (170) 70 passengers, (175) 78 passengers to a maximum of 86 passengers in rows of four-seats with an aisle. Maximum load capacity (170) 20,061 lbs (9,100 kg), (175) 22,508 lbs (10,210 kg).
State of development: The first prototype made its test flight on February 19, 2002 followed by the second (see photo) on April 9, 2002. In all, six aircraft are taking part in the tests. Deliveries to customers began in March 2004. By March 31, 2004, there were 133 firm orders including 85 for US Airways, 15 from Crossair (Switzerland), 13 from Republic (US) and six each for Alitalia and Lot Polish Airlines.
Remarks: With the first flight of its 175 model in June 2003, EMBRAER continues its introduction of four new-generation commercial jets specifically designed for the regional aircraft market. Both the 170 and the 175 models feature the "double bubble hull cross section" which looks like an eight. This allows for considerably more passenger comfort. With four seats next to each other, head and elbowroom are much greater. Additionally, the design is technically up to date to include a cockpit with fluid crystal color monitors, digital electronic engine monitoring, fly-by-wire piloting and so on. Thanks to the four doors, extremely short turn-around times will be possible. Also, both models will be offered in two variants (STD and LR), which will have different range capabilities. Two larger models are planned. The first flight of the 190 model took place on March 12, 2004 with the second flight on May 9, 2004. Delivery will begin in the fourth quarter of 2005 (there are 100 orders plus 195 options, many of these for JetBlue). Delivery of the 195 model is expected to begin in the third quarter of 2006. At present Swiss International Airlines is the only purchaser.
Manufacturer: EMBRAER (**Em**prêsa **Br**asileira de **Aer**onautica SA), Sao José dos Campos, Brazil.

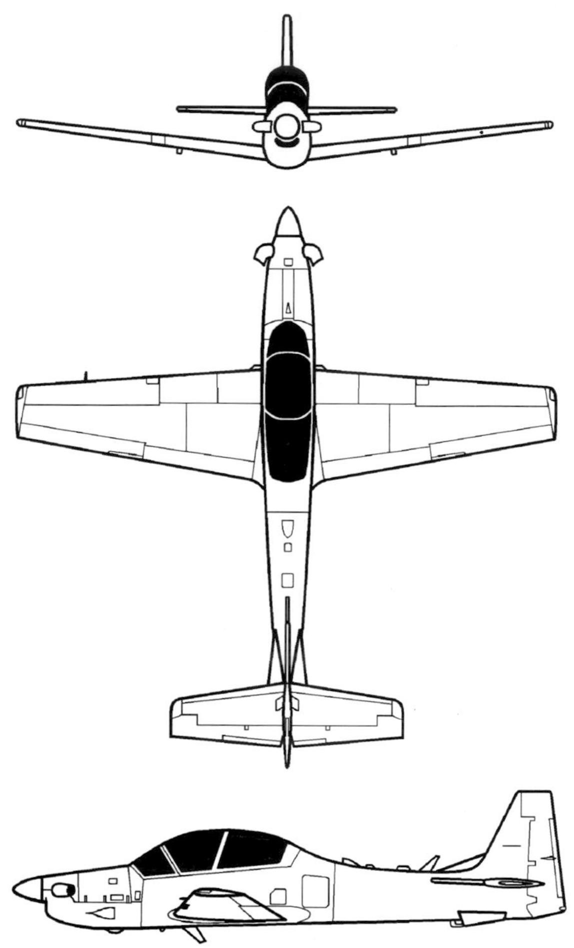

Dimensions:
Wingspan 36.54 ft (11.14 m)
Length 37.33 ft (11.38 m)
Height 13.02 ft (3.97 m)
Wing area 208.82 sq. ft (19.40 m^2)

EMBRAER EMB-314/A-29 SUPER TUCANO

Country of origin: Brazil.
Type (EMB-314): Two-seat basic and advanced trainer (ALX) or light one-seat (A-29) or two-seat (AT-29) ground fighter and surveillance aircraft.
Power Plant: One Pratt & Whitney Canada PT6A-68/3 turboprop engine with 1,600 SHP (1,190 kW) performance.
Performance: Maximum speed 367 mph (590 km/h), maximum cruising speed 332 mph (535 km/h), initial rate of climb 79 ft (24 m)/sec, service ceiling 34,776 ft (10,600 m), tactical operation radius at 10,826 ft (3,300 m) unarmed 466 miles (750 km), fully armed 336 miles (540 km).
Weight: Empty weight 6,944 lbs (3,150 kg), normal take-off weight 7,936 lbs (3,600 kg), with weapons load 11,574 lbs (5,250 kg).
Armament (AT-29): Two 12.7-mm machine guns permanently built into wings and a multitude of various weapon loads of up to 3,306 lbs (1,500 kg) at five mounting points under the fuselage and wings.
State of development: The first YA-29 prototype (see photo), which conforms to the standard series, took its initial test flight on June 2, 1999. The Brazilian Air Force will receive 25 A-29's and 51 AT-29's (+23 options) beginning in December 2003. Latest customer: Dominican Republic (10).
Remarks: The A-29/AT-29 are ground combat or COIN versions of the EMB-314 Super Tucano trainer. Their differences lie mainly in their mission-related equipment including Elbit attack and navigation electronics, GPS, heads-up-display, multifunction monitors and locally reinforced cell and wing structure. The cockpit is armored and air-pressurized. The crew can be equipped with **n**ight **v**ision **g**oggles (NVG) for night deployment. In addition the two-seat AT-29 has a forward mounted FLIR set. Thus equipped, the A-29 will primarily be deployed in the fight against drug smugglers and guerrillas in the Amazon region. They will team up with the AEW version of the EMB-145SA (see pages 158/159).
Manufacturer: EMBRAER (**Em**prêsa **Br**asileira de **Aer**onautica SA), Sao José dos Campos, Brazil.

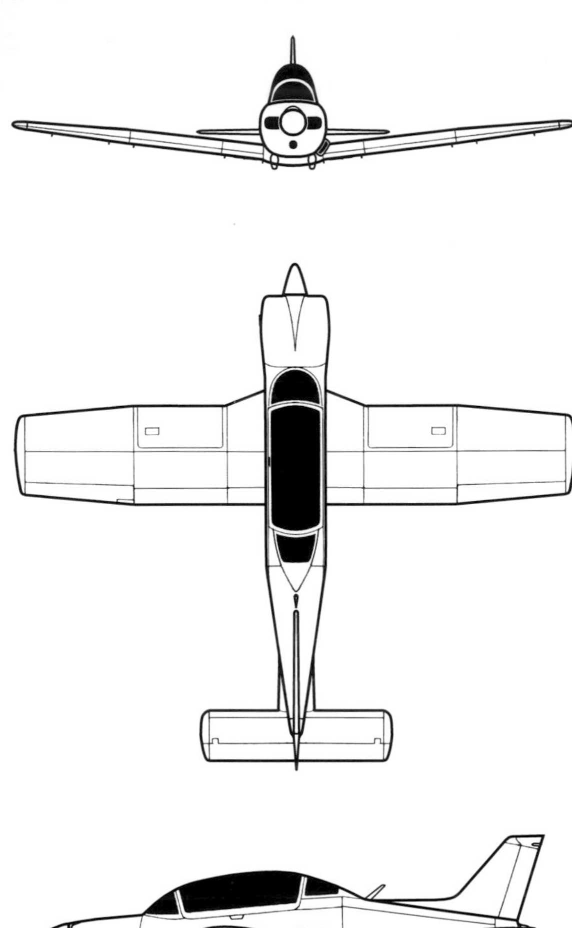

Dimensions:
Wingspan 28.90 ft (8.81 m)
Length 26.14 ft (7.97 m)
Height 7.67 ft (2.34 m)
Wing area 146.82 sq. ft (13.64 m^2)

ENAER T-35B PILLAN

Country of origin: Chile.
Type: Two-seat basic and instrument training aircraft.
Power Plant: One Textron Lycoming IO 540-K1K5 air-cooled six-cylinder horizontally opposed engine with 300 SHP (233 kW) performance.
Performance: Top speed 193 mph (311 km/h) at sea level, cruising speed at 75% capacity 185 mph (298 km/h) at 8,792 ft (2,680 m), initial rate of climb 25 ft (7.7 m)/sec, service ceiling 19,094 ft (5,820 m) range at 75% capacity including 45-minute reserves 679 miles (1,093 km).
Weight: Empty weight 1,834 lbs (832 kg), maximum take-off weight 2,954 lbs (1,340 kg).
Armament (as weapons trainer): Two rocket launchers, each one for four to seven unguided rockets, 250 lb (113 kg) bombs, or 12.7-mm machine gun pods with a maximum weight of 441 lbs (200 kg).
State of development: The first prototype flew on March 6, 1981. Between 1984 and 1991, 146 of these aircraft were produced for, among others, Chile (80), Panama (10) and Spain (40). After an interruption, production was resumed. The latest customers include the Dominican Republic, which received ten of the ECH-52B model, and the Ecuador Navy (see photo), which received four. The Pillan remains in production in small numbers.
Remarks: The Pillan ("the devil") originated under contract with the Piper Company and uses a number of parts from Piper models PA-28, PA-31, and PA-32. The following versions were manufactured: the T-35A/C basic trainer and the T35B/D instrument trainer. Both can be fully used for aerobatics. Development of a model using the RR 250 turboprop engine with 415 SHP (310 kW) performance was offered but found no buyers. A new design with an EFIS cockpit and improved ergonomics is being tested, reportedly for sale to Chile.
Manufacturer: ENAER, **E**mpresa **N**acional de **Aer**onautica de Chile, Santiago, Chile.

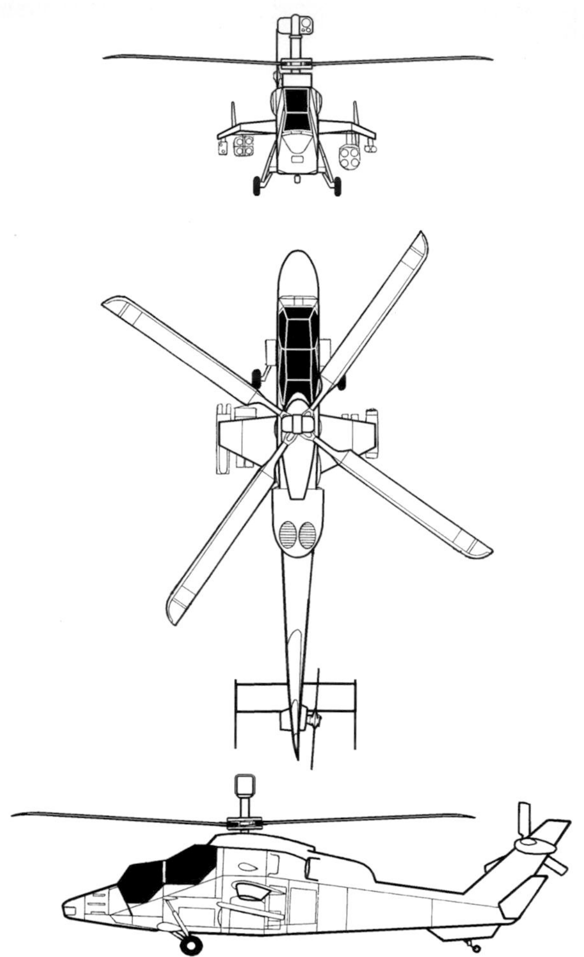

Dimensions:
Rotor diameter 42.65 ft (13.00 m)
Fuselage length (HAP with cannon) 49.21 ft (15.00 m), (UHU) 46.19 ft (14.08 m)
Height including rotor head 12.56 ft (3.83 m), including mast-mounted gun-sight 17.06 ft (5.20 m)

EUROCOPTER TIGER/UHU

Country of origin: France and Germany.
Type: Two-seat anti-tank and ground combat support helicopter.
Power Plant: Two MTU/Rolls Royce/Turboméca MTR 390 turbine engines each with 1,285 SHP (958 kW) performance.
Performance (HAP): Maximum speed 200 mph (322 km/h), maximum cruising speed 178 mph (287 km/h), normal cruising speed 155 mph (250 km/h), maximum rate of climb 38 ft (11.5 m)/sec, service ceiling 12,991 ft (3,960 m), hovering altitude without ground effect 11,482 ft (3,500 m), flight duration 3 hours, range 497 miles (800 km).
Weight: Empty weight 7,495 lbs (3,400 kg), normal take-off weight 11,904 lbs (5,400 kg), maximum overload 13,448 lbs (6,100 kg).
Armament (HAP): 30-mm cannon, up to 68 unguided rockets and four Mistral air-to-air guided missiles, (HAC) eight HOT/Trigat anti-tank weapons and two air-to-air Mistral guided missiles, (UHU) two pods each with 22 unguided 67-mm rockets and two fixed 12.7-mm cannon under the wings as well as Stinger air-to-air guided missiles.
State of development: Five prototypes have been built with the initial flight of the first prototype on April 27, 1991. The French Air Force is expected to receive 215 aircraft (115 HAP and 100 HAC) and the German Army 212 UHU's. For the time being, funds have been allocated for the procurement of 160 units (80 per country). The Australian Army will receive 22 Tigers starting in 2004.
Remarks: Three versions will be built: HAP (**H**éliocoptère d'**A**ppui **P**rotection, a combat support helicopter with optical sighting via TV/infrared camera and laser rangefinder), HAC (**H**éliocoptère **A**nti-**C**har, an anti-tank helicopter with additional Osiris sighting system) for the French Army and UHU (**U**nterstutzungs**hu**bschrauber, with equipment very similar to the HAC version) for the German Army. Over 75% of the cabin consists of composite materials. A large area of the fuselage is furnished with a copper-bronze grid to screen out electro-magnetic influences and for lightning protection. The anti-tank model is equipped with a camera gun-sight atop the rotor mast.
Manufacturer: Eurocopter Hubschrauber GmbH, Munich, Germany.

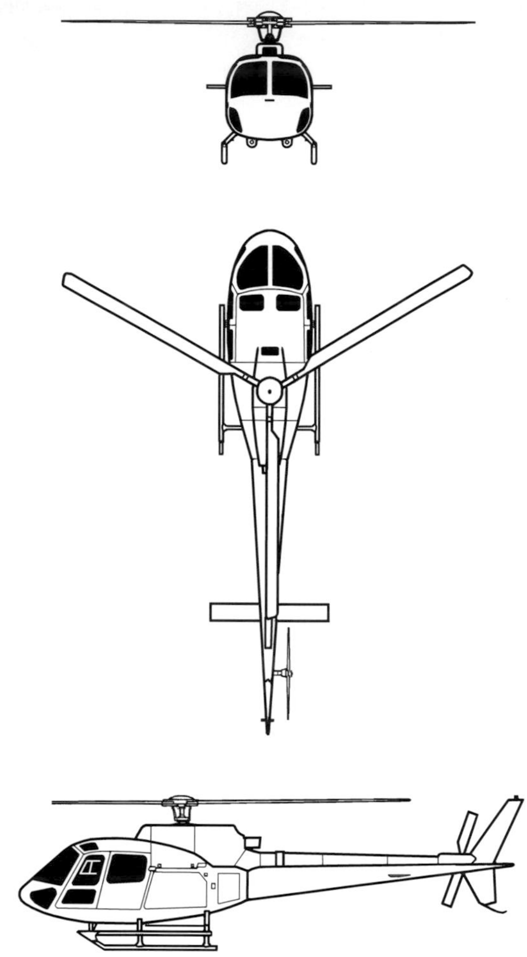

Dimensions:
Rotor diameter 35.07 ft (10.69 m)
Fuselage length including tail rotor 42.45 ft (12.94 m)
Height including rotor head 10.30 ft (3.14 m)

EUROCOPTER AS 350B3 ECUREUIL/AS 550C3 FENNEC

Country of origin: France.
Type: Civil and military multi-purpose light helicopter.
Power Plant: One Turboméca Arriel 2B turbine engine with 848 SHP (632 kW) performance.
Performance (AS 350B3): Maximum speed 178 mph (287 km/h), cruising speed 154 mph (248 km/h) at sea level, maximum rate of climb 33 ft (10.1 m)/sec, service ceiling 17,224 ft (5,250 m), hover altitude 13,583 ft (4,140 m) with ground effect, 12,200 ft (3,720 m) without ground effect, range 383 miles (616 km).
Weight: Empty weight 2,590 lbs (1,175 kg), maximum take-off weight 4,960 lbs (2,250 kg), with external load 6,063 lbs (2,750 kg).
Payload: Six to a maximum of seven people. Maximum capacity with external load 3,087 lbs (1,400 kg).
Armament (AS 550A2): 20-mm GIAT cannon, two 7.62-mm machine guns or 68-mm rocket pods, (AS 550C2) Saab/Emerson HeliTow anti-tank guided weapons system.
State of development: On March 4, 1997 the more powerful AS350B3 version completed its initial test flight. Including all the various models, over 2,300 units (more than 110 of those B3's) have been ordered and, for the most part, delivered. Additionally, the AS350B3 has been built under licence by Helibras in Brazil as the HB 350 (200+). A further 800 units of the twin engine AS355 (see silhouette) have been built.
Remarks: The latest model, AS 350B3, can be distinguished from its B2 forerunner by the strengthened gearbox, digital engine monitoring and tail rotor with an increased surface area to improve controllability. Thanks to the increase in power, the B3 is optimized for deployment at high altitude.
Manufacturer: Eurocopter, Marignane plant, La Courneuve, France.

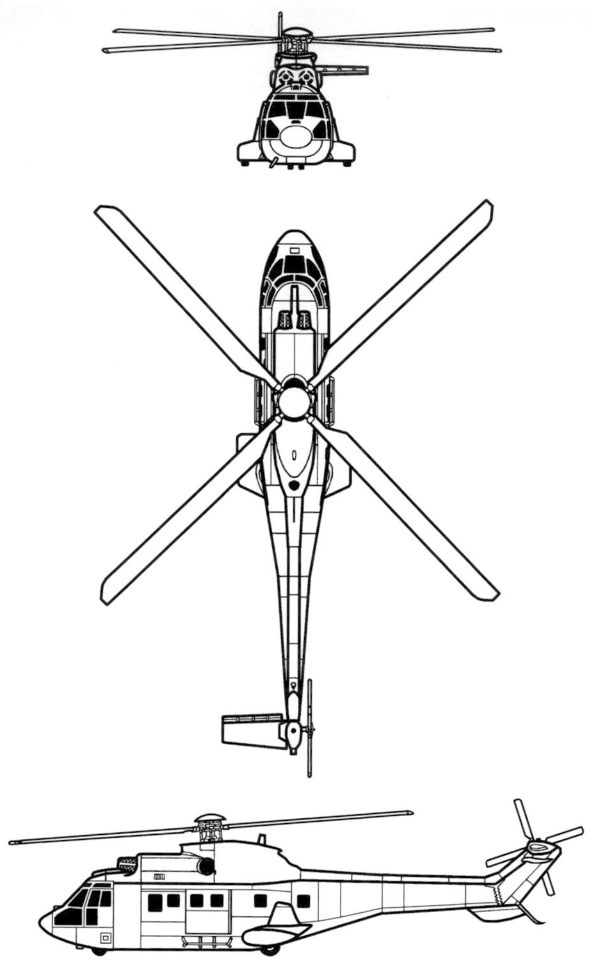

Dimensions:
Rotor diameter 53.15 ft (16.2 m)
Fuselage length including tail rotor 55.08 ft (16.79 m)
Height including rotor head 15.09 ft (4.6 m)

EUROCOPTER EC225 SUPER PUMA / EC725 COUGAR

Country of origin: France.
Type: Medium weight civil (EC 225) and military (EC 725) multi-purpose helicopter.
Power Plant: Two Turboméca Makila 1A2 turbine engines each with 1,959 SHP (1,461 kW) performance.
Performance (EC 225): Maximum speed 196 mph (315 km/h), cruising speed 172 mph (276 km/h) at sea level, maximum rate of climb 21 ft (6.5 m)/sec, hover height with ground effect 8,200 ft (2,500 m), without ground effect 5,250 ft (1,600 m), range with standard fuel load 402 miles (647 km).
Weight: Empty weight 10,250 lbs (4,650 kg), maximum take-off weight 20,500 lbs (9,300 kg), with external load 22,046 lbs (10,000 kg).
Payload: Two pilots and 24 passengers or 29 soldiers (AS 532). Maximum load capacity 9,127 lbs (4,140 kg).
State of development: The prototype's first flight was on February 6, 1987. To date, around 540 Super Pumas in all its variations have been contracted, about two thirds of these from 34 military or paramilitary organizations. Latest customer: Slovenia, 2. The EC 725 has been flying since November 27, 2000. The Armée de l'Air will receive four units by the end of 2004.
Remarks: The EC 725 Cougar Mk II+ Combat SAR (previously designated AS 532 Mk II+) is a recent addition to the available models. In addition to rescue equipment, it has searchlights, FLIR and weather radar. Available since the end of 2001, the EC 225 Super Puma Mk III has been developed by Eurocopter as a competitor to the S-92 (see pages 300/301). Because it is equipped with the more powerful Makila 2A engines (2,413 SHP/1,800 kW), it achieves a higher maximum take-off weight of about 24,250 lbs (11,000 kg). Due to an increase in the fuselage size (length +2.29 ft/70 cm, width +0.82 ft/25 cm, inside height +1.15 ft/35 cm), the cabin volume has increased by around a quarter. Also new are the five-blade rotor and the strengthened gearbox. This model is offered for civil and military service.
Manufacturer: Eurocopter, Marignane plant, La Courneuve, France.

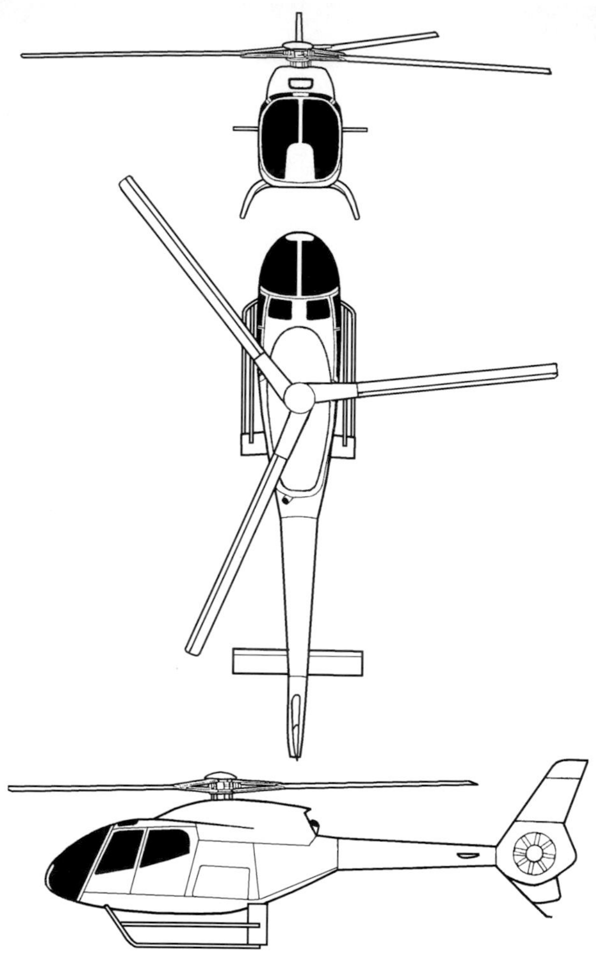

Dimensions:
Rotor diameter 33.46 ft (10.20 m)
Fuselage length including rotor 37.8 ft (11.52 m)
Height including rotor head 11.15 ft (3.4 m)

EUROCOPTER EC120B COLIBRI

Country of origin: France, People's Republic of China and Singapore.
Type: Light civil multi-purpose helicopter.
Power Plant: One Turboméca Arrius 2F turbine engine with 504 SHP (375 kW) performance.
Performance: Maximum speed 173 mph (278 km/h), maximum cruising speed 144 mph (231 km/h), maximum rate of climb 25 ft (7.49 m)/sec, service ceiling 20,000 ft (6,100 m), hover altitude with ground effect 13,600 ft (4,145 m), without ground effect 11,120 ft (3,413 m), range 466 miles (750 km).
Weight: Empty weight 1,973 lbs (895 kg), maximum take-off weight 3,704 lbs (1,680 kg).
Payload: Pilot and four passengers. Maximum load capacity 1,653 lbs (750 kg).
State of development: The first of three prototypes took to the air on June 9, 1995. At present, there are orders for about 260 units, of which 15 are for the Spanish Air Force and 12 for the Indonesian Air Force and three for the Indonesian Navy. The 200th unit was manufactured in March 2001. Current monthly production stands at six EC 120's.
Remarks: Eurocopter, CATIC/HAMAC and Singapore Technologies are partners in the EC 120 joint venture. Eurocopter is the technical leader with a share of 61% (their contribution includes conception, electronics, dynamic components, final assembly and certification). CATIC/HAMAC has a share of 24% and is responsible for the complete fuselage structure. Finally, Singapore Technologies has a share of 15% and contributes the tail rotor, compound material structure and cabin doors. The cabin of this helicopter is made extensively from compound materials. Thanks to the Spheriflex main rotor and the newly developed shrouded Fenestron tail rotor, outstanding flying performance with low noise level has been achieved. The high demands on safety are being fulfilled through, among other things, the use of unbreakable seats and fuel tanks. The EC 120 has been designed for the low end of the helicopter market and hopes to attract a large number of customers due to its quite reasonable asking price of around US$800,000 as well as its very economical operating costs.
Manufacturer: Eurocopter, CATIC/HAMC (China) and Singapore Aerospace, Paris, France.

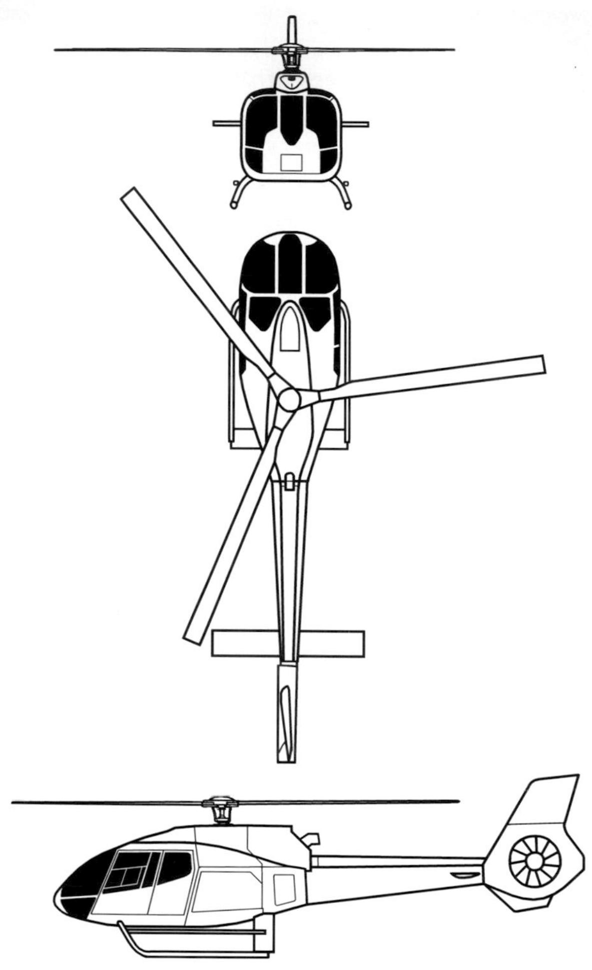

Dimensions:
Rotor diameter 35.07 ft (10.69 m)
Fuselage length 34.71 ft (10.68 m)
Height including rotor head 10.96 ft (3.34 m)
Height including tailplane 11.84 ft (3.61 m)

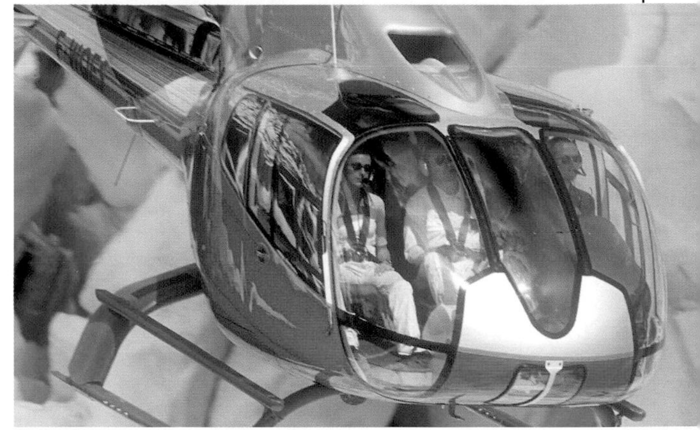

EUROCOPTER EC130

Country of origin: France.
Type: Light civil multi-purpose helicopter.
Power Plant: One Turboméca Arriel 2B1 turbine engine with 848 SHP (375 kW) performance.
Performance: Maximum speed 178 mph (287 km/h), cruising speed 161 mph (259 km/h) at sea level, maximum rate of climb 38 ft (11.6 m)/sec, service ceiling 16,500 ft (5,029 m), hover altitude at maximum load capacity with ground effect 11,900 ft (3,267 m), without ground effect 8,737 ft (2,663 m), range about 373 miles (600 km).
Weight: Empty weight 3,000 lbs (1,360 kg), maximum take-off weight 5,291 lbs (2,400 kg), with external load 6,173 lbs (2,800 kg).
Payload: Normally one pilot and six to a maximum of seven passengers, as EMS helicopter up to two recumbent patients and two attendants, maximum external load capacity 2,557 lbs (1,160 kg).
State of development: The EC 130 was introduced to the public without prior fanfare in February 2001. Test flights had been conducted quietly since June 1999. The first customer deliveries followed at the end of 2001. Reportedly, over 100 units have been ordered to date. The monthly production rate is three units.
Remarks: Although derived from the AS 350B3 (see pages 170/171), the EC 130, originally labelled AS 350B4, appears to be a new design. It has a slightly flatter fuselage that has been widened by 10 inches (25 cm) that provides 23% more interior space for passengers and luggage. Also new is the Fenestron tail rotor. Because of these and other measures, the EC 130 should be especially low on noise. Engine functions are monitored through a two-channel digital control system, which simplifies the work of the pilot. Eurocopter is quoting a base price of US$1.6 million.
Manufacturer: Eurocopter, Marignane plant, La Courneuve, France.

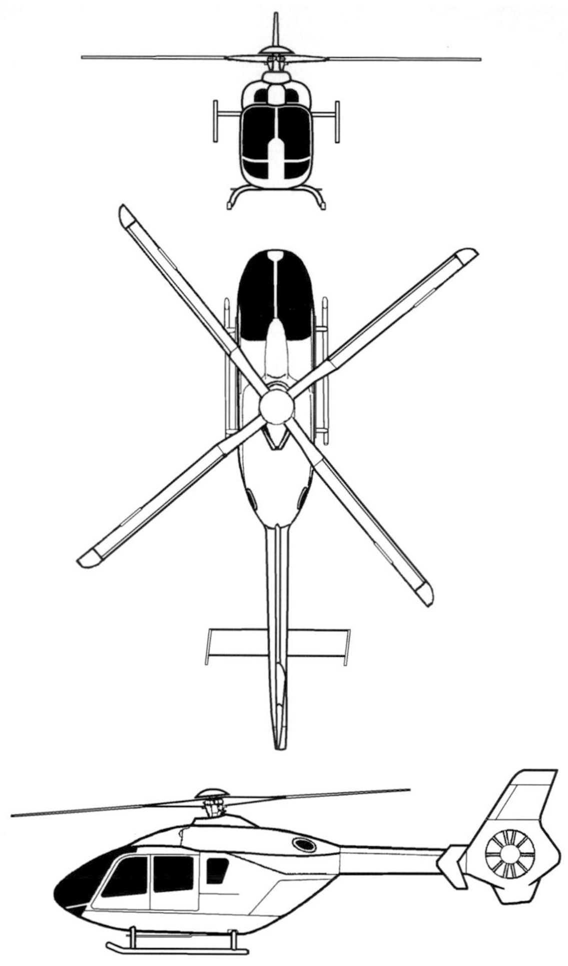

Dimensions:
Rotor diameter 33.46 ft (10.20 m)
Fuselage length 33.37 ft (10.17 m)
Height including rotor head 11 ft (3.35 m)
Height overall 11.65 ft (3.55 m)

EUROCOPTER (MBB) EC135

Country of origin: Germany.
Type: Light multi-purpose helicopter.
Power Plant: Two Turboméca Arrius 2B1A-1 turbine engines each with 606 SHP (452 kW) performance or two Pratt & Whitney Canada PW206B2 turbine engines each with 621 SHP (463 kW) performance.
Performance (PW206B2): Maximum speed 173 mph (278 km/h), maximum cruising speed 159 mph (256 km/h) at sea level, economic cruising speed 140 mph (226 km/h), maximum diagonal rate of climb 28 ft (8.4 m)/sec, service ceiling 17,000 ft (5,180 m), hover altitude with ground effect 13,583 ft (4,140 m), without ground effect 10,695 ft (3,260 m), maximum range 392 miles (630 km).
Weight: Empty weight 3,285 lbs (1,490 kg), maximum take off weight with external load 6,393 lbs (2,900 kg).
Payload: Six to seven people, in rescue deployment two stretchers and two helpers, maximum load capacity 2,756 lbs (1,250 kg).
State of development: The first prototype has been flying since February 15, 1994; deliveries commenced on July 31, 1996. To date, around 250 orders have been received, among them many from police forces and rescue organizations around the world. The orders include the German Border Guard which will receive 13 in addition to the 9 already on order, and 15 EC 135's for the German Army starting in 2000. The latest customer is Jordan, which has ordered up to 16 EC 135's.
Remarks: The EC 135 follows the latest technological principles: main and tail rotors are made from fibrous composite materials without any joints; transmission shaft with special vibration dampers, cabin structure in plastic, Fenestron tail rotor, etc. The rotor head no longer has blade bearings. The adjustment of the individual blades is achieved through elastic distortion of the plastic blade roots. The rotor hub and mast are forged from one single piece. The EC 135's are generally equipped for police work as follows: searchlight, night-sight equipment, TV camera and special navigation tools. A test unit has been flying since the beginning of 2002 with Fly-by-Light control. In this joint research project of Eurocopter and Liebherr, the impulses from optical signals are searched out. With this system all mechanical control elements could be dispensed in the future.
Manufacturer: Eurocopter Hubschrauber, Munich, Germany.

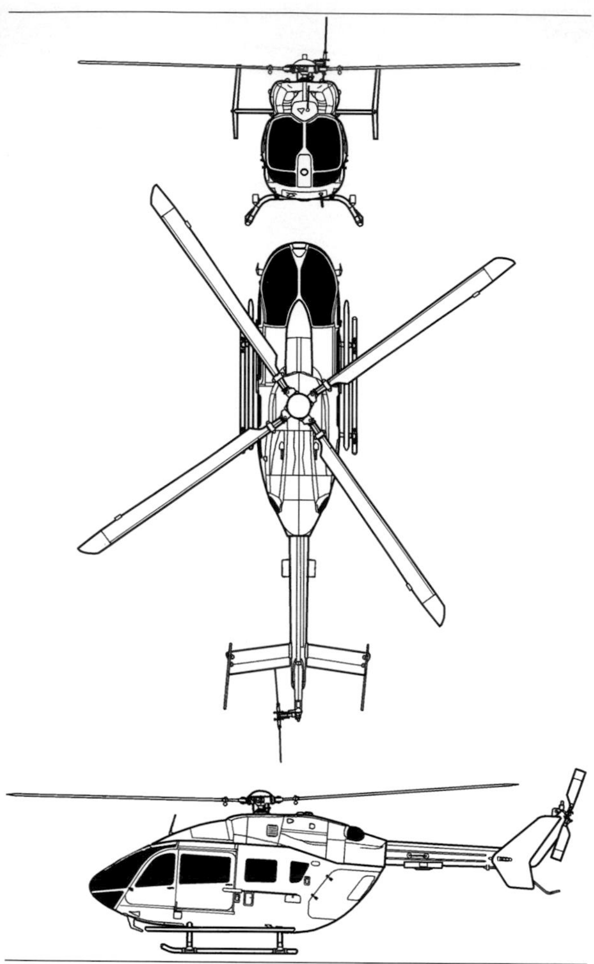

Dimensions:
Rotor diameter 36.09 ft (11.00 m)
Fuselage length 33.43 ft (10.19 m)
Height including rotor head 12.96 ft (3.95 m)

EUROCOPTER (MBB/KAWASAKI) EC145

Country of origin: Germany and Japan.
Type: Multi-purpose helicopter.
Power Plant: Two Turboméca Arriel 1E2 turbine engines each 750 SHP (550 kW) performance.
Performance: Maximum speed 168 mph (270 km/h) at sea-level, maximum cruising speed 152 mph (245 km/h), maximum diagonal rate of climb 28 ft (8.4 m)/sec, service ceiling 17,388 ft (5,300 m), hovering altitude with and without ground effect 6,988 ft (2,130 m), cruising range with normal fuel payload 4,162 miles (6,702 km), maximum deployment time 3.30 hours.
Weight: Empty weight 3,840 lbs (1,742 kg), normal take-off weight 7,385 lbs (3,350 kg), maximum take-off weight 7,826 lbs (3,550 kg).
Payload: Eight to twelve people, including pilots, two recumbent patients and two attendants in EMS operations, maximum payload 3,306 lbs (1,500 kg).
State of development: Maiden flight of the EC 145 on June 12, 1999. Orders to date include French Sécurité Civile 32, Gendarmerie 8, ADAC 2 and REGA 4. The deliveries commenced in the middle of 2001. To date, more than 300 units of the earlier models have been ordered for worldwide use.
Remarks: The latest model was first named BK117 C-2 and later renamed EC 145. It shows substantial improvements. The avionics and cockpit with NVG-equipment are completely new. The size of the cabin has clearly increased thanks to the lengthening of the fuselage by 16 inches (40 cm) and widening by 4 inches (10 cm). Also, lift-up doors simplify the loading procedures. This is why this version is particularly suitable for rescue operations. Because of the increased take-off weight, better cruising range performances have been achieved. The cockpit uses substantial elements of the EC135 (see pages 178/179). The frontal area of this model is particularly similar. The purchase price is approximately 5.9 million Euros. These days the EC 145 is being tested with a three-dimensional information display that increases visibility during night missions.
Manufacturer: Eurocopter Hubschrauber, MBB Division, Munich, Germany, as well as Kawasaki Heavy Industries Ltd., Gifu, Japan.

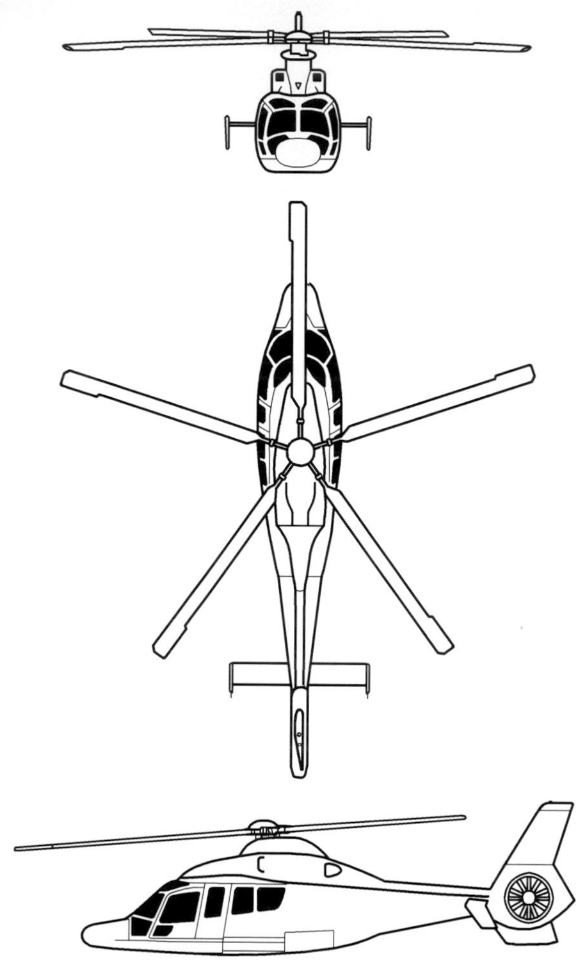

Dimensions:
Rotor diameter 41.34 ft (12.60 m)
Fuselage length 42.09 ft (12.83 m)
Height including rotor head 11.55 ft (3.52 m)
Height including vertical tail 14.27 ft (4.35 m)

EUROCOPTER EC155B

Country of origin: France.
Type: Civil and military multi-purpose helicopter.
Power Plant: Two Turboméca Arriel 2C turbine engines each with 851 SHP (635 kW) performance.
Performance: Maximum cruising speed at sea-level 164 mph (264 km/h), average cruising speed 157 mph (252 km/h) at sea-level, economic cruising speed 162 mph (260 km/h), maximum rate of climb 23 ft (7.0 m)/sec, hovering altitude with ground effect 8,366 ft (2,550 m), without ground effect 5,905 ft (1,800 m), cruising range 516 miles (830 km) at sea-level.
Weight: Empty weight 5,562 lbs (2,523 kg), maximum take-off weight with internal payload 10,582 lbs (4,800 kg), with external payload 11,023 lbs (5,000 kg).
Payload: One to two pilots and a maximum of 13 passengers or 14 soldiers, maximum payload 4,395 lbs (1,994 kg).
State of development: The EC155 has been flying since June 17, 1997. To date, about 40 units have been ordered including the German Federal Border Control 15 and Baden-Württemberg 2 with delivery beginning at the end of 1998.
Remarks: The EC155 represents a substantial advance over model AS 365N2. This model primarily distinguishes itself by a cabin that is 12 inches (30 cm) longer and 7 inches (18 cm) higher. The inside volume has increased by 40% and there is a much larger cargo compartment. The two Arriel 2C engines feature increased performance with a new Spheriflex-five blade rotor that has a diameter that is 24 inches (60 cm) larger. The ten-blade Fenestron-tail rotor has also been modified for noise reduction. The cockpit is completely digitalized. The standard model costs approximately US$5.5 million. A military version for transporting troops is being developed.
Manufacturer: Eurocopter (Aérospatiale), Marignane plant, La Courneuve, France.

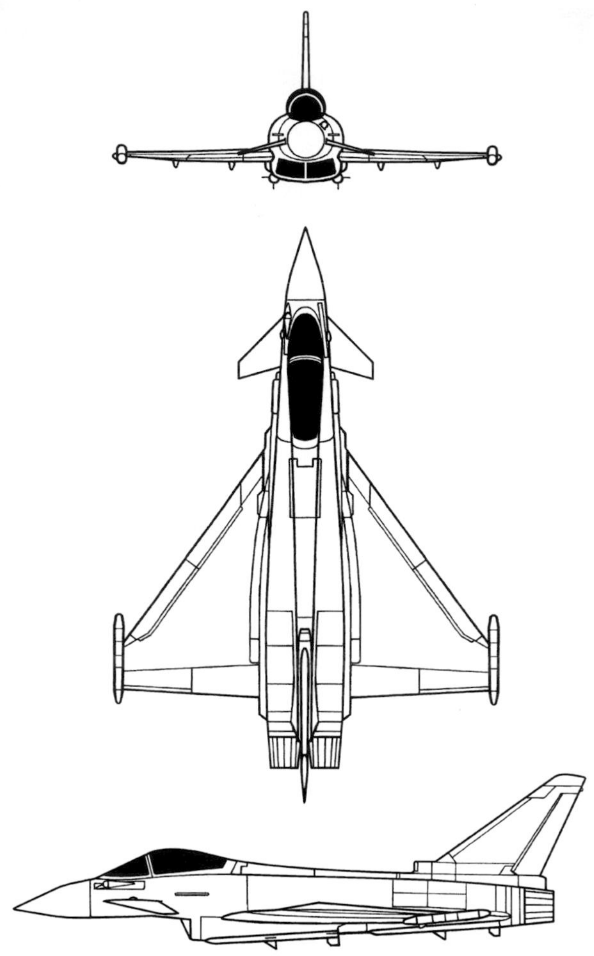

Dimensions:
Wingspan 35.92 ft (10.95 m)
Length 52.36 ft (15.96 m)
Height 17.32 ft (5.28 m)
Wing area 538.2 sq. ft (50.00 m^2)

EUROFIGHTER EJ2000 TYPHOON

Country of origin: United Kingdom, Germany, Italy and Spain.
Type: One-seat interceptor and air superiority fighter.
Power Plant: Two Eurojet EJ200 turbofan engines each with 13,487 lbs (61,000 kp/60 kN) static thrust without afterburner and 20,233 lbs (9,185 kp/90 kN) with afterburner.
Performance: Maximum speed at high altitudes Mach 2.0+, near-surface 864 mph (1,390 km/h), rate of climb to 32,808 ft (10,000 m) approximately two minutes, service ceiling 55,002 ft (16,765 m), action radius with two AIM-120 and AIM-132 air-to-air guided missiles each including external tanks 864 miles (1,390+ km), crossover cruising range with two external tanks 2,299 miles (3,700 km).
Weight: Empty weight 24,239 lbs (10,995 kg), maximum take-off weight 50,705 lbs (23,000 kg).
Armament: One 27-mm Mauser cannon in the fuselage and, for example, one group of six short-range AIM-132 air-to-air guided missiles and four medium-range AIM-120 air-to-air guided missiles. Maximum weapons load 14,329 lbs to 17,636 lbs (6,500 to 8,000 kg) at 13 weapons stations.
State of development: The first of seven prototypes had its initial flight test on March 27, 1994. The first serial models started flying 2002. At this time, 620 units have been ordered including United Kingdom 232, Federal Republic of Germany 180, Italy 121 and Spain 87. Initial deliveries of 148 aircraft have been made. Further orders from Greece (60) and Austria (18 – 24) are currently delayed until 2005 to 2007.
Remarks: The EJ2000 Typhoon is offered as a one- or two-seat fighter. The first units have been configured for interception duties. Beginning in 2004, the entire range of activities has become available. For the export market, Eurofighter is testing a model with additional tanks left and right at the fuselage above the wing. This will significantly increase the cruising range. Offsetting the additional weight will be a 15% increase in the performance of the engines. Tilting final nozzles and a reengineered cockpit with Voice-Control (speech-controlled airplane control) are being considered as further options.
Manufacturer: Eurofighter, Munich, Germany.

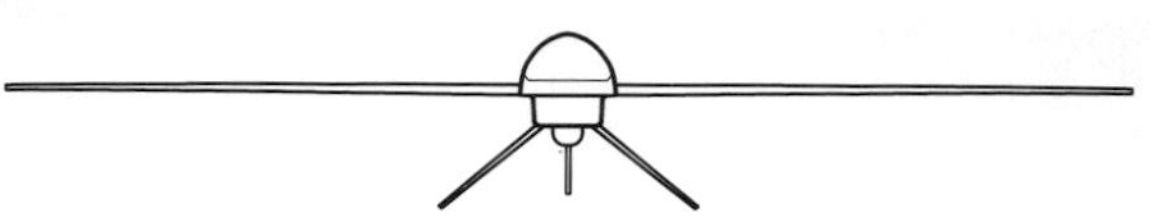

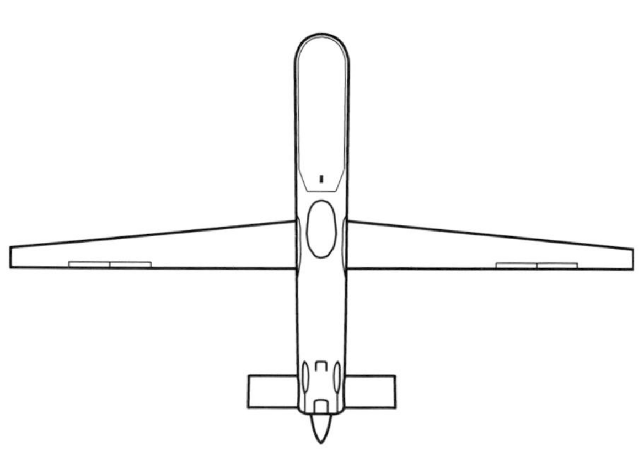

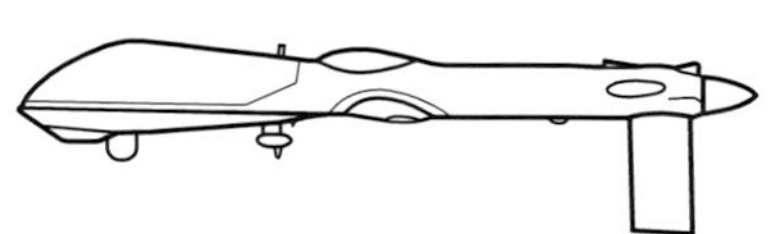

Dimensions:
Wingspan 47.9 ft (14.60 m)
Length 27 ft (8.23 m)

GENERAL ATOMICS RQ-1A PREDATOR

Country of origin: USA.
Type: Unmanned drone for reconnaissance and ELINT tasks at medium altitudes.
Power Plant: One Rotax 914 TC piston engine with thrust propeller with 106 PS (79 kW) performance.
Performance: Maximum speed approximately 140 mph (225 km/h), service ceiling 24,394 ft (7,600 m), flight duration 311 miles (500 km) from the base 24 hours, maximum flight duration 40 to 60 hours.
Weight: Normal take-off weight 1,873 lbs (850 kg), maximum take-off weight 2,292 lbs (1,040 kg).
Payload: Reconnaissance systems with a total weight of 450 lbs (204 kg).
State of development: The first unit was introduced in August 1994. For several years an unknown number of systems have been with the 11th Reconnaissance Wing of the USAF. Including the USN, a total of about 90 units will be acquired. Italy has ordered five (+ three options) systems.
Remarks: The RQ-1A is an improved version of the initial model GNAT-750, which is sporadically being used by the CIA for clandestine reconnaissance. The built-in "synthetic broadband reconnaissance radar" is equipped with a satellite data connection. A high-resolution video recording device enables the commanders of ground troops to obtain information regarding enemy territories by means of Data Link Real Time. The Predator can fly in all weather conditions. It is especially optimized for slow flights at average altitudes. The RQ-1A was frequently used for reconnaissance missions in the Bosnian war and in Afghanistan. One model of this type has a specialized radio-frequency system in order to fulfill ELINT-tasks. Several models are being tested including an armed model that can carry AGM-114 hellfire antitank guided missiles at two wing stations. A further test by the USAF is for a model with an FJ44-2A (MQ-9A) turbofan engine as well as one variant with a Honeywell TPE-331-10T propeller turbine engine. In this way, all flight performances will increase substantially in all fields.
Manufacturer: General Atomics Aeronautical Systems Inc., San Diego, USA.

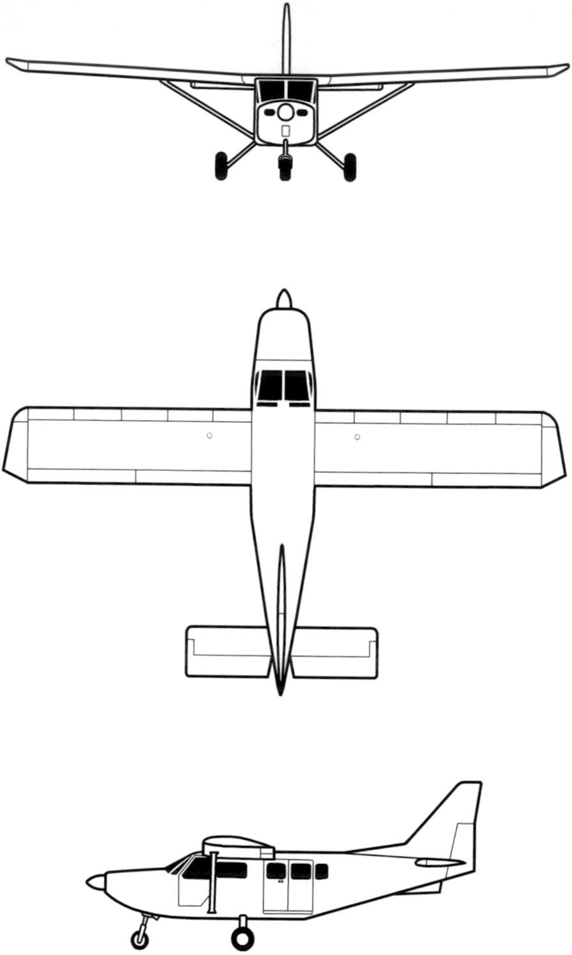

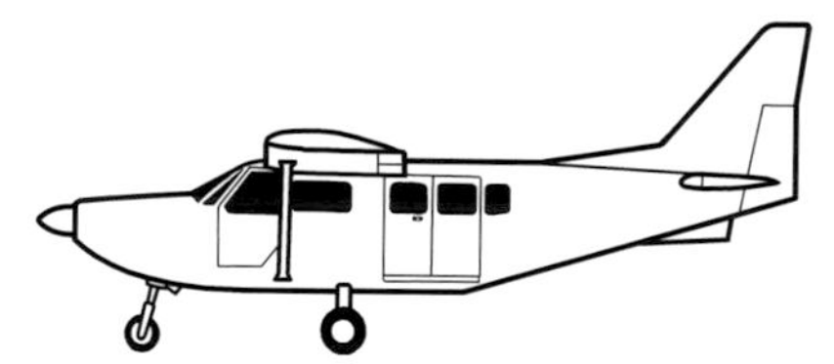

Dimensions:
Wingspan 40.68 ft (12.40 m)
Length 29.53 ft (9.00 m)
Height 12.79 ft (3.90 m)
Wing area 206.66 sq. ft (19.20 m^2)

GIPPSLAND AERONAUTICS GA-8 AIRVAN

Country of origin: Australia.
Type: Single engine STOL-multi-purpose airplane.
Power Plant: An air-cooled six-cylinder Textron Lycoming IO-540-K1A5 boxer engine with 300 PS (223 kW) performance.
Performance: Maximum speed 213 mph (342 km/h), normal cruising speed 139 mph (224 km/h), initial rate of climb 13 ft (4.0 m)/sec, service ceiling 20,012 ft (6,100 m), cruising range 839 miles (1,350 km), maximum 1,068 miles (1,720 km).
Weight: Empty weight 2,197 lbs (997 kg), maximum take-off weight 3,999 lbs (1,814 kg).
Payload: Pilot and up to seven passengers, as freighter maximum payload of about 1,322 lbs (600 kg).
State of development: The first flight of the prototype was on March 3, 1995. The Airvan was certified in December 2000. About 20 aircraft are in operation. Currently, the option of franchised manufacturing by companies outside Australia is being explored.
Remarks: This extremely robust and very simply constructed multi-purpose airplane is intended for use in developing countries. Therefore, this model is being offered at a price unrivaled in its category (about US$310,000). This aircraft utilizes short take-off and landing characteristics and can operate from unprepared runways. Control, avionics and interior design are kept very simple and limited to what is absolutely necessary. The landing gear cannot be retracted. Currently, replacing the Lycoming engine with a Thielert TAE 135 diesel engine with 135 PS (100 kW) performance is being considered. A lengthened ten-passenger variant, equipped with a Rolls-Royce 250 propeller turbine engine with 420 SHP (310 kW) is being developed.
Manufacturer: Gippsland Aeronautics, Morwell Victoria, Australia.

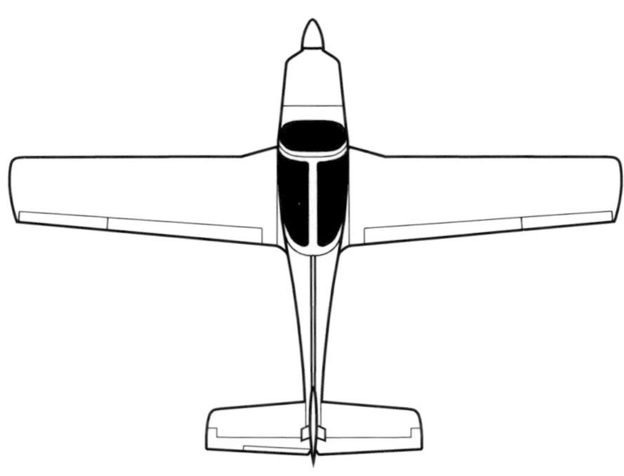

Dimensions:
Wingspan 32.80 ft (10.00 m)
Length 24.93 ft (7.60 m)
Height 7.87 ft (2.40 m)
Wing area 131.42 sq. ft (12.21 m^2)

GROB G 115E TUTOR

Country of origin: Germany.
Type: Basic flight school trainer.
Power Plant: One air-cooled Textron Lycoming AEIO-360 six cylinder horizontally opposed engine with 180 PS (134 kW) performance.
Performance: Maximum permissible speed at sea level 212 mph (341 km/h), cruising speed at 75% output 155 mph (250 km/h) at 8,202 ft (2,500 m), rate of climb 23 ft (7.11 m)/sec, service ceiling 15,994 ft (4,875 m), range 598 miles (963 km), maximum flight duration 5 hours 40 minutes.
Weight: Empty weight 1,455 lbs (660 kg), maximum take-off weight 2,183 lbs (990 kg).
Payload: Flight student and instructor.
State of development: First flight of the initial model G 115A in November 1985, and the G 115T on June 11, 1992. Thus far, over 200 units have been ordered by, among others, the United Arab Emirates. The RAF obtained 99 G 115E for its 15 university air squadrons in September 1999.
Remarks: The G115D and E models that are suitable for acrobatic use (+ 6g / -4 G) are completely manufactured from composite materials. These models are particularly heat and fatigue resistant and have a lifespan of up to 15,000 hours. The following versions are available: G 115C and D with fixed landing gear and an engine in the performance category from 160 to 180 PS (119 to 134 kW), the G 115T with retractable landing gear and the more powerful AE10-540DA5 engine with 260 PS (194 kW) performance and the G115TA with air conditioning. The G115TE complies extensively with the D version, but has been adapted to the requirements of the RAF.
Manufacturer: Grob Luft- und Raumfahrt GmbH & Co. KG., Tussenhausen-Mattsies, Federal Republic of Germany.

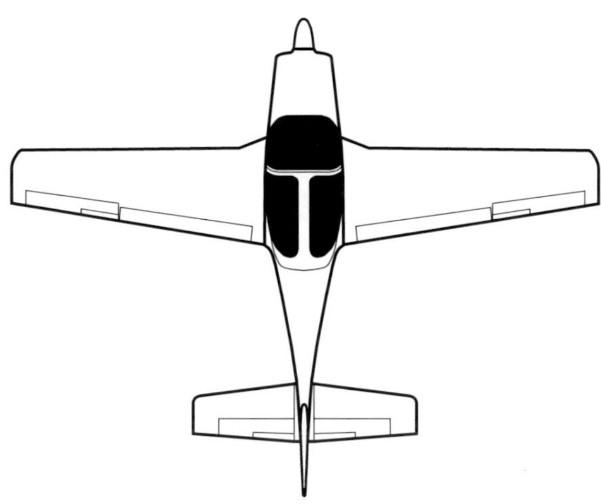

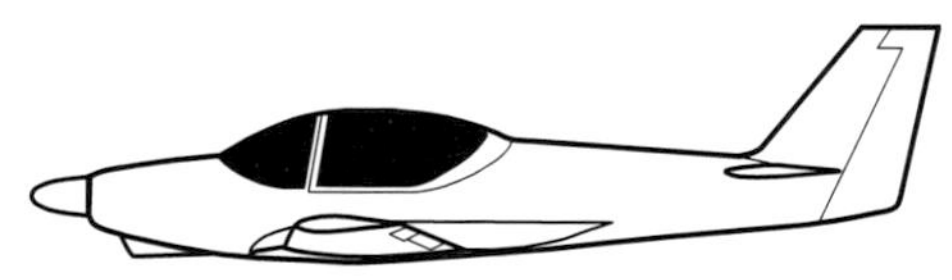

Dimensions:
Wingspan 33.39 ft (10.18 m)
Length 26.44 ft (8.06 m)
Height 8.43 ft (2.57 m)
Wing area 143.16 sq. ft (13.30 m^2)

GROB G 120A

Country of origin: Germany.
Type: Basic, advanced and acrobatic trainer.
Power Plant: One air-cooled Textron Lycoming AEIO-540-D4D5 six cylinder horizontally opposed engine with 260 PS (194 kW) performance.
Performance: Maximum speed at sea level 199 mph (320 km/h), cruising speed at 75% output 191 mph (307 km/h) at 5,003 ft (1,525 m), rate of climb 24 ft (7.21 m)/sec, range 954 miles (1,535 km).
Weight: Maximum take-off weight for acrobatics 2,976 lbs (1,350 kg), for training 3,175 lbs (1,440 kg).
Payload: Flight student and instructor, maximum payload between 705 and 904 lbs (320 and 410 kg).
State of development: The first flight took place in 2000 with production starting the following year. After certification at the beginning of 2002, the first deliveries were made. The Israeli Air Force purchased 17 units of this model as trainers. Before this, Lufthansa had already ordered six G120.
Remarks: With this type of aircraft, Grob wants to cover the entire field from beginner to advanced training to acrobatics. Thanks to the comprehensive avionics and an EFIS cockpit, the model is also suitable for instrument flight training. In contrast to the G 115, the G 120 has retractable landing gear. As with all Grob light airplanes, the construction is mainly made from carbon fiber composite material. This principle enables a high degree of sturdiness, a long lifespan of the airframe, minimum weight and economical usage. The aircraft ordered by Israel will be operated by the private company Elbit Systems Ltd. to create a comprehensive training system for the Air Force.
Manufacturer: Grob Luft- und Raumfahrt GmbH & Co. KG., Tussenhausen-Mattsies, Germany.

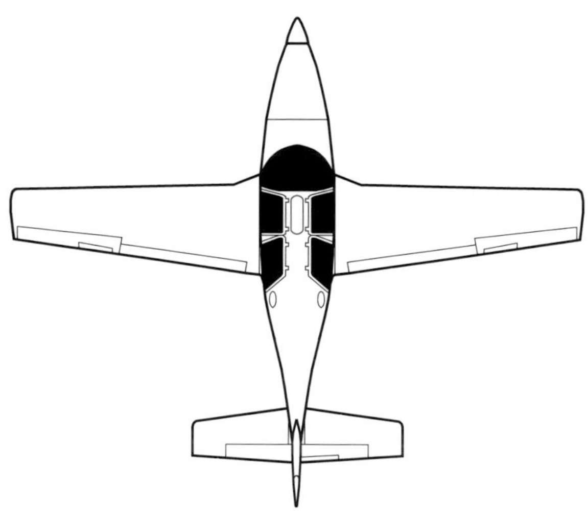

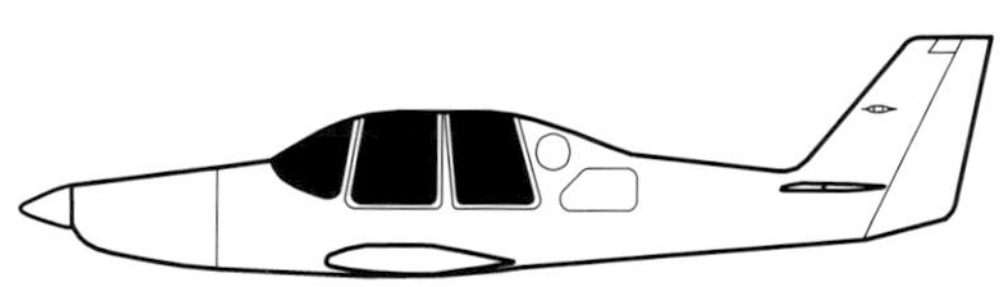

Dimensions:
Wingspan 33.79 ft (10.30 m)
Length 29.19 ft (8.90 m)
Height 9.18 ft (2.80 m)
Wing area 143.16 sq. ft (13.30 m^2)

GROB G 140TP

Country of origin: Germany.
Type: Light multi-purpose aircraft.
Power Plant: One Rolls Royce 250 B17F propeller turbine engine with 450 SHP (335 kW) performance.
Performance: Maximum cruising speed 246 mph (395 km/h) at 10,006 ft (3,050 m), normal cruising speed 196 mph (315 km/h), maximum vertical rate of climb 45 ft (13.70 m)/sec, range with four passengers and 30 minute reserve 662 miles (1,065 km), maximum range 1,324 miles (2,130 km).
Weights: Maximum take-off weight 3,638 lbs (1,650 kg).
Payload: Four people including pilot, maximum payload 1,213 lbs (550 kg).
State of development: The prototype was presented for the first time at the air show in Paris in June 2001. The first flight was on December 12, 2002. The development schedule has been delayed while two fleet orders for the G 120 are filled. For that reason sales are just now beginning and numbers are not yet known.
Remarks: The G 140TP is intended to be a trainer for civilian or military operators as well as for acrobatics. This model is also suitable as a light, highly cost-efficient corporate aircraft. The four- person cabin is spaciously designed to make longer trips more comfortable. The fuselage and wings are completely made from composite material. The G 140TP has retractable landing gear and a five-blade Mühlbauer MTV-5 propeller. The G 140TP can be ordered with or without a pressure cabin, depending on the customer's needs. The purchase price will start at US$890,000.
Manufacturer: Grob Luft- und Raumfahrt GmbH & Co. KG., Tussenhausen-Mattsies, Germany.

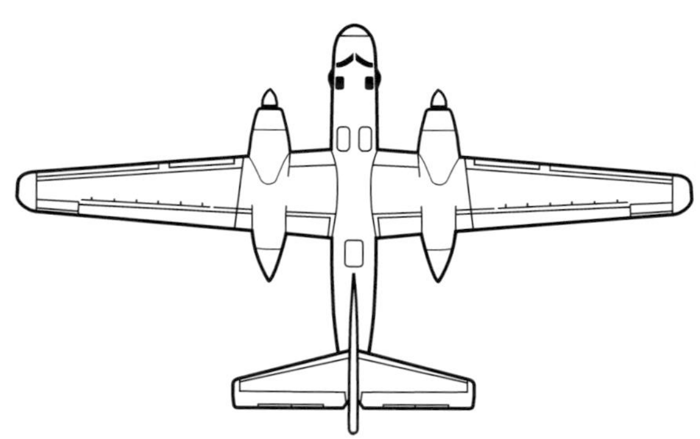

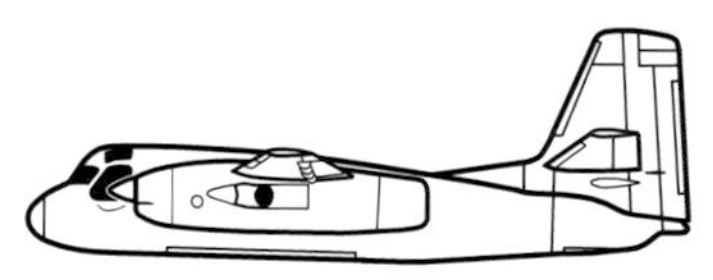

Dimensions:
Wingspan 72.60 ft (22.13 m)
Length 43.50 ft (13.26 m)
Height 16.60 ft (5.06 m)
Wing area 496 sq. ft (46.08 m^2)

MARSH/GRUMMAN S-2T TURBO TRACKER

Country of origin: USA.
Type: Water bomber and submarine tracker.
Power Plant: Two Garret TPE331 propeller turbine engines each with 1,645 SHP (1,227 kW) performance.
Performance: Maximum speed at sea level 300 mph (482 km/h), cruising speed 290 mph (467 km/h), service ceiling 23,996 ft (7,314 m), range without reserves 746 miles (1,200 km).
Weights: Empty weight 13,841 lbs (6,278 kg), maximum take-off weight 29,000 lbs (13,154 kg).
Payload: Two pilots and/or system operators, between 793 and 1,189 gallons (3,000 and 4,500 l) when used as a water bomber.
Armament: Six weapon stations underneath the wings with missiles, torpedoes and bombs.
State of development: The redesigned version of the Turbo Tracker first flew on November 24, 1986, and the submarine tracker model on July 26, 1991. Since then, with a few interruptions, redesigns have been produced for, among others, the Argentine Navy (6 submarine trackers), the French Protection Civile (11 water bombers - redesign by Conair), the Taiwanese Navy (32 submarine trackers), the Turkish Forestry Service (15 water bombers planned) and the US Forestry Service in California (8 water bombers + an option for a further 15). Production continues. Starting with the original design of the Grumman S-2 tracker, almost 1,500 models were built between 1953 and 1967, and operated, among others, by 12 navies and air forces.
Remarks: Over the years, several variants of the proven and robust Grumman S-2 submarine tracker were equipped with propeller turbines. The most significant of these variants is the redesign to a water bomber. Here, among other things, the earlier internal weapons load was replaced and made larger for holding water and chemicals used in extinguishing fires. In addition, these Turbo Trackers received completely new avionics. The redesign was taken even further, e.g., in Argentina for submarine use: EFIS cockpit, avionics from Elbit, search radar, FLIR, MAD and reduced empty weight.
Manufacturer: Marsh Aviation Company, Mesa, Arizona, USA.

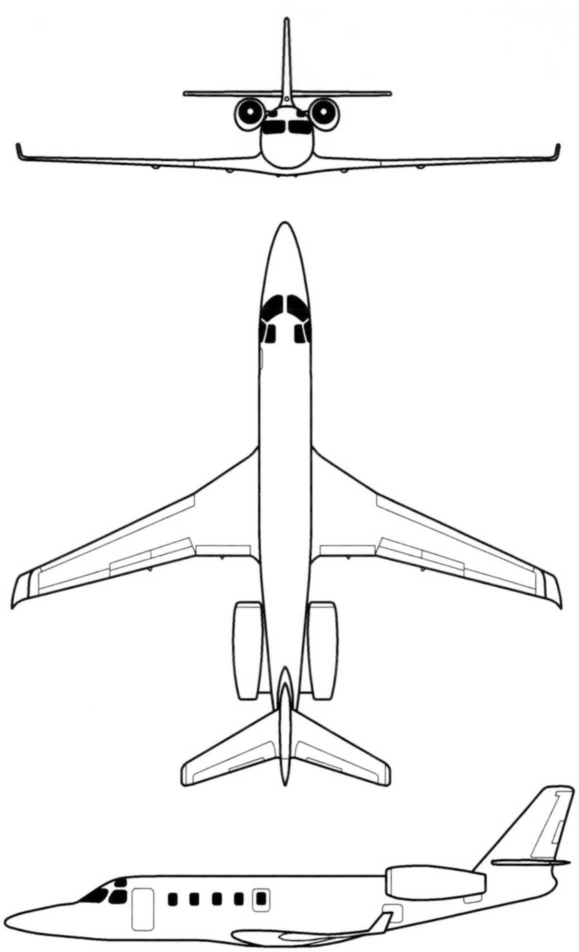

Dimensions:
Wingspan 54.59 ft (16.64 m)
Length 55.57 ft (16.94 m)
Height 18.17 ft (5.54 m)
Wing area 316.46 sq. ft (29.40 m^2)

GULFSTREAM G100

Country of origin: Israel/USA.
Type: Corporate aircraft.
Power Plant: Two Honeywell 731-40R-200G turbofan engines each with 4,249 lbs (1,930 kp/18.90 kN) static thrust.
Performance (SPX): Maximum cruising speed 539 mph (867 km/h [Mach 0.84]), long-haul cruising speed 495 mph (796 km/h [Mach 0.82]), rate of climb 58 ft (17.8 m)/sec, service ceiling 45,000 ft (13,716 m), range at maximum fuel intake with four passengers and IFR reserves (SP) 3,140 miles (5,053 km), (SPX) 3,418 miles (5,500 km).
Weight (SPX): Empty weight 13,700 lbs (6,214 kg), maximum take-off weight 24,645 lbs (11,179 kg).
Payload: Two-crew cockpit and normally six to a maximum of nine passengers depending on the internal configuration, maximum payload 3,329 lbs (1,510 kg).
State of development: The prototype of the IAI Astra SP has been flying since 1989, and the prototype of the SPX since August 16, 1994. Delivery of the SPX began in January 1996. Both the SP and SPX versions are being offered at the same time. Thus far about 180 units have been ordered, and of these about 150 are currently flying. About 12 G 100 are manufactured annually.
Remarks: In comparison to the original Astra design, the G 100, formerly designated as Astra SP (**S**pecial **P**erformance), has a revised internal configuration and aerodynamic improvements for an increased service ceiling and range performance. In addition, the cockpit has been completely redesigned and equipped with EFIS displays. It has TFE731-3A engines each with 3,700 lbs (1,680 kp/16.46 kN) performance. Thanks to its new wings and a higher performance engine, the SPX version achieves a considerably higher cruising speed and has a greater range. It is equipped with the avionics Collins Pro Line 4 set. Recently the manufacturer introduced a new model called the Gulfstream G 150, which combines the wings of the G 100 with a large fuselage. The first flight took place in 2003. NetJet has already ordered 50 units (+50 options) with the first delivery set for the second quarter of 2005 and continuing through 2010.
Manufacturer: Gulfstream Aerospace Corp. (subsidiary of DaimlerChrysler Corp.), Savannah, Georgia, USA and Israel Aircraft Industries Ltd., Ben-Gurion International Airport, Israel.

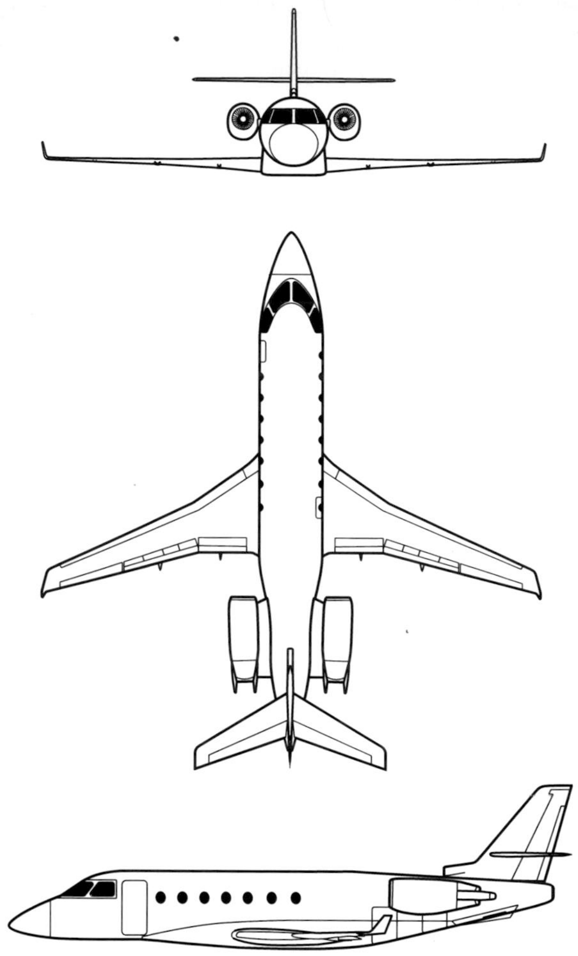

Dimensions:
Wingspan: 58.1 ft (17.71 m)
Length: 62.24 ft (18.97 m)
Height: 21.42 ft (6.53 m)
Wing area: 369 sq. ft (34.28 m^2)

GULFSTREAM G 200

Country of origin: Israel/USA.
Type: Corporate aircraft.
Power Plant: Two Pratt & Whitney Canada PW306A turbofan engines each with 6,065 lbs (2,740 kp/26.98 kN) static thrust.
Performance: Maximum speed 541 mph (870 km/h [Mach 0.85]), long haul cruising speed 497 mph (800 km/h [Mach 0.82]), service ceiling 45,000 ft (13,716 m), range with four passengers and IFR-reserves 4,138 miles (6,660 km).
Weight: Empty weight 19,800 lbs (8,981 kg), maximum take-off weight 35,450 lbs (16,080 kg).
Payload: Two pilots and usually eight passengers in a comfortable configuration or up to 18 persons in narrow rows of three-seats with aisle, maximum load 4,200 lbs (1,905 kg).
State of development: The first of four prototypes flew on December 25, 1997, followed by the second on May 21, 1998. Deliveries began at the beginning of 1999. Over 100 units (with options) have been ordered thus far, half of which have been already produced. 24 units are produced annually in Israel, with subsequent interior configuration in the US.
Remarks: The earlier Galaxy, newly designated as Gulfstream G 200, is a result of the cooperation between Israeli IAI and an American financial group, and is a further development of the Astra SPX/G 100 (see pages 198-199). While the wing is largely that of the earlier aircraft, the G 200 boasts a newly designed, significantly larger fuselage. With interior dimensions of length 24 ft (7.44 m), width 7 ft (2.18 m) and height 6 ft (1.91 m), the G 200 meets considerably higher demands. In keeping with the majority of the latest generation of corporate aircraft, the cockpit is equipped with multifunction displays, in this case, supplied by Rockwell Collins. Purchase price of a fully equipped G 200 amounts to approximately US$17 million. Owing to a weight reduction program of about 661 lbs (300 kg), the aircraft is likely to achieve the originally promised maximum permissible load and the range results.
Manufacturer: Gulfstream Aerospace Corp. (subsidiary of DaimlerChrysler Corp.), Savannah, Georgia, USA, Israel Aircraft Industries Ltd., Ben-Gurion International Airport, Israel.

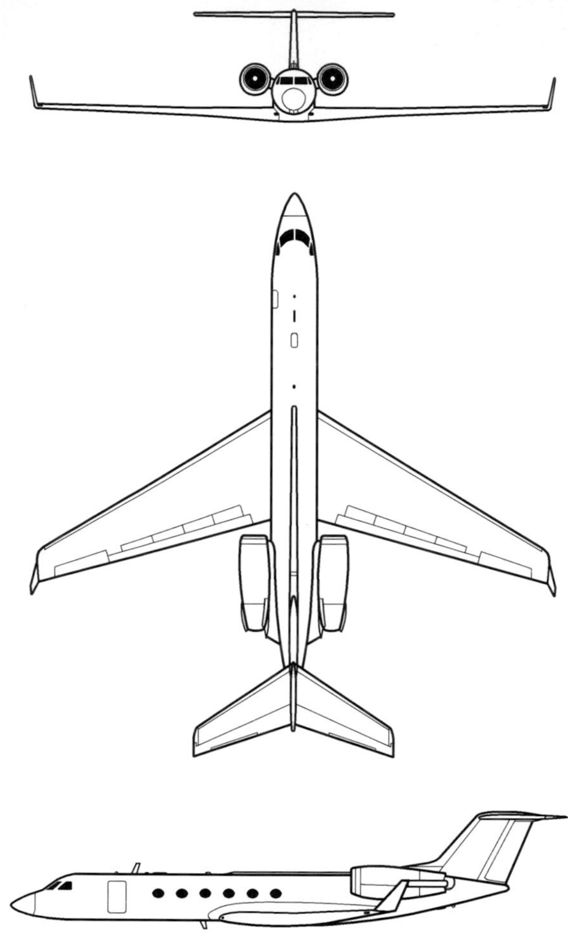

Dimensions:
Wingspan: 93.50 ft (28.50 m)
Length: 96.46 ft (29.40 m)
Height: 25.26 ft (7.70 m)
Wing area: 1,137 sq. ft. (105.63 m^2)

GULFSTREAM AEROSPACE GULFSTREAM V

Country of origin: USA.
Type: Long-haul corporate aircraft.
Power Plant: Two BMW/Rolls-Royce BR 710-48 turbofan engines each with 14,748 lbs (6,690 kp/65.6 kN) static thrust.
Performance: Maximum speed 562 mph (904 km/h), long haul cruising speed 529 mph (851 km/h), initial rate of climb 70 ft (21.3 m)/sec, service ceiling 50,850 ft (15,500 m), range with eight passengers and maximum fuel capacity with IFR-reserves 7,485 miles (12,046 km).
Weight: Empty weight 46,800 lbs (21,228 kg), maximum take-off weight 90,500 lbs (41,050 kg).
Payload: Two pilots in cockpit and usually 13-15 to a maximum of 19 passengers, maximum load 6,504 lbs (2,950 kg).
State of development: The first prototype flew on November 28, 1995 with the initial deliveries beginning in mid-1997. By the end of 2002, approximately 170 units were in service. The USAF operates 20 as the C-37A VIP transporter, while the US Army and the US Coast Guard have one each. The V-SP model (see photo) took off on a maiden flight on July 18, 2002. Thus far, some 40 units have been ordered. Approximately 30 aircraft of both models are produced annually.
Remarks: The largest Gulfstream model is the first corporate aircraft, which, under normal operation, achieves a range of over 6,214 miles (10,000 km). For this purpose, the previous Gulfstream IV model has been completely redesigned. The fuselage boasts an aspect ratio of 7.87 ft (2.40 m) and thus offers significantly higher passenger comfort with higher baggage payload. The cabin now measures 50 ft (15.3 m). The wing is a wholly new construction to optimize it for the required range. The plane is fitted with the digital Honeywell SPZ-8000 avionics system with six multi-function screens. With the V-SP, Gulfstream offers an improved model with a range of 7,767 miles (12,500 km) and a new cockpit. It has an option of incorporating higher output engines. Israel has obtained three Gulfstream V designed for ELINT operations. Furthermore, an AEW version is to be purchased. The Japanese Coast Guard operates two aircraft for sea surveillance and special operations.
Manufacturer: Gulfstream Aerospace Corp. (subsidiary of DaimlerChrysler Corp.), Savannah, Georgia, USA.

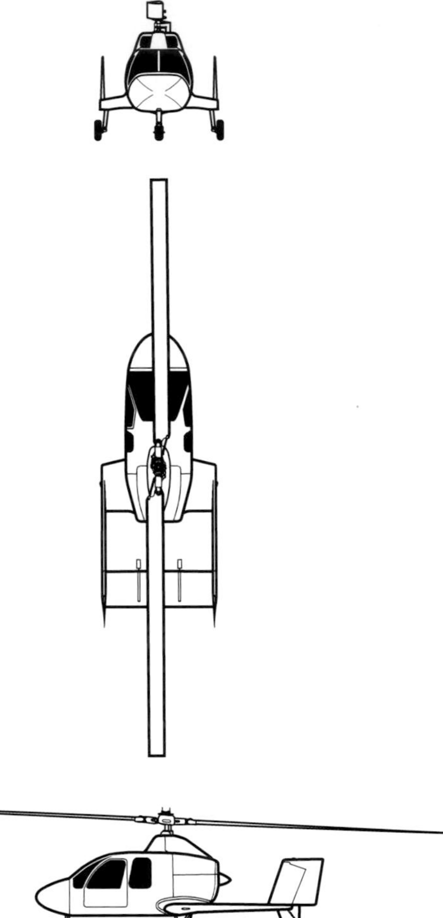

Dimensions:
Rotor diameter 42 ft (12.80 m)
Fuselage length 24 ft (7.32 m)
Height including rotor head 13.5 ft (4.11 m)

GYROPLANE GROEN HAWK 4T

Country of origin: USA.
Type: Light autogyro.
Power Plant: One Rolls-Royce 250 B17C gas turbine engine with 420 SHP (313 kW) performance.
Performance (data supplied by manufacturer): Maximum speed at sea level 148 mph (238 km/h), cruising speed 132 mph (212 km/h) at sea level, lowest possible speed 47 mph (75 km/h), maximum rate of climb 25 ft (7.6 m)/sec, service ceiling 15,990 ft (4,875 m), range 364 miles (585 km).
Weight: Maximum take-off weight 3,307 lbs (1,500 kg).
Payload: Pilot and three passengers.
State of development: To date, the one prototype flew on July 12, 2000. Production decisions have not yet been made. However, reportedly purchase orders for 150 Hawk T4's have already been placed. The PR of China is apparently interested in obtaining 200 units.
Remarks: The Hawk T4 revisits the 80-year-old idea of a combined wing/rotary aircraft, or a gyroplane, in a modern form. Thanks to the robust, simple and cost-effective design, the Hawk 4T is capable of performing diverse tasks which usually require the use of both a helicopter and a winged aircraft. Specifically, these include surveillance and police tasks. The rotor and the thrust propeller are connected to a single engine, which they share depending on the flight status of the aircraft. Therefore, take-off is not totally vertical. It requires a runway of approximately 25 ft (7.5 m) in length. The first units of the Hawk 4T are equipped with fixed landing gear. A standard retractable landing gear is planned for the future. The purchase price for the first units will be about US$750,000. An eight-seat version is currently being tested.
Manufacturer: Groen Brothers Aviation, Glendale plant, Arizona, Salt Lake City, Utah, USA.

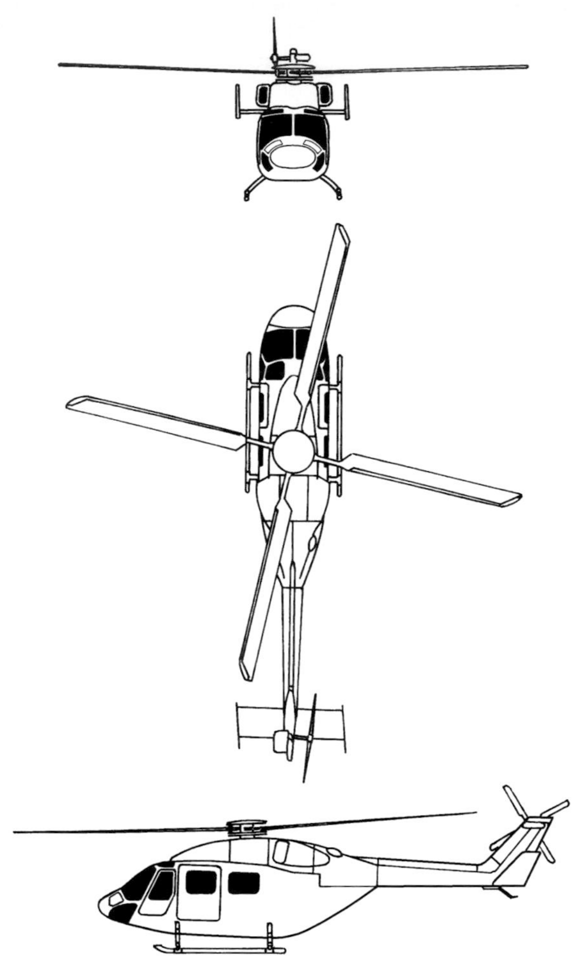

Dimensions:
Rotor diameter 43.31 ft (13.20 m)
Fuselage length 42.29 ft (12.89 m)
Height including rotor head 12.34 ft (3.76 m)

HAL DRUV

Country of origin: India.
Type: Civil and military multi-purpose helicopter.
Power Plant: Two Turboméca TM 333-2B gas turbine engines each with 1,000 SHP (746 kW) performance.
Performance: Maximum speed 174 mph (280 km/h) at sea level, cruising speed 152 mph (245 km/h), maximum diagonal rate of climb 30 ft (9.0 m)/sec, service ceiling 19,690 ft (6,000 m), hovering altitude without ground effect 9,843+ ft (3000+ m), range with 1,543 lbs (700 kg) load 249 miles (400 km) at sea level, maximum range 497 miles (800 km).
Weight: Empty weight (Air Force version) 4,885 lbs (2,216 kg), (Navy version) 5,185 lbs (2,352 kg), maximum take-off weight (Army version) 12,130 lbs (5,500 kg), (Air Force version) 8,818 lbs (4,000 kg), (Navy version) 11,020 lbs (5,000 kg).
Payload: Two pilots and up to 14 passengers, maximum payload as external load 3,307 lbs (1,500 kg).
State of development: The test flight for the first of four prototypes was in August 1992. Indian Armed Forces require 300 ALH's (Army - 120, Air Force - 60, Navy - 120). About 12 units in various versions have been produced, eight of these were delivered by the end of 2002. Production will amount to 24 aircraft the first year and about 36 units annually thereafter.
Remarks: The Druv, initially designated as ALH, is produced in various versions: (Army) troop transporter and supply helicopter, for antitank and mine-laying missions, all equipped with skid chassis; (Navy) communication and evacuation duties as well as SAR and ASW tasks, equipped with a retractable three-point wheel landing gear, collapsible main and tail rotors and sonar; (Air Force) rescue helicopter, multi-purpose transporter. Also, a civilian version, first flown in 1999, is being offered for, normally, up to 12 passengers. Main and tail rotors are jointless, made of fiber composite materials, the fuselage consists of aluminum, carbon and kevlar. At present, tests are being carried out to equip the Navy version with stronger TM332C2 engines, each with 1,200 SHP (895 kW) performance. Generally, it is planned to increase performance at high altitudes by installing more powerful engines.
Manufacturer: HAL Hindustan Aeronautics Ltd., Bangalore, India.

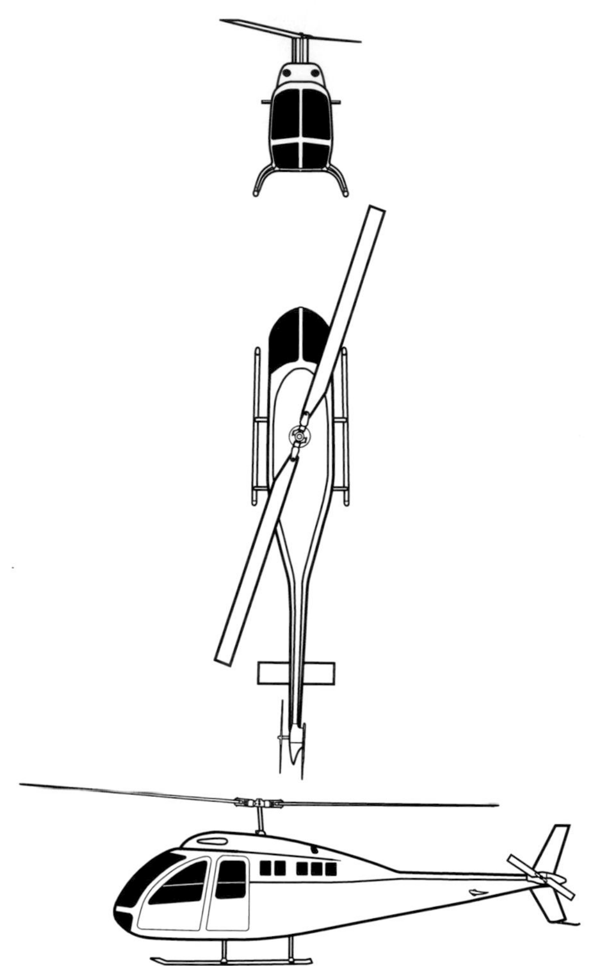

Dimensions:
No data available.

IAC SHAHED 274

Country of origin: Iran.
Type: Civil and military multi-purpose light helicopter.
Power Plant: Two Allison 250-C20B gas turbine engines each with 420 SHP (313 kW) performance.
Performance (very tentative data): Maximum speed 112 mph (180 km/h), service ceiling 16,400 ft (5,000 m), range with maximum internal fuel load 311 miles (500 km).
Weight: No data available.
Payload: Two pilots and up to five passengers.
Armament: Aircraft is expected to carry light weapons.
State of development: It is unknown when the first model, formerly named Shahed X5, underwent its initial flight test. The Islamic Revolutionary Corps (successor to the Iranian Air Force) received 30 units. To date, at least three other units have been delivered.
Remarks: Because of many years of international sanctions, Iran has been forced either to modernize helicopters purchased earlier mainly from the US and Italy or to develop totally new models. The first category includes the Panha 2061 (Bell JetRanger) as well as variants of the Bell models 205 (renamed Shabaviz 2-75) and 212. Shahed 274 is, however, totally new. With the exception of the engines and parts of the avionics, it is a complete Iranian development. It is assumed that it is based on the Bell 206 JetRanger. Fuselage, dynamic components and tail controls represent new design engineering. Since the Shahed 274 conforms to international standards, IAC will be able to offer it for sale abroad.
Manufacturer: Iran Aircraft Company, Iran.

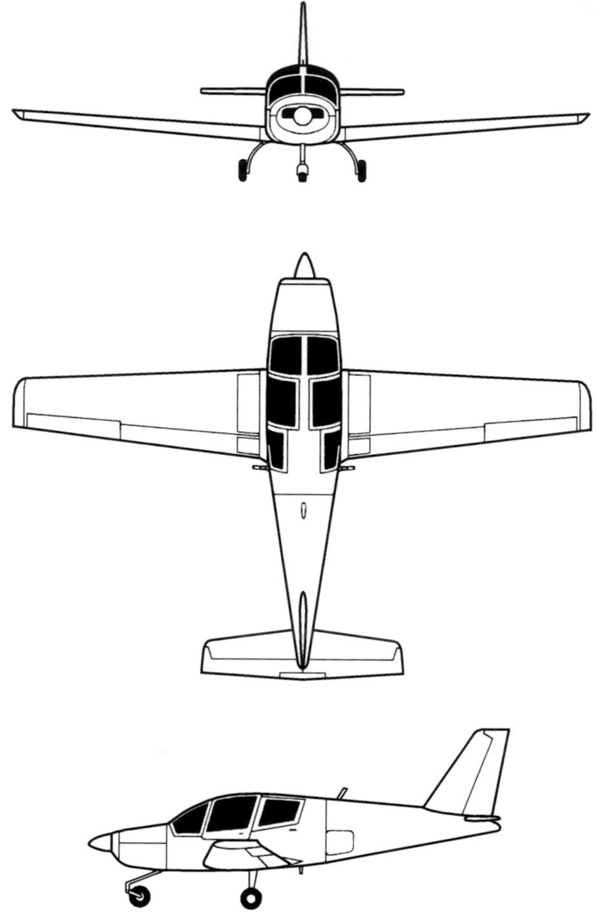

Dimensions:
Wingspan: 34.65 ft (10.56 m)
Length: 26.1 ft (7.95 m)
Height: 10.27 ft (3.13 m)
Wing area: 18.34 sq. ft (14.71 m^2)

ILYUSCHIN IL-103

Country of origin: Russia.
Type: Two-seat beginner trainer or five-seat touring airplane.
Power Plant: One Teledyne Continental IO-360ES air-cooled six-cylinder boxer engine with 210 PS (157 kW) performance.
Performance: Maximum speed 211 mph (340 km/h), cruising speed 137 mph (220 km/h), initial rate of climb 26 ft (8 m)/sec, service ceiling 9,843 ft (3,000 m), range with three passengers about 497 miles (800 km).
Weight: Empty weight 1,984 lbs (900 kg), maximum take-off weight as trainer 2,833 lbs (1,285 kg), as touring airplane 3,219 lbs (1,460 kg).
Additional load: Normally four people including pilot to a maximum of five people, maximum payload 970 lbs (440 kg).
State of development: The test flight of the prototype was on May 17, 1994 and the first of 20 serial aircraft followed in January 1995. Also, in that year, the IL-103 obtained Russian certification. To date, orders for approximately 180 IL-103 (+120 options) have been received, including Uzbekistan (100), Peru (6) and South Korea (23). Ilyuschin hopes to be able to sell over 1,000 IL-103's domestically and overseas.
Remarks: IL-103 is a low wing aircraft with conventional, all-metal construction and fixed, three-point landing gear. Originally developed for civil and military service as a trainer, it is also being offered as a touring airplane. The trainer is equipped with two steering columns and visual flight instrumentation, whereas the touring version features a steering yoke. In cooperation with AlliedSignal, the aircraft offers an integral Western made avionics package. The base price is US$155,000. Aircraft produced for Uzbekistan are built as agricultural crop dusters. The next version will be designated the IL-103RG and will be fitted with retractable landing gear.
Manufacturer: Ilyuschin Design Bureau, Moscow, MAPO-MiG-plant, Lukhovitsy, Russia.

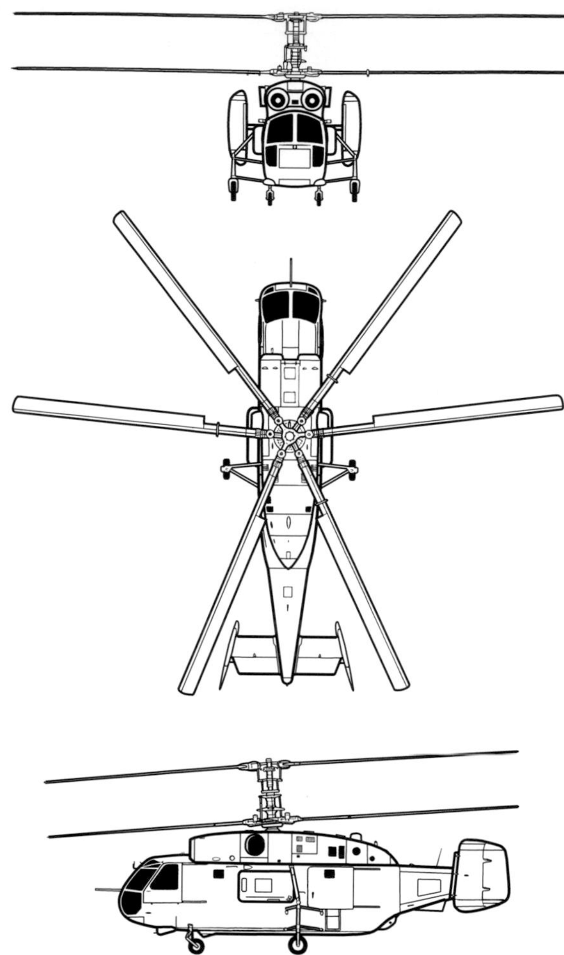

Dimensions:
Rotor diameter (each individual) 52.17 ft (15.90 m)
Fuselage length 37.1 ft (11.30 m)
Height including rotor head 17.72 ft (5.40 m)

KAMOV KA-31/-32

Country of origin: Russia.
Type: (KA-31) carrier-based AEW-helicopter, (KA-32) medium weight civil multi-purpose helicopter.
Power Plant (KA-32A-11BC): Two Klimov TV3-117VMA gas turbine engines each with 2,225 SHP (1,658 kW) performance.
Performance (KA-32 at 24,250 lbs/11,000 kg): Maximum speed 155 mph (250 km/h) at sea level, maximum cruising speed 143 mph (230 km/h), service ceiling 19,690 ft (6,000 m), hovering altitude with ground effect 11,483 ft (3,500 m), without ground effect 5,594 ft (1,705 m), range with maximum fuel load 497 miles (800 km), maximum flight time 4.5 hours.
Weight (KA-32): Empty weight 13,780 lbs (6,250 kg), normal load 24,250 lbs (11,000 kg), maximum take-off weight 27,780 lbs (12,600 kg).
Payload (KA-31): Two pilots and two systems operators, (KA-32) two pilots and 16 passengers in seats along the walls, maximum payload 8,818 lbs (4,000 kg), maximum 11,020 lbs (5,000 kg).
State of development: The original KA-32 version first flew in 1973. The KA-32A-11BC which is the currently offered model and which represents a further development of the original KA-32, was registered in 2002. Roughly 150 helicopters are currently used for civilian purposes. Following a production break of several years, South Korea has ordered 10 new units. Although the KA-31 has been flying since 1988, production began only recently. The Indian Navy has purchased nine units.
Remarks: Both KA-31 and KA-32 versions, as well as their predecessors KA-27, -28, -29 are notable for their stocky fuselage and typical Kamov coaxial, counter-rotating tandem rotor. The KA-32 is utilized in various models for supplying oil platforms, remote outstations, and for transporting heavy external loads as well as a search and rescue helicopter. It features a particularly robust design and can operate under very difficult weather conditions. Under the fuselage the KA-31 AEW model is equipped with the Oko E-801 two-dimensional, 360-degree surveillance radar, which can open while in flight. It simultaneously recognizes up to 200 objects from a distance of 93 miles (150 km).
Manufacturer: Kamov Kompaniya, Lyubertsy plant, Moscow, Russia.

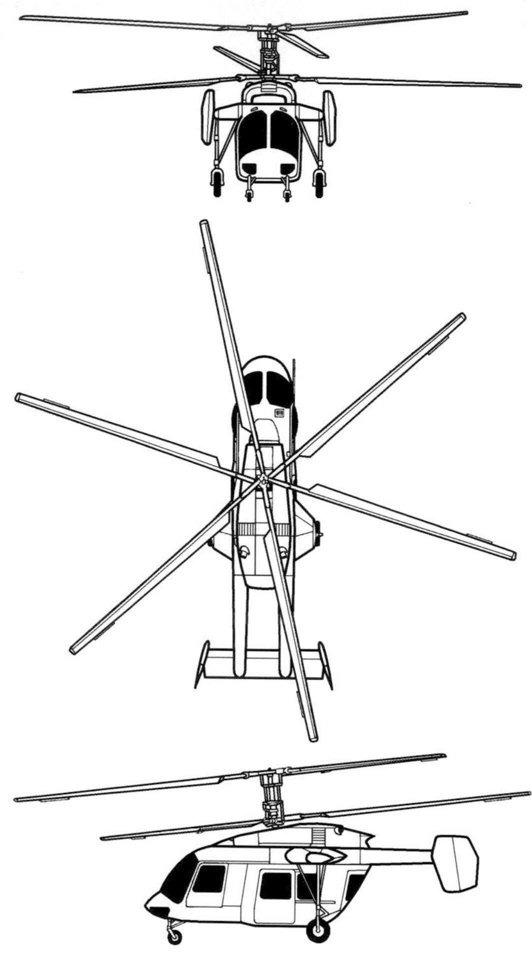

Dimensions:
Rotor diameter (each individual) 42.65 ft (13.00 m)
Fuselage length 26.57 ft (8.10 m)
Height including rotor head 13.94 ft (4.25 m)

KAMOV KA-226

Country of origin: Russia.
Type: Light multi-purpose helicopter.
Power Plant: Two Allison 250-c20B gas turbine engines each with 420 SHP (313 kW) performance.
Performance (approximate): Maximum speed 127 mph (205 km/h), economic cruising speed 115 mph (185 km/h), maximum diagonal rate of climb 33 ft (10.1 m)/sec, service ceiling 16,570 ft (5,050 m), range with maximum load 25 miles (40 km), with maximum fuel load 373 miles (600 km).
Weight: Empty weight 4,303 lbs (1,952 kg), maximum take-off weight 7,496 lbs (3,400 kg).
Payload: One to two pilots and up to eight passengers, maximum load 2,866 lbs (1,300 kg).
State of development: The first flight of this model took place on September 4, 1997. Two further prototypes are supposed to have undergone test flights since then. The Russian Ministry of Civil Defense has ordered five units (+ 20 options) so far. Further prospective buyers include the city of Moscow and the Gazprom Gas Company (50 options) for patrol service along gas pipelines.
Remarks: The KA-226 is a twin motor, vastly improved version of the earlier KA-26/126 model. As with most advanced Russian versions, the KA-226 resorts to Western products for the important elements. In this case this means Allison engines as well as the entire avionics. A distinctive feature of the KA-226 is that the entire passenger cabin is built into the helicopter as a separate module and by replacing the module with other available modules, the helicopter can perform other functions. Thus, the KA-226 is decidedly flexible in purpose, whether as passenger transporter, cargo freighter, ambulance and crop-duster with containers of up to 264 gallons (1,000 l). It boasts a very simple and robust design, and features a coaxial rotor, typical for Kamov.
Manufacturer: OKB Nikolai I. Kamov, Orenburg plant, Russia.

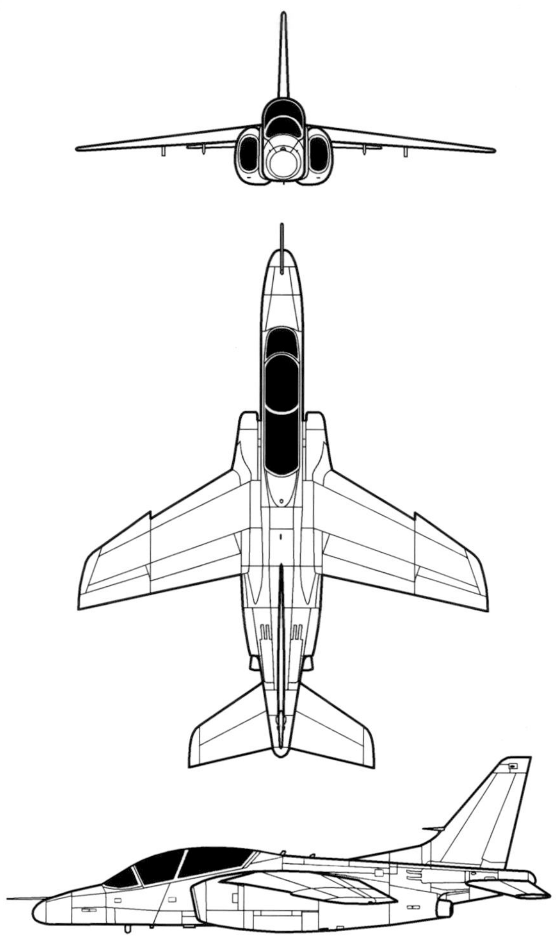

Dimensions:
Wingspan: 32.61 ft (9.94 m)
Length: 42.65 ft (13.00 m)
Height: 15.09 ft (4.60 m)
Wing area: 226 sq. ft (21.00 m^2)

KAWASAKI T-4

Country of origin: Japan.
Type: Two-seat trainer.
Power Plant: Two Ishikawajima-Harima F3-IHI-30 turbofan engines each with 3,680 lbs (1,670 kW/16.37 kN) static thrust.
Performance: Maximum speed at 10,360 lbs (4,700 kg) 645 mph (1,038 km/h) at sea level, 594 mph (956 km/h) at 36,010 ft (10,975 m), maximum sustained speed at 12,130 lbs (5,500 kg) 495 mph (797 km/h), initial rate of climb at 12,130 lbs (5,500 kg) 167 ft (51 m)/sec, service ceiling 40,030 ft (12,200 m), range without external tanks 806 miles (1,297 km), with two 119 gallon (450 l) external tanks 1,036 miles (1,668 km).
Weight: Empty weight 8,157 lbs (3,700 kg), maximum take-off weight 16,530 lbs (7,500 kg).
Armament (as weapons trainer): One 7.6-mm MG module under the fuselage and two AIM-9L Sidewinder air-to-air missiles on both wing pylons, or up to four 500 lb (227 kg) training bombs.
State of development: The initial test flight of the first of four XT-4 prototypes was on July 29, 1985 followed by the first serial T-4 aircraft on June 28, 1988. The Japanese Armed Forces ordered and received 200 T-4's.
Remarks: As a primary contractor, Kawasaki is responsible for the production of the T-4. Mitsubishi supplies the fuselage mid-section, engine intakes and vertical stabilizer, while Fuji provides the fuselage nose and wings. The T-4 replaces the Fuji T-1 and Lockheed T-33 as training aircraft. The T-4 can also be used for a range of other missions, e.g. communications and target towing. The T-4 is the first wholly Japanese construction with domestic power plants in 25 years. The Japanese Air Force has been offered an improved version of the T-4, which can also replace the Mitsubishi T-2 in its duties as advanced trainer.
Manufacturer: Kawasaki Heavy Industries Ltd., Gifu plant, Japan.

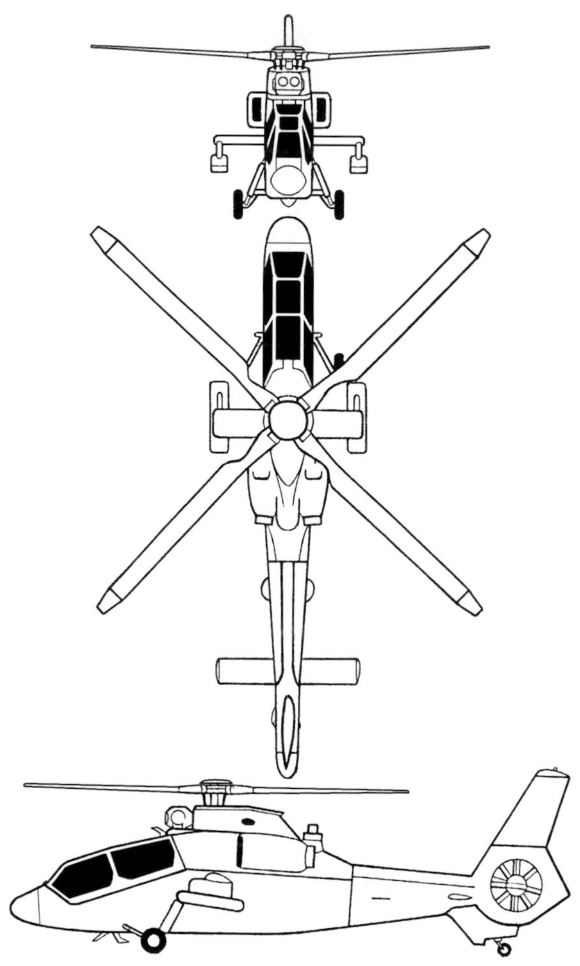

Dimensions:
Rotor diameter 38.06 ft (11.60 m)
Fuselage length 39.37 ft (12.00 m)
Height 12.47 ft (3.80 m)

KAWASAKI OH-1

Country of origin: Japan.
Type: Two-seat light battle and surveillance helicopter.
Power Plant: Two Mitsubishi TS1-10 gas turbine engines each with 888 SHP (313 kW) performance.
Performance (according to provisional data from manufacturer): Maximum speed in horizontal flight 168 mph (270 km/h), operating range without external tanks 124 miles (200 km), range 342 miles (550 km).
Weight: Empty weight 5,401 lbs (2,450 kg), maximum take-off weight around 8,818 lbs (4,000 kg).
Armament: Four short-range Toshiba Type 91 air-to-air infrared missiles on two pylons on the sides of the fuselage as well as two additional tanks with 42 gallons (160 l) each.
State of development: The first of six prototypes (of which two prototypes were non-flying models for stationary testing) completed its initial test flight on August 6, 1996. Deliveries began in January 2000. The Japanese Ground Defense Forces reported the need for approximately 200 OH-1 to replace the Kawasaki/MDD OH-6D, of which the first 18 have been ordered. Additional orders are expected.
Remarks: In addition to Kawasaki, Fuji and Mitsubishi have each contributed 20% of the development of the OH-1. The concept of the originally designated OH-X design follows the currently common model of a slender tandem two-seat helicopter where the pilot sits in the front cockpit while the observer/systems operator sits in the back. The compartment is predominantly made of composite materials and the cockpit is armored. Also, the non-articulated main rotor is made of synthetic material and the tail rotor is encased for security reasons. Field electronics includes, among others, TV, FLIR and laser rangefinder. A MIL-STD-1553B data bus controls all systems. With this equipment, the OH-1 is completely suitable for night and all-weather service.
Manufacturer: Kawasaki Heavy Industries Ltd., Tokyo, Japan.

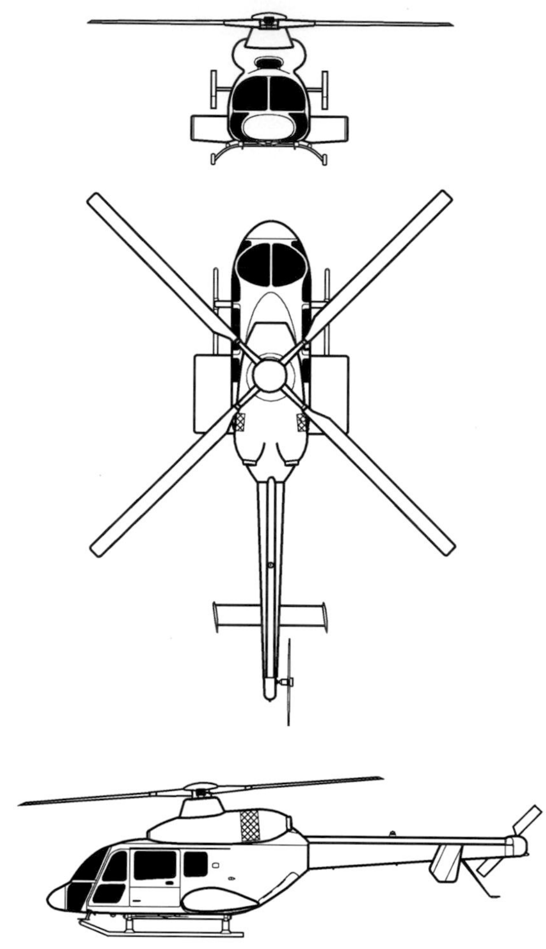

Dimensions:
Rotor diameter 37.73 ft (11.50 m)
Fuselage length including rotating tail rotor 37.86 ft (11.54 m)
Height including rotor 11.29 ft (3.44 m)

KAZAN ANSAT

Country of origin: Russia.
Type: Light civil and military multi-purpose helicopter.
Power Plant: Two Pratt & Whitney Canada (series) PW206K gas turbine engines (manufactured under license by Klimov) each with 650 SHP (480 kW) performance.
Performance (according to manufacturer's claims): Maximum cruising speed 180 mph (290 km/h), normal cruising speed 148 mph (238 km/h), hovering altitude without ground effect 8,858 ft (2,700 m), service ceiling 19,690 ft (6,000 m), range with load of 2,866 lbs (1,300 kg) 323 miles (520 km), maximum range without external tanks 385 miles (620 km), maximum flight duration 3 hours.
Weight: Maximum take-off weight 7,275 lbs (3,300 kg).
Payload: Nine people including pilot, as an ambulance helicopter up to two recumbent patients and two paramedics, normal load as a freight carrier 2,866 lbs (1,300 kg) with a maximum of 3,638 lbs (1,650 kg).
State of development: Three prototypes have flown thus far, with the initial prototype having its first test flight on August 17, 1999. Certification is expected in the immediate future. The Russian Border Guard intends to order up to 100 Ansats and the Russian Air Force has selected this model as a future training helicopter.
Remarks: The Ansat helicopter complies with all international requirements and can be sold to all countries. It is suitable for multiple purposes and, for that reason, can carry a variety of additional equipment. At the same time, it is particularly valued for its cost-effective construction and economic operation. The Ansat is in direct competition to the EC145 (see pages 180/181), but costs about a third of the price. Clients have a choice of Western or Russian avionics. The helicopter is equipped with a fly-by-wire system and many of its structural parts consist of composite materials. An advanced armed version is in the works as is a reconnaissance model.
Manufacturer: Kazan Helicopter plant, Kazan, Russia.

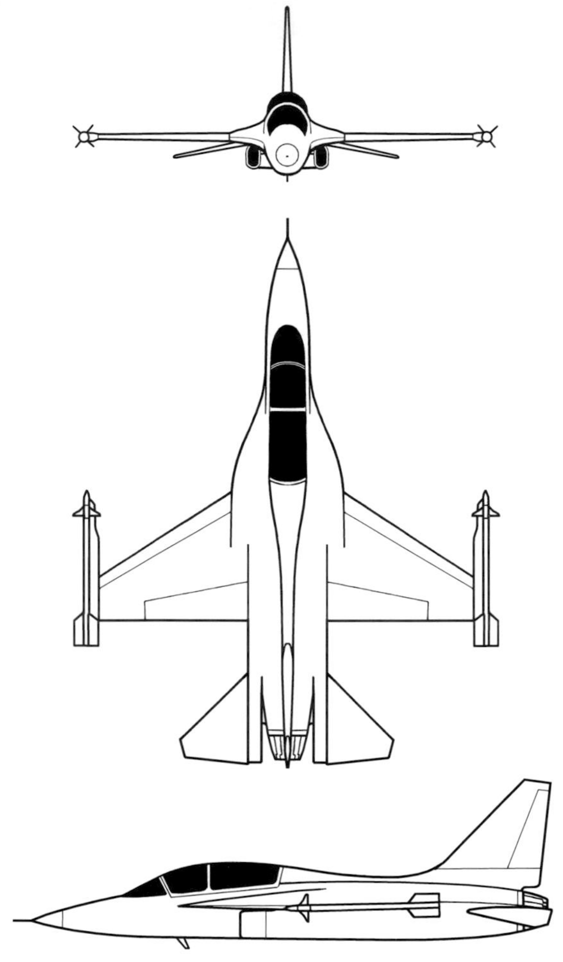

Dimensions:
Wingspan including missiles at wing tips 30 ft (9.17 m)
Length: 43 ft (13.13 m)
Height: 16 ft (4.90 m)

KOREAN AEROSPACE INDUSTRIES T-50/A-50 GOLDEN EAGLE

Country of origin: South Korea.
Type: Two-seat T-50 trainer and light multi-purpose A50 tactical aircraft.
Power Plant: One General Electric F404-GE-402 turbofan engine with 17,693 lbs (8,000 kp/78.7 kN) static thrust with afterburner.
Performance (according to manufacturer's claims): Maximum speed Mach 1.4, initial rate of climb 541 ft (165 m)/sec, service ceiling 48,000 ft (14,630 m).
Weight: Empty weight 14,200 lbs (6,441 kg), maximum take-off weight without external load 19,600 lbs (8,890 kg), with external load 26,400 lbs (11,974 kg).
Armament: One 20-mm cannon in front of the fuselage with muzzle under the leading edge of the left wing. Seven attachment points, one under the fuselage, four under the wings and two on wing tips, support air-to-air or air-to-ground missiles as well as an assortment of bombs.
State of development: On August 20, 2002, the first of four prototypes flew, followed by the second on November 8, 2002. To date, the Korean Air Force plans to order 47 T-50A advanced trainers, 47 T-50B fighter-trainers and later up to 100 A-50 light tactical aircraft. Deliveries are expected to begin in 2005.
Remarks: The T-50/A-50 Golden Eagle is a joint venture between Korea Aerospace Industries and Lockheed Martin. The American Company has developed the wings and flight control system as well the avionics. Three versions are planned: the T-50A advanced trainer, the so called T 50B Lead-in Fighter-Trainer with AGP-67 on-board radar as well as the A-50 light single-seat tactical aircraft. The A-50 may be compared to the F-50, a light multi-purpose fighter equipped with better on-board radar, combat electronics and greater fuel capacity. In terms of design and engineering, these versions hardly differ from one another, the differences being almost entirely in their equipment. All are fitted with a fly-by-wire steering system and cockpit equipment with HUD made by Honeywell.
Manufacturer: Korea Aerospace Industries (KAI), Inchon, Sachon plant, Republic of South Korea.

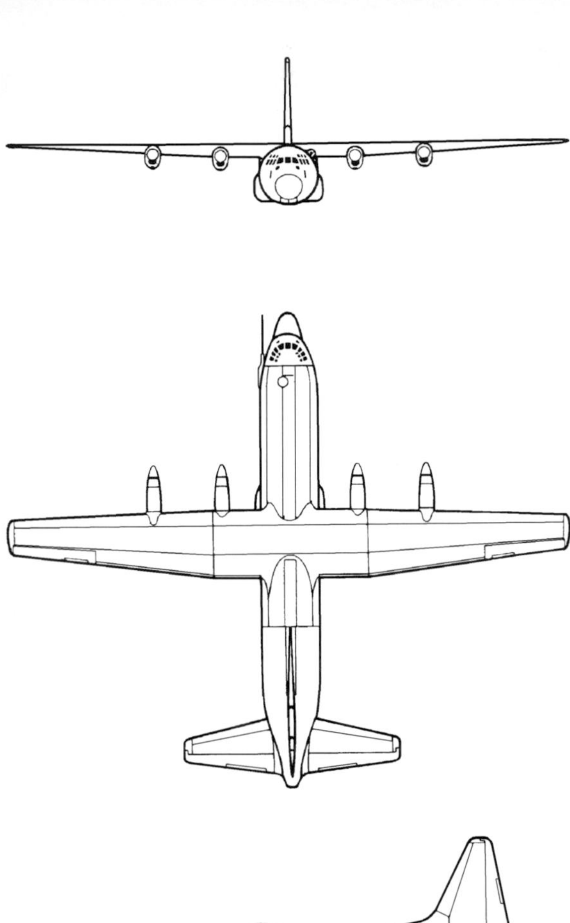

Dimensions:
Wingspan: 132.6 ft (40.41 m)
Length (C-130J) 97.74 ft (29.79 m), (C-130J-30) 112.7 ft (34.36 m)
Height: 38.42 ft (11.71 m)
Wing area: 1,745 sq. ft (162.12 m^2)

LOCKHEED C-130J HERCULES II

Country of origin: USA.
Type: Medium-heavy military and civilian transporter.
Power Plant: Four Allison AE2100 turboprop engines each with 6,000 SHP (4,500 kW) performance.
Performance: Maximum cruising speed 401 mph (645 km/h), normal cruising speed 346 mph (556 km/h), initial rate of climb 35 ft (10.7 m)/sec, service ceiling 30,560 ft (9,315 m), range with payload of 47,670 lbs (21,625 kg) over 1,616 miles (2,600 km), with 40,000 lbs (18,144 kg) 3,262 miles (5,250 km).
Weight: Empty weight (J) 75,560 lbs (34,274 kg), (J-30) 79,290 lbs (35,965 kg), maximum take-off weight 175,000 lbs (79,380 kg).
Payload: Two pilots and a load of 48,5oo lbs (22,000 kg).
State of development: The first C-130J flew on April 5, 1996. Until now, 182 have been ordered including Denmark 3, RAF 25, RAAF 12 C-130J-30, Italy 24 C-130J/-30, USAF/USMC/USCG 119 comprising of 71 CC-130J/-30, 10 WC-130J, 32 KC-130J and 6 HC-130J. In addition, the USCG has a demand for 168 new C-130J units. The C-130 is the only aircraft that, in its many variants, has been produced continuously for 43 years resulting in the construction of 2,180 units. Through 2002, 95 units of the C-130J version have been produced.
Remarks: Compared to the previous C-130H model, the C-130J version has been greatly redesigned and improved. In addition to new engines with technologically advanced six-blade rotors, a wholly new two-person cockpit with four large LCD displays and a HUD have been installed. To further increase performance and simplify maintenance, Lockheed has redesigned the entire electronics as well as the electric and refueling systems. All these measures have reduced fuel consumption by 17% and increased speed by 15%. In turn, the payload/range performance has improved by an astonishing 61%. Also, structural parts have been strengthened. The C-130J and C-130J-30 variants differ only in the length of the fuselage. Lockheed is developing a civilian version L-100J that, in addition to the tail-loading ramp, is fitted with an 12 ft (3.55 m) wide freight gate on the front right side of the fuselage.
Manufacturer: Lockheed Martin Marietta Corp., Marietta, Georgia, USA.

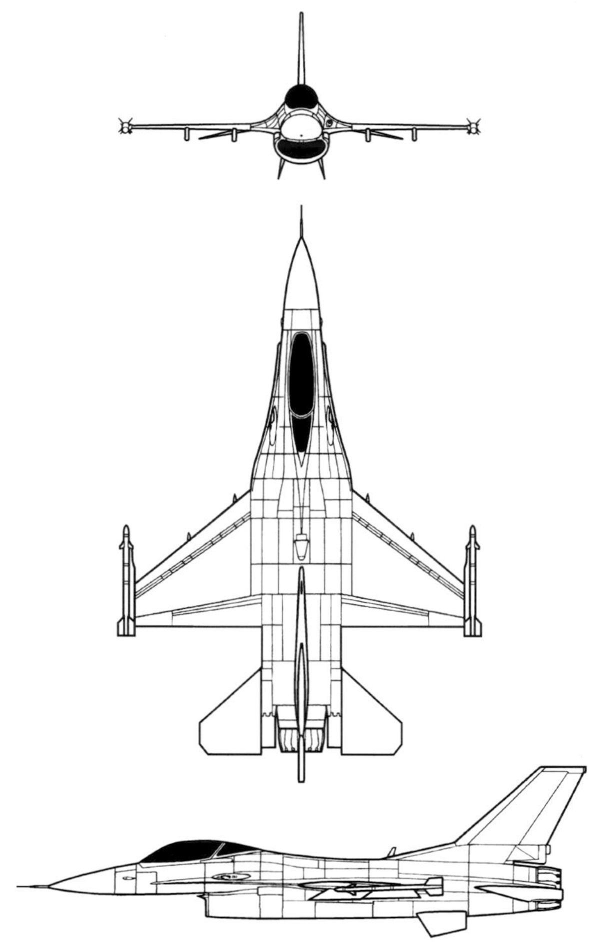

Dimensions:
Wingspan: 31 ft (9.45 m)
Length 49.31 ft (15.03 m)
Height: 16.7 ft (5.09 m)
Wing area: 300 sq. ft (27.87 m^2)

LOCKHEED F-16C/D BLOCK 50/52/60 FIGHTING FALCON

Country of origin: USA.
Type: One-seat multi-purpose fighter (F-16C) and two-seat operational trainer (F-16D).
Power Plant: One Pratt & Whitney F100-PW-229 turbofan engine with 17,805 lbs (8,075 kp/ 79.2 kN) static thrust without afterburner or 29,090 lbs (13,150 kp/129.4 kN) with afterburner or one General Electric F110-GE-129 turbofan engine with 17,738 lbs (8,043 kp/78.9 kN) static thrust without afterburner and 29,585 lbs (13,416 kp/131.6 kN) with afterburner.
Performance (F-100): Short-burst maximum speed at 39,990 ft (12,190 m) 1,333 mph (2,145 km/h [Mach 2.02]), maximum sustained speed 1,247 mph (2,007 km/h [Mach 1.89]), tactical operation radius with six 500 lb (227 kg) bombs 360 miles (580 km), deployment range with external tanks 2,450 miles (3,943 km).
Weight: Empty weight 18,240 lbs (8,273 kg), maximum take-off weight 42,300 lbs (19,187 kg), (Block 60) 50,000 lbs (22,680 kg).
Armament: One M61A-1 20-mm multi-barrel revolving cannon and, as an interceptor, up to six AIM-9L/M air-to-air missiles, as ground attack airplane up to 12,430 lbs (5,638 kg) external load.
State of development: The F-16C Block 50/52 has been in operation since 1991. Of all versions, roughly 4,350 units, both new and used, have been ordered by air forces of 20 countries. The 4,000th unit left the assembly hangar on April 28, 2000. The most recent orders for F-16C/D come from Poland for 48 Block 50/52. Currently, approximately 50 units are produced each year.
Remarks: Current deliveries include Blocks 50/52 and 60. The former contains improved electronics including APG-68(V)X radar and laser gyroscope. In 2001, the F-16C/D (Block 60) model went into production. Aside from more powerful F110-129EFE power plants with 31,473 lbs (14,270 kp/140 kN) static thrust with afterburner or Pratt & Whitney F100-PW-229A with somewhat similar performance, the F-16C/D (Block 60) is equipped with the most modern “Active-Array” radar. The cockpit has been improved and a display has been built into the pilot’s helmet. To increase range, conforming external tanks have been planned, which will significantly reduce wind resistance when compared to conventional external tanks.
Manufacturer: Lockheed Martin Marietta Corp., Fort Worth Division, Fort Worth, Texas, USA.

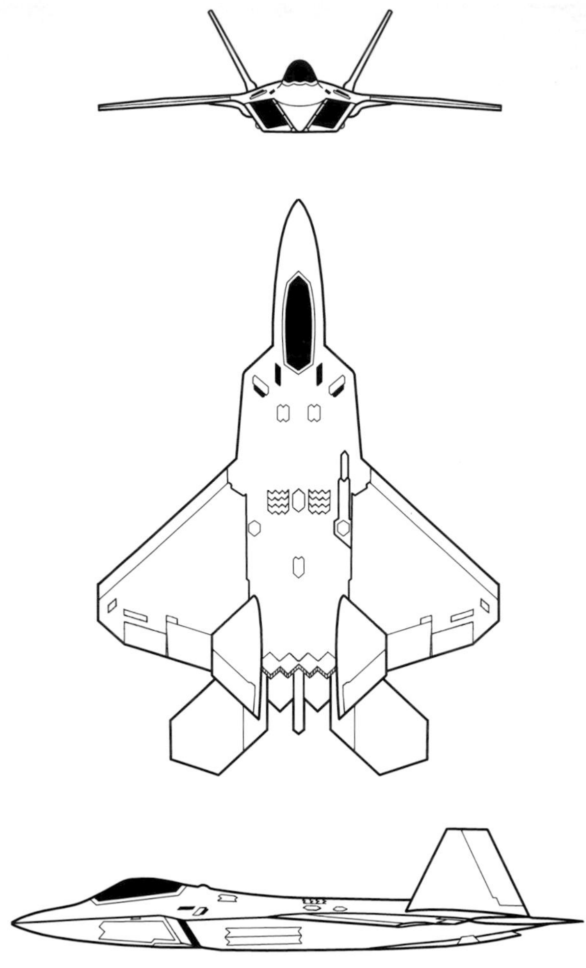

Dimensions:
Wingspan: 44.50 ft (13.56 m)
Length 61.91 ft (18.87 m)
Height: 16.57 ft (5.05 m)
Wing area: 829.9 sq. ft (77.1 m^2)

LOCKHEED / BOEING F/A-22 RAPTOR

Country of origin: USA.
Type: Air superiority and multi-purpose tactical aircraft.
Power Plant: Two Pratt & Whitney YF119-PW-100 turbofan engines each with 35,070 lbs (15,900 kp/156 kN) static thrust with afterburner and swiveling exhaust nozzle.
Performance (estimated): Maximum speed at low altitude 913 mph (1,470 km/h [Mach 1.20]) or 1,190 mph (1,915 km/h [Mach 1.80]) above 36,010 ft (10,975 m), maximum sustained speed 991 mph (1,595 km/h [Mach 1.50]) above 36,010 ft (10,975 m), service ceiling 54,790+ ft (16,700+ m), tactical operation radius with internal fuel load and full air-to-air missile complement 901 miles (1,450 km).
Weight (estimated): Empty weight 31,670 lbs (14,365 kg), maximum take-off weight 60,000 lbs (27,216 kg).
Armament: One six-barrel 20-mm revolving cannon and two short-range AIM-9 air-to-air missiles in a separate bay on the side of the fuselage, as well as up to six medium-range AIM-120 air-to-air missiles in the central weapons bay. For ground support missions, it can carry special 1,000 lb (450 kg) bombs, or additional tanks can be carried on four suspension pylons below the wings.
State of development: The F-22 series prototype took off on its maiden flight on September 7, 1997 and the first serial aircraft flew on September 16, 2002. Some 12 F-22's flew by the end of 2002. The first squadron will be operational by 2005. The USAF is testing the aircraft through the first quarter of 2004. With satisfactory results, it is expected that the USAF will purchase up to 295 planes with deliveries to begin by the end of 2004.
Remarks: The Raptor is also designed for low-level attack and can carry corresponding weapons in weapon bays and on support points under the wings. For that reason the Raptor, originally designated as F-22, has been renamed F/A-22. Stealth characteristics, high and almost unlimited agility, the most modern combat electronics and the ability to achieve sustained speed of Mach 1.5 without afterburner make the Raptor the most powerful fighter aircraft in the world. Lockheed is testing the development of a twin-seat variant for long-range air raids.
Manufacturer: Lockheed Martin Marietta Corp., Marietta, Georgia and Boeing Military Airplanes, Seattle, Washington, USA.

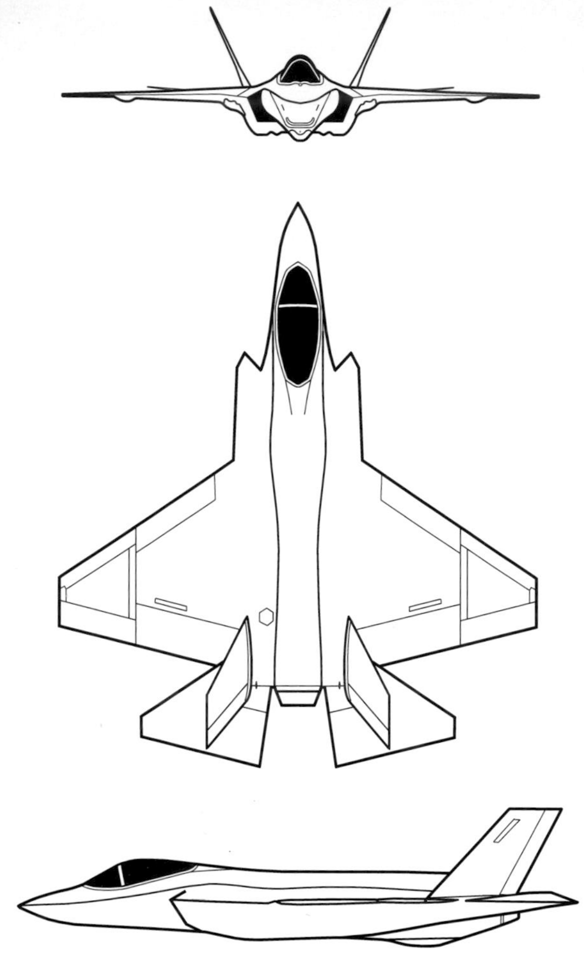

Dimensions:
Wingspan (X-35A) 35.1 ft (10.70 m), (X-35C) 40 ft (12.19 m)
Length 50.75 ft (15.47 m)
Wing area (X-35A) 459.6 sq. ft (42.70 m^2), (X-35C) 620 sq. ft (57.60 m^2)

LOCKHEED MARTIN X-35A/C JOINT STRIKE FIGHTER

Country of origin: USA (Great Britain).
Type: Experimental model for (X-35A) land-based or (X-35C) carrier-based multi-purpose tactical aircraft.
Power Plant: One Pratt & Whitney PW611 turbofan engine (derived from F119) with 25,000 lbs (11,400 kp/111.20 kN) static thrust without afterburner and 35,084 lbs (15,910 kp/156.06 kN) with afterburner and thrust control steering. Also available is an alternative General Electric YF-120-FX turbofan engine with approximately similar performance and design.
Performance: Maximum speed approximately Mach 1.5, service ceiling 50,000+ ft (15,240+ m), tactical combat radius 932 miles (1,500 km).
Weight: Empty weight 25,000 lbs (11,340 kg), maximum take-off weight 49,120 lbs (22,280 kg).
Armament: One 27-mm BK-27 Mauser cannon and approximately 15,430 lbs (7,000 kg) of weapons.
State of development: The maiden flight of the X-35C took place on December 16, 2000, after the land-based X-35A version had its test flight on October 24, 2000. As a winner of the competition for a new Joint-Strike-Fighter (JSF), X 35 was further developed for serial production. The USAF wants to order 1,736 F-35A's, and the USN 480 F-35C's. Deliveries should begin in 2008.
Remarks: The land-based CTOL 230A (X-35A) version is intended for the USAF, while 230C/X-35C is meant for the USN as a carrier-based multi-purpose tactical aircraft. Common to all models (including the X-35B, see pages 232/233) are the wings, vertical tails and the tailplane (with a large area for the 230C in order to achieve better take-off and landing performance). Aside from Lockheed, the development team also includes Northrop Grumman and British Aerospace as well as Australia, Denmark and Canada. In terms of engineering and design, the three versions are nearly 90% identical. The technologically advanced cockpit features high-resolution screens. Numerous functions can be performed with voice commands or via the pilot's helmet display. The serial production aircraft show only minor external changes when compared with the prototypes.
Manufacturer: Lockheed Martin Marietta Corp., Marietta, Georgia, Fort Worth plant, Texas, USA.

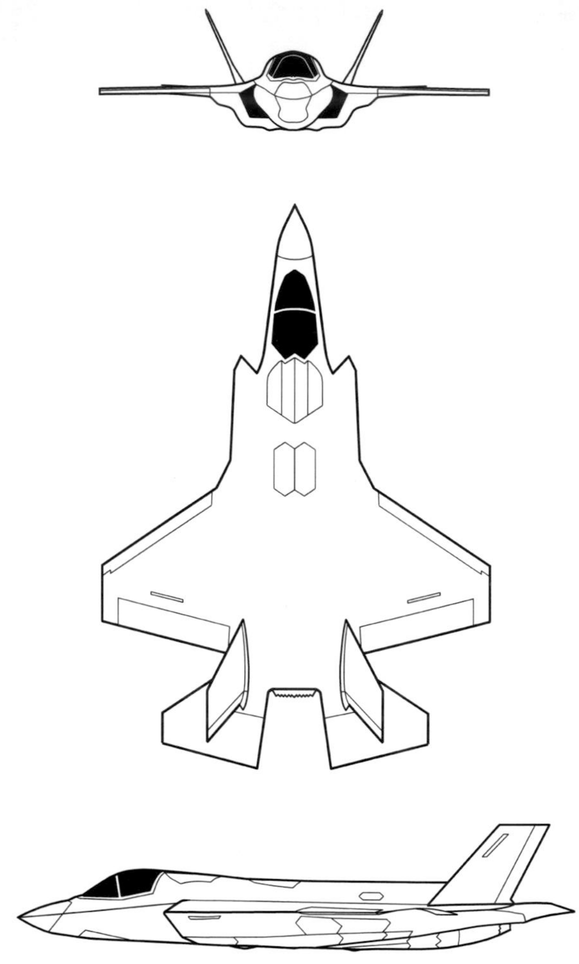

Dimensions:
Wingspan 35.1 ft (10.70 m)
Length 50.75 ft (15.47 m)
Wing area 459.6 sq. ft (42.70 m^2)

LOCKHEED MARTIN X-35B JOINT STRIKE FIGHTER

Country of origin: USA (Great Britain).
Type: Experimental model for a carrier-based CTOL multi-purpose tactical aircraft.
Power Plant: One Pratt & Whitney PW611 turbofan engine (derived from F119) with 25,000 lbs (11,400 kp/111.20 kN) static thrust without afterburner and 34,888 lbs (15,910 kp/155.19 kN) with afterburner and up to 110° downward swiveling exhaust nozzle. Also available is an alternative General Electric YF-120-FX turbofan engine with approximately similar performance and design.
Performance: Maximum speed approximately Mach 1.5, service ceiling 50,000+ ft (15,240+ m), tactical combat radius 932 miles (1,500 km).
Weight: Empty weight 25,000 lbs (11,340 kg), maximum take-off weight 49,120 lbs (22,280 kg).
Armament: One 27-mm BK-27 Mauser cannon and approximately 15,430 lbs (7,000 kg) of weapons.
State of development: The X-35B originated from the conversion of the X-35C and flew for the first time in this configuration on June 24, 2001. The USMC will order 609 units and the RAF and RN 150 units of the serial F-35B version. Deliveries to the USMC should begin in 2008, RAF/RN will obtain their aircraft starting in 2010.
Remarks: The STOVL X-35B version is equipped with a power plant connected, via a cardan shaft, to a Lift-Fan, with an intake above and the exhaust nozzle below the front part of the fuselage. The three X-35A, B and C versions are nearly 90% identical in their engineering and design. The technologically advance cockpit features high-resolution screens. Numerous functions can be performed with voice commands or via the pilot's helmet display. Aside from Lockheed, the development team also includes Northrop Grumman and British Aerospace. The RN has decided upon the F-35B STOVL variant for service abroad aircraft carriers while the USN plans to order the F-35C for the same service.
Manufacturer: Lockheed Martin Marietta Corp., Marietta, Georgia, Fort Worth plant, Texas, USA.

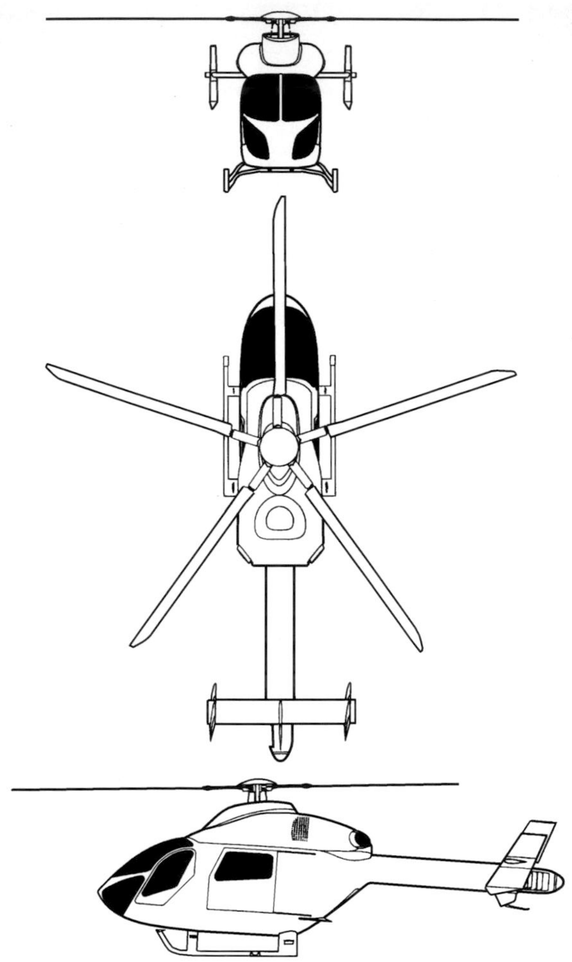

Dimensions:
Rotor diameter 33.83 ft (10.31 m)
Fuselage length 32.32 ft (9.85 m)
Height including rotor head 12 ft (3.66 m)

MD HELICOPTERS MD 902 EXPLORER

Country of origin: USA (Netherlands).
Type: Multi-purpose helicopter.
Power Plant: Two Pratt & Whitney Canada PW207E gas turbine engines each with 730 SHP (530 kW) performance or two Turboméca Arrius-2C engines each with 605 SHP (451 kW) performance.
Performance: Maximum speed 184 mph (296 km/h), maximum cruising speed 161 mph (259 km/h) at sea level, diagonal rate of climb 47 ft (14.2 m)/sec, service ceiling 18,500 ft (5,638 m), hovering altitude without ground effect 10,990 ft (3,350 m), range 360 miles (580 km).
Weight: Empty weight 3,214 lbs (1,458 kg), normal take-off weight 6,504 lbs (2,950 kg), maximum weight with external load 6,790 lbs (3,080 kg).
Payload: Eight to ten people including pilots, maximum load 3,086 lbs (1,400 kg).
Armament (Combat Explorer): One 12.7-mm GAU-19/A Gatling cannon and a container for unguided 70-mm rocket missiles.
State of development: The latest MD 902 version has been flying since September 5, 1997 and the first deliveries to clients took place in mid-1998. After completing 30 MD 900's for, among others, ADA, the Belgian Gendarmerie and the British Police Aviation Services, production was switched over to MD 902. Current orders to date are for 100 units. Latest buyers include U.S. Department of Justice for anti-drug duties and Aero Care, Texas (3). Approximately 20 helicopters are produced annually.
Remarks: The MD 902 uses NOTAR technology that was originally used in the MD 520N. One distinguishing feature of the Explorer is the jointless five-blade rotor made of composite materials. The complete equipment contains, among others, EFIS, weather radar, GPS, FADEC digital engine management and flight control system. The Explorer can be obtained with both wheeled landing gear as well as with skids. Numerous operators use a specially equipped rescue version. Purchase price is about US$3.1 million. The PW207E engine, which began production at the beginning of 2000, improves flight performance in single-engine flight as well as in hot climate regions. The Mexican Navy operates six MD 902 Combat Explorers.
Manufacturer: MD Helicopters, a subsidiary of RDM, Netherlands, Mesa plant, Arizona, USA.

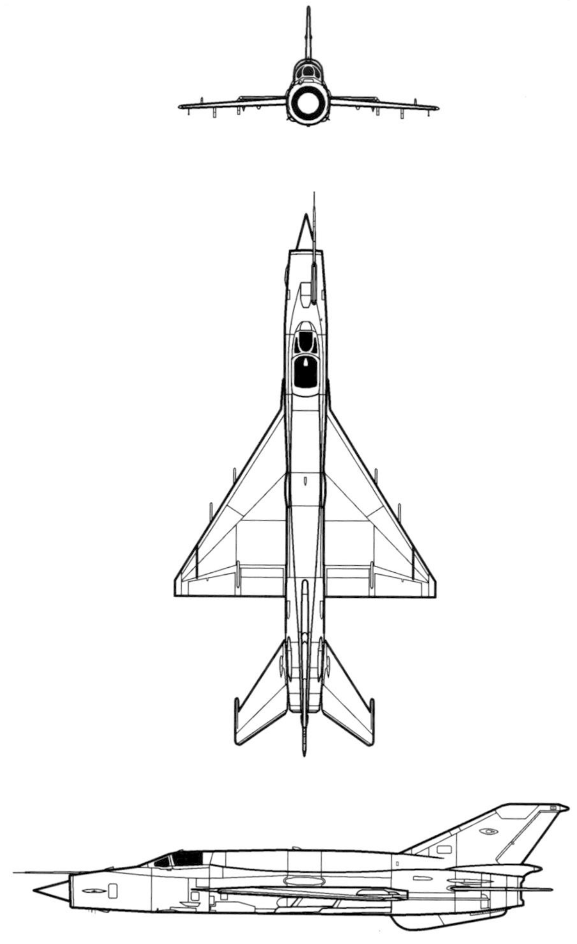

Dimensions:
Wingspan 23.46 ft (7.15 m)
Length 47.51 (14.48 m)
Height 14.76 ft (4.50 m)
Wing area 248 sq. ft (23.04 m^2)

MIKOYAN MiG-21-93

Country of origin: Russia.
Type: One-seat multi-purpose fighter and two-seat operational trainer.
Power Plant (MiG-21bis): One Tumanskiy R-13 turbofan engine with 9,037 lbs (4,100 kp/40.20 kN) static thrust without afterburner and 15,647 lbs (7,100 kp/69.6 kN) with afterburner.
Performance (MiG-21bis): Maximum speed at sea level 808 mph (1,300 km/h), 1,352 mph (2,175 km/h [Mach 2.04]) at 42,650 ft (13,000 m), time to reach 55,770 ft (17,000 m) 8.5 minutes, service ceiling 58,400 ft (17,800 m), range with two air-to-air missiles and a 211 gallon (800 l) external tank 913 miles (1,470 km).
Weight (MiG-21bis): Empty weight 13,000 lbs (5,895 kg), maximum take-off weight 22,970 lbs (10,420 kg).
Armament (MiG-21bis): One 23-mm GSH-23L twin-barrel cannon and, for interceptor use, up to eight R-60 short-range air-to-air missiles, as ground attack aircraft an assortment of air-to-surface rockets and bombs.
State of development: The first YE-4 prototype in its final configuration flew for the first time on June 16, 1955. With approximately 13,500 units in all its versions, the MiG-21 is the most produced Mach-2 capable tactical aircraft in the world. This includes production under licensing arrangements with CSSR 194, India 657, and PR China approximately 2,400. Air forces of at least 38 countries have received one or more versions of the MiG-21.
Remarks: Air forces throughout the world continue to fly the MiG-21 in large numbers. Programs have been initiated to keep the older aircraft updated. The most important of these are for India (see photo) where approximately 125 aircraft have been equipped with new Kopyo radar, Elta avionics, ECM, GPS etc. (the updated aircraft first flew on October 6, 1998). Under the designation MiG-2000 Lancer, IAR Romania and IAI Israel modified some 110 aircraft for Romania (this version first flew on March 29, 1998) with a Tumanskiy R-25-300 power plant, Aerostar and Elbit avionics, Elta EL-2032M multi-purpose on-board radar, INS/GPS etc. Russia has attempted to sell an updated version under the name MiG-21-93. The Chinese F-7MG advanced model is described on pages 138/139.
Manufacturer: OKB Mikoyan/Gurevich, Gorkiy plant, Moscow and Tbilisi, Russia.

Dimensions:
Wingspan 37.27 ft (11.36 m), with folded wings 27.82 ft (8.48 m)
Length 56.32 ft (17.32 m)
Height 14.76 ft (5.18 m)
Wing area 452.1 sq. ft (42.00 m^2)

MIKOYAN MiG-29K

Country of origin: Russia.
Type: One-seat carrier-based multi-purpose tactical aircraft.
Power Plant: Two Klimov/Sarkisov RD-33 (Mod) turbofan engines each with 11,106 lbs (5,035 kp/49.40 kN) static thrust without afterburner and 20,458 lbs (9,300 kp/91.00 kN) with afterburner.
Performance (MiG-29SMT): Maximum speed with four air-to-air missiles 1,519 mph (2,445 km/h [Mach 2.3]) at 36,090 ft (11,000 m) or 932 mph (1,500 km/h [Mach 1.3]) at sea level, maximum initial rate of climb rate 1,083 ft (330 m)/sec, service ceiling 55,770 ft (17,000 m), tactical operation radius (intercept mission with 396 gallon/1,500-l additional tanks and four air-to-air missiles) 631 miles (1,015 km), maximum range with three external tanks 2,175 miles (3,500 km).
Weight: Normal take-off weight 40,790 lbs (18,500 kg), maximum take-off weight 49,380 lbs (22,400 kg).
Armament: One 30-mm GSh-301 revolving cannon and a maximum weapons load of 12,130 lbs (5,500 kg) at ten external stations. Eight various air-to-air or air-to-surface missiles can be carried together with anti-radar missiles and TV-guided glide-bombs.
State of development: The converted MiG-29SMT version has been flying since April 12, 1998. 200 older versions in the Russian Air Force will be similarly converted. Approximately 1,200 MiG-29's in all versions have been built for 29 air forces. Production still continues in limited numbers. The latest order is for 12 units from the Sudan.
Remarks: The carrier-borne version of the MiG-29K aircraft obtained by the Indian Navy come equipped with collapsible wings, strengthened landing gear and additional adjustments to suit its intended duties. The main wing is somewhat bigger. Avionics correspond to that of MiG-29SMT. This model is steered with the help of a digital triple fly-by-wire system with a mechanical backup. A number of two-seat MiG-29KUB have been purchased as a trainer for take-off and landing on aircraft carriers. Under the MiG-29M2 designation, the manufacturer offers a two-seat multi-purpose tactical version that was first flown on September 26, 2001 with a new front section and multifunction Phasotron Zhuk-M radar. No orders have been placed as yet.
Manufacturer: RSK-MiG and MAPO, Moscow, Russia.

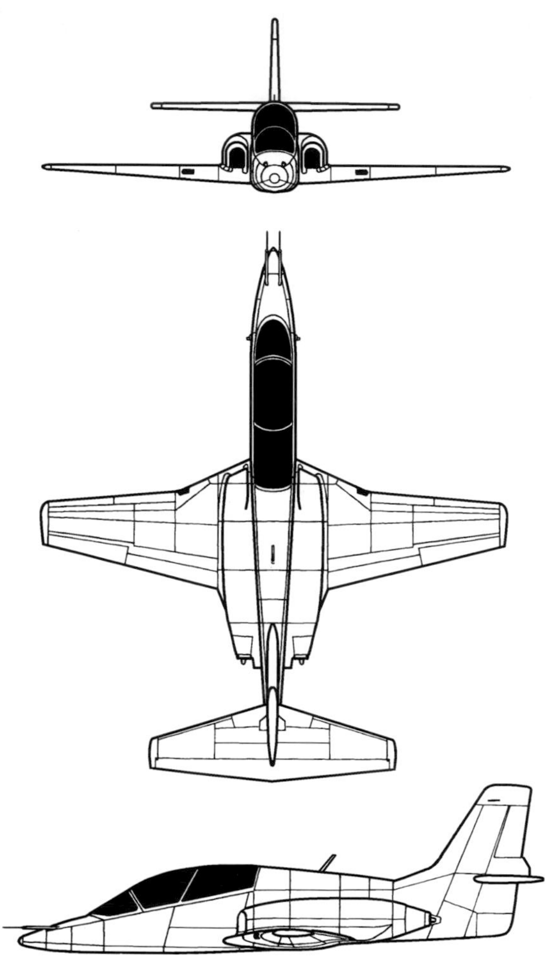

Dimensions:
Wingspan 33.33 ft (10.16 m)
Length 39.4 ft (12.01 m)
Height 14.5 ft (4.42 m)
Wing area 190.2 sq. ft (17.67 m^2)

MIKOYAN MiG-AT

Country of origin: Russia.
Type: Two-seat advanced trainer.
Power Plant: Two Turboméca-SNECMA Lazarc 04-R20 turbofan engines each with 3,170 lbs (1,437 kp/14.10 kN) static thrust.
Performance: Maximum speed 528 mph (850 km/h) at sea level, 621 mph (1,000 km/h) at 8,202 ft (2,500 m), initial rate of climb 220 ft (67 m)/sec, service ceiling 50,850 ft (15,500 m), deployment range 1,616 miles (2,600 km).
Weight: Empty weight at least 7,275 lbs (3,300 kg), normal take-off weight 10,160 lbs (4,610 kg), maximum weight 15,430 (7,000 kg).
Armament: Serial aircraft will be equipped with seven support points on wings and fuselage for 4,409 lbs (2,000 kg) of all types of weapons, (ATS) combination of air-to-air missiles and precision bombs.
State of development: Two prototypes have been built, one with French (designation -F) or Russian (designation -R) electronics. The first one had its test flight on March 21, 1996. Reportedly, six other pre-production aircraft have been built. Apparently, the Russian Air Force has decided not to obtain this model. However, Algeria is thought to have ordered an unknown number of this aircraft.
Remarks: The MiG-AT has been developed in cooperation with French companies. The power plant comes from France but is built under license in Russia. The sextant-avionics are also a French contribution. It's been reported that the composite material wings have been manufactured in South Korea. The aircraft is capable of performing exactly the same combat maneuvers as MiG-29 and Su-27 and was therefore designed for G-forces up to +8 or -3. MiG has designed a single-seat MTS ground attack version. Instead of Lazarc engines, this model, first flown in October 1997, is equipped with two Klimow RD-1700 turbofan engines each with 3,754 lbs (1,700 kp/16.7 kN) performance and Russian avionics including Phazotron Moskit Lightweight radar. This engine model is expected to be installed in the serial production AT training version aircraft.
Manufacturer: MiG, Moskovskiy Mashinostroitelnyi Zavod Imeni A.I. Mikoyana, Moscow, Russia.

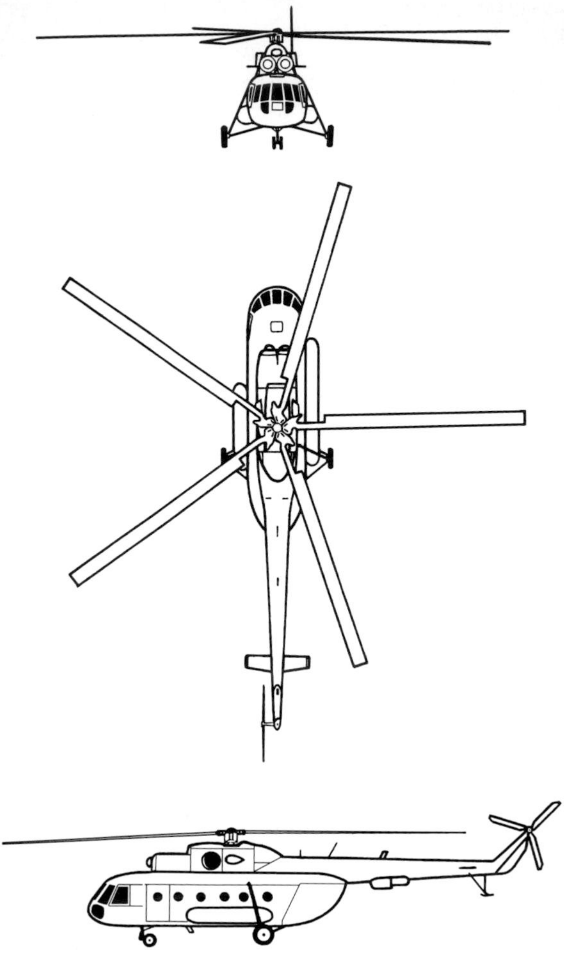

Dimensions:
Rotor diameter 69.85 ft (21.29 m)
Fuselage length without rotating tail rotor 60.7 ft (18.50 m)
Height including rotor head 15.58 ft (4.75 m)

MIL/KAZAN MI-17M/MD

Country of origin: Russia.
Type: Medium-heavy military and civil multi-purpose helicopter.
Power Plant: Two Klimov TV3-117VM gas turbine engines each with 2,200 SHP (1,620 kW) performance.
Performance: Maximum speed at 3,281 ft (1,000 m) 155 mph (250 km/h), with maximum take-off weight 143 mph (230 km/h), cruising speed 137 mph (220 km/h), service ceiling 19,690 ft (6,000 m), hovering altitude with ground effect 13,120 ft (4,000 m), without ground effect 5,774 ft (1,760 m), range without normal load 311 miles (500 km), with four external additional tanks up to 994 miles (1,600 km).
Weight: Empty weight 15,650 lbs (7,100 kg), normal take-off weight 24,250 lbs (11,000 kg), maximum 28,660 lbs (13,000 kg).
Payload: Two pilots in cockpit and up to 36 soldiers or 40 passengers, maximum internal payload 8,818 lbs (4,000 kg), maximum external payload 11,020 lbs (5,000 kg).
State of development: One prototype of the MD version has been flying since 1995. The demand for the MI-17 in its many versions is still growing. In 2002, the following reorders were placed: Malaysia 10, Indonesian Navy 2, Iran 30, and Nepal 2.
Remarks: With the Mi-17MD, the Kazan factory offers the latest version of the Mi-17 helicopter, of which over 11,000 units have been built. Externally, the Mi-17D differs noticeably in its new nose design with color weather radar. Other features include rescue equipment with inflatable balloons, large sliding doors on both sides, mechanical freight transport equipment in tail, and a place for four additional passengers. A rescue winch with the capacity of 661 lbs (300 kg) can be installed as an option. A decision is imminent on whether or not to produce the Mi-17 under license in Mexico. An improved version, designated the Mi-172, comes with a Honeywell glass cockpit, 1553 data bus, multi-sensor optic system and a BAE mission system as an option.
Manufacturer: Mil/Kazan Helicopters, Moscow/Kazan, Russia.

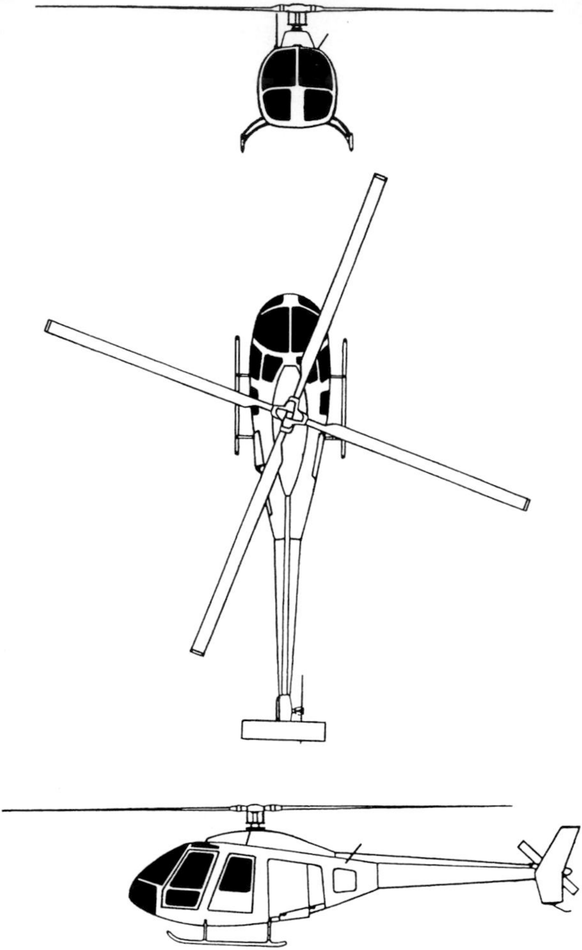

Dimensions:
Rotor diameter 32.81 ft (10.00 m)
Fuselage length 29.04 ft (8.85 m)
Height including rotor head 9.02 ft (2.75 m)

MIL MI-34

Country of origin: Russia.
Type: Light multi-purpose helicopter.
Power Plant: One Vedeneyev M-14V26 air-cooled nine-cylinder radial engine with 325 PS (242 kW) performance.
Performance: Maximum speed 131 mph (210 km/h), maximum cruising speed 112 mph (180 km/h), service ceiling 13,120 ft (4,000 m), hover altitude without ground effect 4,921 ft (1,500 m), range with 364 lbs (165 kg) payload 112 miles (180 km), maximum range 280 miles (450 km).
Weight: Empty weight 2,084 lbs (950 kg), take-off weight in aerobatic flight 2,381 lbs (1,080 kg), maximum take-off weight 3,197 lbs (1,450 kg).
Payload: Pilot and up to four people, maximum payload 992 lbs (450 kg).
State of development: The first of two prototypes had its test flight at the end of 1986. About 15 units have been built so far, including nine for the Nigerian Air Force and one Mi-34 for Bosnia.
Remarks: The Mi-34 is designed primarily for training and aerobatic flight duties, but it can also be used for transport, surveillance and communications duties. It will replace the Mil Mi-1, which is still used in great numbers in Russian flight clubs and schools. Additionally, different versions of the above described basic Mi-34S model are offered such as the Mi-34P for police and patrol duties, the Mi-34L with a TIO-540J Textron-Lycoming power plant with 350 PS (161 kW) as well as the new Mi-34A with a Turboméca Arrius 2F gas turbine with 504 SHP (376 kW) performance. This aircraft could carry one additional passenger. Finally, Mil is testing a design of a twin-motor Mi-34M1/M2 version for six passengers.
Manufacturer: OKB Mikhail L. Mil, Arseneyev plant, Moscow, Russia.

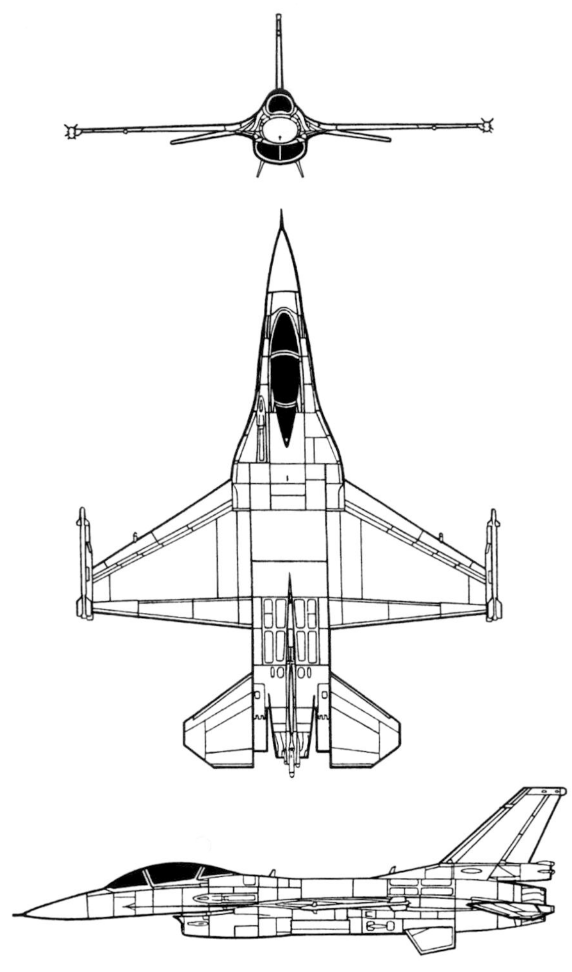

Dimensions:
Wingspan 36.52 ft (11.13 m)
Length 50.92 ft (15.52 m)
Height 16.27 ft (4.96 m)
Wing area 375 sq. ft (34.84 m^2)

MITSUBISHI F-2

Country of origin: Japan (USA).
Type: (F-2A) one-seat or (F-2B) two-seat multi-purpose fighter.
Power Plant: One General Electric F110-GE-129 turbofan engine with 16,973 lbs (7,711 kp/75.5 kN) static thrust without afterburner or 29,607 lbs (13,880 kp/131.7 kN) with afterburner.
Performance (estimated): Maximum speed at high altitude Mach 2.0, near the ground over Mach 1.0, tactical operating radius with anti-ship missiles 516 miles (830 km).
Weight: Empty weight 21,000 lbs (9,527 kg), maximum take-off weight ca. 48,500 lbs (22,000 kg).
Armament: The maximum weapons load is reported at 19,840 lbs (9,000 kg), including Japanese developed Mitsubishi AAM-3 air-to-air missiles as well as XASM-2 anti-ship missiles.
State of development: The maiden flight of the first of four FS-X prototypes took place on October 7, 1995 and last one on May 24, 1996. Deliveries to the Japanese Air Forces began in September 2000. To date, about 65 units have been ordered and approximately 20 delivered. The first squadron became operational in 2001. Altogether, 130 F-2's will be obtained (including 47 two-seaters).
Remarks: The F-2 is derived from the Lockheed F-16 (see pages 226/227). Over the course of its technical development, the F-2 has moved further away from the initial model, so that today it can be totally regarded as a newly developed type. The fuselage front and tail are slightly longer and the wing comprised of synthetic material is a new development. A new multi-purpose on-board radar with active control and a range of up to 118 miles (190 km), which can simultaneously track ten targets, was a result of American Japanese cooperation. The remaining electronics are completely Japanese developed, including the wide-angle Head-up-Display, five Liquid Crystal Displays in the cockpit as well as a substantial integrated system for electronic combat control. Various parts of the fuselage are covered with radar-absorbing material. Currently, Mitsubishi is testing the development of a fighter version with extensive weapons electronics.
Manufacturer: Mitsubishi Heavy Industries Ltd., Nagoya plant, Tokyo, Japan.

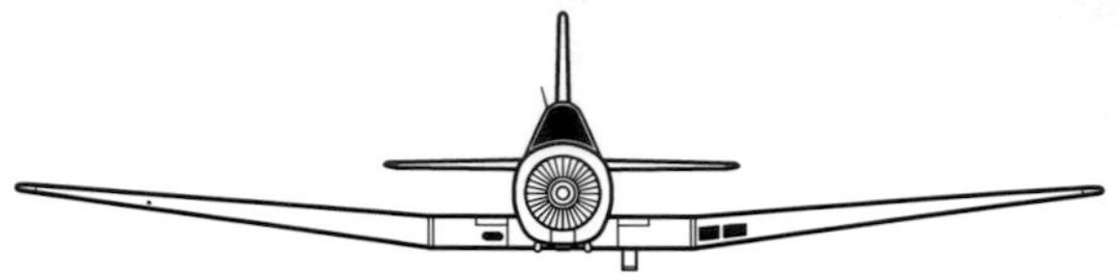

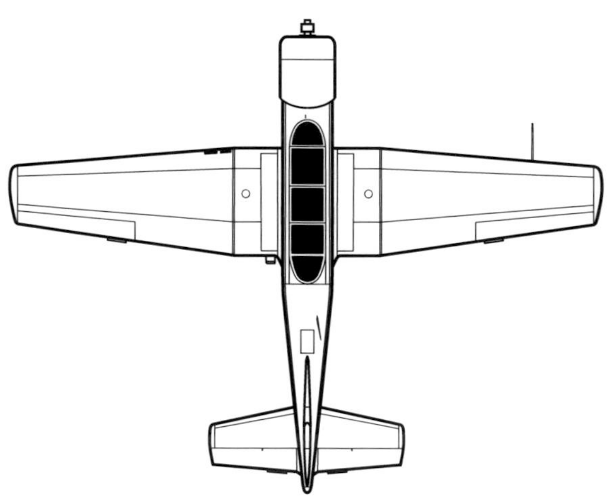

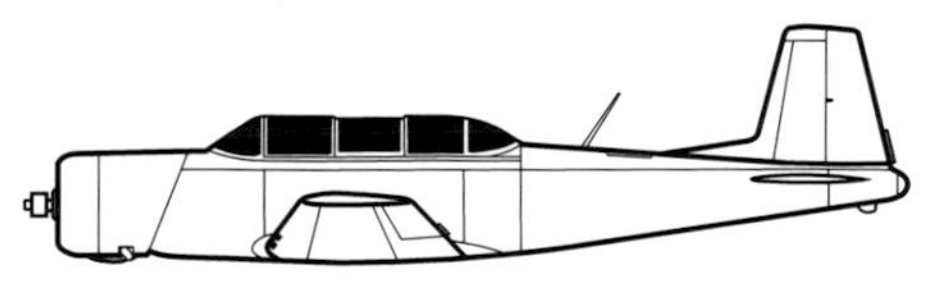

Dimensions:
Wingspan 33.53 ft (10.22 m)
Length 27.76 ft (8.46 m)
Height 10.66 ft (3.25 m)

NANCHANG CJ-6

Country of origin: People's Republic of China.
Type: Two-seat basic trainer.
Power Plant: One SAEC (Zhuzhou) HS6A air-cooled nine-cylinder radial engine with 285 PS (212 kW) performance.
Performance: Maximum speed 185 mph (297 km/h), initial rate of climb 21 ft (6.3 m)/sec, service ceiling 20,510 ft (6,250 m), maximum flight duration 3.5 hours, range 429 miles (690 km).
Weight: Empty weight 2,414 lbs (1,095 kg), maximum take-off weight 3,086 lbs (1,400 kg).
Armament (CJ-6B): Various light weapons for training purposes.
State of development: The first flight of the CJ-6 version was made prior to the end of 1961. Since then, more than 2,100 units of this trainer have been built, probably with interruptions. The principal buyer has been the Chinese Air Force. Some 200 units were exported to Bangladesh, Cambodia and North Korea, among others. The latest purchase has been made by Sri Lanka (10).
Remarks: The Nanchang CJ-6 is a Chinese replica of the Russian Yakovlev Yak-18 basic trainer. Its construction represents the technology of the fifties: full metal structure, radial engine with twin-blade propeller, and cockpit with conventional displays. There have been limited improvements over the long-term production period. Because of this, the aircraft is promoted for its very robust, long-life construction and its distinguishable very good flight characteristics. The retractable landing gear with low-pressure tires allows for take offs and landings on unpaved fields.
Manufacturer: NAMC (**N**anchang **A**ircraft **M**anufacturing **C**ompany), Nanchang, PR China.

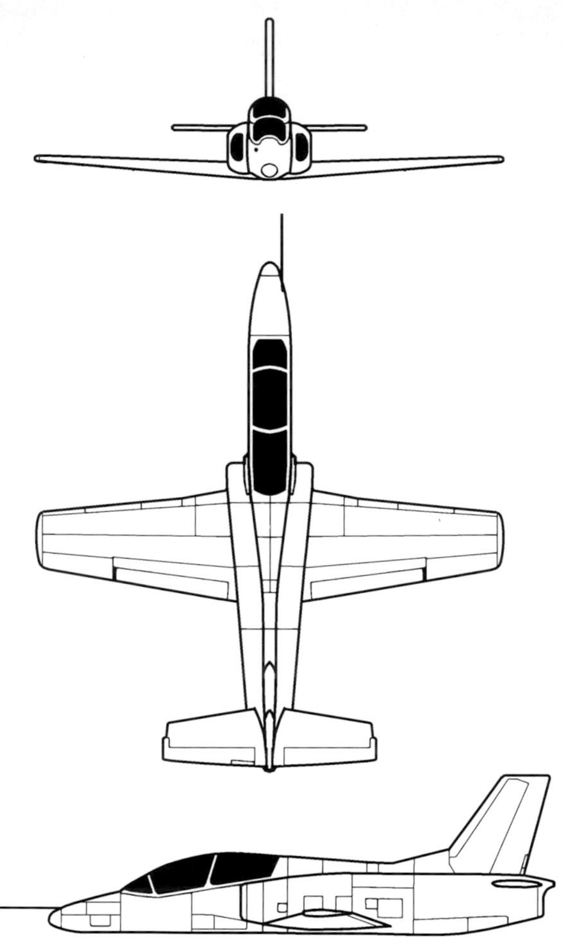

Dimensions:
Wingspan 31.59 ft (9.63 m)
Length including probe 38.06 ft (11.60 m)
Height 13.81 ft (4.21 m)
Wing area 191.8 sq. ft (17.02 m^2)

NANCHANG K-8 JET TRAINER

Country of origin: People's Republic of China and Pakistan.
Type: Two-seat basic trainer and light ground attack aircraft.
Power Plant: One AlliedSignal TFE731-2A-2A turbofan engine with 3,597 lbs (1,632 kp/16.0 kN) static thrust or (K-8J) Progress AI-25 turbofan engine with approximately 4,946 lbs (2,200 kp/22.0 kN) static thrust.
Performance: Maximum speed 497 mph (800 km/h) at sea level, initial rate of climb 89 ft (27 m)/sec, service ceiling 42,650 ft (13,000 m), maximum flight duration 3.0 hours, range with two 66 gallon (250 l) external drop-tanks 1,398 miles (2,250 km), with internal fuel 924 miles (1,487 km).
Weight: Empty weight 5,924 lbs (2,687 kg), normal load without external load 8,003 lbs (3,630 kg), maximum take-off weight 9,546 lbs (4,330 kg).
Armament (as ground attack aircraft): One 23-mm cannon bay under the fuselage and four wing pylons for bombs, rocket pods, or missiles. Maximum weapons load 2,079 lbs (943 kg).
State of development: The initial flight test of the first of six prototypes (of which two were only for stationary tests) was on November 21, 1990. To date, Pakistan has purchased six and the PR China 30 units. Pakistan would like to purchase up to 100 K-8's. However, PR China doesn't intend to make any further purchases. Other customers include Egypt 80 (licensed construction), Morocco, Myanmar 12, Namibia 4, Sri Lanka 6, and Zambia 8.
Remarks: The K-8 is a Chinese-Pakistani co-development that is designed for particularly high reliability and ease of service. Initially, all K-8's destined for Pakistan were to be assembled in the Kamra plant. However, for financial reasons, the production remains solely in China. The Pakistani K-8, when compared to the Chinese version, exhibits some modifications: EFIS cockpit, different electronic components and new anti-centrifugal brakes. Collins makes the avionics while the ejector seats are the Martin Baker Mk.10L type. It's not known whether the version equipped with the Ukrainian Ivchenko Progress ZMKB AI-25TL/DV-2 engine, relinquished by China, is still in production.
Manufacturer: NAMC (**N**anchang **A**ircraft **M**anufacturing **C**ompany), Nanchang, PR China and Pakistan Aeronautical Complex.

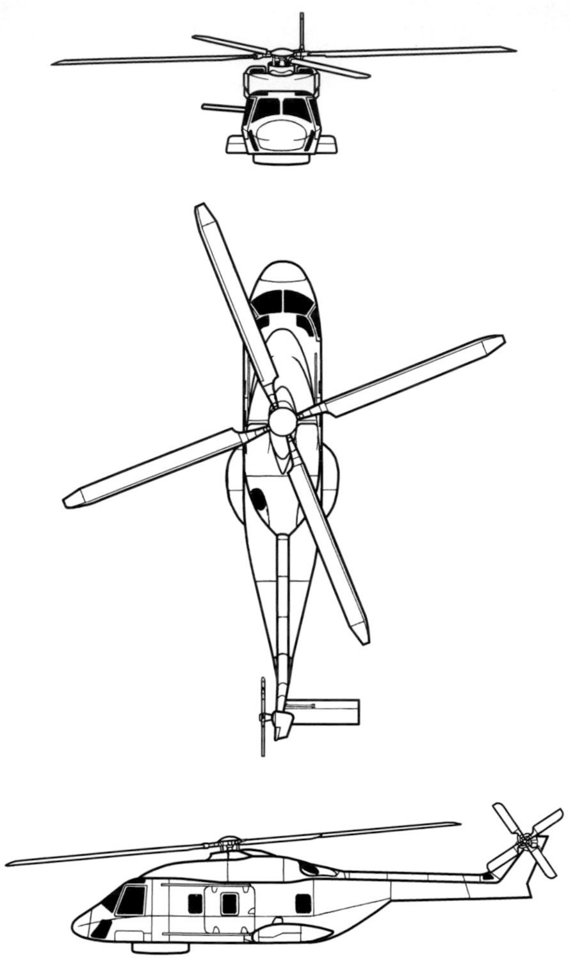

Dimensions:
Rotor diameter 53.48 ft (16.30 m)
Fuselage length 52.1 ft (15.88 m)
Height above tail rotor 17.85 ft (5.44 m)

NH INDUSTRIES NH90

Country of origin: Germany, France, Italy, Netherlands.
Type: Medium-heavy military multi-purpose helicopter (TTH) and ship-based submarine hunter (NFH).
Power Plant: Two Rolls-Royce-Turboméca RTM322-01/9 gas turbine engines or General Electric T700-T6E engines each with 1,680 SHP (1,253 kW) performance.
Performance: Maximum speed nearly 186 mph (300 km/h), normal cruising speed 162 mph (260 km/h), service ceiling 19,690 ft (6,000 m), diagonal rate of climb 36 ft (11 m)/sec, hover altitude with ground effect 11,480 ft (3,500 m), without ground effect 9,514 ft (2,900 m), tactical operation radius with 4,409 lb (2,000 kg) load 155 miles (250 km), deployment range 746 miles (1,200 km), tactical operation duration 4 hours.
Weight: Empty weight between 11,900 lbs (5,400 kg) and 14,110 lbs (6,400 kg), normal take-off weight 19,180 lbs (8,700 kg) to 20,500 lbs (9,300 kg), maximum weight 22,050 lbs (10,000 kg).
Payload (TTH): Two pilots and 20 soldiers or 20 wounded, payload 5,512 lbs (2,500 kg), (NFH) two pilots and up to four systems operators.
Armament (NFH): Two torpedoes or anti-ship missiles each on carriers on fuselage sides.
State of development: The first of five test versions (four TTH, one NFH) has been flying since December 18, 1995. Planned purchases: Germany a total of 215, France 133/27, Italy 150/46, Netherlands 0/20. The first lot of 200 helicopters in both versions was ordered in 2000 with deliveries expected by the end of 2004. Further orders: Finland 20 TTH, Greece 42 TTH, Norway 14 NFH, Portugal 10 TTH, and Sweden 18 TTH + NFH.
Remarks: Two versions, extremely similar in basic concept, are being offered: The TTH, designed for tactical duties, with a tail loading ramp, as well as the NFH naval version. The latter lacks the ramp, has collapsible rotors, automatic folding tail and two buoyancy chambers. On-board avionics contains, among others, tactical radar, FLIR, sonar and numerous other sensor systems. The back of the fuselage contains an ejection system for chaff, infrared flares and sonar buoys. The NH90 has a fuselage composed extensively of composite materials and a fly-by-wire flight control.
Manufacturer: NH Industries, Aix-en-Provence, France.

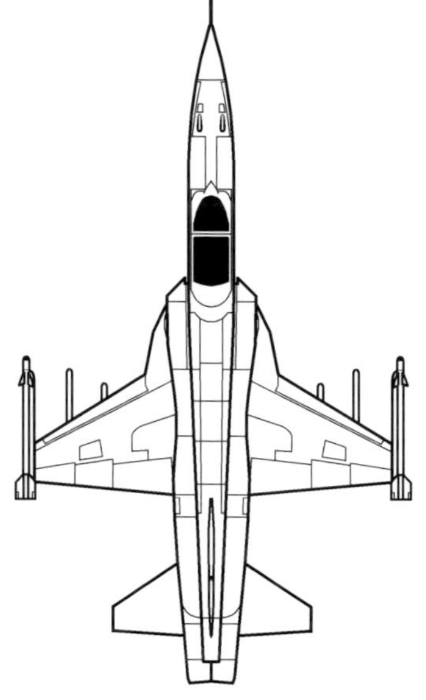

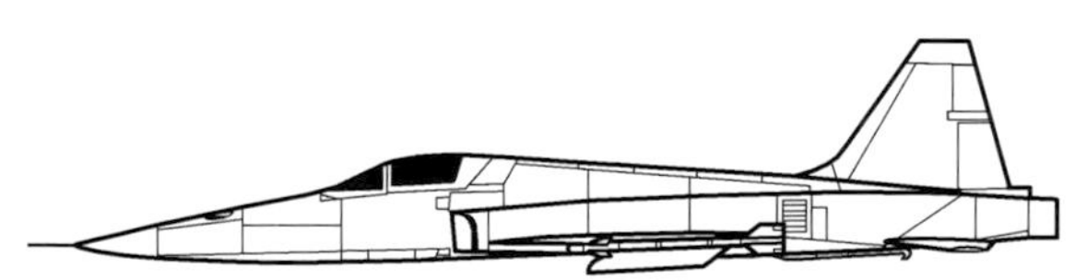

Dimensions:
Wingspan 26.67 ft (8.13 m)
Length (F-5E) 48.16 ft (14.68 m), (F-5F) 51.57 ft (15.72 m)
Height 13.32 ft (4.06 m)
Wing area 186.2 sq. ft (17.30 m^2)

NORTHROP F-5E TIGER

Country of origin: USA.
Type: Light multi-purpose tactical aircraft.
Power Plant: Two General Electric J85-GE-21A turbojet engines each with 3,500 lbs (1,588 kp/ 15.57 kN) static thrust without afterburner or 5,000 lbs (2,270 kp/22.24 kN) with afterburner.
Performance (F-5E): Maximum speed 1,056 mph (1,700 km/h [Mach 1.64]) at 36,010 ft (10,975 m), normal cruising speed Mach 0.98, initial rate of climb 574 ft (175 m)/sec, service ceiling 51,804 ft (15,790 m), tactical operating radius with a weapons load of 5,176 lbs (2,348 kg) around 155 miles (250 km), range with external tanks 1,543 miles (2,483 km).
Weight: Empty weight 9,700 lbs (4,400 kg), maximum take-off weight 24,680 lbs (11,193 kg).
Armament: Two M-39 20-mm cannons on the sides of the fuselage tip and up to 7,000 lbs (3,175 kg) of weapons under the fuselage on four wing pylons and on the wingtips.
State of development: Between 1972 and 1987, 1,410 units of the F-5E/F and RF-5E were built in the US and by licensees for air forces of 20 countries. A large number of the Tigers are still in use today. There have been various conversion programs to keep the aircraft updated. Some have been terminated, while some are still in progress or are in planning.
Remarks: The Tiger has undergone various modernization programs worldwide. A typical conversion has been executed for the F-5E/F in Singapore where 48 units were updated by the Singapore Technologies Aerospace as follows: New Elbit avionics with reworked cockpit, including, among others, HUD, HOTAS controls and a Ring-Laser-Gyro. Further, the previous on-board radar has been replaced with FIAR Grifo F/X Pulse radar. This enables the plane to carry the most modern AMRAAM air-to-air missiles. Finally, this version features MIL-STD-1553B databus architecture that allows for the possibility of carrying the FLIR and ECM systems.
Manufacturer: Northrop Grumman Corporation, Hawthorne plant, Los Angeles, California, USA.

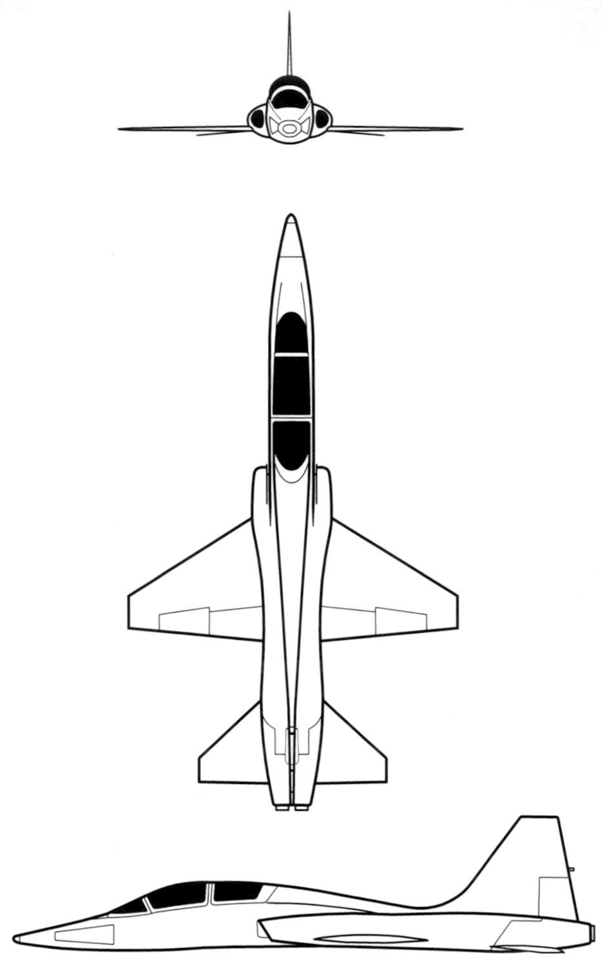

Dimensions:
Wingspan 25.26 ft (7.70 m)
Length 46.39 (14.14 m)
Height 12.86 ft (3.92 m)
Wing area 170 sq. ft (15.79 m^2)

NORTHROP T-38C

Country of origin: USA.
Type: Light multi-purpose tactical aircraft.
Power Plant: Two General Electric J85-GE-5A turbojet engines each with 2,675 lbs (1,215 kp/ 11.9 kN) static thrust without afterburner or 3,844 lbs (1,750 kp/17.1 kN) with afterburner.
Performance: Maximum speed 858 mph (1,380 km/h) at 36,000 ft (10,975 m), 751 mph (1,209 km/h) at 5,000 ft (1,525 m), initial rate of climb 561 ft (171 m)/sec, service ceiling 53,480 ft (16,300 m), typical tactical operation radius 367 miles (590 km), deployment range with maximum internal fuel 1,264 miles (2,035 km).
Weight: Empty weight 7,165 lbs (3,250 kg), maximum take-off weight 12,050 lbs (5,465 kg).
Armament (as AT-38B weapons trainer): One SUU-11 machine gun pod or SUU-20A dispenser for training bombs and unguided rockets under the fuselage.
State of development: The T-38C has been flying since July 8, 1998. It is expected that the over 500 units of the T-38A that are still in service with the USAF, USN and NASA will be modified. On July 23, 2000, the 14th Training Wing was the first unit to obtain the new version. Over 100 units have already been delivered. Between 1959 and 1972, a total of 1,187 aircraft of the original T-38A version were manufactured, which, aside from the USAF units, are or were in service in Portugal, Turkey, Taiwan, South Korea, and Germany (the latter with USAF markings).
Remarks: The original T-38A has had approximately 40 years of heavy training use. Further, the life span is anticipated to be through 2020. Because of these factors, a lasting modernization became necessary. The modernization included a completely new glass cockpit that is better able to match the requirements of newer combat aircraft. Also installed were the GPS, an anti-collision system and a head-up display. The navigation system has been modified and part of the structure renewed and strengthened. All T-38C's include US16LN Martin Baker ejection seats. A further step will be to install new power plants of a type still to be determined.
Manufacturer: Northrop Grumman Corporation, Hawthorne plant, Los Angeles, California; conversion contractor: Boeing Aerospace Support, USA.

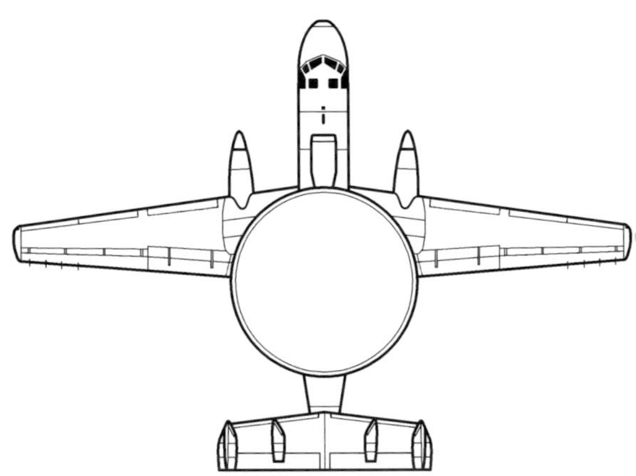

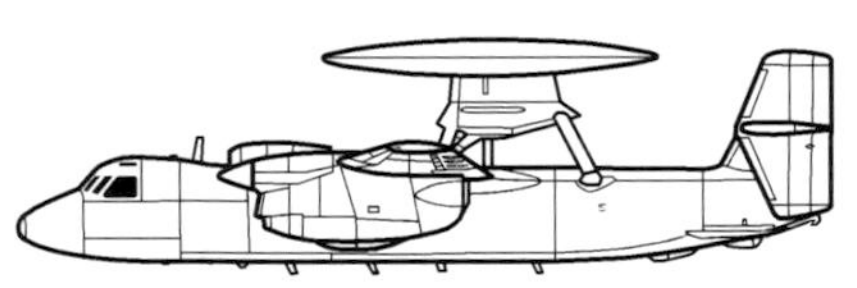

Dimensions:
Wingspan 80.58 ft (24.56 m)
Length 57.58 ft (17.55 m)
Height 18.67 ft (5.69 m)
Wing area 700 sq. ft (65.03 m^2)

NORTHROP GRUMMAN HAWKEYE 2000

Country of origin: USA.
Type: Carrier-based early warning and control system aircraft as well as an airborne command and control center.
Power Plant: Two Allison T56-A-427 turboprop engines each with 5,250 SHP (3,917 kW) performance.
Performance: Maximum speed 372 mph (598 km/h), maximum cruising speed 358 mph (576 km/h), initial rate of climb 42 ft (12.8 m)/sec, service ceiling 30,810 ft (9,390 m), operational duration 4 hrs with a tactical operation radius of 230 miles (370 km), maximum flight duration 6 hours, deployment range 1,603 miles (2,580 km).
Weight: Empty 38,060 lbs (17,265 kg); maximum take-off weight 54,000 lbs (24,494 kg).
Payload: Five-man crew, consisting of two pilots and three engineers in the central operational compartment.
State of development: By 1995, the US Navy obtained a total of 148 aircraft before a production break. Since 1997, Hawkeyes have been delivered in an annual quota of three to four E-2C's. Additionally, the Hawkeye is operated in various versions in Egypt 6, France 3, Israel 4, Japan 13, Singapore 4 and Taiwan 4. The US Coast Guard uses four and the US Customs Service one E-2C loaned from the US Navy for Drug War operations.
Remarks: The latest version, currently known as Hawkeye 2000, had its first flight test on April 11, 1998. Between 2001 and 2006, the US Navy will obtain 21 new units. A maximum of 54 additional aircraft will be built in this version by 2010. Differing from the E-2C Group 2 standard, the Hawkeye 2000 has a new central computer with so-called "open IT architecture" which makes subsequent updates significantly easier, new user-friendly workstations, satellite communications, better navigation systems, airborne refueling capability and an infrared sensor for passive surveillance. All Hawkeye 2000's are also fitted with a new eight-blade propeller.
Manufacturer: Northrop Grumman Corporation, St. Augustine plant, Florida, Los Angeles, California, USA.

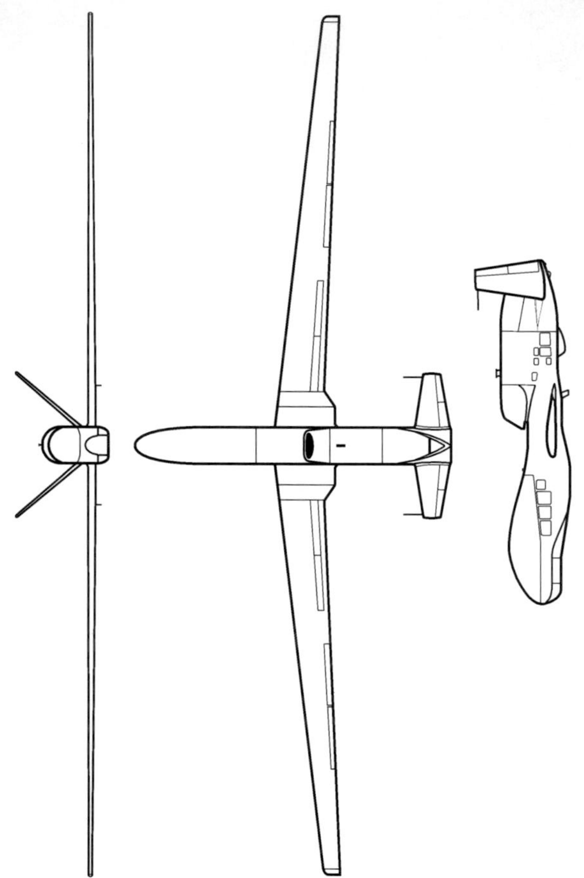

Dimensions:
Wingspan 116.2 ft (35.42 m)
Length 44.4 ft (13.53 m)
Height 15.2 ft (4.63 m)
Wing area 539.3 sq. ft (50.1 m^2)

NORTHROP GRUMMAN RQ-4A GLOBAL HAWK

Country of origin: USA.
Type: Unmanned high-altitude long-range reconnaissance aircraft.
Power Plant: One Rolls-Royce Allison AE3007H turbofan engine with 6,407 lbs (2,900 kp/28.5 kN) performance.
Performance: Maximum speed around Mach 0.60, patrol speed 395 mph (635 km/h), service ceiling 64,960 ft (19,800 m), maximum flight duration 36 hours, tactical operation radius with a 24-hour duration of stay over the target 3,418 miles (5,500 km), range up to 15,540 miles (25,015 km).
Weight: Empty weight 9,200 lbs (4,173 kg), maximum take-off weight 25,600 lbs (11,612 kg).
Payload: Reconnaissance systems with a total weight of 2,000 lbs (907 kg).
State of development: The initial test flight of the first of two prototypes was on February 28, 1998. To date, the USAF has ordered 17 units with an expectation of ordering a total of 51. Five of those have already been delivered. Also, the USN and the USCG plan to order up to 75 and 25 RQ-4A's, respectively. The USAF units were deployed in 2002 and have flown missions during the Afghanistan conflict.
Remarks: In a 24 hour period, the unmanned Global Hawk can provide broad area reconnaissance coverage of a territory the size of Greece from the altitude of 12 miles (20 km), and transfer obtained data worldwide online via satellite. In order to complete this task, the RQ-4A is equipped with the most modern systems, including all-weather lateral view radar, CCD camera for high-resolution photographs, thermal-imaging sensors etc. While the fuselage is conventionally built of aluminum, the wings are made exclusively of carbon fibers with extremely firm construction even though the wingspan is greater. Under load, they bend by a maximum of 2 feet (60 cm). Also, the entire tailpiece is made exclusively of composite materials. In order to achieve a higher measure of reliability, the entire flight control system exists in duplicate. This is true, also, of most of the computers. Currently, tests are being carried out to see whether the Global Hawk could be used as a complement to the Lockheed U-2 manned reconnaissance system, particularly during SIGINT missions.
Manufacturer: Northrop Grumman Corp., San Diego plant, California, USA.

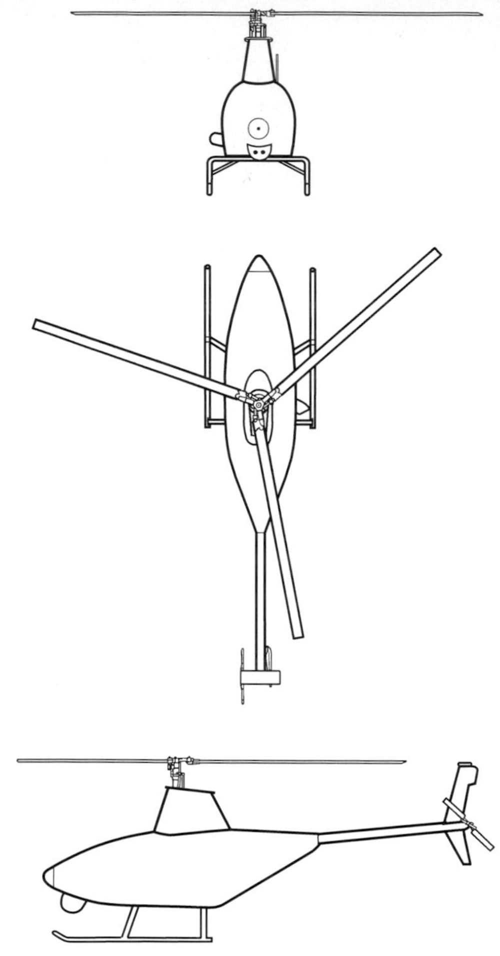

Dimensions:
Rotor diameter 27.49 ft (8.38 m)
Fuselage length 23 ft (7.01 m)
Height 9.42 ft (2.87 m)

NORTHROP GRUMMAN RQ-8A FIRE SCOUT

Country of origin: USA.
Type: Unmanned surveillance and reconnaissance helicopter.
Power Plant: One Rolls-Royce Allison 250-C20W turboshaft engine with 420 SHP reduced to 250 SHP (186.3 kW) performance.
Performance: Maximum speed 143 mph (230 km/h), service ceiling 20,010 ft (6,100 m). The Fire Scout is capable of extended continuous operations and will be able to fly 124 miles (200 km) from launch site, stay aloft for three hours, and then return.
Weight: Take-off weight 2,646 lbs (1,200 kg).
Payload: Maximum 126 lbs (57 kg) of reconnaissance, electronics and sensor equipment.
State of development: The prototype began testing on May 19, 2002. Currently, three of them are in the experimental flight stage. While initial interest came from the USN, it appears that the USCG is planning to order a yet unknown number of Fire Scouts in connection with the "Deepwater" program.
Remarks: The RQ-8A unmanned rotorcraft derives from the Schweizer 333 light helicopter. Its scope of operation includes real-time reconnaissance and surveillance missions as well as target display of small vessels in a radius of approximately 124 miles (200 km). For that purpose, it is equipped with electro-optical sensors, infrared equipment and a laser target designator. Aside from the aircraft, the overall integral system includes a containerized S-280 ground or ship station for mission control and data reception. The helicopter and receiving station can be quickly moved aboard a C-17 transporter. Light weapons operations are also conceivable in the future and, to that end, tests with AGM-114 Hellfire air-to-surface missiles are being scheduled.
Manufacturer: Northrop Grumman Corp., Los Angeles, California, USA.

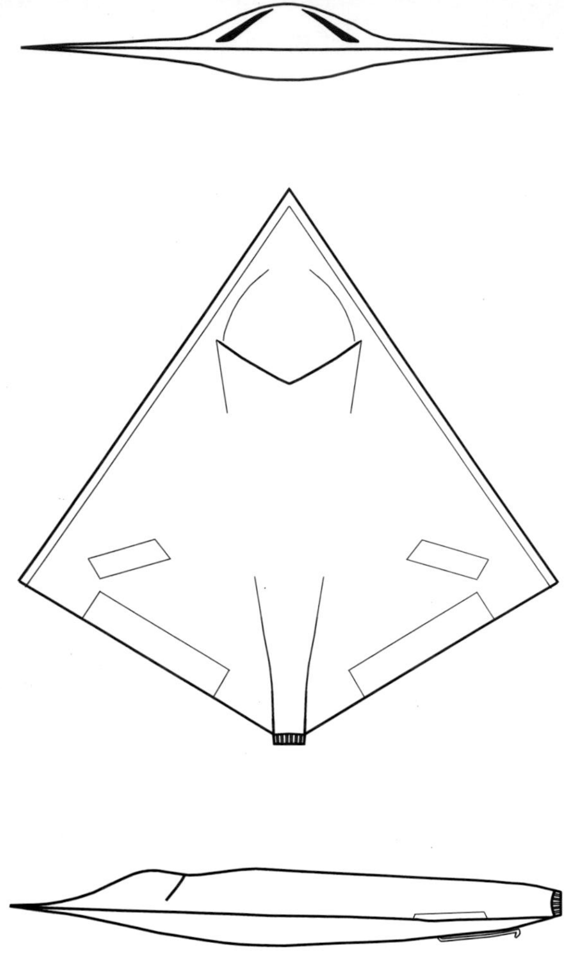

Dimensions:
Wingspan 27.89 ft (8.50 m)
Length 27.72 ft (8.45 m)

NORTHROP GRUMMAN X-47A PEGASUS

Country of origin: USA.
Type: Unmanned carrier-based test aircraft.
Power Plant: One Pratt & Whitney JT15D-5C turbofan engine with 3,192 lbs (1,450 kp/14.2 kN) static thrust.
Performance: No data available yet.
Weight: Maximum take-off weight 3,858 lbs (1,750 kg).
State of development: The X-47A test aircraft, entirely financed by the manufacturer, had its first test flight on February 23, 2003. Only one prototype is planned.
Remarks: Northrop Grumman developed the X-47A with the aid of the Mojave based company Scaled Composites. Constructed largely of composite materials, the Pegasus is mainly intended to test unmanned take-off and landings on aircraft carriers. The entire design provides this test aircraft excellent "stealth" capability. Since it lacks a tail, Pegasus maneuvers by way of six control surfaces (two elevons and four "inlays" placed two above and two below the fuselage). The X-47A will later serve as the development basis for a larger UAV-N X-47B model intended for "first hour" reconnaissance and combat duties, i.e. particularly dangerous missions, which often take place at the beginning of a conflict. It is intended to carry a weapons load of 3,968 lbs (1,800 kg) and be able to fly missions of up to 12 hours. The open-systems electronics are designed by BAE Systems and allow for very precise landings aboard aircraft carriers. In May 2003 Northrop Grumman was awarded a contract from the Defense Advanced Research Projects Agency to produce and demonstrate a minimum of two full-scale X-47Bs. Development is expected to continue through 2006.
Manufacturer: Northrop Grumman Corp., San Diego plant and Scaled Composites Corp., Mojave, California, USA.

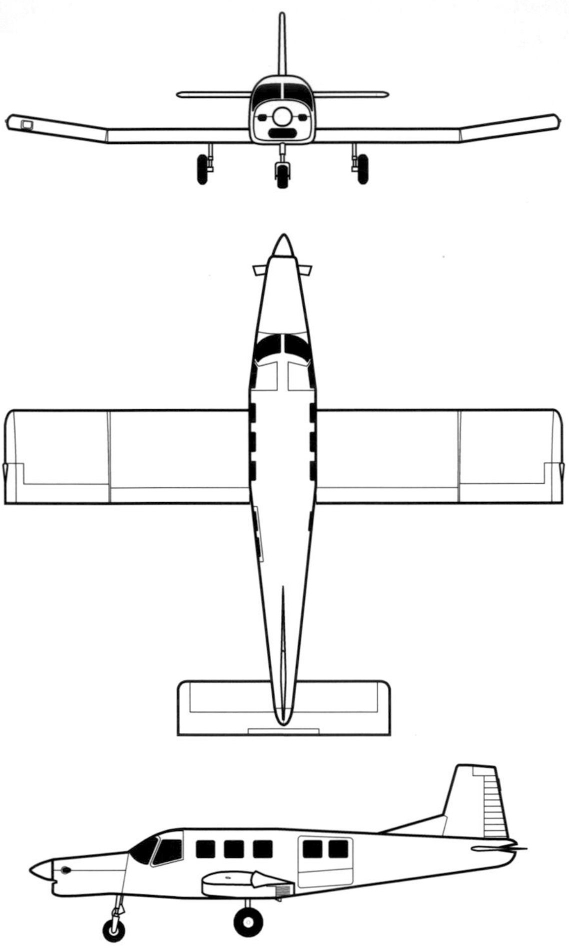

Dimensions:
Wingspan 42 ft (12.80 m)
Length 38 ft (11.58 m)
Height 11.91 ft (3.63 m)
Wing area 294 sq. ft (27.31 m^2)

PACIFIC AEROSPACE PAC-750XL

Country of origin: New Zealand.
Type: Multi-purpose aircraft.
Power Plant: One Pratt & Whitney Canada PT6-34 turboprop engine with 750 SHP (559 kW) performance.
Performance: Maximum speed 203 mph (326 km/h), cruising speed 178 mph (287 km/h), initial rate of climb 28 ft (8.64 m)/sec, service ceiling 30,000 (9,144 m), range with 75% output 682 miles (1,098 km), maximum flight duration 4 hours.
Weight: Empty weight 3,071 lbs (1,393 kg), maximum take-off weight 7,500 lbs (3,402 kg).
Payload: One to two pilots and nine passengers in standard configuration or a maximum of 17 parachute jumpers without seats, payload as a cargo plane 4,427 lbs (2,008 kg).
State of development: The only prototype had its first flight on September 5, 2001. After certification in June 2003, the first units were delivered.
Remarks: The PAC-750XL adopted important elements from the Aerospace Fletcher FU-24 agricultural aircraft including the wings, tail and engine. The fuselage is brand new. The entire structure consists mainly of aluminum and is particularly robust for the numerous prescribed applications. Its intended duties are in freight and general transportation services, as well as transporting parachute jumpers. A wide freight door behind the main wings facilitates these tasks. Thanks to the robust fixed landing gear and short take-off and landing capability, the PAC-750XL can also operate from unpaved fields. In general, this version is designed for a very economic operation while offering sufficient comfort. The basic price is US$925,000.
Manufacturer: Pacific Aerospace Corp. Ltd., Hamilton, New Zealand.

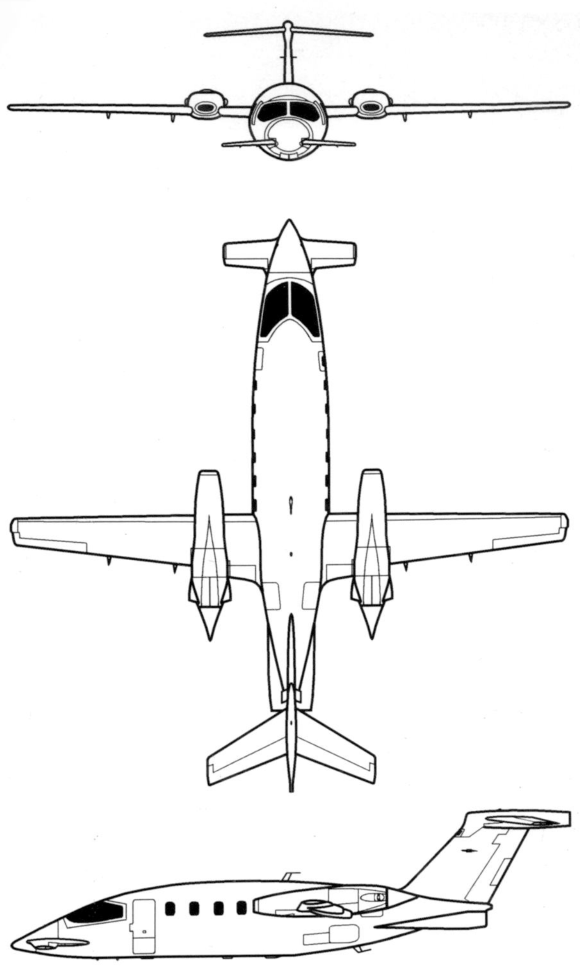

Dimensions:
Wingspan 46.03 ft (14.03 m)
Length 47.28 ft (14.41 m)
Height 13.06 ft (3.98 m)
Wing area 172.2 sq. ft (16.00 m^2)

PIAGGIO P180 AVANTI

Country of origin: Italy.
Type: Corporate and military multi-purpose aircraft.
Power Plant: Two Pratt & Whitney Canada PT6A-66 turboprop engines each with output reduced to 850 SHP (634 kW).
Performance: Maximum speed 455 mph (732 km/h) at 28,300 ft (8,625 m), maximum sustained speed 400 mph (644 km/h) at 38,993 ft (11,885 m), initial rate of climb 49 ft (15.0 m)/sec, service ceiling 39,010 ft (11,890 m), range with a load of six people and IFR-reserves 1,639 miles (2,637 km), maximum range with VFR reserves 1,956 miles (3,148 km).
Weight: Empty weight 7,500 lbs (3,402 kg), maximum take-off weight 11,550 lbs (5,239 kg).
Payload: One or two pilots and seven to eight passengers in standard interior configuration, for EMS operations two recumbent wounded, as a cargo plane maximum 4,100 lbs (1,860 kg).
State of development: The maiden flight of the first of two prototypes took place on September 23, 1986 with the first serial aircraft following on January 29, 1990. By the end of 1998, 36 Avantis were manufactured, after which production was temporarily suspended. Production was resumed in 2000 after orders were received for 33 further units, nine of which were for the Italian Air Force.
Remarks: The Avanti, with its futuristic look, is based on the so-called "three-surface-concept", where forward placed small support wings balance the aircraft in all flight phases and the tailplane is required only for change of direction. The wings have a laminar airfoil and bear a high load due to their comparatively small area. For the most part, the Avanti is made of light metals, though synthetic material parts are used in the tail unit, engine cowl, on the fuselage nose, support wings and the main wings. Its unconventional form gives the Avanti one of the largest cabins in its class with a length of 15 ft (4.55 m), a width of 6 ft (1.85 m), and a height of 6 ft (1.75 m). There is more than ample headroom throughout. Because of this, the aircraft is particularly suitable for ambulance operation. The most recent units to be delivered have an increased fuel capacity.
Manufacturer: Rinaldo Piaggio S.p.A., Genoa-Sestri, Italy.

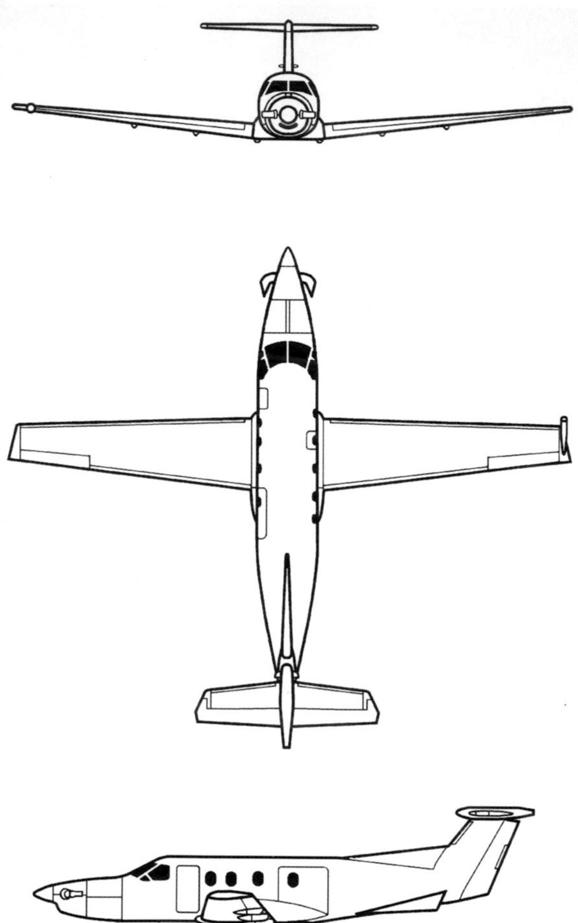

Dimensions:
Wingspan 53.24 ft (16.23 m)
Length 47.24 ft (14.40 m)
Height 13.97 ft (4.26 m)
Wing area 277.8 sq. ft (25.81 m^2)

PILATUS PC-12/45

Country of origin: Switzerland.
Type: Light multi-purpose and corporate aircraft.
Power Plant: One Pratt & Whitney Canada PT6A-67B turboprop engine with output reduced from 1,605 SHP to 1,200 SHP (895 kW).
Performance: Maximum cruising speed 309 mph (498 km/h) at 25,000 ft (7,620 m), initial rate of climb 28 ft (8.50 m)/sec, service ceiling 30,020 ft (9,150 m), range at 30,020 ft (9,150 m) 2,647 miles (4,260 km), with nine passengers 1,877 miles (3,020 km).
Weight: Empty weight for cargo version 5,476 lbs (2,484 kg), in passenger configuration 5,732 lbs (2,600 kg), maximum take-off weight 9,921 lbs (4,500 kg).
Payload: Pilot and co-pilot in cockpit and up to nine passengers in individual seats, as a corporate aircraft six to eight passengers, load with full fuel tanks up to 1,764 lbs (800 kg), maximum payload 3,109 lbs (1,410 kg).
State of development: The first of two prototypes had its maiden flight on May 31, 1991. Deliveries to customers began in May 1994. By the end of 2002, 370 units have been delivered.
Remarks: This multi-purpose aircraft is suitable for a variety of operations from business travel to freight transportation. The cabin of the single-engine PC-12 is longer and wider than, for example, that of twin-motor Beech King Air and allows for freight up to 100 sq. ft (9.34 m^3) in volume. A combined version for four passengers and 64 sq. ft (5.95 m^3) of freight is also offered. A front passenger door and a large freight door in the back facilitate the loading process. The PC-12 is equipped with a substantial avionics package by Allied Signal Bendix/King. The currently produced PC-12/45 version features strengthened landing gear with larger wheels.
Manufacturer: Pilatus Flugzeugwerke AG, Stans, Switzerland.

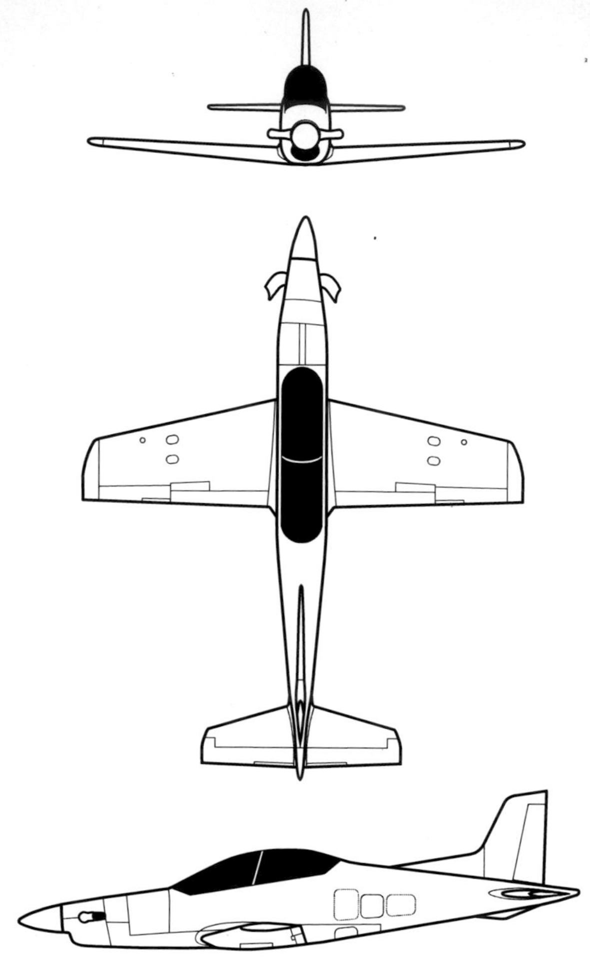

Dimensions:
Wingspan 28.77 ft (8.77 m)
Length 36.71 ft (11.19 m)
Height 12.83 ft (3.91 m)
Wing area 160.4 sq. ft (14.90 m^2)

PILATUS PC-21

Country of origin: Switzerland.
Type: Two-seat training aircraft for basic, advanced and fighter lead-in training.
Power Plant: One Pratt & Whitney Canada PT6A-68B turboprop engine with 1,609 SHP (1,200 kW) performance.
Performance (according to manufacturer's data): Maximum speed 483 mph (778 km/h), cruising speed 426 mph (685 km/h), initial rate of climb 72 ft (22 m)/sec, service ceiling 37,401 ft (11,400 m), range 746 miles (1,200 km).
Weight: Empty weight 4,960 lbs (2,250 kg), maximum take-off weight 9,370 lbs (4,250 kg).
State of development: While there have been test aircraft flying since May 2001, the actual prototype had its flight test on July 1, 2001. An additional pre-production sample is anticipated in the near future. Certification is expected by the end of 2004 with the first orders to follow.
Remarks: Under the designation PC-21, Pilatus has developed a completely new aircraft as a successor to the PC-7/9. A distinctive feature of the integrated, flexible PC-21 training system is that one single model can cover the entire spectrum of training from initial flight training to advanced training. Operational software has been programmed in such a way that various categories of aircraft can be realistically simulated for training. Each cockpit has three EFIS main displays that are fully digitized and compatible with NVG. A HUD is installed in the front cockpit. System input is delivered via HOTAS. In addition to the latest aircraft structure, the PC-21 differs from the PC-9 in its higher output engine with electronic output control, five-blade propeller, high performance swept back wings with spoilers, pressurized cabin with automatic climate control and an anti-G system. Also included is the latest Mk.16L model ejection seat by Martin Baker with zero-zero rejection percentage.
Manufacturer: Pilatus Flugzeugwerke AG, Stans, Switzerland.

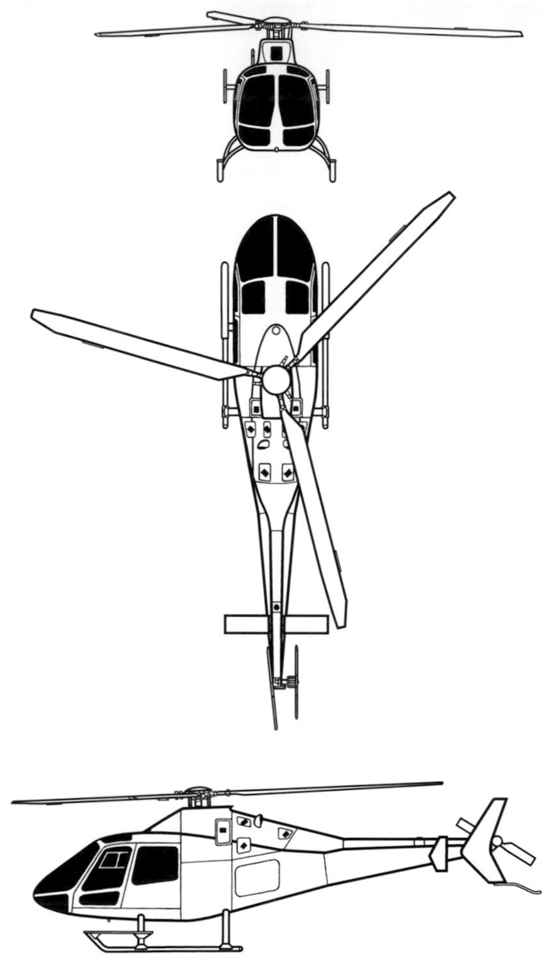

Dimensions:
Rotor diameter 29.52 ft (9.00 m)
Fuselage length including rotor 34.58 ft (10.54 m)
Height 9.68 ft (2.95 m)

PZL SWIDNIK SW-4

Country of origin: Poland.
Type: Light multi-purpose helicopter.
Power Plant: One Rolls-Royce 250-C20R turboshaft engine with 475 SHP (354 kW) performance.
Performance: Maximum speed 179 mph (288 km/h), normal cruising speed 143 mph (230 km/h), maximum diagonal rate of climb 36 ft (11 m)/sec, service ceiling 22,966 ft (7,000 m), hovering altitude with ground effect 11,483 ft (3,500 m), range with maximum internal fuel load approximately 472 miles (760 km), flight duration 5.5 hours.
Weight: Empty weight 1,874 lbs (850 kg), maximum take-off weight 3,748 lbs (1,700 kg).
Payload: One pilot and four passengers, internal payload 882 lbs (400 kg), external payload 1,323 lbs (600 kg).
State of development: The first of two prototypes had its initial test flight on October 26, 1996, after a fairly long delay caused by technical problems. Certification wasn't achieved until November 2003. The initial production is reserved for the Polish Air Force, which will receive 47 units to use as training helicopters by 2010.
Remarks: With the SW-4, PZL offers a cost-efficient alternative to the already well-known competitor models. The purchase price is expected to be approximately US$700,000. The rotor system features a classic construction with conventional three-blade rotor made of fiberglass/epoxy resin. Compound materials (fiberglass and carbon) make up 20% of the fuselage. The helicopter is equipped with AlliedSignal Bendix/King avionics and can therefore be flown under IFR regulations. Aside from actual communications operations, the SW-4 will also be suitable for EMS and patrol duties. As an option, this model can also be obtained with a Pratt & Whitney Canada PW206 turboshaft engine with 615 SHP (459 kW) output.
Manufacturer: PZL Swidnik, Swidnik, Poland.

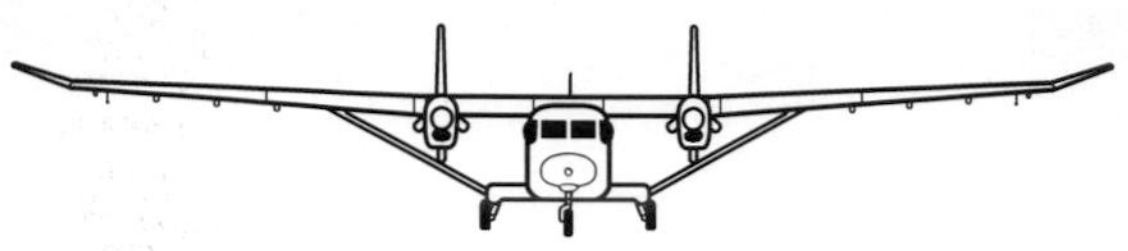

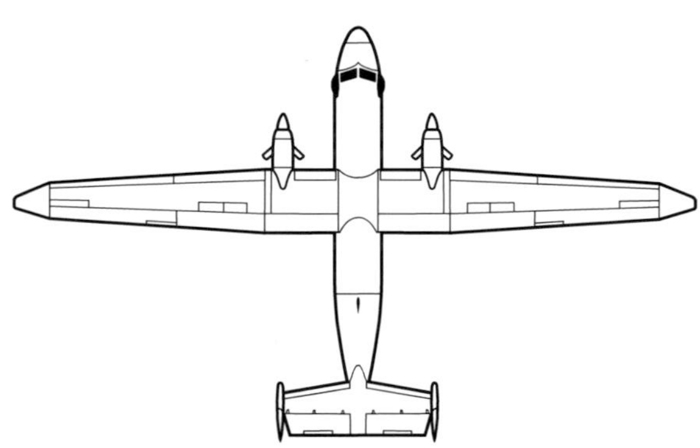

Dimensions:
Wingspan 72.38 ft (22.06 m)
Length 49.02 ft (14.94 m)
Height 16.01 ft (4.90 m)
Wing area 427.54 sq. ft (39.72 m^2)

PZL MIELEC M-28 SKYTRUCK PLUS

Country of origin: Poland.
Type: Civil and military light multi-purpose STOL transporter.
Power Plant: Two Pratt & Whitney Canada PT6A-65B turboprop engines each with 1,200 SHP (880 kW) performance.
Performance: Maximum speed 242 mph (390 km/h), maximum cruising speed 213 mph (342 km/h), service ceiling 20,341 ft (6,200 m), range with maximum payload 435 miles (700 km), maximum range 540 miles (870 km).
Weight: Empty weight 9,304 lbs (4,220 kg), maximum take-off weight 18,960 lbs (8,600 kg).
Payload: Two-person cockpit crew and up to 30 passengers, 21 fully equipped soldiers or, as a freighter, three standard LD-3 containers.
State of development: The first of two prototypes had its maiden flight in 1998. Deliveries began in 2000. The actual order status is not known. To date, the Skytruck Plus has been purchased by Poland (two M-28TD, two M-28E), Nepal (1), Peru (Navy 2), and Venezuela (18 for National Guard, Army 10).
Remarks: The Skytruck Plus is an advanced design version of the original An-28 and is partially fitted with Western equipment. It is primarily designed for military operations and comes equipped with a rear-loading ramp. Additionally, a civilian version with a freight door on the side of the fuselage will also be offered. The avionics package includes, among others, EFIS displays, GPS and weather radar. For the rest, the Skytruck Plus has adopted the very robust and simple, fixed landing gear construction of the An-28. The sea surveillance and ELINT version An-28R, or the M-28E of the Polish Navy, is, among others, equipped with PIT ASR-400 surveillance radar. In the near future, a new version with retractable landing gear will be offered.
Manufacturer: PZL Mielec Aircraft, Mielec, Poland.

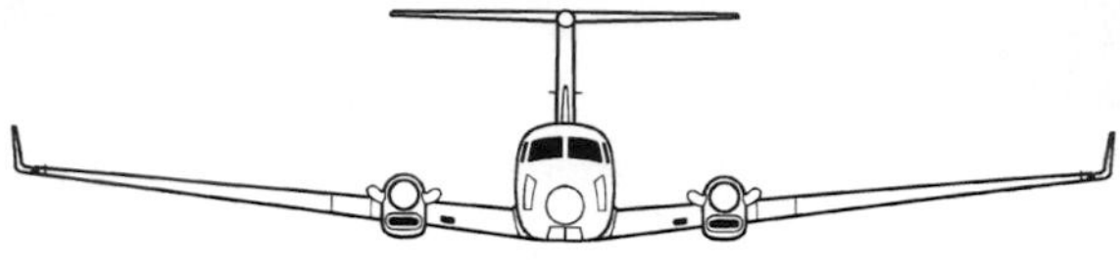

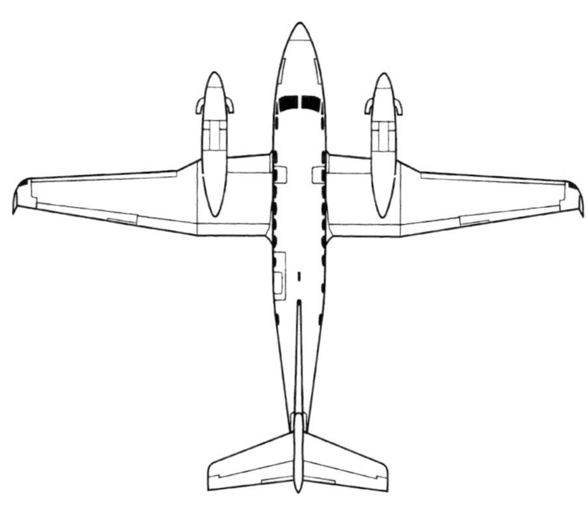

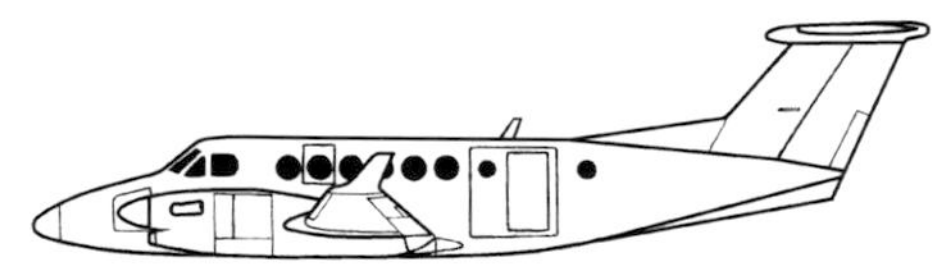

Dimensions:
Wingspan 57.91 ft (17.65 m)
Length 46.65 ft (14.22 m)
Height 14.34 ft (4.37 m)
Wing area 310 sq. ft (28.80 m^2)

RAYTHEON BEECHCRAFT KING AIR 350

Country of origin: USA.
Type: Corporate aircraft.
Power Plant: Two Pratt & Whitney Canada PT6A-60A turboprop engines each with 1,050 SHP (783 kW) performance.
Performance: Maximum speed 362 mph (583 km/h), maximum cruising speed at 18,000 ft (5,486 m) 354 mph (570 km/h), initial rate of climb 45 ft (13.8 m)/sec, service ceiling 35,105 ft (10,700 m), maximum range with 45 minute reserves 2,082 miles (3,350 km)
Weight: Empty weight 9,110 lbs (4,132 kg), maximum take-off weight 15,000 lbs (6,804 kg).
Payload: One to two-person cockpit crew and normally nine individual seats along the cabin facing each other with a maximum of 15 passengers.
State of development: The King Air 350 has been flying since September 1988 and was first delivered to customers in March 1990. To date, over 350 units have been produced. With approximately 5,300 aircraft (17 variants) in 30 years of uninterrupted production, the King Air family has sold the most twin-motor turboprop airplanes in its class. Current production is 20 units annually.
Remarks: The King Air 350 represents the top of a long line of variants. It is the largest and best-equipped model. Since 1993 all models manufactured have been further improved, particularly in the area of take-off power. The cockpit features an EFIS Collins Pro Line II Flight Deck. Cabin comfort has been enhanced. The 350C version is available for freight transportation, with a freight gate on one side of the fuselage. Between 2000 and 2006, the US Army is expected to obtain 45 units of the RC-12 Guardrail military surveillance version. The Israeli Navy has purchased five planes of the B200 sea surveillance version, equipped with Elta radar and other sensors. Sri Lanka ordered a similarly equipped unit. Recently, the Israeli Air Force obtained eight units for general transportation duties, while the Greek Air Force received two units.
Manufacturer: Raytheon Aircraft, Beech Aircraft Division, Wichita, Kansas, USA.

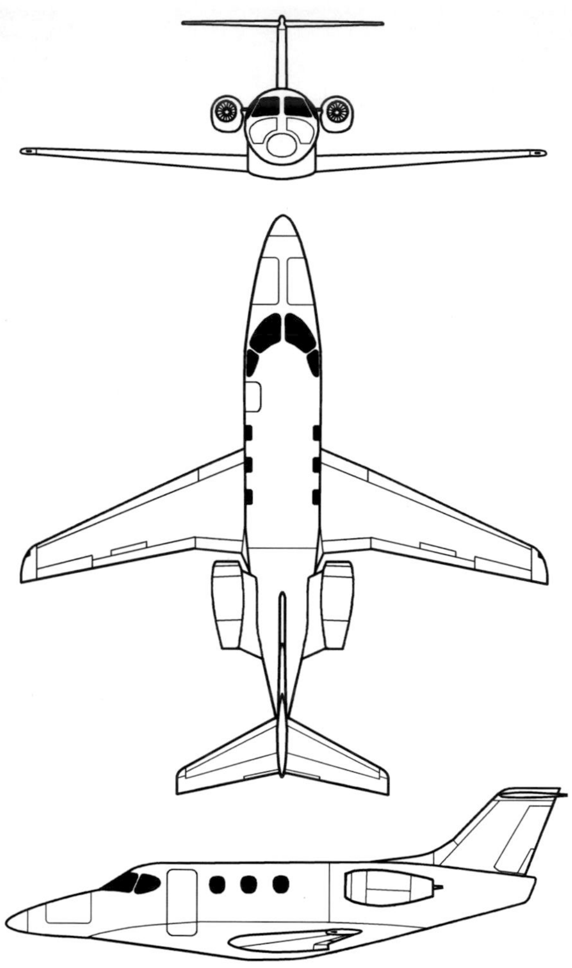

Dimensions:
Wingspan 44.49 ft (13.56 m)
Length 46.00 ft (14.02 m)
Height 15.78 ft (4.81 m)
Wing area 225 sq. ft (20.90 m^2)

RAYTHEON BEECHCRAFT 300 PREMIER I

Country of origin: USA.
Type: Corporate aircraft.
Power Plant: Two Williams/Rolls-Royce FJ44-2A turbofan engines each with 2,300 lbs (1,050 kp/10.23 kN) static thrust.
Performance: Maximum cruising speed 528 mph (850 km/h), normal cruising speed 423 mph (680 km/h), service ceiling 44,010 ft (12,500 m), range with four passengers and IFR reserves 1,616 miles (2,600 km).
Weight: Empty weight 8,245 lbs (3,740 kg), maximum take-off weight 12,700 lbs (5,760 kg).
Payload: One to two pilots and up to six passengers in a standard club configuration, payload with maximum fuel load 805 lbs (365 kg).
State of development: The first of four test models took on its maiden flight on December 22, 1998. To date, orders have been placed for over 300 units. Deliveries began in June 2001 after long technical delays and the 100th unit was delivered in May 2004. Annual production is about 58 units.
Remarks: While the entire fuselage is made of composite materials (combination of honeycomb Nomex structure and carbon fiber), the swept wings are still made of aluminum. However, based on recent calculations, the wings will need to be redrawn in order to achieve the guaranteed aircraft performance. The construction of the entire aircraft is deliberately kept very simple in order to maximize production automation. As a result of and thanks to new production technologies, the Premier I can be offered at a reasonable price of approximately US$5.26 million. The internal cabin volume is distinctly larger than comparable models from competitors. The Premier I cabin length is 14 ft (4.10 m), the width is 6 ft (1.70 m), and the height is 5 ft (1.60 m). The cockpit, equipped with ProLine 21 avionics, is designed for one-pilot operation. The Premier I is to be the base model of an entire family of corporate jets.
Manufacturer: Raytheon Aircraft, Beechcraft Division, Wichita, Kansas, USA.

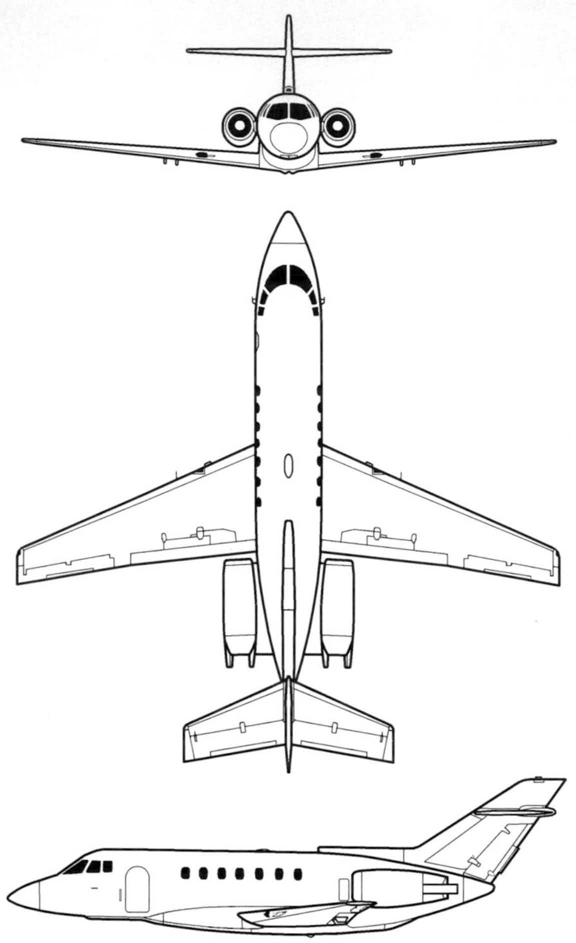

Dimensions:
Wingspan 51.38 ft (15.66 m)
Length 51.18 ft (15.60 m)
Height 17.59 ft (5.36 m)
Wing area 374.05 sq. ft (34.75 m^2)

RAYTHEON HAWKER 800XP

Country of origin: Great Britain/USA.
Type: Corporate aircraft.
Power Plant: Two AlliedSignal TFE731-5BR turbofan engines each with 4,666 lbs (2,113 kp/20.73 kN) static thrust.
Performance: Maximum cruising speed 525 mph (845 km/h) at 29,003 ft (8,840 m), economic cruising speed 460 mph (741 km/h) at 39,009 up to 42,979 ft (11,890 up to 13,100 m), initial rate of climb 52 ft (15.75 m)/sec, service ceiling 42,979 ft (13,100 m), range with maximum payload 2,969 miles (4,778 km), with maximum fuel load and VFR reserves 3,251 miles (5,232 km).
Weight: Empty weight 15,600 lbs (7,076 kg), maximum take-off weight 28,000 lbs (12,701 kg).
Payload: Two pilots and normally eight passengers in single seats or up to 14 passengers in narrow seating, maximum payload 2,879 lbs (1,306 kg).
State of development: The initial flight of the prototype of the latest 800XP version took place in June 1995. The U-125A SAR version, developed from Series 800, is destined for the Japanese Air Force, which requires 27 aircraft (21 of which have been ordered to date). More than 1,050 units have been manufactured in all versions thus far, which is why, worldwide, this model is the most successful corporate aircraft in this class. Production in 2003 reached 46 aircraft.
Remarks: The 800XP is the latest model in a long series. Thanks to more powerful engines it achieves distinctly higher performance, particularly with regard to speed, rate of climb at high temperature and a longer range. The new 800XP features Pro Line 21 avionics made by Rockwell Collins. One aircraft is currently being used to test the effect of winglets, which will eventually be available in all new as well as retrofitted aircraft. At present, Korea will receive a derived version of the 800XP for espionage and surveillance duties (SIGINT). Four have been equipped with radio monitoring systems built by E-Systems, and an additional four with radar made by Loral.
Manufacturer: Raytheon Corporate Jets, Hawker Division, Wichita, Kansas, USA.

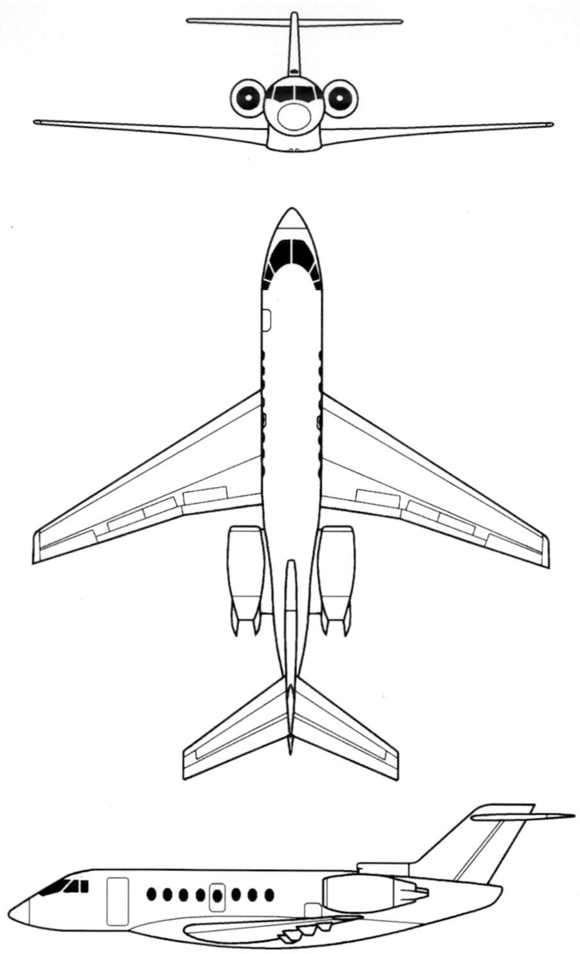

Dimensions:
Wingspan 61.70 ft (18.80 m)
Length 69.16 ft (21.08 m)
Height 19.59 ft (5.97 m)

RAYTHEON HAWKER HORIZON

Country of origin: USA.
Type: Corporate aircraft.
Power Plant: Two Pratt & Whitney PW308A turbofan engines each with 6,497 lbs (2,950 kp/28.9 kN) static thrust.
Performance (according to manufacturer's data): Maximum cruising speed Mach 0.84, service ceiling 45,000 ft (13,716 m), range with IFR reserves 3,573 miles (5,750 km), maximum range 3,915 miles (6,300 km).
Weight: Empty weight 20,931 lbs (9,494 kg), maximum take-off weight 36,001 lbs (16,330 kg).
Payload: Two pilots and normally eight passengers in club seating to a maximum of 12 people, payload 3,569 lbs (1,619 kg).
State of development: After continued delays, testing began on August 11, 2001. The second prototype has been flying since May 10, 2002. To date, the manufacturer has received orders for 100 Horizons (+ 50 options). The largest single order thus far has been placed by NetJet, which ordered 50 aircraft and an option for 50 additional ones. Deliveries of the first aircraft began in 2003. 36 units are produced annually.
Remarks: Although there are certain similarities with the Hawker 800XP (pages 282/283), the Horizon is a completely new construction. With this model, Raytheon intends to set a new comfort standard for the middle segment of the corporate aircraft market. To help achieve this, the cabin is markedly spacious for this class with a length of 29 ft (8.87 m), a width of 7 ft (2.01 m), and a height of 6 ft (1.83 m). Also, the center wing runs completely under the fuselage, so that it never reduces the passenger area. As in the Premier I, the Horizon has a fuselage crafted completely out of composite materials. The wing consists of aluminum and a large part is crafted out of one piece of material. The cockpit features five large flat LCD displays, and, for the first time, the Honeywell Primus Epic Flight Management System has been installed in an aircraft. The avionics, which is placed entirely behind the cockpit, is easily accessible. The basic price is US$15.8 million.
Manufacturer: Raytheon Corporate Jets, Hawker Division, Wichita, Kansas, USA.

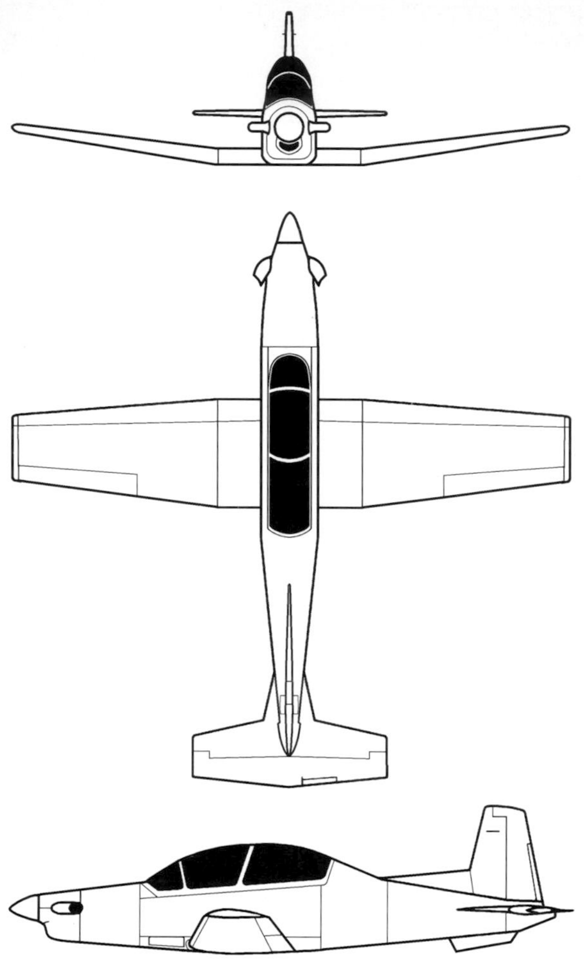

Dimensions:
Wingspan 33.30 ft (10.15 m)
Length 33.27 ft (10.14 m)
Height 10.70 ft (3.26 m)
Wing area 175.34 ft (16.29 m^2)

RAYTHEON BEECHCRAFT T-6A TEXAN II

Country of origin: USA/Switzerland.
Type: Two-seat basic and advanced trainer.
Power Plant: One Pratt & Whitney Canada PT6A-68 turboprop engine with output up to 1,708 SHP (1,275 kW) reduced to 1,100 SHP (820 kW).
Performance: Maximum speed at high altitudes 357 mph (575 km/h), at sea level 311 mph (500 km/h), cruising speed at 7,497 ft (2,285 m) 265 mph (426 km/h), initial rate of climb 67 ft (20.3 m)/sec, service ceiling 35,007 ft (10,670 m), range 978 miles (1,574 km), maximum flight duration 3 hours.
Weight: Empty weight 4,604 lbs (2,087 kg), maximum take-off weight 6,299 lbs (2,857 kg).
State of development: The first test model (a rebuilt PC-9) originally flew in September 1992. After that, Beech manufactured two additional production prototypes (first flight on December 23, 1993), followed by the first serial aircraft on July 15, 1998. It is expected that the American Armed Forces will order 782 planes through 2014, including USAF 454 and USN 328. To date, 167 units have been ordered (USAF 137, USN 30). Deliveries to the USAF began in 1999 with service starting in 2001. The USN began using the T-6A for training in 2003. Other orders include Greece 45 and NATO Flying Training (NFTC) 24.
Remarks: Although very similar to the PC-9, roughly 70% of the T-6A construction has been redefined. The fundamental differences are strengthened fuselage structure and cockpit hood, pressurized cabin, zero-zero ejection seats, new digital electronics (GPS, MLS, anti-collision display, HUD), and one-point fueling. The T-6A is part of an integrated training system, which also comprises simulators and other logistics. The general contractor is Beech Aircraft, a subsidiary of Raytheon. The 47th Flying Training Wing in Laughlin, Texas was the first USAF unit to obtain the T-6A at the end of 2001. 20 of the 45 Texan II units ordered by Greece have been equipped with weapon supports under the wings.
Manufacturer: Raytheon Aircraft, Beech Aircraft Division, Pilatus, Wichita plant, Kansas, USA.

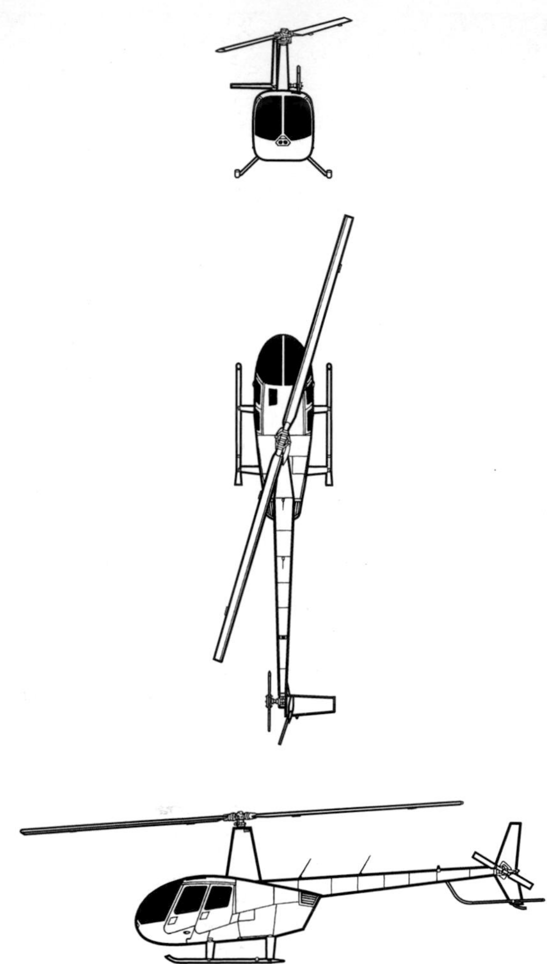

Dimensions:
(R-22/R-44) Rotor diameter 25.16/33.01 ft (7.67/10.06 m)
Fuselage length including rotor 28.74/38.58 ft (8.76/11.76 m)
Height 8.92/10.75 ft (2.72/3.28 m)

ROBINSON R22/44

Country of origin: USA.
Type: Light training and multi-purpose helicopter.
Power Plant (R-22): One Textron Lycoming O-320-B2C four cylinder horizontally opposed engine with 160 PS (119 kW) performance, (R-44) one Textron Lycoming O-540 six cylinder horizontally opposed engine with 260 PS (194 kW) performance.
Performance (R-22/R-44): Cruising speed at 75% output 110/130 mph (177/209 km/h), maximum diagonal rate of climb 20/17 ft (6.1/5.1 m)/sec, service ceiling 13,862/14,009 ft (4,225/4,270 m), hovering altitude with ground effect 6,955/6,398 ft (2,120/1,950 m), range with maximum internal fuel load 368/400 miles (592/643 km).
Weight (R-22/R-44): Empty weight 836/1,400 lbs (379/635 kg), maximum take-off weight 1,369/2,399 lbs (621/1,088 kg).
Payload (R-22/R-44): Two and four people respectively including one pilot.
State of development: The R-22 has been flying since 1975, the R-44 since 1990. Since then numerous improvements have been made. To date, some 3,400 units of the R-22 and 1,250 units of the R-44 have been manufactured. Most have been built for the civilian market. Approximately 400 aircraft are being built annually.
Remarks: Both models are market leaders in the field of simple light helicopters. The helicopters have an extremely diverse range of uses. Aside from the R-22's primary function as a training helicopter, many units are used in agriculture and for police and traffic duties as well as for general transportation purposes. The R-22 fuselage is largely an aluminum tube construction covered with synthetic material and the rotor features a sandwich construction covered with aluminum skin. The R-44 (see photo) is similarly popular. The extended fuselage and other parts have been strengthened accordingly to allow for increased weight. Various avionics sets are available. An improved R-44 Raven II version is brand new, with a stronger IO-540 engine, higher take-off weight and a payload of 1,036 lbs (470 kg). The base price is US$335,000.
Manufacturer: Robinson Aircraft Company, Torrance, California, USA.

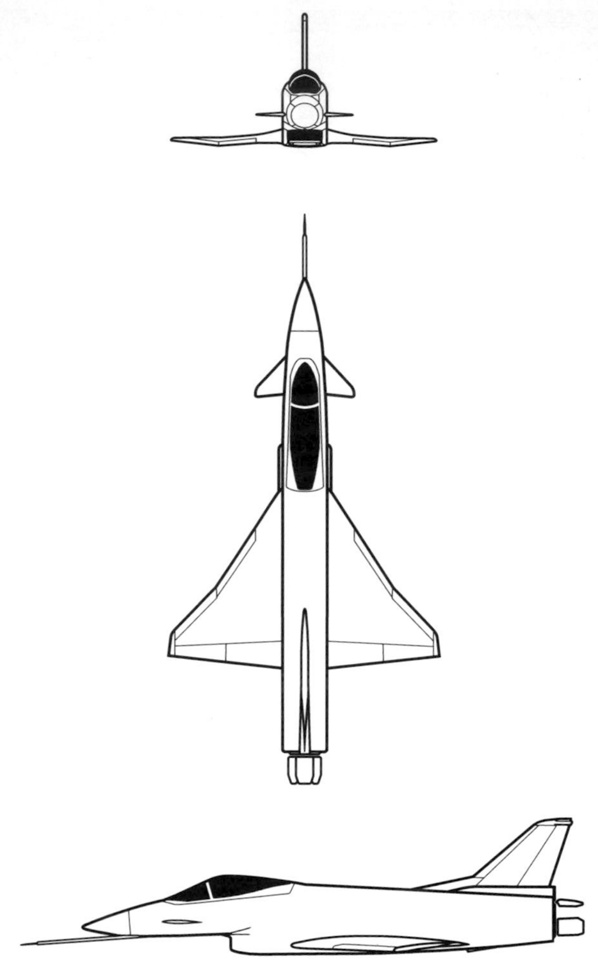

Dimensions:
Wingspan 23.82 ft (7.26 m)
Length with probe 48.72 ft (14.85 m), without probe 40.65 ft (12.39 m)
Height 14.57 ft (4.44 m)
Wing area 226.04 sq. ft (21.00 m^2)

ROCKWELL/DASA X-31

Country of origin: USA/Germany.
Type: Experimental aircraft for extremely short take-off and landing (ESTOL).
Power Plant: One General Electric F404-GE-400 turbofan engine with 16,000 lbs (7,257 kp/71.17 kN) static thrust with afterburner.
Performance: Maximum speed approximately Mach 1.30, initial rate of climb 715 ft (218 m)/sec, service ceiling 40,026 ft (12,200 m).
Weight: Empty weight 11,409 lbs (5,175 kg), normal take-off weight 14,595 lbs (6,620 kg), maximum weight 15,939 lbs (7,230 kg).
State of development: Two experimental aircraft were originally built. Their initial flights were on October 11, 1990 and January 19, 1991 respectively. One of them was lost. The X-31, in its new configuration, had a second test flight on May 17, 2002.
Remarks: The German company MBB/DASA (which has since become EADS) initiated this project with what was then the American company Rockwell International. Working together the companies formed a research program whose goal was to advance the range of maneuverability of potential combat aircraft. Thanks to vector control the program succeeded in flying with attack angles of up to 70° as well as in testing tight turns and other flight maneuvers which to date have not been possible for a fixed-wing aircraft. The project was then suspended for many years before the remaining prototype was converted for new operations. Under the term VECTOR (**V**ectoring **E**xtremely short take-off and landing **C**ontrol **T**ail-less **O**peration **R**esearch), it will probe the possibility of extremely short take-off and landing (ESTOL). With the help of thrust vector steering, it is possible, for example, to carry out landing approaches with the attack angle of up to 25° (normally 12°). The approach speed can then be reduced from the usual 186 mph (300 km/h) to around 124 mph (200 km/h). This would be greatly advantageous when operating from an aircraft carrier without a catapult or arresting wires. Aside from the engine exhaust nozzle that consists of three paddle-shaped guide vanes, new steering software has been developed. To achieve the desired objectives, the X-31 is additionally equipped with an integrated Beacon Landing System (IBLS) and a triple redundant inertial navigational system with GPS.
Manufacturer: Rockwell International Corporation, Palmdale (now Boeing Phantom Works, Seal Beach, California, USA) and MBB/DASA (now EADS, Munich, Germany).

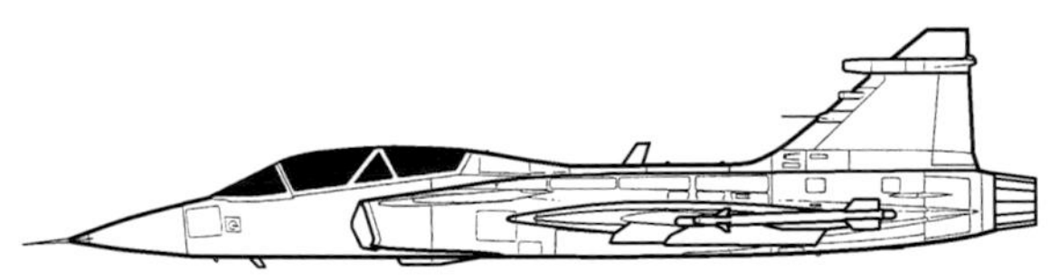

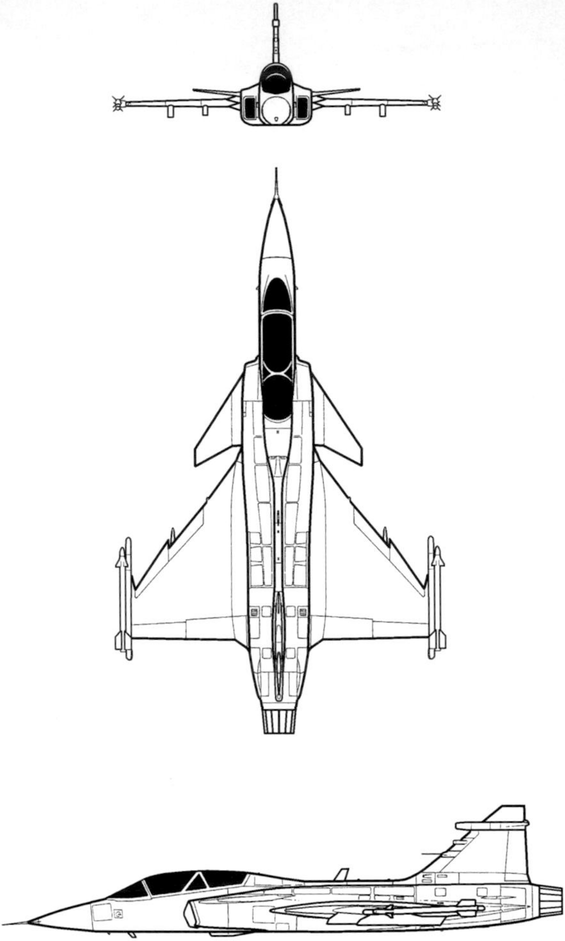

Dimensions:
Wingspan 27.56 ft (8.40 m)
Length (one-seat) 46.26 ft (14.10 m), (two-seat) 48.56 ft (14.80 m)
Height 14.76 ft (4.50 m)
Wing area 322.92 sq. ft (30 m^2)

SAAB JAS 39 GRIPEN

Country of origin: Sweden.
Type: One or two-seat multi-purpose fighter.
Power Plant: One General Electric/Volvo Flygmotor RM12 turbofan engine with 12,140 lbs (5,510 kp/54 kN) static thrust without afterburner and 18,097 lbs (8,210 kp/80.5 kN) with afterburner.
Performance (approximate): Maximum speed at sea level 913 mph (1,470 km/h [Mach 1.2]), at 36,089 ft (11,000 m) 1,588 mph (2,555 km/h [Mach 2.2]), service ceiling 65,617 ft (20,000 m), tactical operation radius as intercept fighter with two Rb24 Sidewinder and Rb72 Sky Flash missiles 249 miles (400 km), deployment range 1,864 miles (3,000 km).
Weight: Empty weight 14,599 lbs (6,622 kg), maximum take-off weight 30,865 lbs (14,000 kg).
Armament: One BK27 27-mm Mauser cannon, six wing supports including two at wingtips for up to four Rb72 Sky Flash and two Rb24 Sidewinder or AIM-120 AMRAAM air-to-air missiles. Air-to-surface and anti-ship weapons can be carried under the wings; maximum weapons load 9,259 lbs (4,200 kg).
State of development: The first of five prototypes had its initial flight test on December 9, 1988. The first serial aircraft was handed over to the Swedish Air Force on June 8, 1993. To date, some 130 units have been delivered. 218 aircraft are on order, of which 190 are the one-seat model and 28 are JAS 39B two-seat models. 20 Gripens are built annually. The South African Air Force has obtained 9 two-seat models (+ options for 19 one-seat units). Hungary has leased 14 aircraft for 12 years with an option to buy.
Remarks: The Gripen, or JAS 39 (**J**akt/**A**ttack/**S**paning), eliminates the need for additional special versions for handling specific tasks. Each Gripen carries the appropriate software in its on-board computer and the accompanying equipment is designed to be modular and easily interchangeable. The two-seat JAS 39B-training version has been built for pilot training. The third lot of 84 aircraft, designated as JAS 39C, features some improvements including FADEC engine controls, color multifunction displays and optional airborne refueling equipment. Currently, more advanced possibilities are being tested.
Manufacturer: Saab-Scania Aktiebolag, Linköping, Sweden.

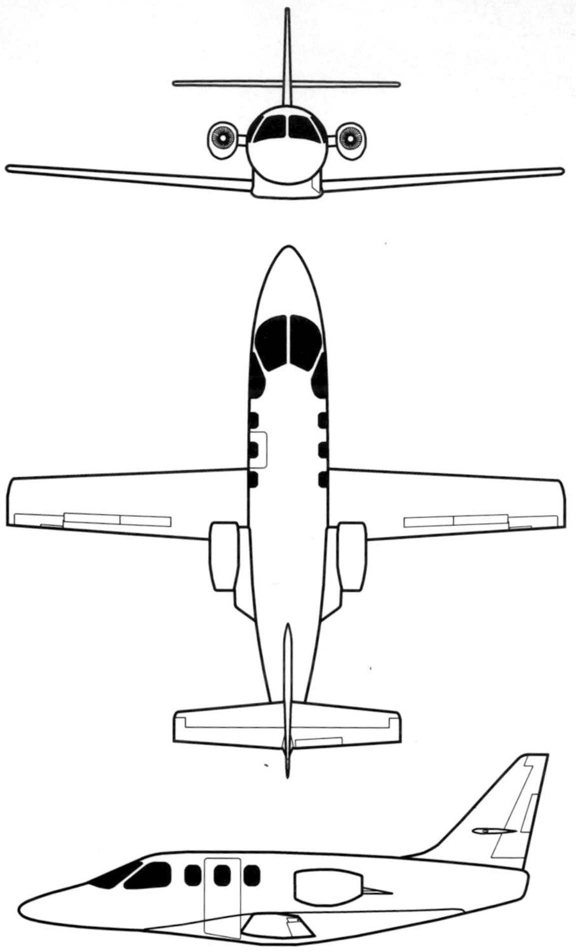

Dimensions:
Wingspan 38.06 ft (11.60 m)
Length 36.09 ft (11.00 m)
Height 14.44 ft (4.40 m)

SAFIRE S-26

Country of origin: USA.
Type: Light corporate aircraft.
Power Plant: Two turbofan engines of yet unselected type each with approximately 1,012 lbs (450 kp/ 4.50 kN) static thrust.
Performance (according to manufacturer's data): Maximum cruising speed 390 mph (628 km/h), initial rate of climb 48 ft (14.7 m)/sec, service ceiling 37,073 ft (11,300 m), range with a payload of 794 lbs (360 kg) 1,174 miles (1,890 km), maximum range 1,616 miles (2,600 km).
Weight: Empty weight 3,646 lbs (1,654 kg), maximum take-off weight 5,900 lbs (2,676 kg).
Payload: Six passengers including pilot in club seating. Maximum payload 1,400 lbs (635 kg).
State of development: On June 10, 2004, the Safire Aircraft Company suspended operations while it attempts to secure additional funding. It is unclear how this will affect the continued development of this aircraft. After many delays, the prototype was scheduled to have its first test flight by the end of 2004. Certification was expected in 2006 with deliveries beginning that same year. It is reported that, to date, over 900 units have been ordered.
Remarks: With the S-26, the manufacturer wants to offer a corporate jet which, despite the typical business jet performance and comfort, costs only as much as the standard sports and touring aircraft. The expected purchase price of US$1.395 million will be, for example, only a quarter of the price of the Cessna Citation CJ1. The operational cost is calculated at US$280 per hour. Large parts of the basic construction are made of aluminum and only a limited use is made of composite materials. The cockpit features EFIS instruments. Although the cockpit is furnished for two pilots, the Safire S-26 is expected to receive certification for one pilot. Originally, it was to be fitted with two Agilis TF-1000 power plants. Currently this issue remains unresolved. A Swiss investment group has financed the initial phase. An actual production site has not yet been determined.
Manufacturer: Safire Aircraft Company, West Palm Beach, Florida, USA.

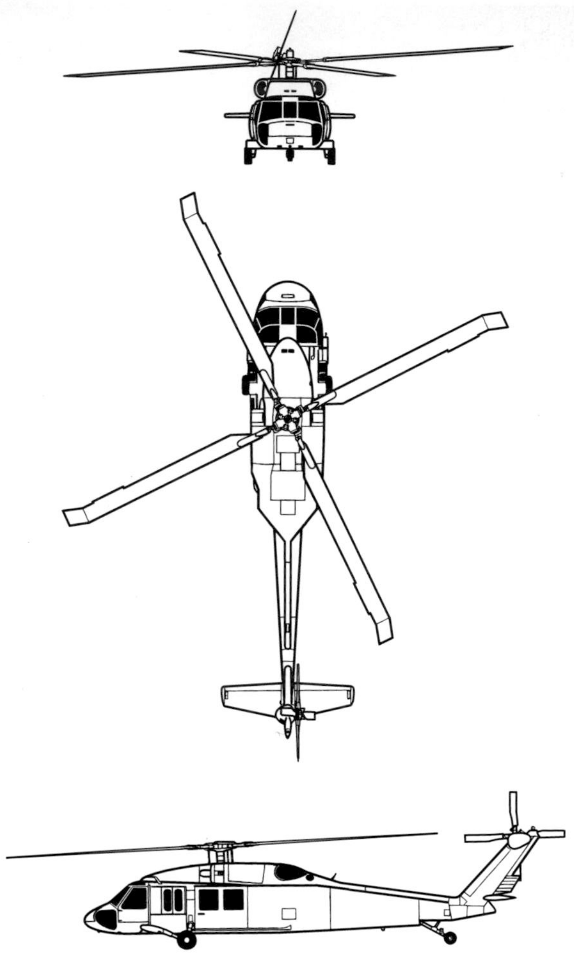

Dimensions:
Rotor diameter 53.67 (16.36 m)
Fuselage length 50.07 ft (15.26 m)
Height including rotor column 12.34 ft (3.76 m)

SIKORSKY MH-60S NIGHTHAWK

Country of origin: USA.
Type: Multi-purpose and ship-based fleet supply helicopter.
Power Plant: Two General Electric T700-GE-701C turboshaft engines each with 1,947 SHP (1,448 kW) performance.
Performance: Maximum speed 183 mph (295 km/h) at 2,001 ft (610 m), maximum cruising speed 167 mph (268 km/h) at 4,019 ft (1,225 m), service ceiling 19,150 ft (5,837 m), hovering altitude without ground effect 11,122 ft (3,390 m), range with 30-minute reserves 373 miles (600 km), range with two 230-gallon (870 l) external tanks 1,013 miles (1,630 km).
Weight: Empty weight 11, 519 lbs (5,225 kg), maximum take-off weight without external load 21,991 lbs (9,975 kg), with external load 23,000 lbs (10,433 kg).
Payload: Three-man crew and 13 people and as a transporter up to 3,999 lbs (1,814 kg) of internal or up to 9,039 lbs (4,100 kg) of external load on freight hooks.
State of development: The Nighthawk prototype, then designated the CH-60S, had its maiden flight on October 6, 1997, followed by the first serial model on January 27, 2000. The US Navy requires 237 helicopters, of which 117 units have been ordered. In addition, 14 of the US Army's UH-60L's will be converted to the MH-60S version. The first HC-5's became operational in 2002. Approximately 30 units have been delivered thus far.
Remarks: This version is a combination of the SH-60 for naval operations and the UH-60L. The fuselage and landing gear come from the UH-60L, while the dynamic systems including the folding mechanism are taken from the SH-60. In addition, the MH-60S is equipped with an EFIS glass cockpit. Aside from freight transportation between US Navy ships, the MH-60S is also intended for SAR and supply operations in combat zones. For long-haul operations, up to four external tanks can be carried on the fuselage on the so-called ESSS supports. A MH-60S advanced version is intended as a replacement for the MH-53E Airborne Mine Countermeasure helicopter.
Manufacturer: Sikorsky Aircraft, Stratford, Connecticut, USA.

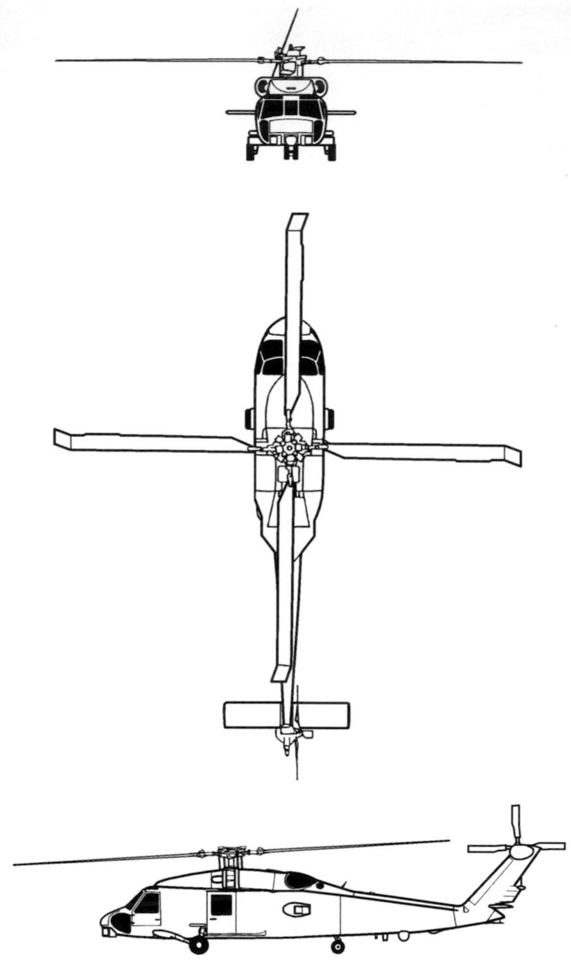

Dimensions:
Rotor diameter 53.67 ft (16.36 m)
Fuselage length 50.07 ft (15.26 m)
Height including rotor column 12.43 ft (3.79 m)

SIKORSKY SH-60R STRIKEHAWK

Country of origin: USA.
Type: Carrier-based submarine hunter and multi-purpose helicopter.
Power Plant: Two General Electric T700-GE-401C turboshaft engines each with 1,900 SHP (1417 kW) performance.
Performance: Maximum speed 169 mph (272 km/h) at sea level, maximum cruising speed 155 mph (249 km/h) at 5,003 ft (1,525 m), on-target duration 3 hrs 50 min. at 60 miles (92 km) or 45 minutes at 300 miles (483 km) away from base.
Weight: Empty weight 13,649 lbs (6191 kg), maximum take-off weight 23,590 lbs (10,700 kg).
Armament: Two Mk.46 torpedoes or two Penguin anti-ship missiles, as well as AGM-114 Hellfire anti-tank missiles and a 7.62-mm machine gun.
State of development: The MH-60R, converted from SH-60B, first flew on July 19, 2001, followed by the first fully equipped model on April 4, 2002. The US Navy would like to have 243 new Strikehawks in service by 2006. To date, over 500 units of all the various versions of the SH/HH-60 helicopters have been delivered to nine navies and coast guards. The latest reorders come from Japan (three SH-60J).
Remarks: While the basic structure of the MH-60R is almost identical to the original version, it is, in many areas, a newly designed construction. Among the new features, it is equipped with an EFIS glass cockpit, APS-147 multi-mode radar, AQS-22 sonar and an acoustic processor. FLIR sensor and ECM equipment are completely new as well. In the future, new engines of the 3000-SHP class (2,240 kW) will be installed, which will improve both flight performance and economic viability. The MH-60R's equipment enables it to combine several tasks of the previous SH-60B/SH-60F/HH-60H versions within one helicopter model.
Manufacturer: Sikorsky Aircraft, Stratford, Connecticut, USA.

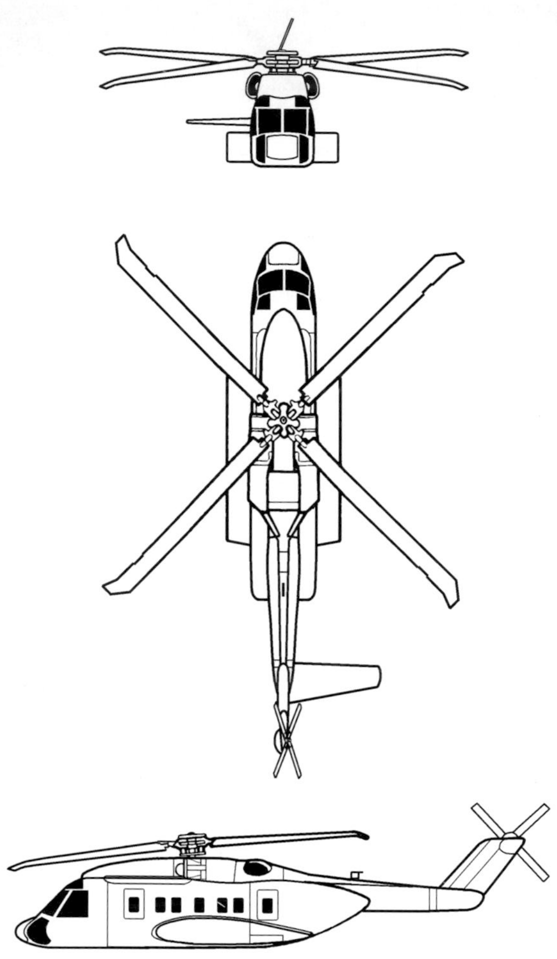

Dimensions:
Rotor diameter 58.10 ft (17.71 m)
Fuselage length 56.82 ft (17.32 m)
Height including rotor head 15.16 ft (4.62 m)

SIKORSKY S-92 HELIBUS

Country of origin: USA.
Type: Passenger and utility helicopter.
Power Plant: Two General Electric CT7-8 turboshaft engines each with 2,400 SHP (1,790 kW) performance.
Performance: Maximum speed 190 mph (305 km/h), maximum cruising speed 179 mph (288 km/h), normal cruising speed 162 mph (260 km/h), service ceiling 14,993 ft (4,570 m), hovering altitude with ground effect 10,171 ft (3,100 m), without ground effect 5,495 ft (1,675 m), range 547 miles (880 km).
Weight: Empty weight 15,498 lbs (7,030 kg), maximum take-off weight with internal payload 25,199 lbs (11,430 kg), with external payload 26,500 lbs (12,020 kg).
Payload: Two pilots and between 19 and 22 passengers, maximum external payload 11,020 lbs (5,000 kg).
State of development: The first of four S-92A testing units took off for its maiden flight on December 23, 1998. According to the latest plans, customer deliveries are expected to begin mid-summer 2004 with a total of 12 units being delivered by the end of the year. To date, orders and purchase intentions for 18 units are known to have been placed.
Remarks: While the fuselage is a completely new construction, the most dynamic components (main and tail rotors, rotor head) were adopted from the S-70. The cabin is spacious with a length of 19 ft (5.67 m), a width of 7 ft (2.00 m), and a height of 6 ft (1.83 m). This will offer as much comfort as an airliner, as will the attention paid to noise and vibration reduction. The landing gear is retractable. A rear-loading ramp is available for easier loading. In addition to its electronics, the S-92 is equipped with one other distinctive feature. Thanks to a digital flight control system (AFCS), the helicopter can also be steered automatically when hovering. When the serial version is manufactured, Sikorsky plans to extend the fuselage by a little more than 1 ft (40 cm) behind the cockpit. Additionally, the Pro Line 21 avionics will be installed. Because of its various components, the S-92 will be deployable for a variety of tasks, including offshore operations, SAR and ASW duties as well as for VIP and commuter flights.
Manufacturer: Sikorsky Aircraft, Stratford, Connecticut, USA.

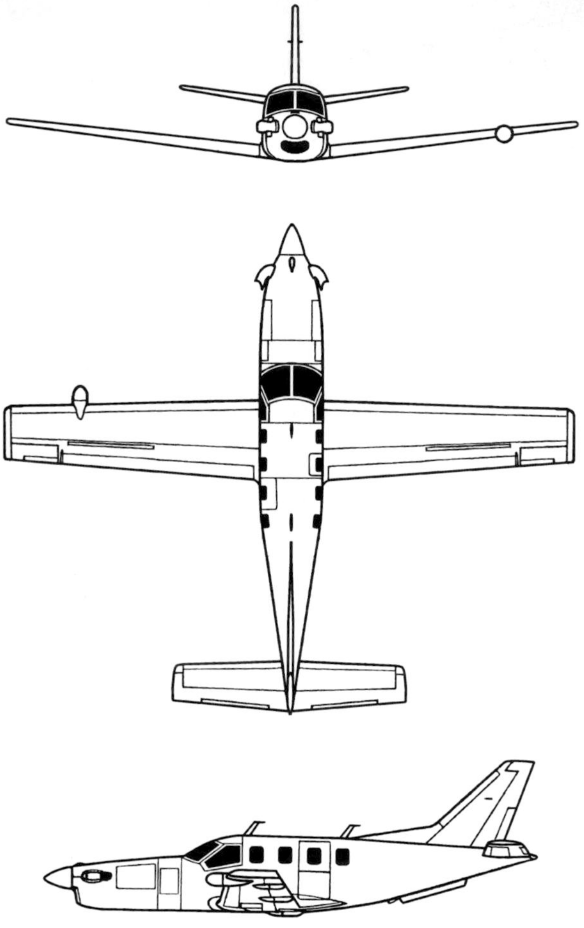

Dimensions:
Wingspan 41.60 ft (12.68 m)
Length 34.90 ft (10.64 m)
Height 14.27 (4.35 m)
Wing area 193.75 sq. ft (18.00 m^2)

SOCATA TBM 700

Country of origin: France.
Type: Light multi-purpose aircraft.
Power Plant: One Pratt & Whitney Canada PT6A-64 turboprop engine with 700 SHP (522 kW) performance.
Performance: Maximum speed 345 mph (556 km/h) at 26,000 ft (7,925 m), normal cruising speed 325 mph (523 km/h) at 30,003 ft (9,145 m), long-range cruising speed 281 mph (452 km/h) at 30,003 ft (9,145 m), initial rate of climb 38.39 ft (11.7 m)/sec, service ceiling 30,003 ft (9,145 m), range with six passengers 1,180 miles (1,900 km), range with maximum fuel load 1,784 miles (2,871 km).
Weight: Empty weight 4,100 lbs (1,860 kg), maximum take-off weight 6,581 lbs (2,985 kg).
Payload: One to two pilots and up to six passengers. The "club" version seats four passengers with a center aisle. Maximum payload as freighter 1,598 lbs (725 kg).
State of development: The TBM 700 prototype first flew on July 14, 1988, followed by the second in August and the third in October 1989. The first serial aircraft had its maiden flight on August 21, 1990. Through 2002, approximately 230 TBM 700's have been ordered and some 190 of those delivered. The French Air Force has obtained 19 TBM 700's so far and plans to purchase a total of 35 aircraft. In 2002, 35 TBM's were produced.
Remarks: The TBM 700 is a joint development of Socata (a subsidiary of Aérospatiale) and Mooney Aircraft. As a pressurized touring airplane, the TBM 700 benefits from the Mooney M301, from which its fuselage was largely adopted. However, Socata has developed new wings and a new tail unit. Socata also offers a number of military versions to be used, for example, as communications aircraft, freighter, ECM-operations plane or target designator. Also offered is a freight version designated TB700B, which has larger loading doors and quickly re-configurable interior equipment. The first model was delivered at the end of 2001. An advanced TBM700C2 became available for delivery in March 2003. This model has a larger baggage compartment and the take-off weight increased to 7,408 lbs (3,360 kg).
Manufacturer: Socata, Groupe Aérospatiale, Tarbes plant, Suresnes, France.

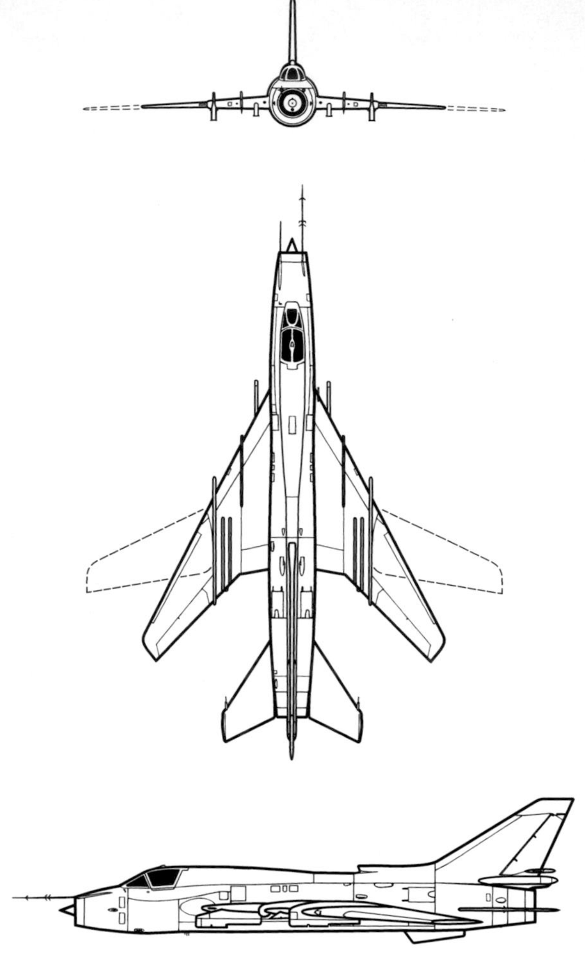

Dimensions:
Wingspan 32.81 ft (10.00 m)/63° up to 45.23 ft (13.80 m)/30°
Length 62.40 ft (19.02 m)
Height 16.40 ft (5.00 m)
Wing area 370.82 sq. ft (34.45 m^2)/ 63°, 414.30 sq. ft (38.49 m^2)/30°

SUKHOI SU-22M4

Country of origin: Russia.
Type: One-seat low-level attack airplane (Su-22M4), tactical reconnaissance aircraft (Su-20R) and two-seat combat trainer (Su-22M3).
Power Plant: One Lyulka/Saturn AL-23F-3 jet engine with 17,198 lbs (7,800 kp/76.5 kN) static thrust without afterburner and 24,842 lbs (11,200 kp/110.5 kN) with afterburner.
Performance: Maximum speed 1,156 mph (1,860 km/h [Mach 1.7]) at high altitude, 839 mph (1,350 km/h) at sea level, initial rate of climb 738 ft (225 m)/sec, service ceiling 49,868 ft (15,200 m), range with external tanks 1,243 miles (2,000 km).
Weight: Empty weight 26,810 lbs (12,161 kg), normal take-off weight 36,156 lbs (16,400 kg), maximum take-off weight 42,990 lbs (19,500 kg).
Armament: Two NR-30 30-mm cannons and a weapons load of up to 8,973 lbs (4,070 kg).
State of development: Approximately 770 units of this version of the Su-17, once operated exclusively by the armed forces of the Soviet Union (now Russia), have been exported to 17 countries including Angola, Egypt, the former DDR, Libya, Poland, and the former Czechoslovakia. This model was manufactured between 1983 and 1991.
Remarks: As the last in a long line of low-level attack aircraft of the Su-7/Su-17 family, the Su-22M4 features a new degree of maturity. Unlike its predecessor, the Su-17M4, the SU-22M4 has updated weapons equipment and electronics. Because of this, fuel capacity has had to be slightly reduced. Aircraft still operated in large numbers by the Polish Air Force have been partially modernized by receiving NATO-compatible communications and navigation systems. The modernization will continue in the near future with the addition of a digital attack system connected with a MIL-STD-1553B data bus. Finally, the cockpit is to be modernized and equipped with a HUD. The first converted SU-22 flew in 2003. Similar programs for Bulgaria and Slovakia are also being discussed in cooperation with Sukhoi, EADS and Russian Rosoboronexport in order to extend the operational capability of the aircraft until 2015.
Manufacturer: OKB Pavel O. Sukhoi, Russia.

Dimensions (Su-30MK)**:**
Wingspan 48.22 ft (14.70 m)
Length 71.95 ft (21.93 m)
Height 20.83 ft (6.35 m)
Wing area 680.28 sq. ft (63.20 m^2)

SUKHOI SU-30MKK/MKI

Country of origin: Russia.
Type: Two-seat multi-purpose tactical aircraft.
Power Plant: Two Saturn (Lyulka) AL-31F turbofan engines each with 17,857 lbs (8,100 kp/ 79.43 kN) static thrust without afterburner and 27,562 lbs (12,500 kp/122.60 kN) with afterburner.
Performance (Su-30MK): Maximum speed Mach 2, 839 mph (1,350 km/h [Mach 1.1]) at sea level, initial rate of climb 1,083 ft (330 m)/sec, service ceiling 56,759 ft (17,300 m), tactical operation radius in low-level flight 789 miles (1,270 km), at high altitude 1,864 miles (3,000 km), with flight refueling 3,231 miles (5,200 km).
Weight (Su-30MK): Normal take-off weight 57,519 lbs (26,090 kg), maximum weight 72,753 lbs (33,000 kg).
Armament: One six-barrel 30-mm revolving cannon and a variety of weapons up to 17,637 lbs (8,000 kg) on twelve support points under the fuselage and wings.
State of development: The multi-purpose Su-30M has been flying since December 30, 1989, followed by the Su-30MKK in 1993 and the Su-30MKI on November 26, 2000. China has purchased 45 Su-30MKK's. Other buyers of this version include India 50 (18 Su-30K, 32 Su-30MKI + 140 MKI from licensed production).
Remarks: The two-seat Su-30M is primarily intended for fighter/bomber operations. To maximize the wide range of operations, a new combat electronics system and a Loran navigation system have been installed rather than an all-weather radar system. The tail section particularly has been reworked and strengthened. The Su-30M is equipped with the same slats as the Su-27 M. The export version has been designated Su-30MK and is likewise equipped with slats and, on request, with additional vector steering (Su-27MKI). A further distinction from the Su-30M lies in the combat electronics. An advanced version with digital cockpit, new mission computer and updated weapons control systems has been introduced recently. The Russian Air Force will obtain six units. The initial Sukhoi Su-27SK version remains in production.
Manufacturer: Sukhoi Design Bureau/KnAAPO, Komsomolsk and Irkutsk plants, Moscow, Russia.

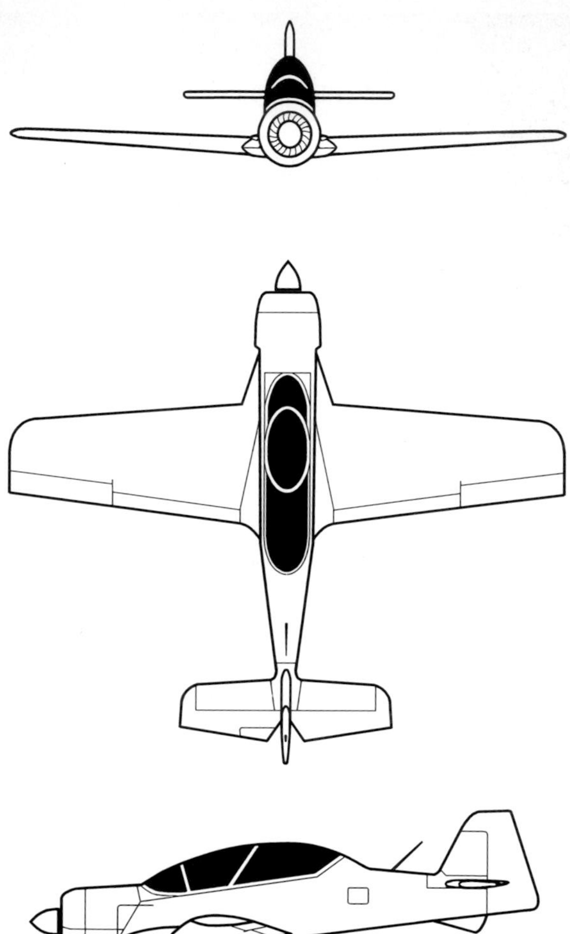

Dimensions:
Wingspan 30.15 ft (9.19 m)
Length 25.72 ft (7.84 m)

SUKHOI SU-49

Country of origin: Russia.
Type: Two-seat basic trainer.
Power Plant: One Voronezh M-9F nine-cylinder radial engine with 420 PS (3.13 kW) performance.
Performance (according to manufacturer's data): Maximum speed 311 mph (500 km/h), range 746 miles (1,200 km).
Weight: No available data yet.
Armament: It is anticipated that a machine gun pod, exercise bombs and similar weapons will be transported under the wings for light weapons training.
State of development: As recently as 2003, it appeared that the Russian Air Force was prepared to commit to purchasing 300 units of the Su-49. However, constant production delays have resulted in a rethinking of the order. At present, it is likely the Russian Air Force prefers to upgrade its fleet of Yak-52 piston-engine basic trainers to the contemporary Yak-52M standard rather than replacing them with the Su-49.
Remarks: The competition to replace the Yakovlev Yak-52 basic trainer, which has been in operation for many years, seemed to be between Sukhoi Su-49 and the Yak-152 model. The Su-49 is an aluminum version with three-point landing gear closely modeled on the Su-26/29/31 series of aerobatic aircraft. Generally, the Su-49 is an attempt to develop a very simple, robust construction that is highly cost-effective. In order to make training as compatible as possible to the latest deployed combat aircraft, the cockpit features, among others, liquid crystal displays, HUD and navigation equipment, which significantly simplify training for the MiG-29 or Su-27 for example. The Su-49 will be capable to carry out flight maneuvers with high G-force.
Manufacturer: Sukhoi Development Bureau, Novosibirsk plant, Russia.

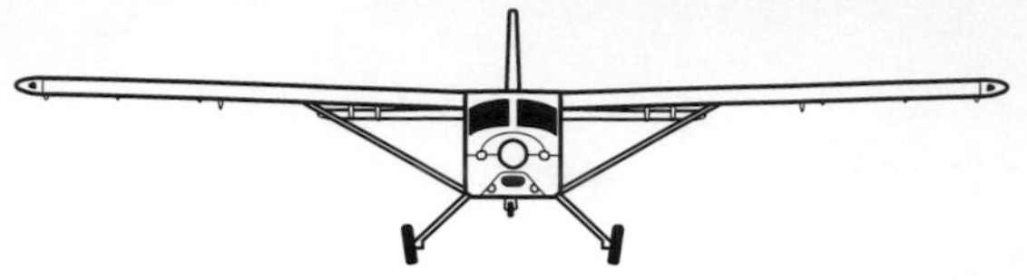

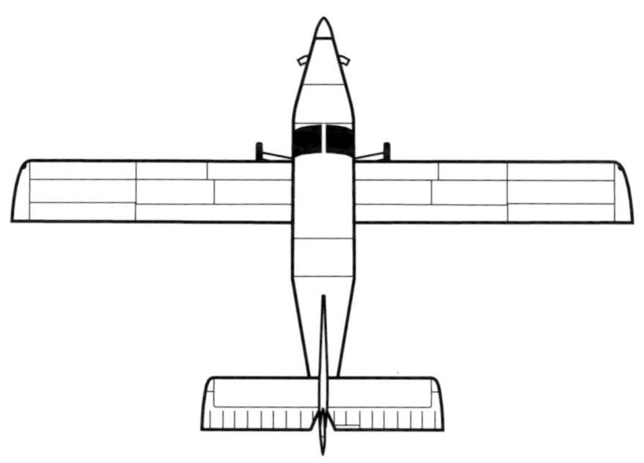

Dimensions:
Wingspan 47.90 ft (14.60 m)
Length 32.71 ft (9.97 m)
Height 10.10 ft (3.08 m)

TECHNOAVIA SMG-92 TURBO FINIST

Country of origin: Russia/Slovakia.
Type: Multi-purpose STOL utility aircraft.
Power Plant: One Walter M-601D2 turboshaft engine with 520 SHP (403 kW) performance.
Performance: Maximum 190 mph (305 km/h), maximum cruising speed 165 mph (265 km/h), recommended cruising speed 149 mph (240 km/h), initial rate of climb 25 ft (7.61 m)/sec, service ceiling 19,501 ft (5,944 m), maximum range 373 miles (600 km).
Weight: Empty weight 3,197 lbs (1,450 kg), maximum take-off weight between 5,181 and 5,952 lbs (2,350 and 2,700 kg).
Payload: Pilot and seven passengers or up to ten parachute jumpers, maximum payload as a freighter 1,543 lbs (700 kg).
State of development: The first test flight was at the end of 2000. Slovakian Aerotech built the SMG-92. Until now, only a few units have been sold in several countries.
Remarks: The SMG-92 is an advanced version of the SM 92 Finist, still equipped with a radial engine. From the earlier aircraft, the SMG-92 has adopted the wings, elevator and fuselage. In order to install a lighter engine, the nose section has been extended and therefore resembles its competing model Pilatus PC-6 Turbo Porter. Wings with a high lift ratio give the Turbo Finist very short take-off and landing characteristics and enable good gliding ability with turned off engine. Bendix King makes the avionics. In general, the Turbo Finist is a simple and robust construction with fixed landing gear and a tail wheel. Aside from general transportation, it is particularly suited for parachute jumpers, ambulance duties and glider towing. A large door facilitates loading and unloading.
Manufacturer: Technoavia, Smolensk, Russia and Aerotech Slovakia, Slovakia.

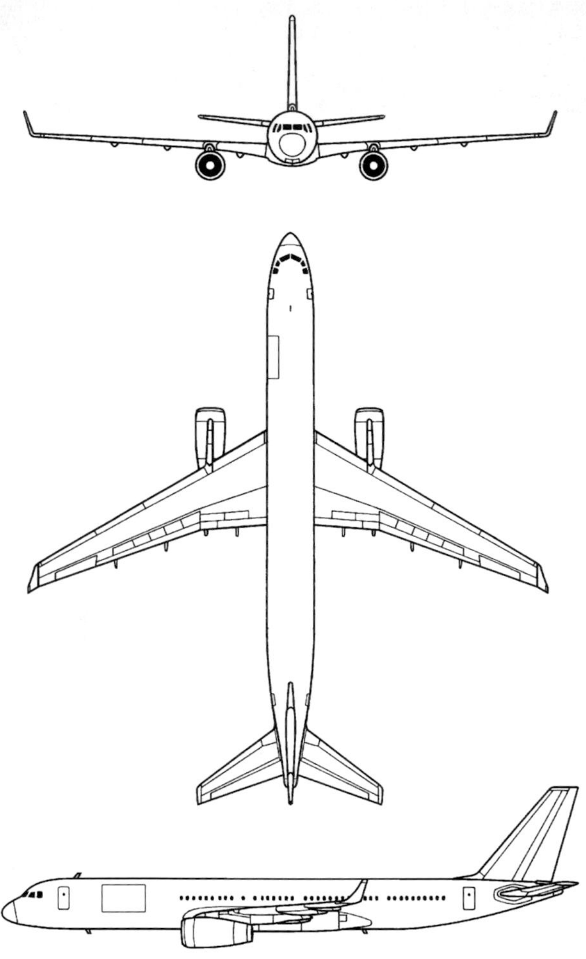

Dimensions:
Wingspan 137.80 ft (42.00 m)
Length 157.48 ft (48.00 m)
Height 45.60 ft (13.90 m)
Wing area 1,981.64 sq. ft (184.1 m^2)

TUPOLEV TU-204/TU-214

Country of origin: Russia.
Type: Medium (Tu-204) to long-range (Tu-214) commercial airliner.
Power Plant: Two Perm (Solovyev) PS-90 turbofan engines (Tu-204-100) each with 35,273 lbs (16,000 kp/156.9 kN) static thrust or two Rolls-Royce RB.211-535E4 turbofan engines each with 43,388 lbs (19,580 kp/193 kN) static thrust.
Performance (Tu-204-100): Maximum cruising speed 528 mph (850 km/h) at 34,941 ft (10,650 m), service ceiling 41,027 ft (12,505 m), range with 196 passengers 2,392 miles (3,850 km), range with maximum payload 1,553 miles (2,500 km).
Weight: Empty weight 124,561 lbs (56,500 kg), maximum take-off weight 227,071 lbs (103,000 kg).
Payload: Two-person cockpit crew and normally 170 passengers in three-class seating or a maximum of 214 passengers in one-class seating in six rows, maximum payload as cargo plane 63,934 lbs (29,000 kg).
State of development: The first Tu-204 prototype flew on January 2, 1989. In 1997, customer deliveries began. Of the 39 Tu-204's and 8 Tu-214's ordered thus far, about 30 were delivered by the end of 2002. The maiden flight of the first Tu-214 serial aircraft took place at the beginning of 2001. In 2002, six aircraft were built in all versions.
Remarks: In order to achieve the lowest possible empty weight, new materials, mainly plastics, have been used in many areas. The cockpit is equipped with six color-screen displays. Equipment also includes fully electric controls, a supercritical wing profile and a triple inertial navigation system. Because of its higher take-off weight of 242,508 lbs (110,000 kg), the Tu-214 achieves a higher range than the Tu-204. Both are equipped with Russian avionics. Optionally, the Tu-214 can also be delivered furnished with Rolls-Royce power plants and with Western avionics. Finally, a Tu-204C cargo plane is also available, as is the nearly 20 ft (6 m) shorter Tu-204-300 version.
Manufacturer: Tupolev Joint Stock Company, Ulyanovsk plant (Tu-204) and Kazan plant, Tatarstan (Tu-214) Moscow, Russia.

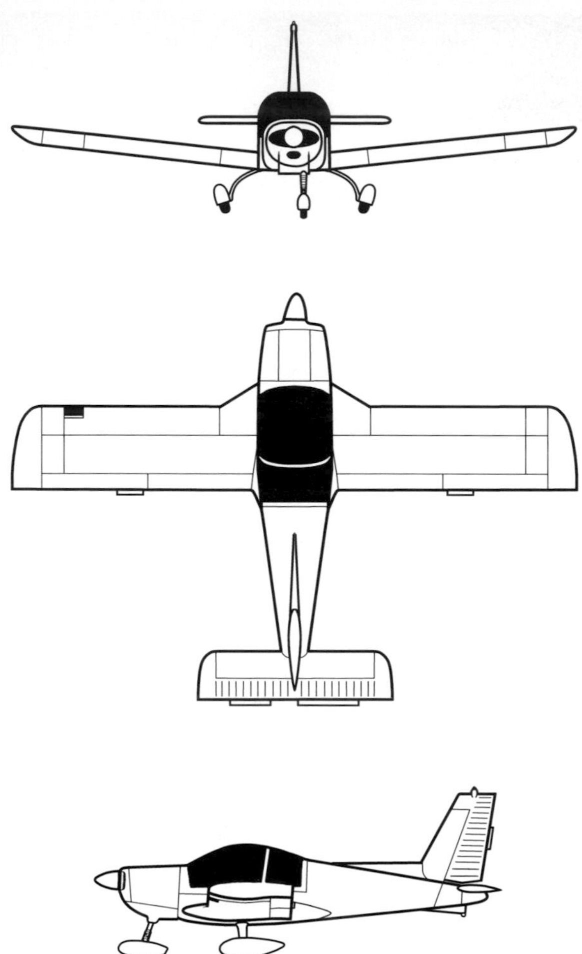

Dimensions (242L/143L):
Wingspan 30.64/33.27 ft (9.34/10.14 m)
Length 22.77/24.87 ft (6.94/7.58 m)
Height 9.68/9.55 ft (2.95/2.91 m)
Wing area 148.11/159.09 sq. ft (13.76/14.78 m^2)

ZLIN 242L/143

Country of origin: Czech Republic.
Type: (242L) Civil and military beginner training touring aircraft, (143L) touring aircraft.
Power Plant: One Textron Lycoming AEIO-360A1B6 air-cooled four cylinder horizontally opposed engine (242L) with 200 PS (149 kW) performance or one Textron Lycoming O-540-J3A5 air-cooled six cylinder horizontally opposed engine (143L) with 235 PS (175 kW) performance.
Performance: (242L/143L) Maximum speed 144/163 mph (231/262 km/h), cruising speed at 75% output 129/142 mph (207/228 km/h), initial rate of climb 14.76/16.08 ft (4.5/4.9 m)/sec, service ceiling 14,764/13,681 ft (4,500/4,170 m), range at 65% output 581/727 miles (935/1,170 km).
Weight: (242L/143L) Empty weight 1,609/1,830 lbs (730/830 kg), maximum take-off weight 2,403/2,976 lbs (1,090/1,350 kg).
Payload: (242L) Two people, (143L) four people including pilot.
State of development: The maiden flight of the 242L took place on February 14, 1990, followed by the 143L on April 24, 1992. Both models are still in production. Some 100 units of the 242L version have been ordered and, for the most part, delivered to, among others, air forces in Yemen, Macedonia, Peru, Slovenia, and the Mexican Navy. Some 50 units of the 143L have been built to date. Approximately 800 units of the earlier Zlin sports aircraft have been manufactured.
Remarks: The 242L and 143L represent the latest versions in a long line of proven sports and training aircraft. In many areas, both models are widely identical. While the 242L (see the three side sketches) represents a fully aerobatics-suitable trainer, the 143L (see photo) is intended more as a touring aircraft and also as an advanced trainer. Both models are simply designed and cost effective low-wing monoplanes with metal construction and three-point fixed landing gear. Both models are offered as normal as well as aerobatic versions with somewhat different flight performance.
Manufacturer: Zlin-Morovan Aeroplanes Inc., Otrokovice, Czech Republic.

➤ INDEX OF AIRCRAFT

A-29/AT-29, EMBRAER EMB-314 Super Tucano, 164
AB139, Agusta Westland, 26
ADA (HAL) LCA, 8
Adam Aircraft Industries A500, 10
Aermacchi M-346, 12
Aero L-159 Albatros, 14
  AE 270, 16
Agusta Westland A109 Power, 18
  A119 Koala, 20
  Super Lynx 300, 22
  EH 101, 24
  -Bell AB139, 26
AH-64D Longbow Apache, Boeing (MDD), 100
Airbus A310MRTT, 28
  A321, 30
  A320, 30
  A319, 30
  A318, 32
  A330-300, -200, 32
  A340-600/-500, 36
AH-1Z, Bell, 58
Airborne Laser, Boeing YAL-1A, 74
Airtech (CASA/IPTN) CN-235-200, 38
Airvan, Gippsland Aeronautics GA-8, 188
Albatros, Aero L-159, 14
Alenia C-27J Spartan, 38
ALH, HAL Druv, 206
AL-29 Super Tucano, Embraer EMB-314, 164
Ansat, Kazan, 220
Antonow An-74TK-300, 42
  An-72/-72P, 42
  An-74T/-74TK, 42
  An-70/-70T, 44
  An-140, 46
Apache, Longbow, McDonnell Douglas AH-64D, 100
AS 332/EC 225 Super Puma Mk. II, 172
AS 350 Ecureuil, 170
AS 355 Ecureuil 2, 170
AS 550 Fennec, 170
AS 555 Fennec, 170
Astor, Bombardier Global Express, 110
AT/ATS, MiG, 240
ATR 42-500, 48
  72-500, 48
Avanti, Piaggio P180, 269

Battlefield Lynx, AgustaWestland, 22
BD-10 Continental, Bombardier, 114
Bell (Tridair) 206 TwinRanger, 50
  OH-58D, 50
  407, 50
  427, 52
  430, 54
  412EP/UH-1Y, 56
  AH-1Z, 58
  Eagle Eye, 60
  -Agusta AB139, 26
  -Boeing V-22/CV-22B Osprey, 62
Boeing (Bell) V-22 Osprey, 62
BK 117/EC 145 Eurocopter (MBB/Kawasaki), 180
Beriew Be-103, 66
  Be-200, 64
Boeing 737-900, 70
  737BBj, 68
  747-400ER, 72
  YAL-1A Airborne Laser, 74
  757-200/300, 76
  767-300/400ER, 78
  767T-T/KC-767, 78
  777-300/200ER/300ER, 80
  Sonic Cruiser, 6
  X-45A Spiral o, 92
  X-50A Dragonfly
  -Helicopters CH-47D/SD/ICH Chinook, 96
  /Lockheed Martin F/A-22 Raptor, 228
  (MDD) C-17A Globemaster III, 84
  (MDD) F-15S Eagle, 86
  (MDD) F/A-18E/F Super Hornet, 88
  (MDD) 717-200, 82
  (MDD/Bae) T-45A Goshawk, 90
  (MDD) AH-64D Longbow Apache, 100
  /Sikorsky RAH-66 Comanche, 98
Bombardier (Canadair) CL-415/MP, 102
  CL-215, 102
  Regional Jet 200/200ER/200LR/440 104
  CRJ 700, 106
  CRJ 900, 108
  Global Express, 110
  Global Express Astor, 110
  Global 5000, 112
  Challenger 300, 114
  Continental BD-10, 112
  (De Havilland Canada) Q400 Dash 8, 116
  (Learjet) 45/45 XR/40, 118
British Aerospace Hawk LIFT 100/200, 120
  Nimrod MRA.4, 122

C-17A Globemaster III, Boeing (MDD), 84
C-27J Spartan, Alenia, 40
C-130J Hercules, Lockheed Martin, 224
C-295, CASA, 124

CH-47D/SD/ICH Chinook,
Boeing Helicopters, 96
CH-60S, Sikorsky, 296
CJ-6, Nanchang, 248
CN-235-100, CASA/IPTN, Airtech, 36
Canadair, see Bombardier
CASA C-295, 124
CASA/IPTN CN-235-100, Airtech, 36
Cessna 172R/SP Skyhawk, 126
182S Skylane, 126
206H Stationair/T206H Turbo S, 126
208B Grand Caravan, 128
208B Grand Commander, 128
525 Citation CJ1, 130
525 Citation CJ2, 130
525 Citation CJ3, 130
560XL Excel, 132
680 Citation Sovereign, 134
750 Citation X, 136
CH-60S Nighthawk, Sikorsky, 296
Challenger 300, Bombardier, 114
Chengdu F-7MG/PG, 138
F-10, 140
China Nanchang K-8 Jet Trainer,
s. Nanchang, 250
Chinook, Boeing Helicopters
CH-47D/SD/JA/F, 96
Cirrus SR20/-22, 142
Citation, Cessna 525 CJ1/2/3, 130
Citation, Sovereign, Cessna, 134
Citation X, Cessna, 136
CL-415, Bombardier (Canadair), 102
CL-215, Bombardier (Canadair), 102
CN-235-200, Airtech (CASA/IPTN), 38
Colibri, Eurocopter (MBB) EC 102B, 174
Comanche, Boeing-Sikorsky RAH-66, 98
Combat Explorer, MD Helicopters MD 902,
234
Continental, Bombardier, 112
Cougar II, Eurocopter AS 532/EC 725, 172
CRJ 200/440 Bombardier (Canadair), 104
CRJ 700, Bombardier (Canadair), 106
CRJ 900, Bombardier (Canadair), 108
CV-22 Osprey, Bell-Boeing, 62

DA-42, Diamond Twin Star, 154
DASA, Rockwell X-31, 290
Dauphin, Eurocopter EC155, 182
Dash 8, Bombardier (de Havilland
Canada) Q400, 116
Dassault Falcon 900C/900EX, 146
Falcon 2000/200EX, 148
Mirage 2000-5, -5 Mk. II, -9, 150
Rafale F1 (M), F2 (B), 152
De Havilland Canada, see Bombardier
Diamond DA-42 Twin Star, 154
Dragonfly, Boeing X-50A, 94

E-2C Hawkeye 2000, Northrop Grumman,
250
Eagle, Boeing (MDD) F-15E/S, 86
Eagle Eye, Bell, 60
EC-37SM, 188
EC-120B Colibri, Eurocopter (MBB), 162
EC 135/EC 635, Eurocopter (MBB), 166
EC 145, Eurocopter (MBB/Kawasaki), 168
EC 225, Eurocopter AS 332 Super Puma
Mk. II+, 156
EC 725, Eurocopter AS 531 Cougar, 172
Eclipse 500, 156
Ecureuiil (2), Eurocopter AS 350/355, 160
EJ2000 Typhoon, Eurofighter, 184
EH Industries EH 101, s.AgustaWestland,
24
EMBAER EMB-314/A-29/AT-9 Super
Tucano, 164
ERJ-145SA/RS Amazon, 158
Legacy, 160
ERJ-135, 160
ERJ-140, 160
170/175, 162
190/195, 162
ENAER T-35B Pillan, 166
Eurocopter EC 225 (AS 332) Super Puma
II, 172
EC 725 (AS 532) Cougar II, 172
Tiger/UHU, 168
AS 350 Ecureuil, 170
AS 355 Ecureuil 2, 170
AS 550 Fennec, 170
AS 555 Fennec, 170
EC 120B Colibri, 174
EC 130, 176
EC 135/EC 635 (MBB), 178
EC 145 (MBB/Kawasaki BV-117), 180
EC 155, 182
EC 635, 178
Eurofighter EJ2000 Typhoon, 184
Explorer, MD 902, MD Helicopters, 234
Excel, Cessna 560XL, 132

F1, Dassault Rafale M, 152
F2, Dassault Rafale B, 152
F-2, Mitsubishi, 242
F-7MG/PG, Chengdu, 138
F-10, Chengdu, 140
F-15E/S Eagle, Boeing (MDD), 86
F-16 Fighting Falcon, Lockheed Martin, 226
F/A-18E/F Super Hornet, Boeing (MDD), 88
F/A-22 Raptor, Lockheed Martin/Boeing,
228
F-356, Lockheed X-35A, B, C Joint Strike
Fighter 230, 232
Falcon 900C/900EX, Dassault, 146
2000/2000EX, Dassault, 148

Fennec, Eurocopter AS 550, 555, 170
Fighting Falcon, Lockheed Martin F-16, 226
Fire Scout, Northrop Grumman RQ-8A, 262

GA-8 Airvan, Gippsland Aeronautics, 188
Galaxy Aerospace (IAI), see Gulfstream
General Atomics RQ-1A, Predator, 186
Gippsland Aeronautics GA-8 Airvan, 188
Global Express, Bombardier (Canadair), 110
Global 5000, 112
Global Hawk, Northrop Grumman RQ-4A, 260
Globemaster III, Boeing (MDD) C-17A, 84
Golden Eagle, Korean Aerospace T-50, 222
Goshawk, Boeing (MDD)/Bae) T-45A, 90
Grand Caravan 208B, 128
Grand Commander 208B, 128
Gripen, Saab 39, 292
Grob G 115E Tutor, 190
  G 120A, 192
  G 140TP, 194
Grumman, see Northrop Grumman
Grumman/Marsh S-2T Turbo Tracker, 196
Gulfstream Aerospace G 100, 98
  G 200, 200
  Gulfstream V/V-SP, 202
Groen Hawk 4T, 204

HAL Druv, 206
  ALH, 206
  LCA, see ADA
Hawk, Groen 4T, 204
Hawk LIFT 100/200, British Aerospace, 120
Hawker, see Raytheon
Hawker 800XP, Raytheon, 282
  Horizon, 284
Hawkeye, Northrop Grumman E-2C/2000, 258
Helibus, Sikorsky S-92, 300
Hercules, Lockheed Martin C-130J, 224
Horizon, Raytheon Hawker, 284

IAI, see Gulfstream Aerospace
IAC Shahed 274, 208
Ilyuschin IL-103, 210

JAS 39 Gripen, Saab, 292
Jet Trainer, Nanchang K-8, 250
Joint Strike Fighter, Lockheed Martin X-35, 230/232

K-8 Jet Trainer, Nanchang, 250
Kamov Ka-31/-32, 212
  Ka-226, 214
Kawasaki T-4, 216
  OH-1, 218
Kawasaki (MBB), see Eurocopter
Kazan Ansat, 220
KC-767, Boeing 78
King Air 350, Raytheon/Beechcraft, 278
Koala, AgustaWestland A 119, 20
Korea Aerospace Industries T-50 Golden Eagle, 222

L-159 Albatros, Aero, 14
LCA, ADA (HAL), 6
Learjet, see Bombardier
Legacy, EMBRAER, 160
LIFT 100/200, British Aerospace Hawk, 120
Lockheed Martin C-130J Hercules, 224
  F-16C/D Fighting Falcon, 226
  /Boeing F/A-22 Raptor, 228
  X-35A/C Joint Strike Fighter, 230
  X-35B Joint Strike Fighter, 232
Longbow Apache, Boeing (MDD) AH-64D, 100
Lynx 300, AgustaWestland, 22

M-28 Skytruck Plus, PZL Mieler, 276
M-346, Aermacchi, 12
Marsh/Grumman S-2T Turbo Tracker, 196
MBB, see Eurocopter
MD Helicopters MD902 Explorer, Combat Explorer, 234
McDonnell Douglas, see Boeing
Merlin, AgustaWestland EH 101, 24
MH-60S, Sikorsky Nighthawk, 296
Mikoyan MiG 21-93, 236
  MiG-29K/SMT, 238
  MiG-AT/-ATS, 240
Mil/Kazan Mi-17M/MD, 242
  Mi-34, 244
Mirage 2000-5, -5 Mk. II, -9, Dassault, 150
Mitsubishi F-2, 246
MRA.4, British Aerospace Nimrod, 12X
MV-22 Osprey, Bell-Boeing, 66

Nanchang CJ-6, 248
  K-8 Jet Trainer, China, 250
NH Industries NH90, 252
Nighthawk, Sikorsky MH-60S, 296
Nimrod, British Aerospace MRA.4, 122
Northrop F-5E Tiger, 254
  T-38C, 256
Northrop Grumman Hawkeye 2000, 258
  RQ-4A Global Hawk, 260
  RG-88A Fire Scout, 262
  X-47A/B Pegasus, 264

OH-1, Kawasaki, 218
OH-58D, Kiowa, Bell, 50
Osprey, Bell-Boeing V-22, 62

Pacific Aerospace PAC-750XL, 266
P180 Avanti, Piaggio, 268
PC-7MK. II Turbo Trainer, Pilatus, 272
PC-9M Turbo Trainer, Pilatus, 272
PC-9Mk. II, Raytheon Beechcraft T-6 Texan II, 272
PC-12, Pilatus, 270
PC-21, 272
Pegasus, Northrop Grumman X-47A/B, 264
Piaggio P180 Avanti, 256
Pilatus PC-7Mk. II Turbo Trainer, 272
PC-9M Turbo Trainer, 272
/Raytheon T-6A Texan II, 286
PC-12, 270
PC-21, 272
Pillan, ENAER T-35B, 166
Power, AgustaWestland A 109, 18
Predator, General Atomics RQ-1A, 186
Premier I, Raytheon 300, 280
PZL Swidnik SW-4, 274
Mielec M-28 Skytruck Plus, 276

Q490 Dash 8, Bombardier (de Havilland Canada), 116

Rafale F1 (M), F2 (B), Dassault, 152
RAH 66, Boeing Sikorsky Comanche, 98
Raptor, Lockheed Martin/Boeing F/A-22, 228
Raytheon/Beechcraft King Air 350, 278
300 Premier I, 280
Hawker 800XP, 282
Hawker Horizon, 284
/Beechcraft-Pilatus T-6A Texan II, 286
Robinson R22/44, 288
Regional jet, Bombardier (Canadair), 104/106/108
Rockwell/DASA X-31, 290
RQ-1A, General Atomics Predator, 186
RQ-4A, Northrop Grumman Global Hawk, 260
RQ-8A Northrop Grumman Fire Scout, 262

S-2T, Marsh/Grumman Turbo Tracker, 196
S-70A/UH-60L Blackhawk, 278
S-92 Helibus, Sikorsky, 286
Saab JAS 39 Gripen, 292
Safire S-26, 294
Shahed, IAC 274, 208
Sikorsky MH-60S Nighthawk, 296
SH-60R Strikehawk, 298
S-92 Helibus, 300
-Boeing RAH-66 Comanche, 98
Skyhawk, Cessna 172R/SP, 126
Skylane, Cessna 182S, 126
Skytruck Plus, PZL Mielec M-28, 276
SMG-92 Turbo Finist, Technoavia, 310
Socata TBM 700, 302
Sonic Cruiser, Boeing, 6
Spartan, Alenia C-27J, 40
Spiral o. Boeing X-45A, 92
SR20/SR-22, Cirrus, 142
Stationair, Cessna 206H, 126
Strikehawk, Sikorsky SH-60R, 282
Sukhoi Su-22M4, 304
Su-27SK/Su-30M/MK/MKI, 306
Su-49, 308
Super Hornet, Boeing (MDD) F/A-18E/F, 88
Super Lynx 300, AgustaWestland, 22
Super Puma II, Eurocopter EC 225 (AS 232), 172
Super Tucano, Embraer EMB-314/ A-29/AT-29, 164
SW-4, PZL Swidnik, 274

T-4, Kawasaki, 216
T-6A Texan II, Ratytheon/Beech/Pilatus, 286
T-35B, ENAER Pillan, 166
T-45A Goshawk, Boeing (MDD/Bae), 90
T-50, Korean Aerospace Golden Eagle, 222
Technoavia SMG-92 Turbo Finist, 310
TMB 700, Socata, 302
Texan II, Raytheon/Beech/Pilatus T-6A, 286
Tiger, Eurocopter, 168
Tupolev Tu-204, 312
Tu-214, 312
Turbo Finist, Technoavia SMG-92, 310
Turbo Trainer, Pilatus PC-9M, 272
Turbo Stationair, Cessna T206H, 126
Turbo Tracker, Marsh/Grumman S-2T, 196
Turbo Trainer, Pilatus PC-9M/Mk. II, 250
Tutor, Grob G 115E, 190
Twin Star, Diamond DA-42, 154
Typhoon, Eurofighter EJ2000, 184

UH-1Y, Bell 412EP, 56
UHU, Eurocopter, 168

V-22 Osprey, Bell-Boeing, 62

Westland, see Agusta Westland

X-21, Rockwell/DASA, 290
X-35 Joint Strike Fighter, Lockheed Martin, 230/232
X-45A, Boeing Spiral o, 92
X-47A, Pegasus, Northrop Grumman, 264
X-50A, Boeing Dragonfly, 94

YAL-1A, Boeing Attack Laser, 74

Zlin 242L/143, 314

➤ ABBREVIATIONS IN THE TEXT

Aéronavale = French Naval Air Force
AEW/C = **A**irborne **E**arly **W**arning/**C**ommand
ALAT = **A**viation **L**égère de l'**A**rmée de **T**erre, French military air force
Armée de l'Air = French Air Force
ASTOR = **A**irborne **St**and-**O**ff **R**adar
ASW = **A**nti-**S**ubmarine **W**arfare
AWACS = **A**irborne **W**arning **A**nd **C**ontrol **S**ystem
CTOL = **C**onventional **T**ake-**O**ff and **L**anding
CRT = **C**athode-**R**ay-**T**ube
ECM = **E**lectronic **C**ounter **M**easures
EFIS = **E**lectronic **F**light **I**nstrument **S**ystem
Elint = **El**ectronics **Int**elligence
FADEC = **F**ull **A**uthority **D**igital **E**ngine **C**ontrol
FBW = **F**ly **B**y **W**ire
FLIR = **F**orward-**L**ooking **I**nfra**R**ed
GFK = **G**las**f**aserverstärkterlter **K**unststoff
GPS = **G**lobal **P**ositioning **S**ystem
HOTAS = **H**ands-**O**n-**T**hrottle-**A**nd-**S**tick
HUD = **H**ead-**U**p **D**isplay
IFR = **I**nstrument **F**light **R**ules
LANTIRN = **L**ow-**A**ltitude **N**avigation **T**argeting **IR** for **N**ight
MAD = **M**agnetic **A**nomaly **D**etection
NVG = **N**ight **V**ision **G**oggles
RAAF = **R**oyal **A**ustralian **A**ir **F**orce
RAF = **R**oyal **A**ir **F**orce
RN = **R**oyal **N**avy
SAR = **S**earch **a**nd **R**escue
SIGINT = **Sig**nals **Int**elligence
STOL = **S**hort **T**ake-**O**ff and **L**anding
STOVL = **S**hort **T**ake-**O**ff and **V**ertical **L**anding
USAF = **U**nited **S**tates **A**ir **F**orce
USCG = **U**nited **S**tates **C**oast **G**uard
USMC = **U**nited **S**tates **M**arine **C**orps
USN = **U**nited **S**tates **N**avy
VFR = **V**isual **F**light **R**ules
VTOL = **V**ertical **T**ake-**O**ff and **L**anding
WPS = **W**ellen-**PS**, performance of a propeller or turboshaft engine, measured at the shaft; the residual thrust is not taken into account; English: SHP (**S**haft **H**orse **P**ower)